German Submarine Warfare in World War I

The Onset of Total War at Sea

LAWRENCE SONDHAUS

ROWMAN & LITTLEFIELD
Lanham • Boulder • New York • London

Published by Rowman & Littlefield
A wholly owned subsidiary of The Rowman & Littlefield Publishing Group, Inc.
4501 Forbes Boulevard, Suite 200, Lanham, Maryland 20706
www.rowman.com

Unit A, Whitacre Mews, 26-34 Stannary Street, London SE11 4AB, United Kingdom

British Library Cataloguing in Publication Information Available

Library of Congress Cataloging-in-Publication Data

Names: Sondhaus, Lawrence, 1958– author.
Title: German submarine warfare in World War I : the onset of total war at
    sea / Lawrence Sondhaus.
Description: Lanham : Rowman & Littlefield, 2017. | Series: Total war |
    Includes bibliographical references and index.
Identifiers: LCCN 2017011988 (print) | LCCN 2017013908 (ebook) | ISBN
    9781442269552 (electronic) | ISBN 9781442269545 (cloth : alk. paper)
Subjects: LCSH: World War, 1914–1918—Naval operations—Submarine. | World
    War, 1914–1918—Naval operations, German.
Classification: LCC D591 (ebook) | LCC D591 .S66 2017 (print) | DDC
    940.4/512—dc23
LC record available at https://lccn.loc.gov/2017011988

Printed in the United States of America

Contents

Preface   xv

1 Origins   1

   22 September 1914: Context and Consequences   4
   Commerce Raiding: From the Privateer to the Torpedo Era 6
   The Advent of the Submarine   8
   Toward Unrestricted Submarine Warfare   14

2 False Start   23

   "Threat of Great Submarine War Made by Naval Chief
     of Germany"   26
   Unrestricted Submarine Warfare: The First Months   30
   "Heinrich"   37
   The Sinking of the *Lusitania*   41
   From the *Lusitania* to the *Arabic* Pledge   46

3 Interlude   57

   Tirpitz's Last Stand   60
   The Mediterranean (1916)   65
   More Minelayers   70
   Antisubmarine Warfare: Detection, Destruction, Containment 73

4 Preparation 85

Scheer, U-Boats, and the Shift in German Strategy 86
U-Boat Construction (1915–17) 95
The Decision 101

5 The Sharpest Weapon 109

"An Effect as Strong as Possible" 112
April 1917: American Intervention and the Record Month 115
The United States, Britain, and the Allied Convoy System 119
Hopeful Spring 127

6 Falling Short 135

The Peace Resolution, the Navy, and Unrestricted
Submarine Warfare 137
Diminishing Returns 144
Antisubmarine Warfare and Escalating U-Boat Losses 152

7 Anxious Months 163

The Tonnage War 166
The Final Allied Counterattack: Convoys, Countermeasures,
and Barrages 175
The Navy and the Turning Point in the War on Land 183

8 Defeat 189

The Scheer Program: Reality or Fantasy? 190
The End of the War in the Atlantic 192
The End of the War in European Waters 198
Reform, Revolution, and Running for Home 202

9 Aftermath 215

U-Boats, the Armistice, and the Treaty of Versailles 216
Former Submariners under the Republic 221
Former Submariners under the Third Reich 223
Unrestricted Submarine Warfare in Two World Wars 225
Conclusion 227

Bibliography 233

Index 241

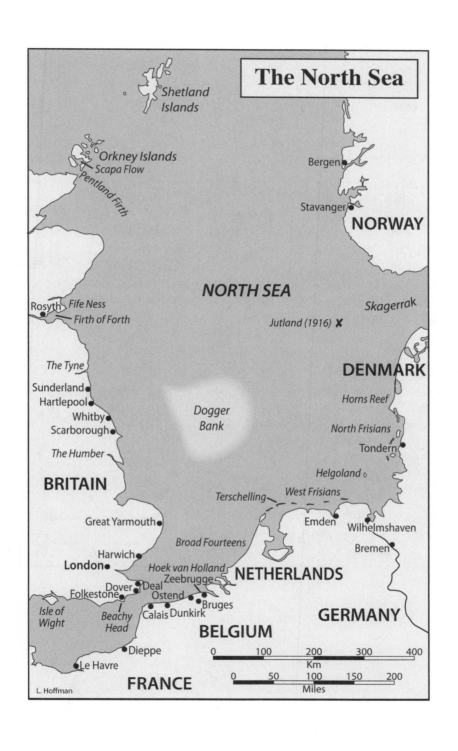

The North Sea

Shetland Islands

Orkney Islands
Scapa Flow
Pentland Firth

Bergen

Stavanger

NORWAY

NORTH SEA

Skagerrak

Rosyth Fife Ness
Firth of Forth

Jutland (1916) ✗

DENMARK

The Tyne
Sunderland
Hartlepool
Whitby
Scarborough

Dogger
Bank

Horns Reef

North Frisians

The Humber

Tondern

Helgoland ◦

BRITAIN

Terschelling West Frisians

Great Yarmouth

Emden
Wilhelmshaven

Broad Fourteens

Bremen

Harwich

London

Hoek van Holland
Zeebrugge

NETHERLANDS

Dover Deal
Folkestone Ostend
Bruges

Calais Dunkirk

Isle of
Wight
Beachy
Head

GERMANY

BELGIUM

0   100   200   300   400
Km

Dieppe

0   50   100   150   200
Miles

Le Havre

FRANCE

L. Hoffman

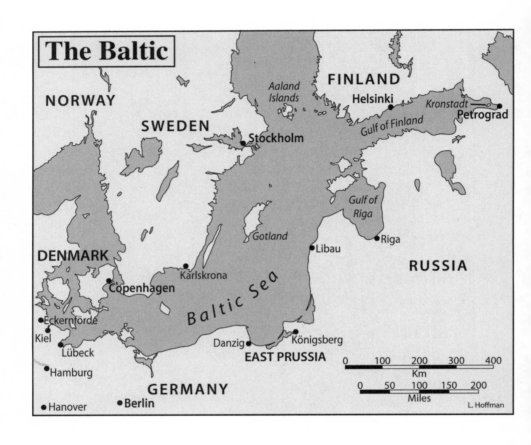

The Baltic

NORWAY

SWEDEN

FINLAND

Aaland Islands

Helsinki

Kronstadt

Petrograd

Stockholm

Gulf of Finland

Gulf of Riga

Gotland

Libau

Riga

DENMARK

RUSSIA

Karlskrona

Copenhagen

Baltic Sea

Eckernförde

Kiel

Lübeck

Danzig

Königsberg

Hamburg

EAST PRUSSIA

GERMANY

Hanover

Berlin

0	100	200	300	400

Km

0	50	100	150	200

Miles

L. Hoffman

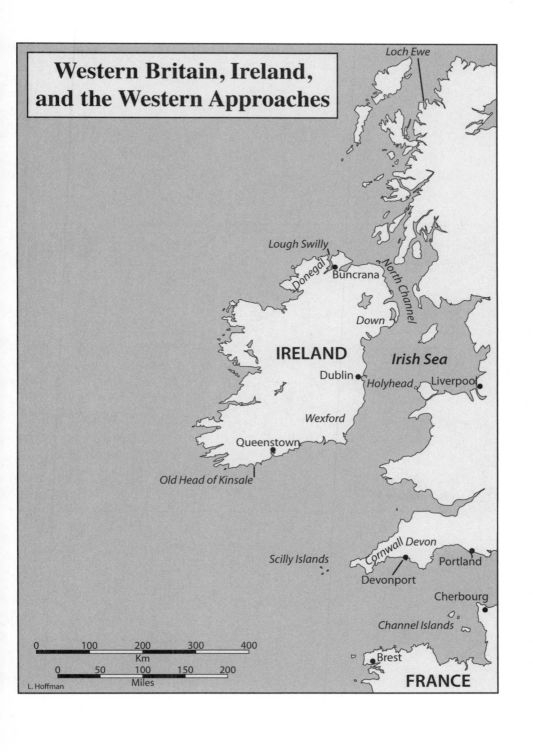

Western Britain, Ireland, and the Western Approaches

Loch Ewe

Lough Swilly
Donegal
Buncrana
North Channel

Down

IRELAND

Irish Sea

Dublin
Holyhead
Liverpool

Wexford

Queenstown

Old Head of Kinsale

Scilly Islands

Cornwall   Devon
Devonport
Portland

Cherbourg

Channel Islands

Brest

FRANCE

0   100   200   300   400
Km
0   50   100   150   200
Miles

L. Hoffman

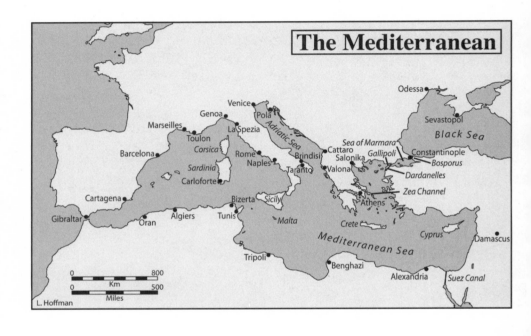

The Mediterranean

Odessa

Sevastopol

Black Sea

Venice
Pola
Marseilles
Genoa
La Spezia
Adriatic Sea
Toulon
Corsica
Barcelona
Rome
Naples
Sardinia
Carloforte
Cartagena
Bizerta
Sicily
Gibraltar
Oran
Algiers
Tunis
Malta
Brindisi
Taranto
Cattaro
Salonika
Valona
Sea of Marmara
Gallipoli
Constantinople
Bosporus
Dardanelles
Zea Channel
Athens
Crete
Cyprus
Damascus
Mediterranean Sea
Tripoli
Benghazi
Alexandria
Suez Canal

0   800
Km
0   500
Miles

L. Hoffman

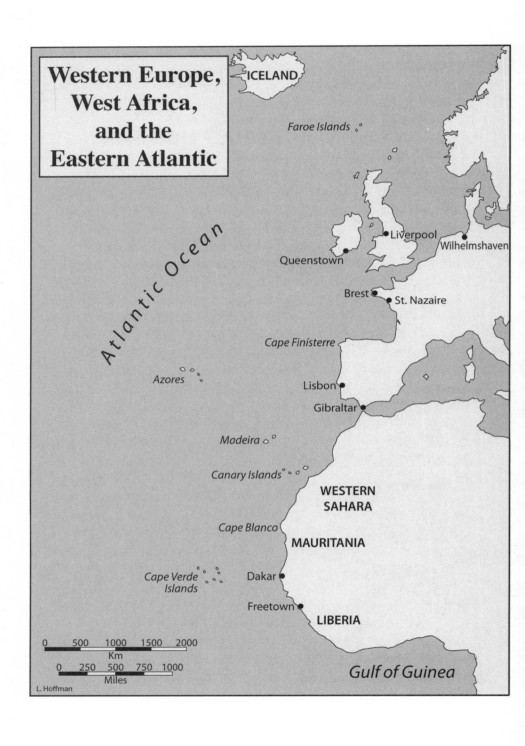

Western Europe, West Africa, and the Eastern Atlantic

ICELAND

Faroe Islands

Atlantic Ocean

Liverpool

Wilhelmshaven

Queenstown

Brest

St. Nazaire

Cape Finisterre

Azores

Lisbon

Gibraltar

Madeira

Canary Islands

WESTERN SAHARA

Cape Blanco

MAURITANIA

Cape Verde Islands

Dakar

Freetown

LIBERIA

Gulf of Guinea

0   500   1000   1500   2000
Km
0   250   500   750   1000
Miles

L. Hoffman

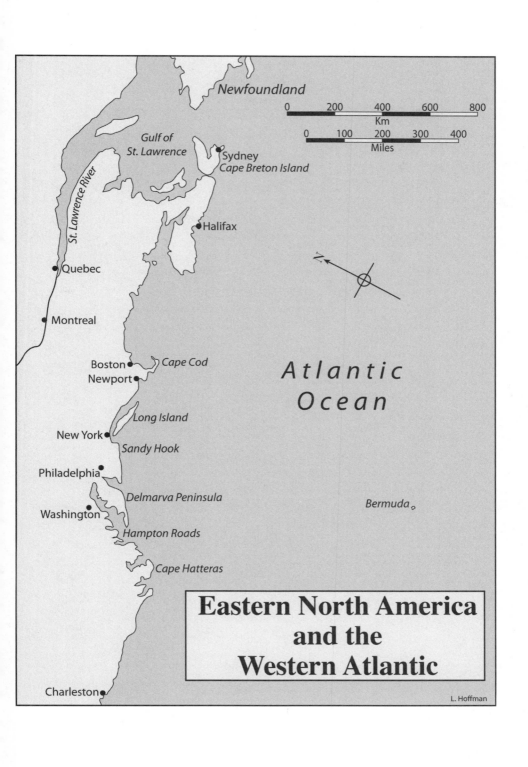

Newfoundland

0 200 400 600 800
Km
0 100 200 300 400
Miles

Gulf of
St. Lawrence

Sydney
Cape Breton Island

Halifax

Quebec

Montreal

Boston ● ● Cape Cod
Newport ●

Long Island

New York ●

Sandy Hook

Philadelphia ●

Delmarva Peninsula

Washington

Hampton Roads

Cape Hatteras

Charleston ●

St. Lawrence River

*Atlantic
Ocean*

Bermuda ○

Eastern North America
and the
Western Atlantic

L. Hoffman

Preface

Germany's campaign of unrestricted submarine warfare in World War I marked the onset of total war at sea. The German people readily embraced the argument that an "undersea blockade" of Britain enforced by their navy's *Unterseeboote* (U-boats) was the moral equivalent of the British navy's more conventional blockade of German ports, but international opinion never accepted its legitimacy, even though the campaign began as an ad hoc response to Britain's plan to achieve victory by strangling Germany economically. During the war the Allies also torpedoed unarmed ships, just as they also used poison gas on the battlefield and dropped bombs on cities from the air, but the Germans ultimately bore the stigma of having done each of these things first. In their initial, somewhat confused rollout of unrestricted submarine warfare in February 1915, German leaders underestimated the extent to which the policy would alienate the most important neutral power, the United States. In rationalizing the risk of resuming the unrestricted campaign in February 1917, they took for granted that, should the United States join the Allies, their U-boats would be able to stop the transport of an American army to France. But by bringing the United States into the war while also failing to stop the deployment of its troops to Europe, unrestricted submarine warfare caused Germany to lose the war. Because American manpower proved decisive in breaking the stalemate on the western front and securing victory for the Allies, Germany's decision to stake its fate on the U-boat campaign ranks among the greatest blunders of modern history.

The unrestricted German campaign of World War I was revolutionary in that it applied a relatively new weapon to an age-old strategy. In the war's first weeks, dramatic successes of submarines against surface warships raised the possibility that they would be even more lethally effective if deployed as commerce raiders against unarmed targets. Following the initial false start of 1915, plagued by insufficient resources and insufficient resolve, German submarine warfare entered a "restricted" phase, an interlude during which traditional "cruiser rules" were followed (albeit sometimes loosely) in a campaign focusing on the Mediterranean. After the German surface fleet's tactical victory at Jutland in 1916 failed to alter the strategic reality of the war at sea, navy leaders prepared for the resumption of unrestricted submarine warfare, which Chancellor Bethmann Hollweg announced early the following year, characterizing it as Germany's "best and sharpest weapon." But the improvement of Allied countermeasures, most notably the development of a comprehensive convoy system after the United States entered the war, caused the unrestricted campaign to fall short of sinking enough tonnage to force the Allies to sue for peace. Even though the U-boats failed to deliver on their promise—a failure that contributed to a decline of morale on the home front as well as within the navy—the campaign continued through anxious months of diminishing returns until just three weeks before Germany's final defeat, when it was abandoned in a belated attempt to appease the United States and secure armistice terms based on Woodrow Wilson's Fourteen Points. The Versailles Treaty prohibited Germany from having submarines and thus made the revival of the undersea service a matter of principle for Adolf Hitler after the establishment of the Third Reich. The ultimate failure of unrestricted submarine warfare in World War I did not deter Germany from trying it again in World War II, when the United States likewise waged a ruthless unrestricted undersea campaign against Japan.

This book leans heavily on the memoirs of Germany's naval and political leaders as well as its U-boat commanders, a remarkable number of whom survived the war to publish their recollections. Their accounts have been cross-checked against resources available in the National Archives of the United Kingdom, most notably convoy reports and the interrogation files of captured German submariners, as well as statistical studies produced in the decades-long quest by historians and history buffs to account for every German submarine that sortied in either world war. The latter effort has culminated in recent years in the work of information technology specialist Guðmundur Helgason of Reykjavik, Iceland, whose u-boat.net database has become an invaluable resource for scholars. Above all, this book is supported by a synthesis of the best scholarship on the subject, benefiting from my insights into the German perspective and German decision making, which throughout the war served as the primary driver for the action at sea as well as on land. My prior experience in researching and writing on German and Austrian naval and military topics, most of which have been from the era of World War I, naturally informs my explanations of the factors shaping the strategies and operations of the Central Powers. It has led me to the broader conclusion that in the naval war, no less than in the trenches, World War I may be conceptualized as a series of Allied reactions to the actions of the Central Powers; thus, understanding their actions is key to understanding the war as a whole.

I would like to thank Michael Barrett and Kyle Sinisi for their willingness to include this book in Rowman & Littlefield's "Total War" series, and my editor, Susan McEachern, for her patience and understanding as I brought the project to completion. I am especially grateful to Larry Hoffman for his excellent work on the maps. This book is dedicated to the memory of my mother, my first teacher, who passed away while the manuscript was in preparation.

Origins

By the time dawn broke on 22 September 1914, *Kapitänleutnant* Otto Weddigen had charted a homeward course for *U 9*. After leaving Helgoland two days earlier, the 493-ton submarine had cruised some 250 miles (400 km) through heavy seas to the eastern approaches of the English Channel, waters British mariners called the Broad Fourteens, and had reached the limit of its operational range without encountering an enemy ship. With Weddigen aboard *U 9* were his first officer, *Oberleutnant* Johannes Spiess, a crew of twenty-four, and six torpedoes that seemed destined to go unused. But at 06:10 GMT (07:10 German Summer Time), as their boat cruised on the surface twenty-one miles (33 km) northwest of Hoek van Holland off the Dutch coast, Spiess reported a plume of smoke in the distance. Weddigen's spyglass soon confirmed not just one but three four-funneled warships of the British navy's Seventh Cruiser Squadron steaming toward *U 9* in line abreast: the 12,000-ton armored cruiser *Aboukir*, flanked by its sister ships *Hogue* and *Cressy*. For submariners eager to demonstrate the usefulness of the undersea boat as a weapon of war, the circumstances could not have been much better. The day had dawned clear and the waters were calm, leaving no natural obstacles to a successful attack, but owing to the rough weather of recent days, the destroyers that should have been escorting the British cruisers had been recalled to port.[1]

Weddigen took *U 9* below, to periscope depth, and set a course toward the approaching cruisers, straining his boat's electric motors to their maximum underwater speed of 8 knots. By 06:20, he had closed to within 550 yards (500 m) of the *Aboukir* without being detected. He fired a torpedo which struck the enemy ship at the waterline, then dove deeper to keep his boat hidden from the *Hogue* and *Cressy*, which he assumed would close to assist their stricken sister. Within minutes the *Aboukir*'s commander, Captain John Drummond, played into Weddigen's hands, reacting to the cruiser's increasing list by ordering his crew to abandon ship and signaling the *Hogue* and *Cressy* to commence rescue operations. As they lowered their boats and began to pick up the *Aboukir*'s survivors, Weddigen kept *U 9* submerged, waiting for his next opportunity to strike. At 06:55, roughly ten minutes after the *Aboukir* capsized and sank, he had maneuvered to a spot three hundred yards (270 m) off the beam of the *Hogue*, which he targeted with two torpedoes. The first shot missed its mark, but the second sufficed to doom its prey, which capsized and sank fifteen minutes later. Meanwhile, Weddigen had failed to anticipate the consequences of the sudden loss of the weight of two torpedoes from a vessel as light as his and was surprised when *U 9* lurched abruptly to the surface just as the *Hogue* was struck. Only then did the British realize that they had not blundered into a minefield but were being attacked by a German submarine. Fortunately for the U-boat, the *Cressy*'s gunners had virtually no chance of hitting such a small target with shell fire, even at close range, though Weddigen recalled afterward that "one shot went unpleasantly near us." He continued to circle the chaotic scene, seeking the right moment to use his remaining three torpedoes against the *Cressy*, which "stood her ground as if more anxious to help the many sailors who were in the water than to save herself," thus making his task much easier. At 07:20, while the *Hogue* went under nearby, he targeted the *Cressy* at a range of one thousand yards (910 m). His first shot hit the ship starboard, close to its bow; then, after missing with a second, at 07:35 he closed to 550 yards (500 m) off its port side and used his last torpedo to deal the cruiser a fatal blow amidships. Like its sister ships, the *Cressy* capsized before sinking, but its overturned hull remained afloat until 07:55, by which time *U 9* had slipped away for home. Despite the relatively calm weather and the proximity of the coast, barely a third of the men aboard the three cruisers survived to be rescued by Dutch steamers and fishing boats. The dead numbered 1,459.

Weddigen maintained radio silence until *U 9* was safely away from the scene, sending his initial message home only after he had passed the island of Terschelling. Having exhausted his battery power by operating submerged for so long, he had to cruise on the surface much of the day, a risky proposition

FIGURE 1.1.
Otto Weddigen

owing to the smoke put off by his boat's kerosene engines. He was fortunate to have a good head start on the British destroyers that eventually pursued him, but with a top surfaced speed of just 14 knots, barely half that of a destroyer, Weddigen chose the prudent course of hugging the Dutch coast to avoid detection, then spent the night of 22–23 September submerged. By the time U 9 reached Helgoland late on the 23rd, the German navy had issued an official release detailing the action of the previous day, and Weddigen's first telegram to his wife, sent that evening, reveals that he had already been notified of his reward: "Received Iron Cross First and Second Class. Am healthy. Meet me tomorrow in Wilhelmshaven."[2] The thirty-two-year-old *Kapitänleutnant* soon became a national hero, but the accolades to come did not top his initial reception. On the 24th, when U 9 passed through the main anchorage of the High Sea Fleet, the crews of the battleships and cruisers lined the rails, each in turn giving Weddigen and his men three cheers as their boat chugged past them.[3] No one then could have imagined that, less than two and a half years later, Germany would stake its entire war effort on such tiny vessels, all but abandoning the battle fleet built at great cost over the past two decades. U-boat commanders such as Weddigen, at the rank of *Kapitän-leutnant* and *Oberleutnant* (equivalent to the Anglo-American lieutenant and sub-lieutenant or lieutenant junior grade), median age early thirties, would become the navy's greatest heroes.

22 SEPTEMBER 1914: CONTEXT AND CONSEQUENCES

Observers at the time, and historians over the decades that followed, struggled to put the unprecedented action off Hoek van Holland into perspective. The war was just weeks old, but Weddigen's feat was not the first instance of a U-boat sinking an enemy ship, as submarines on both sides already had registered their first successes. On 5 September, *U 21* (*Kapitänleutnant* Otto Hersing), cruising off the Firth of Forth, sank the 3,000-ton light cruiser *Pathfinder*, history's first victim of a self-propelled torpedo fired by a submerged submarine. Then, on 13 September, the British submarine *E 9* (Lieutenant Commander Max Horton), cruising in the waters between Helgoland and Wilhelmshaven, torpedoed and sank the 2,050-ton light cruiser *Hela*. While the *Pathfinder* exploded after being struck near its magazine, causing the loss of nearly all hands (261 dead), the *Hela* went under so slowly that just three of her crew perished.[4] In these instances, of course, the size of the ship and numbers of men lost stood in sharp contrast to the toll taken subsequently by Weddigen's *U 9*. Though the *Aboukir*, *Hogue*, and *Cressy* were considered obsolete by the standards of 1914 (and, indeed, had been manned by reservists), the sinking of three 12,000-ton warships within the span of barely an hour served notice of what a single U-boat could do to a squadron of battleships or a convoy of troopships.

The implications were so clear that the state secretary of the Imperial Navy Office, Admiral Alfred von Tirpitz, felt compelled to issue a spirited defense of the German battle fleet he had done so much to build up over the past seventeen years since becoming the Second Reich's equivalent of First Lord of the Admiralty (or secretary of the navy) in 1897. Tirpitz had secured the Reichstag's approval for navy laws in 1898 and 1900, funding the expansion of the German navy to a size roughly two-thirds that of the British navy and larger than any other. When the British raised the stakes with their innovative battleship HMS *Dreadnought* (1906) and battle cruiser designs, ships of unprecedented size and cost, the Germans did not shrink from the challenge and ultimately spent one-quarter of their defense outlay on the fleet, leaving their army with little margin for error against the Russians and the French.

Tirpitz's memorandum of 1 October 1914, addressed to the chief of the *Admiralstab* Hugo von Pohl one week after *U 9*'s safe return to Wilhelmshaven, was prefaced by a pointed rebuttal of Weddigen's accomplishment, in which Tirpitz explained to Pohl that "firing from a submarine is extraordinarily difficult," especially if the target of the torpedo "maintains a higher speed and changes course frequently."[5] He noted that the *Aboukir* was steaming "at ten knots" and that "the *Hogue* and *Cressy* were stationary when attacked," making all three extraordinarily easy to sink. Tirpitz admitted that, prior to 1914, the offensive potential of Germany's U-boats had been "underestimated" by battle fleet proponents, but he cautioned, "It is now exaggerated as a result of the success of *U 9*."[6]

Meanwhile, on the British side, concern for the danger from German torpedoes and mines had begun to affect naval operations even before the sinkings of 22 September. After the main body of the British Expeditionary Force (BEF) crossed safely to France, the commander of Britain's Grand Fleet, Admiral Sir John Jellicoe, moved his base temporarily from Scapa Flow in the Orkney Islands to Loch Ewe, 120 miles (190 km) to the southwest, on the northwest coast of Scotland. Over the weeks that followed, while antisubmarine barriers were put in place at Scapa Flow, the ships of the fleet visited the base there only when en route to and from patrols maintaining Britain's "distant blockade" in the North Sea, from the Orkneys eastward to the coast of Norway. On 22 October, a week after Weddigen's *U 9* torpedoed and sank a fourth cruiser, the 7,890-ton *Hawke*, off Aberdeen, drowning all but 70 of the 594 men aboard, Jellicoe thought it prudent to move his dreadnoughts from Loch Ewe all the way to Lough Swilly in Northern Ireland, another 155 miles (250 km) to the southwest, but even that remote location proved not to be secure. On 27 October, the dreadnought *Audacious* sank after striking a mine laid by a German auxiliary cruiser off Lough Swilly, reinforcing Jellicoe's paranoia. The torpedo and mine threat remained his primary focus at least until February 1915, when the antisubmarine barriers at Scapa Flow were finally completed and the dreadnoughts redeployed to their intended base.[7]

Amid the British navy's concern for the safety of its larger warships, a more significant development occurred on 20 October, fourteen miles (23 km) off Skudesnes, Norway, where *U 17* (*Kapitänleutnant* Johannes Feldkirchner) used a shot across the bow from its deck gun to stop the 866-ton British merchant steamer *Glitra*, bound for Stavanger with a cargo consisting mostly of coal. After inspecting the ship and ordering its crew to their lifeboats, Feldkirchner had his men scuttle the *Glitra*, then slipped away. The incident was witnessed by Norwegian vessels, which closed to rescue the *Glitra*'s crew.[8] In the first instance of a U-boat functioning as a commerce-raiding cruiser, Feldkirchner had conducted the search and sinking of an enemy vessel under standards commonly known as cruiser rules or prize rules. Since international law required cruisers destroying the prizes they had taken to allow the crews to abandon ship and then make reasonable provision for their safety—something a submarine, on its own, could not do—it remained to be seen what would happen when a U-boat attempted commerce raiding in circumstances where no surface vessels were nearby to rescue those forced to abandon ship.

COMMERCE RAIDING: FROM THE PRIVATEER TO THE TORPEDO ERA

The use of commerce-raiding cruisers as weapons of war became common in the early modern period, especially for a weaker naval power facing a superior foe. As late as the era of the French Revolution and Napoleon, privateers—privately owned warships licensed by governments to prey upon enemy shipping—accounted for the majority of armed vessels afloat. At the end of the Crimean War, the Declaration of Paris (1856) abolished privateering and established the body of international law that was still in effect in 1914 for cases of merchantmen being seized by naval vessels. Thereafter, during the American Civil War, a handful of Confederate warships provided a sobering example of the damage that could be inflicted by steam-powered naval vessels commissioned to function as commerce-raiding cruisers; the most successful of these, the CSS *Shenandoah*, claimed thirty-eight Union ships while circumnavigating the globe in 1864–65. A dozen years later, a Russian Empire barred from having a Black Sea fleet after the Crimean War used boats armed with spar torpedoes against the Ottoman navy during the Russo-Turkish War of 1877–78, demonstrating that flotillas of inexpensive torpedo boats could immobilize a fleet of ironclads. As the Industrial Revolution continued to transform the world's leading fleets, the French navy, despairing at its inability to keep pace with its British rival in numbers of armored battleships, built upon these developments to craft the strategy of the Jeune École, or "Young School," centered on cruisers and torpedo boats rather than battleships. The Jeune École reached its peak when the school's founder, Admiral Théophile Aube, served as French navy minister in 1886–87. The self-propelled torpedo, invented in Austria by naval officer Johann Luppis in 1864 and developed there by British expatriate Robert Whitehead, became the Jeune École's featured weapon.[9] Though early models performed unpredictably, they extended

the theoretical fighting range of torpedo boats and provided a lethal complement to gunfire for cruisers.

The school had a near-universal impact, and by the 1880s the building
programs of most navies emphasized unarmored steel cruisers and flotillas
of torpedo boats. The navy of the newly unified German Empire (1871), after
assembling the third-largest ironclad fleet behind the British and French, embraced the Jeune École wholeheartedly and soon fell from third place to fifth
in armored tonnage. Like the submarine service later, the torpedo flotillas offered the opportunity for warship commands at junior rank, thus making the
Jeune École especially popular with younger officers, including Tirpitz, head
of the German navy's Torpedo Inspection during the 1880s before becoming
a battleship proponent once again in the 1890s. While the strategy initially
assumed that torpedo flotillas would only operate near the coast to harass
a blockading enemy and create opportunities for cruisers to sortie into the
sea-lanes, maneuvers conducted with torpedo boats led their proponents to
conclude that such small vessels could function as high-seas raiders alongside
cruisers and could also pose a torpedo threat to battleships amid the man-
made fog of war hanging over any exchange of naval gunfire.

In the early 1890s, a combination of factors caused the Jeune École to lose
popularity. The advantage in speed that smaller, lighter vessels had enjoyed in
the 1870s and 1880s eroded rapidly when the new engine and boiler technolo-
gies first introduced in cruisers and torpedo boats were applied to battleships.
Quick-firing guns, likewise initially unique to smaller warships, were introduced to battleships, and in heavier caliber. The advent of smokeless powder
also robbed Jeune École advocates of the artificial fog of war as a factor that
could allow torpedo boats to engage a battleship, and simple enhancements
such as electric searchlights and broadside torpedo netting provided larger
vessels with further protection against torpedo attack. At the same time,
improvements in armor-piercing steel shells gave new life to bigger guns
and to the battleships needed as platforms for them, while Germany's Krupp
works led the way in manufacturing lighter, stronger armor plate to solve
the problem of how to protect such vessels without making them too heavy,
slow, or unseaworthy. These developments touched off a new spiral of technological competition in heavy artillery and armor plate that left unarmored
and smaller warships in its wake. Finally, evidence from repeated maneuvers
caused widespread doubt that torpedo boats could function independently on
the high seas. The turn away from the Jeune École was as rapid as the initial

embrace. By 1894 all of the world's great navies had resumed the construction of battleships, and they would continue to build ever-larger classes of them until the outbreak of the First World War. During the same years, a series of historical works by American naval officer Alfred Thayer Mahan, starting with *The Influence of Sea Power upon History* (1890), downplayed the significance of cruiser warfare and provided justification for the renewed primacy of the battle fleet.

THE ADVENT OF THE SUBMARINE

During the heyday of the Jeune École, concern about the shortcomings of torpedo boats fueled an interest in submarines as a delivery platform for self-propelled torpedoes. Even though the submarine failed to evolve quickly enough to replace the torpedo boat as a linchpin of the strategy, developments in the late 1870s and throughout the 1880s provided a foundation for things to come. Experimentation with submarines featured trial-and-error stories in several different countries—so many, indeed, that the developmental timeline remains contested ground for historians. An unmistakable breakthrough came in 1879 when George Garrett of Liverpool, a private entrepreneur, built the first submarine powered by its own engine, the 30-ton *Resurgam*. In partnership with Swedish arms manufacturer Thorsten Nordenfelt, Garrett went on to build four more submarines, culminating in the 245-ton *Nordenfelt IV* (1888). All five boats were steam powered and could move underwater only by releasing air that had been pressurized by their engines before diving; as for armament, *Nordenfelt I* (1885) and the three subsequent Garrett-Nordenfelt submarines carried self-propelled Whitehead torpedoes. *Nordenfelt I* was sold to Greece, the next two boats to Turkey, and *Nordenfelt IV* to Russia, but none ever served in active commission. It fell to French naval engineer Gustave Zédé to develop the first truly operational submarine, the *Gymnôte* (1888), a 31-ton vessel that featured a battery-powered electric motor providing a submerged speed of 4 knots and a surfaced speed of 8. In contrast to the short life of every earlier submarine, the *Gymnôte* remained in service for nineteen years, making two thousand dives.[10]

During the battleship renaissance of the 1890s, submarines remained attractive in circles that still believed in the Jeune École, with French naval engineers and American entrepreneurs responsible for most of the breakthroughs. After Zédé died in 1891, his colleagues built on the success of the *Gymnôte*. Ultimately, Maxime Lebeuf's 202-ton *Narval* (1900) served as the general prototype for most of the seventy-six French submarines built by the outbreak of the First World War. While submerged, it used a battery-powered electric motor and, when surfaced, an oil-burning engine which also recharged the batteries for further underwater operations. Concurrent with Lebeuf's work on the *Narval*, Irish expatriate John Philip Holland built a 65-ton submarine of similar design in the United States, ultimately commissioned by the American navy as USS *Holland* (1900). It featured a gasoline engine for surface propulsion that, likewise, recharged batteries to operate an electric motor underwater. The paradigm of pairing an internal combustion engine for surface operations and an electric engine for submerged operations, with the former charging the batteries for the latter, would remain intact for over half a century until the application of nuclear power to submarines starting in the 1950s.

The Electric Boat Company, formed to build Holland's boats, became the primary producer of submarines for the American navy and partnered with Vickers to build five similar boats for the British navy in 1901–2. The Holland partnership formed the basis of Vickers's own expertise in submarine construction; by the outbreak of the First World War, Britain commissioned eighty-nine submarines, more than any other country, most of which were built by Vickers. Holland also played a role in launching the submarine programs of Russia and Japan, selling boats to both sides during the Russo-Japanese War (1904–5). The Russians purchased the Holland prototype *Fulton* (1904), then built nine more submarines designed by Holland in their own shipyards. The Japanese navy's first five submarines were built by Electric Boat, disassembled, and shipped to Japan, where they were reassembled and launched in 1905. After the war, Holland's firm supervised the construction of two more submarines in Japan before the Japanese switched mostly to British Vickers designs. Russia also patronized Holland's main American rival, Simon Lake, who built just three boats for his own country's navy before the First World War but fared much better in Europe. Lake sold his prototype *Protector* (1902) to the Russian navy, which built nine more Lake submarines in Russian shipyards. Lake also designed Austria-Hungary's *U 1* and *U 2*, built at Pola (Pula) in 1909.

While Americans thus played a key part in the proliferation of submarine technology, the French at least initially were far more circumspect in sharing what they had developed, for example, providing nothing even to their Russian allies (whose armed forces otherwise benefited a great deal from French military and naval technology). Nevertheless, French expertise played at least an indirect role in the extension of submarine building to Germany thanks to Raimundo d'Equevilley-Montjustin, a Spanish engineer who worked under Lebeuf on the *Narval*. In 1902 Krupp's Germania shipyard in Kiel hired d'Equevilley-Montjustin to design and build a submarine for demonstration purposes in the hope of sparking an interest in undersea boats in the German navy. D'Equevilley-Montjustin's 17-ton midget submarine *Forelle* impressed Russian observers so much that they bought the boat in the summer of 1904 and contracted with Germania to build three 235-ton submarines, their future *Karp* class, eventually completed in 1907. Tirpitz, likewise impressed, responded a bit more slowly, ordering the future *U 1* from Germania in December 1904, while also directing the navy's Torpedo Inspection to develop its own submarine designs. D'Equevilley-Montjustin built *U 1* as a modified *Karp*, displacing 238 tons surfaced, with safer kerosene rather than gasoline engines. The shipyard also made *U 1* a priority, delivering the boat in time for it to be commissioned in December 1906, several months before its Russian half-sisters were completed. The navy's own engineers followed with the 341-ton *U 2* (1908), built in the Kiel navy yard, and the 421-ton *U 3* and *U 4* (1909), built in the Danzig navy yard, which thereafter became the only navy-owned shipyard to build submarines. D'Equevilley-Montjustin, meanwhile, designed Austria-Hungary's *U 3* and *U 4*, which Germania delivered in 1908. Tirpitz envisioned the German navy and Germania cooperating in the further development of undersea boats, but personal differences between d'Equevilley-Montjustin and German naval engineers made this difficult until after he left the firm in 1909. Between January 1910 and the outbreak of the war, the German navy commissioned another thirty-two U-boats of various designs, each slightly larger than the one before, culminating in the first six units of the 685-ton *U 31* class. Fifteen were built by Germania, the remaining seventeen in the Danzig navy yard.[11]

Thus, during the same quarter century that found the great naval powers embroiled in an arms race centered on capital ships (ultimately battleships on the model of Britain's *Dreadnought*, along with the battleship-sized cruisers known as battle cruisers), the same navies engaged in a much less heralded competition to construct submarines. Whereas the German navy, in the race to build dreadnoughts and battle cruisers, ultimately ranked second only to the British, in the undersea competition the British and French far surpassed the Germans, who by 1914 even trailed the Russians, albeit by just one submarine, thirty-seven to thirty-six. After joining the submarine race later than the navies of the Triple Entente, the prewar German navy also lagged behind its future adversaries in adapting the diesel engine to its undersea boats,

FIGURE 1.2. *U 1*

ironically so, since its inventor, Rudolf Diesel, was German. The French
launched their first diesel-electric submarine in 1904, just twelve years after Diesel built his first engine. The Russians followed suit in 1907 and the
British in 1908, but the Germans did not make the switch to diesel engines
until *U 19*, launched in 1912. Before then, Körting of Hannover provided the
kerosene engines for every German submarine except *U 2*, which had engines
built by Daimler. The diesel engines of the *U 19* class were produced by the
Maschinenfabrik Augsburg-Nürnberg (MAN), which thereafter shared the
navy's submarine engine contracts with Germania's own machine shop. During the war years, Körting and Daimler started to produce diesel engines as
well, supplementing the output of MAN and Germania.[12]

The prewar German navy never envisioned its U-boats as heirs to the high-
seas torpedo boats of the Jeune École and thus attached less importance than
most other navies to turn-of-the-century improvements in torpedo technology. The invention of the torpedo gyroscope by Austrian naval officer Ludwig
Obry (1896) doubled the effective range of self-propelled torpedoes, and by
1904 demonstrations had been conducted in which Whitehead torpedoes
hit targets as far away as three thousand yards (2,750 m), leading some to
predict, once again, the demise of the battleship, on the grounds that effective
torpedo ranges would soon outstrip the range of naval gunfire.[13] But during
the Russo-Japanese War, the biggest guns of both fleets scored hits at ranges

of up to 9,850 yards (9,000 m); thanks to further improvements in gun sights and range finding, the maximum reach of naval gunfire nearly doubled again by 1914. In the same years, evidence of the operational efficacy of submarine-launched torpedoes remained meager. While both Russia and Japan had added submarines in 1904–5, their war ended before either attempted to use them. Greece had the only submarine active in the Balkan Wars of 1912–13, the French-built *Delfin*, which became the first undersea boat to fire a self-propelled torpedo in action. In the attack, on 22 December 1912, the *Delfin* targeted the Ottoman cruiser *Mecidiye* from a distance of 875 yards (800 m), but the torpedo missed its mark.[14] Submariners on both sides of the First World War would learn from experience that a successful attack required a range even shorter than that, confirming that the effective-range assumptions of the early years of the century had been wildly optimistic.

In the decade before 1914, the British led the way in conceptualizing the submarine as a harbor-defense weapon that, along with the extensive use of more lethal mines, would prevent an enemy fleet from attempting a close blockade. The same assumption about the threat from submarine torpedoes and mines shaped Britain's decision to impose a "distant blockade" in the North Sea in 1914 rather than attempt more aggressive operations along the German coasts. The German High Sea Fleet drew similar conclusions from its first extensive maneuvers with U-boats in 1910–11. The prewar goal of seventy submarines (set in 1912) included just twelve for North Sea offensive operations, compared to thirty-six for the North Sea defensive perimeter in the Helgoland Bight, twelve to defend the navy's main Baltic base at Kiel, and ten in reserve.[15] Thus, little thought was given to deploying U-boats for offensive purposes against enemy warships, much less as commerce raiders.

The thirty-six U-boats in commission at the outbreak of the war were manned by sailors and machinists who had volunteered for the submarine service, and run by officers who sacrificed most personal comforts for the sake of independent command at junior rank. The U-boats of 1914 were so small that only the officers had bunks, located forward, where they slept with torpedoes next to or underneath them. The crew slept in shifts, in shared hammocks hung throughout the interior, near their duty stations; machinists, for example, slept in the engine room amid the noise of the machinery for which they were responsible. At the start of a cruise, "every available corner and space" was "filled with provisions," including food, leaving the cook to "hunt . . . in every conceivable place for his vegetables and meats." The re-alities of daily life were the same for all aboard, veterans and novices alike.

The commander of one U-boat observed that, when submerged, "the crew is entirely ignorant of their surroundings," because "only the commander" or "the officer of the watch" ever used the periscope.[16] Cruising on the surface of the ocean in such a small vessel was hardly more pleasant, as "the heads and stomachs of the men . . . began to be affected." They looked forward to their time in the open air of the conning tower, where they could "get a breath of fresh air and . . . light up a cigar or cigarette." The humidity inside the hull of a submarine made everyone's clothing and bedding perpetually damp; in warm weather, commanders took advantage of calm seas to surface for "a great drying-out," during which "every man brought up his damp things . . . to be aired above deck" while "the men lay about . . . and sunned themselves like lizards." When operating submerged or when all hatches had to remain closed because of heavy seas, "a frightful smell of oil . . . kept whipping and whirling through all the chambers of the boat."[17] Submariners home on leave reported that their wives and sweethearts complained of their breath smelling like gasoline or kerosene. Ultimately, aboard the typical U-boat the smells of fuel and unwashed bodies were superseded only by the odors of the toilet. Some early submarines (for example, in the British navy) had no toilets at all, reflecting the harbor-defense role everyone assumed they would play; when it became clear that most cruises would last longer than just an hour or two, provisions were made for toilets, but aboard a boat operating submerged in wartime, these were flushed infrequently for fear that the telltale air bubbles would give away its location to enemy surface vessels.[18] Throughout the war, as all navies introduced larger submarines, conditions would remain spartan (especially for the crews), but with greater consideration given to the basic needs of sleep and hygiene. When missions grew longer and more dangerous, providing for the physical and psychological well-being of those aboard involved new challenges which, if not resolved, at least generated lessons to be acted upon before the next war.

None of these problems deterred junior officers from entering the submarine service. Weddigen's class at the naval school (known as Crew 01, after the year of their entry, 1901) included twenty-six eventual U-boat commanders; Crew 09, with fifty-six, ultimately provided more than any other class. At the start of the war the boats they commanded were divided into four half-flotillas, one based at Wilhelmshaven, one at Helgoland, and two at Emden on the Dutch border. In October 1914 a Baltic half-flotilla was created, based at Danzig. All five eventually were expanded into flotillas. Because just eight years passed between the commissioning of *U 1* and the outbreak of the First

World War, as of 1914 no one with experience commanding U-boats was senior enough to lead a group of them, leaving their overall command in the hands of officers who had never served undersea. Throughout the war, the North Sea U-boats under the High Sea Fleet were led by such officers, first *Korvettenkapitän* (later *Fregattenkapitän*) Hermann Bauer, then, from June 1917, *Fregattenkapitän* (later *Kapitän zur See*) Andreas Michelsen, who held the designation of *Kommodore* at war's end.

TOWARD UNRESTRICTED SUBMARINE WARFARE

While the sinking of the British steamer *Glitra* by *U 17* set an example for the eventual deployment of U-boats against enemy shipping, in the autumn of 1914 most German submarines continued to target warships, though none came close to repeating the earlier successes of Weddigen's *U 9*. A daring raid all the way to the Gulf of Finland by *U 26* (*Kapitänleutnant* Baron Egewolf von Berckheim) resulted on 11 October in the sinking of the 7,775-ton Russian cruiser *Pallada* with all hands (597 dead). Another early example of the range and durability of U-boats came on 1–18 October, when *U 20* (*Kapitänleutnant* Otto Dröscher) circumnavigated Great Britain and returned safely home (albeit without sinking an enemy vessel), a feat that, for the time being, remained a closely guarded secret.[19] In further action against the British navy, *U 27* (*Kapitänleutnant* Bernd Wegener) sank the submarine *E 3* on 18 October at the mouth of the Ems River, then the 5,600-ton seaplane carrier *Hermes* on 31 October, off Calais, after which *U 12* (*Kapitänleutnant* Walter Forstmann) sank the 810-ton minesweeper *Niger* on 11 November off Deal in the Downs, three actions that, combined, claimed just fifty-one lives, most of them aboard *E 3*. Actions against merchantmen were limited to Hersing's *U 21*, which followed its earlier destruction of the light cruiser HMS *Pathfinder* by sinking two British steamers off Le Havre, the 718-ton *Malachite* on 23 November and the 1,366-ton *Primo* on 26 November. In both cases Hersing followed international law applicable to cruisers, allowing those aboard to abandon ship, and as with the earlier sinking of the *Glitra*, no lives were lost.[20] The first case of a U-boat targeting a passenger ship, and the only such incident during 1914, came on 26 October, when *U 24* (*Kapitänleutnant* Rudolf Schneider) torpedoed the 4,590-ton French steamer *Amiral Ganteaume*, en route from Calais to Le Havre with 2,500 Belgian refugees aboard. The ship did not sink and was soon assisted by a British railway ferry crossing the Channel nearby, but not before at least thirty passengers went overboard in the panic and drowned. In contrast to the harsh rhetoric and condemnation accompanying future such incidents, the Allies at the time accepted the explanation that Schneider had targeted the *Amiral Ganteaume* in error, thinking it was an auxiliary cruiser.[21]

As winter approached, it became clear that Britain, in imposing its "distant blockade" in the North Sea, had no intention of honoring the provisions of the prewar Declaration of London (1909) that would have allowed the free passage of food and other nonmilitary cargoes to Germany's ports. Indeed, under the prewar First Sea Lord, Admiral Sir John Fisher (in office 1904–10), the Admiralty's plans for the contingency of war against Germany assumed a no-holds-barred economic warfare, with the blockade being the most conventional aspect of an overall strategy that included ruining the German economy through a controlled collapse of the world economy, manipulated to cause minimal damage to the British Empire and Britain's allies. The Foreign Office, under Sir Edward Grey, opposed such schemes; having hosted the conference leading to the Declaration of London, Grey considered it part of a body of international law that Britain was bound to uphold, even though Parliament had never ratified it. Fisher, in contrast, had no intention of having the British navy abide by the declaration, reasoning that, in the event of war, the German navy would violate it too. While Britain's political leaders in 1914 refused to go through with the more grandiose aspects of the Admiralty's economic warfare strategy—fearing the reaction of neutrals, in particular the United States, along with the inevitable unintended consequences—they shared the Admiralty's lack of scruples when it came to how the blockade might affect German civilians. Even within the Foreign Office, its strictness was debated only for pragmatic reasons, out of concern for American opinion.[22]

After the First Lord of the Admiralty, Winston Churchill, brought Fisher out of retirement on 30 October to serve, once again, as First Sea Lord, it did not take long for Britain to raise the stakes. On 2 November, ostensibly in response to the mining of the dreadnought *Audacious* off Lough Swilly six days earlier, the British declared the entire North Sea a military zone. Ostensibly a general warning of the danger from German mines sown in the area, the declaration conveniently provided cover for the British navy's own extensive mining operations, undertaken to support the blockade.[23] Five days later, and just eighteen days after *U 17*'s sinking of the *Glitra*, Admiral Pohl, in his capacity as operational head of the navy, responded to the British declaration by circulating what Tirpitz later characterized as "a draft of a declaration for a submarine blockade of the whole coast of Great Britain and Ireland," the first draft of the policy that eventually evolved into unrestricted submarine warfare.[24] Thus, at least in the economic dimension of the naval war, Britain's premeditated actions sparked an ad hoc reaction that would soon, and forever, cast Germany in the villain's role.[25]

Pohl's document reflected less faith in U-boats than frustration at the navy's general record of failure up to that point. While the submarine war had gone their way, the Germans were losing the naval war on the surface. Immediately after the declarations of war, the navy's Mediterranean Division, consisting of the battle cruiser *Goeben* and its escort *Breslau*, had evaded destruction at the hands of superior Allied forces by fleeing to Constantinople (10 August), a triumph that proved bittersweet when the two ships remained bottled up in the Black Sea for the remainder of the war, transferring to the Turkish flag (under the names *Yavuz Sultan Selim* and *Midilli*) after the Ottoman Empire joined the Central Powers. In the North Sea, the First Battle of Helgoland Bight (28 August) resulted in a decisive victory for British battle cruisers and light cruisers over a German force of light cruisers, in which three of the latter were sunk. Then, in the Battle of Texel Island (17 October), a British light cruiser and its destroyer escorts sank a half-flotilla of German destroyers. In both engagements, the British did not lose a ship. Later in the year, the Germans sent Rear Admiral Franz von Hipper's battle cruiser squadron, officially the I Scouting Group (*I. Aufklärungsgruppe*), on two sorties against English coastal towns, hoping to draw British capital ships far enough to the south for the main body of the High Sea Fleet, under Admiral Friedrich von Ingenohl, to engage them. In the first raid (3 November) Hipper shelled Great Yarmouth, to little effect. A second raid (16 December) targeted Scarborough, Whitby, and Hartlepool, inflicting considerable damage, including 137 deaths and nearly 600 injuries, most of them civilian. Neither action provoked the desired encounter at sea, leaving the Germans frustrated yet again.[26]

Aside from the early successes of its U-boats, the navy could take heart only in the successful flight of the cruisers of Vice Admiral Count Maximilian von Spee's East Asiatic Squadron from their base at Tsingtao (Qingdao), China, across the Pacific to the coast of Chile, where they defeated a British squadron at Coronel (1 November), sinking two armored cruisers. But Spee's triumph was followed by disaster at the Battle of the Falklands (8 December), where British battle cruisers sank four of his five cruisers, killing the admiral and 1,869 of his men. Aside from the light cruiser *Dresden*, the lone survivor of Spee's squadron, by the end of 1914 the Allies had sunk or blockaded every other German warship attempting to operate beyond European waters. Plans to supplement the navy's modest overseas forces with auxiliary cruisers fared no better. In all, sixteen civilian vessels were armed and commissioned, most of them passenger liners of various sizes, of which thirteen were sunk, scuttled, shipwrecked, or interned by the spring of 1915, when the *Dresden*, too, was scuttled in the Juan Fernandez Islands off the coast of Chile.[27]

In their abortive attempt to put the world's sea-lanes into play, Germany's cruisers faced a harsh reality that Spee acknowledged in the aftermath of his victory at Coronel, by which time Tsingtao and every other German colonial port had been blockaded or occupied by the Allies: "I am quite homeless. I cannot reach Germany. We possess no other secure harbor anywhere in the world. I must fight my way through the seas of the world doing as much mischief as I can, until my ammunition is exhausted, or a foe far superior in power succeeds in catching me."[28] By wasting little time in ending the naval war outside of European waters and the North Atlantic, the Allies facilitated their subsequent transport of troops from India to Africa and the Middle East, and additional manpower from the British dominions, French colonies, and later the United States, to fight on the battlefields of Europe. The Allies would also be able to ship food, fuel, and other supplies worldwide thanks to their absolute domination of the sea-lanes.

The navy's early failures rankled no one more than Tirpitz, the architect of the High Sea Fleet. During his many years as state secretary of the Imperial Navy Office, Tirpitz had used his considerable political skills to make Germany the world's second naval power behind Britain. He became a fixture in the inner circle of Emperor William II, no mean feat for a strong personality, given the monarch's preference for sycophants. He had channeled the emperor's enthusiasm for a strong fleet and had built and managed a broad coalition of political parties and industrial interests to support a long-term program of naval expansion. His office made him the most powerful man in the peacetime navy, but, with no command authority, the state secretary had no voice in naval operations once the fighting started. This, understandably, frustrated him a great deal. "I have worked like a horse my entire life for the navy," he confided to his wife, "and now . . . I am not allowed to influence its use." He had little faith in the chief of the *Admiralstab* or the fleet commander, complaining that "neither Pohl nor Ingenohl have the necessary genius."[29] His relationship with William II became increasingly strained, and he lamented that the emperor, who held the ultimate authority of supreme commander, "won't run any risks with the fleet."[30] He reserved his harshest criticism for the "very incompetent" chancellor, Theobald von Bethmann Hollweg, whom he considered "not equal to the stupendous times."[31] But he also believed that the High Sea Fleet, which entered the war inferior in capital ships by a ratio of 2:3 to Britain's Grand Fleet, had already missed its chance for victory in the North Sea. He admonished Pohl that "our best opportunity for a successful battle was in the first two or three weeks after the declaration of war" and argued that "as time goes on, our chance of success will grow worse, not better."[32] Once the *Goeben* was bottled up in the Black Sea, Britain brought two of its battle cruisers home from the Mediterranean, and after Spee's defeat at the Falklands, the four battle cruisers detached to various stations to intercept him likewise would be recalled to home waters. Meanwhile, one Chilean and two Turkish dreadnoughts nearing completion in British shipyards were expropriated for commissioning as British warships. Early in the new year, these further additions to the Grand Fleet (combined with Germany's loss of the *Goeben*) would reduce the High Sea Fleet to a 1:2 ratio of inferiority in capital ships stationed in the North Sea.[33]

Thus, in the last weeks of 1914, the context for Germany's initial experiment with unrestricted submarine warfare had taken shape. The impending failure of the navy's overseas raiders left it searching for some other means to interdict Allied shipping. This practical need coincided with frustrations over the ineffective performance of the surface fleet closer to home and its deteriorating prospects for future victory. Because Tirpitz had persuaded the Reichstag to invest well over a billion Marks in that surface fleet, any alternative hope for relevance had to be cost effective. Submarines met that standard; indeed, the thirty-six U-boats Germany commissioned by 1914 had been built for just 87.9 million Marks, less than the cost of its two newest dreadnoughts alone.[34] Finally, the British blockade, though considered ridiculously leaky by the Admiralty's advocates of no-holds-barred economic warfare, nevertheless had been effective enough for the German people to experience their first hardships. The latter alone would suffice to mobilize popular opinion behind an aggressive undersea campaign, but Tirpitz recognized that a policy focusing on retribution would be problematic, satisfying the public while doing no real harm to the British or the overall Allied war effort, all while risking Germany's relations with neutral powers, in particular the United States. Tirpitz's reaction to Pohl's initial (7 November) proposal for a submarine blockade of the British Isles was to caution "that we ought not to select a date for such a declaration of blockade until such time as we had available a number of submarines more or less sufficient to maintain it." He feared that "the blockade of all England looks too much like bluff" and suggested the more modest alternative of blockading the Thames estuary, which would have the added benefit of "not touching the Atlantic passenger vessels, which always sailed to Liverpool" from the seaports of the eastern United States.[35]

Thus, just as the British Foreign Office worried that the Admiralty's approach to economic warfare against Germany might offend the United States, the Germans likewise were concerned about the American reaction to their possible use of a U-boat campaign as a countermeasure. Alone among the world's eight leading powers, the United States in 1914 had no alliance commitments and no particular motive for entering the war, unless one side or the other violated its security or its interests. Their concerns notwithstanding, the Germans had good reason to take American neutrality for granted. In the 1910 US Census, 10 percent of Americans listed German as their first language. In addition to the millions of immigrants from Germany and Austria-Hungary, Americans born in Ireland (overwhelmingly Catholic and anti-British) and Russia (almost all Jews escaping tsarist persecution) were more likely to favor the Central Powers over the Entente, as were many more American-born citizens of German or Irish heritage. But Britain, too, had reasons to take the neutrality of the United States for granted. The American elite was decidedly anglophile, and in an economic sense the nineteenth-century United States had functioned as part of Britain's "informal empire," using British capital to develop everything from its railways to its cattle ranches. After being second only to the British merchant marine in the age of sail, the American merchant marine lagged far behind it in the age of steam, even in carrying its own country's trade; by 1914 Britain's massive merchant fleet carried six times as many US cargoes to overseas destinations as its American counterpart. With such a small merchant marine for the size of its economy, the United States traded at Britain's mercy.[36] Thus, any effort by Germany to sink large numbers of British merchantmen would have a profound effect on the American economy. By mid-November, Tirpitz resolved to test American public opinion on the matter by granting an interview to German-American journalist Karl von Wiegand, the Berlin bureau chief for the United Press. A seasoned reporter previously employed by the Associated Press and the Hearst chain, Wiegand came highly recommended by Catholic politician Matthias Erzberger, whose Center Party had been a key supporter of Tirpitz's prewar fleet plans. Wiegand's fluency in German and ingenuity in circumventing British censorship already had made him a leading source of war news for the American public.[37] Tirpitz could be sure that an article published under Wiegand's byline would get the widest circulation in the American press, with the likely added benefit of forcing the hand of those within the German leadership who opposed his desire for more decisive action at sea.

NOTES

1. Sources for this paragraph and the following paragraph are Hermann Kirchhoff, ed., *Otto Weddigen und seine Waffe: Aus seinen Tagebüchern und nachgelassenen Papieren* (Berlin: Marinedank-verlag, 1915), 12–20; Otto Weddigen, "The First Submarine Blow Is Struck," text at http://wwi.lib.byu.edu/index.php/U-9_Submarine_Attack; Johannes Spiess, *U 9 auf Kriegsfahrt* (Gütersloh: C. Bertelsmann Verlag, n.d.), 12–20; Robert Massie, *Castles of Steel* (New York: Random House, 2003), 133–35.

2. Otto Weddigen to Frau Weddigen, Helgoland, 23 September 1914 (telegram), text in Kirchhoff, *Weddigen*, 8.

3. Kirchhoff, *Weddigen*, 16–18.

4. Otto Hersing, *U 21 rettet die Dardanellen* (Zürich: Amalthea-Verlag, 1932), 7–16; Edwyn Gray, *The Killing Time* (1972), reprinted as *The U-Boat War, 1914–1918* (London: Leo Cooper, 1994), 46.

5. Tirpitz to Pohl, October 1, 1914, text in Alfred von Tirpitz, *Erinnerungen* (Leipzig: Verlag von K. F. Koehler, 1920), 313. Note: The English translation of this key sentence, in Tirpitz, *My Memoirs*, 2 vols. (New York: Dodd, Mead, 1919), 2:97, reads, "Shooting from a submarine is extraordinarily difficult if the vessel attacked maintains a good speed and changes direction frequently when near submarines."

6. Tirpitz to Pohl, 1 October 1914, text in Tirpitz, *My Memoirs*, 2:97.

7. Lawrence Sondhaus, *The Great War at Sea: A Naval History of the First World War* (Cambridge: Cambridge University Press, 2014), 116.

8. R. H. Gibson and Maurice Prendergast, *The German Submarine War, 1914–1918* (London: Constable, 1931), 13; see also Guðmundur Helgason, "U-Boat War in World War One," http://www.uboat.net/wwi/ships_hit/2544.html (cited hereafter as http://uboat.net/wwi, with full URL for specific page).

9. Lawrence Sondhaus, "Strategy, Tactics, and the Politics of Penury: The Austro-Hungarian Navy and the *Jeune Ecole*," *Journal of Military History* 56 (1992): 587–602.

10. For the broader context of the developments discussed in this paragraph and the following paragraphs, see Lawrence Sondhaus, *Naval Warfare, 1815–1914* (London: Routledge, 2001), 155–56, 168, 182–83, 205–6.

11. *Conway's All the World's Fighting Ships, 1906–1921* (London: Conway Maritime Press, 1985), 173–76 (source cited hereafter as *Conway, 1906–21*).

12. Gordon Williamson, *U-Boats of the Kaiser's Navy* (Oxford: Osprey, 2002), 4–8; *Conway, 1906–21*, 173–76, 180.

13. On Ludwig Obry, see Lawrence Sondhaus, *The Naval Policy of Austria-Hungary: Navalism, Industrial Development, and the Politics of Dualism, 1867–1918* (West Lafayette, IN: Purdue University Press, 1994), 48, 72n42.

14. Bernd Langensiepen and Ahmet Güleryüz, *The Ottoman Steam Navy, 1828–1923* (London: Conway Maritime Press, 1995), 22.

15. *Conway, 1906–21*, 173.

16. Georg-Günther von Forstner, *The Journal of Submarine Commander von Forstner*, trans. Anna Crafts Codman (Boston: Houghton Mifflin, 1917), 14, 56.

17. Paul König, *Voyage of the Deutschland: The First Merchant Submarine* (New York: Hearst's International Library, 1917), 40, 81, 115.

18. Richard Compton-Hall, *Submarines and the War at Sea, 1914–1918* (London: Macmillan, 1991), 23.

19. Gibson and Prendergast, *The German Submarine War*, 13–14.

20. Hersing, *U 21 rettet die Dardanellen*, 29–31; http://uboat.net/wwi/boats/successes/u21.html.

21. http://www.archivespasdecalais.fr/Activites-culturelles/Chroniques-de-la-Grande-Guerre/A-l-ecoute-des-temoins/1914/Le-26-octobre-1914-le-torpillage-de-l-Amiral-Ganteaume. After the onset of unrestricted submarine warfare, the Allies viewed the sinking of the *Amiral Ganteaume* differently; as early as 30 March 1915, British foreign secretary Sir Edward Grey categorized it as a deliberate action, and later in the war it was listed as the first submarine crime in Jean Gabriel Domergue's *The Crimes of Germany: Being an Illustrated Synopsis of the Violations of International Law and of Humanity by the Armed Forces of the German Empire* (New York: American Defense Society, 1918), 171.

22. Nicholas A. Lambert, *Planning Armageddon: British Economic Warfare and the First World War* (Cambridge, MA: Harvard University Press, 2012), 121–81.

23. "All North Sea Made War Zone," *Chicago Tribune*, 3 November 1914, http://archives.chicagotribune.com/1914/11/03/page/2/article/display-ad-1-no-title; see also Gray, *The U-Boat War*, 47.

24. Tirpitz, *My Memoirs*, 2:139.

25. Lambert, *Planning Armageddon*, 7–15, explains that because Britain's pre-1914 planning for economic warfare against Germany did not fit the postwar narrative of the victors, it remained classified and effectively censored from histories and memoirs until the 1960s.

26. Sondhaus, *The Great War at Sea*, 95–120.

27. Ibid., 62–90.

28. Quoted in Hermann Kirchhoff, ed., *Maximilian Graf von Spee, Der Sieger von Coronel: Das Lebensbild und die Erinnerungen eines deutschen Seemanns* (Berlin: Marinedank-Verlag, 1915), 73.

29. Tirpitz to Marie von Tirpitz, 28 September 1914, text in Tirpitz, *My Memoirs*, 2:243.

30. Tirpitz to Marie von Tirpitz, 3 September 1914, text in ibid., 2:224.

31. Tirpitz to Marie von Tirpitz, 20 August 1914, text in ibid., 2:218; Tirpitz to Marie von Tirpitz, 4 September 1914, text in ibid., 2:225.

32. Tirpitz to Pohl, 16 September 1914, text in ibid., 2:95.

33. In addition to Vice Admiral Sir Doveton Sturdee's *Invincible* and *Inflexible*, which engaged Spee at the Falklands, battle cruisers deployed against the East Asiatic Squadron included the *Princess Royal*, ordered to the West Indies, and *Australia*, ordered from the South Pacific to the Pacific coast of Central America, in case Spee had decided to steam for the Panama Canal. See Sondhaus, *The Great War at Sea*, 122–23.

34. Erich Gröner, *Die deutschen Kriegsschiffe 1815–1945*, 8 vols. (Coblenz: Bernard & Graefe Verlag, 1982–94), 1:50, 3:26–30. The dreadnoughts *König* and *Grosser Kurfürst*, which joined the High Sea Fleet in the summer of 1914, each cost 45 million Marks.

35. Tirpitz, *My Memoirs*, 2:139–40.

36. Lambert, *Planning Armageddon*, 239–40.

37. Dale E. Zacher, *The Scripps Newspapers Go to War, 1914–1918* (Urbana: University of Illinois Press, 2008), 39, 40–42; Alfred von Tirpitz, *Deutsche Ohnmachtspolitik im Weltkriege* (Hamburg: Hanseatische Verlagsanstalt, 1926), 621n1.

2

False Start

In order to interview Tirpitz, Wiegand had to travel to Charleville in occupied France, where the headquarters of the German High Command had
been established in September 1914. While Ingenohl commanded the High
Sea Fleet from its main base at Wilhelmshaven, the outbreak of war had
transformed both Tirpitz, the political head of the navy, and Pohl, the chief
of naval operations, into itinerant courtiers, a fate they shared with the chancellor, Bethmann Hollweg, and foreign secretary, Gottlieb von Jagow, who
likewise abandoned their offices in Berlin to follow William II whenever he
left the capital to be in closer daily contact with his generals. Wiegand found
Tirpitz at the address 1 Place Carnot, in what the admiral characterized as
the "well-to-do household" of a "rich captain of industry," which "had been
deserted by the family . . . with everything in it."[1] Their interview took place
on the morning of 21 November. Tirpitz made a very positive first impression
on Wiegand, eventually reflected in a flattering preamble to the published
interview in which the journalist credited the admiral with possessing "more
Bismarckian force and iron in his nature than any other German official I
have met."[2] For his part, Tirpitz sensed that Wiegand was "rather dissatisfied"
with the administration of President Woodrow Wilson and its approach to
the war so far, and thus he felt confident that he had chosen the right man to
state Germany's case to an American audience.[3] Indeed, Wiegand's articles on
the war had provided such an effective articulation of the German point of

FIGURE 2.1.
Alfred von Tirpitz

view that the management of United Press was self-conscious about the news service "speaking with a German accent."[4]

Ultimately, Wiegand let Tirpitz speak for himself. The interview, when published, consisted mostly of direct quotes from the admiral, some of them paragraph length. Tirpitz got to the point right away: "America has not raised her voice in protest . . . against England's closing of the North Sea to neutral shipping. What would America say, if Germany declares submarine war on all enemy merchant ships?" Wiegand asked if Germany was considering such a thing, to which Tirpitz replied, "If pressed to the limit, why not? England wants to starve us. We can play the same game. We can bottle her up and torpedo every English or Allied ship which nears any harbor in Great Britain, thereby cutting off . . . food supplies. Would not such action be only the meting out to England of what she is doing to us?" When asked if Germany had enough submarines to implement his vision of a total war at sea, Tirpitz responded in the affirmative: "Yes, in submarines of the largest type we are superior to England." On the meaning of the emergence of the submarine for the future of the battle fleet, Tirpitz reiterated the same argument he had made to Pohl in his memorandum of 1 October, that the early successes of U-boats "do not warrant the conclusion that the day of large ships is past." He qualified his remarks, however, with an extensive explanation of how and why his prewar views had changed: "We have learned a great deal about submarines in this war. We thought that they would not be able to remain much longer than three days away from their base, as the crew would then necessarily be exhausted. But we soon learned that the larger type of these boats can navigate round the whole of England and can remain absent as long as a fortnight," provided that "the crew gets an opportunity of resting and recuperating," which could happen easily enough, for at night a submarine could "rest on the bottom and remain still, in order that the crew can have a good sleep." For most of the rest of the interview, Tirpitz gave a highly partisan German perspective of the war in general, its origins and possible outcomes, all tinged with the Social Darwinism common to the era, which he had used in the past to characterize the necessity of German naval expansion in the "struggle for existence." Britain posed an existential threat to Germany, reflected in the policy of "encirclement" culminating in the formation of the Triple Entente. "England alone is responsible for this war," he assured Wiegand's readers.[5]

Notwithstanding Tirpitz's boast that German U-boats could "torpedo every English or Allied ship which nears any harbor in Great Britain," Wiegand came away from the interview believing Tirpitz thought it would be sufficient for Germany to provide a series of examples, against Allied shipping, of the destructive capacity U-boats had already shown against Allied warships: "He contemplated torpedoing several large merchant ships, with the result that other ships would not venture out to approach England, which would thus be bottled up and starved out."[6] From the time of Tirpitz's first tentative embrace of unrestricted submarine warfare, a key assumption was that the fear of being sunk would suffice to reduce or stop altogether the flow of Allied shipping, making it unnecessary for Germany to have the capability to actually "torpedo every English or Allied ship." In any event, contrary to Tirpitz's assertions to Wiegand, at the time the navy had too few U-boats large enough to do much practical damage to Allied shipping, and Tirpitz knew it. His articulation of the role submarines would play in a total war at sea was part trial balloon but also part bluff, ironically so for a man who, in his internal correspondence, warned his colleagues against bluffing. Nevertheless, the interview caused a sensation as soon as it was published, not just in the United States but in Germany, where it had an electrifying effect on the public.

"THREAT OF GREAT SUBMARINE WAR MADE
BY NAVAL CHIEF OF GERMANY"

The headline in the *Cleveland Press* reflected the reaction of many American newspaper editors to the text of Tirpitz's interview with Wiegand.[7] The admiral's remarks struck them as inflammatory, and they framed the story accordingly for audiences across the United States, in cities large and small: "Foe to Starve Albion: German Submarines Will Isolate England, Says Von Tirpitz" (*Washington Post*, 23 December), "Will Give England War to the Hilt, Says German Navy Head in Sensational Interview" (Marshall [MI] *Evening Chronicle*, 22 December), and "German Navy Chief Threatens to Cut Off British Food" (*La Crosse* [WI] *Tribune*, 22 December). Others were more matter-of-fact in highlighting the content of the article, with headlines including "Submarines May Raid British Commerce" (*New York Times*, 23 December), "Germany May Attack Merchant Ships with Submarines" (*Xenia* [OH] *Daily Gazette*, 22 December), and "Submarine Blockade of England Possible, Says Germany's Naval Head" (*Cedar Falls* [IA] *Record*, 24 December). One banner headline reproduced, in its entirety, Tirpitz's central question from the interview: "What Will America Say if Germany Blockades England and Declares Submarine War on All Merchant Ships?" (*Des Moines News*, 22 December). Few chose to highlight Tirpitz's criticism of the British blockade, with headlines such as "England Wants to Starve Us, Says Head of Germany's Navy" (*Altoona* [PA] *Mirror*, 22 December). Fewer still framed the article as the trial balloon that Tirpitz had intended, using words as benign as "German Admiral Opens a New Channel of Thought on War" (*Victoria* [TX] *Daily Advocate*, 22 December). Most newspapers excerpted the lengthy interview. Few published it in its entirety, and those that did serialized it over a period of several days.[8] Regardless, the general effect was the same: it failed to elicit much sympathy. The vast majority of the American people, like the Wilson administration, would never accept Tirpitz's argument that German unrestricted submarine warfare against Britain was no less moral or legal than the British blockade of Germany.

The interview was published in the German press on 21 December, the day after it was cleared by Foreign Office censors and a day or two before it appeared in most American newspapers. The reception on the home front could hardly have been more enthusiastic, in a country that just one month later (25

January 1915) would become the first of the great powers to implement war-time food rationing. The Second Reich's own foreign policy, post-Bismarck, had created the context for the shortages by leading Germany into war against both Russia, its main provider of grain, and Britain, the only country capable of closing most of its alternative sources of food. Indeed, the loss of trade with Russia and the wartime reduction of imports from Austria-Hungary (where Hungary was barely feeding Austria, passing on little to Germany) arguably caused greater problems than the North Sea blockade. The German government also had done very little before the war to prepare for food shortages, and at least some of the responsibility rested with Tirpitz, who had long warned of a British blockade in order to justify a larger battle fleet and yet had "discouraged economic preparations," which would have been less expensive than building more battleships.[9] But none of that mattered now. Tirpitz's accusation that "England wants to starve us" had a galvanizing effect, calling out the British for their no-holds-barred pursuit of victory and advocating an equally ruthless antidote to their treachery. Britain thus replaced Russia as the primary enemy in the minds of the German people, and the underlying fear of starvation supplanted the specter of Russian invasion that, in August 1914, had driven even the traditionally antimilitary Social Democratic Party (SPD) to support the initial decisions for war. As the war went on, German rationing would become increasingly complex and inefficient, and by failing to account for the basic factors of age, gender, and economic inequality, it distributed the burden less equitably across society than rationing in the leading Allied countries.[10] But thanks largely to Tirpitz, from the start the German public focused on the British as the cause of their suffering. Because the blockade effectively prevented Germany from seeking relief overseas, throughout the war it would remain the symbol of their hardship, with submarine warfare their remedy of choice. Recalling the Wiegand interview after the war, Bethmann Hollweg did not underestimate its impact, abroad or at home. "Thus, the first and decisive step had been taken. Publicly the enemy had been alerted to prepare for a submarine blockade. Publicly the German people had been informed of the possession of an infallible means of war. From that point onward, submarine warfare could not be torn from the hearts of the nation."[11]

The publication of the interview caught Tirpitz's leading naval and political rivals by surprise. Pohl condemned it as a security breach, noting that because the expansion of U-boat operations was a "secret" and "still in preparation . . . it is neither politically nor militarily correct to speak of it."[12] While speaking in general terms, Tirpitz had carelessly revealed to Wiegand's audience that a U-boat could "navigate round the whole of England," the heretofore secret achievement of Dröscher's *U 20*, along with the practice of "rest[ing] on the bottom," confirming British speculation on how U-boat missions were extended. Pohl also noted William II's displeasure over the interview and concluded that "Tirpitz has damaged himself a great deal."[13] Bethmann Hollweg likewise condemned the interview, refuting later suggestions that he had been complicit in it (as a trial balloon) by stating categorically that Tirpitz had spoken to Wiegand "without my knowledge."[14] But in the chancellor's case, no less than with Pohl or Ingenohl, Tirpitz had no scruples when it came to undermining a rival. In personal letters during the autumn of 1914 he had reserved his harshest criticism for Bethmann Hollweg, reflecting a hubris fueled by his allies in the Reichstag and among Germany's leading industrialists, who had begun to tout him as a prospective wartime chancellor. Pohl, notwithstanding his own differences with Tirpitz, counted among those who thought he would make a good chancellor, at least in the wartime context, because "he has a great deal of understanding of international politics and hates England."[15] There had even been public speculation about it, reflected in the introduction to the Wiegand interview, in which the journalist called Tirpitz "the strongest man in the German government, and possible future chancellor."[16] In any event, constitutionally it was up to William II to appoint a chancellor, and given the state of Tirpitz's relationship with the emperor, any hopes he may have had for succeeding Bethmann Hollweg appear to have been unrealistic, despite the wave of popularity he enjoyed after the publication of the interview in Germany.

Thus, to the extent that his ambitions for higher office figured into his motives behind the interview, Tirpitz failed, but in making it far more likely that Germany would adopt unrestricted submarine warfare, he succeeded. The immediate aftermath found him occupying an unaccustomed position on the prospective U-boat campaign that appeared moderate, between extremes represented by Pohl and Bethmann Hollweg. On 15 December, the chief of the *Admiralstab* had gone beyond his proposal of 7 November to call for an unleashing of Germany's U-boats at the end of January 1915, with no warning at all. Tirpitz responded, just days before the publication of the Wiegand interview, by cautioning Pohl that "submarine warfare without a declaration of blockade . . . is . . . considerably more dangerous politically." Nevertheless, he agreed with Pohl that "a systematic attack on a large scale against English trade by means of submarines must be prepared . . . with the utmost energy and all possible resources," and assured him that the Imperial Navy Office was doing everything within its power to make such preparations.[17] Meanwhile, Bethmann Hollweg, as early as 3 January, cited the backlash from the Wiegand interview in reiterating his opposition to unrestricted submarine warfare, noting that "in America, a storm has already risen against [our] introduction of a war on commerce."[18] Amid the daily meetings and exchanges that followed, Tirpitz took full advantage of the middle ground, preaching delay to Pohl in order for the requisite force of U-boats to be prepared, a delay that also had the benefit of allowing time for public pressure to change Bethmann Hollweg's position.

The final decision in the matter, like all others in the Second Reich, rested with the emperor. Apparently William II had been intrigued by the prospect of an unrestricted U-boat campaign ever since the early days of the war, and from a most unlikely source: Sir Arthur Conan Doyle, creator of the Sherlock Holmes series. Doyle's 1913 short story *Danger! A Story of England's Peril*, had been brought to the emperor's attention by Captain Magnus von Levetzow, commander of the battle cruiser *Moltke* and later operations chief of the High Sea Fleet. The dramatic page-turner included a surprise twist to the ending of a future war, in which Britain defeated an enemy fleet only to have a mere eight enemy submarines suffice to starve her into submission, and in only six weeks' time.[19] While public opinion figured most prominently in bringing Bethmann Hollweg around to supporting a more aggressive submarine campaign, for William II the navy's defeat at Dogger Bank (24 January 1915) proved to be the key event. The war's first battle between German and British capital ships resulted from another attempt, on the model of the inconclusive raids of 3 November and 16 December, to draw part of the Grand Fleet into an engagement with the main body of the High Sea Fleet by using Hipper's battle cruiser squadron as bait. On this occasion Hipper drew a force of British battle cruisers under Vice Admiral Sir David Beatty into a running battle that started in the relatively shallow fishing grounds of the central North Sea and continued southward in the direction of the Helgoland Bight. Ultimately Ingenohl failed to sortie from Wilhelmshaven with the main body of the fleet in time to take advantage of the situation, and Hipper lost the slowest ship in his column, the 15,590-ton armored cruiser *Blücher*, with nearly all hands (792 dead). As in the previous engagements at First Helgoland and Texel Island, the British lost no ships and, on this occasion, suffered a mere eleven fatalities. While the *Blücher* was not a capital ship, it was the largest unit of the High Sea Fleet other than the dreadnoughts and battle cruisers, and its loss affected William II profoundly. He soon sacked

Ingenohl and, to everyone's surprise, appointed Pohl to succeed him as fleet commander, effective 2 February. More significant to the course of the war at sea, the emperor became less willing to allow his admirals to take risks with capital ships. Thus, unrestricted submarine warfare became even more palatable to him as a means for the navy to damage the Allied war effort without risking its dreadnoughts and battle cruisers.[20]

William II, Bethmann Hollweg, and Pohl, all angered by Tirpitz's lack of discretion in the Wiegand interview, deliberately excluded him from the ultimate decision, with the resulting irony that the man most associated with unrestricted submarine warfare, both within Germany and internationally, had no voice in the timing of its introduction. The chancellor, eager to please the emperor, embraced the strategy in the days after Dogger Bank, but as late as 27 January he indicated to Tirpitz that he would not approve the onset of unrestricted submarine warfare "before the spring or summer of 1915," leaving the admiral shocked when Pohl announced it to the world one week later, shortly after taking command of the High Sea Fleet. Admiral Gustav Bachmann, an old friend and ally of Tirpitz who succeeded Pohl as chief of the *Admiralstab* on 2 February, likewise was not consulted. Bachmann later recalled that he "expressed unreservedly to Admiral von Pohl [his] objections to so early an introduction of submarine warfare," owing to "the small number of our submarines, the lack of bases in Flanders or elsewhere, inexperience of submarine warfare against merchant ships, etc." He protested that Germany had too few U-boats to conduct the campaign as envisioned and that their extensive use in the new role meant that strategy and tactics would have to be developed on the fly, only to have his concerns dismissed by Pohl, "who stated that the matter was already decided."[21]

UNRESTRICTED SUBMARINE WARFARE: THE FIRST MONTHS

On 4 February, Pohl issued the official declaration of Germany's undersea blockade of the British Isles, to take effect in two weeks: "The waters around Great Britain and Ireland, including the English Channel, are hereby proclaimed a war region. On and after February 18 every enemy merchant vessel found in this region will be destroyed, without it always being possible to warn the crews or passengers of the dangers threatening." The declaration further warned that "attacks intended for hostile ships may affect neutral ships also," but in a concession to neutral Norway and the Netherlands, it exempted "the sea passage to the north of the Shetland Islands" and a strip of the North Sea along the Dutch coast.[22]

Tirpitz joined Bachmann in condemning the declaration as premature and worried that it "had the appearance of bluff." In particular, he anticipated problems in "the ambiguity arising from our obvious efforts to spare neutrals, coupled with our threats not to spare them."[23] The US government issued its response on 10 February, not waiting for the campaign to actually begin. President Wilson's note asked the German government "to consider, before action is taken, the critical situation . . . which might arise were the German naval force[s] . . . to destroy any merchant vessel of the United States or cause the death of American citizens." The president clearly appreciated the revolutionary nature of the policy, as articulated in Pohl's proclamation: "To declare or exercise a right to attack and destroy any vessel entering a prescribed area of the high seas without first certainly determining its belligerent nationality and the contraband character of its cargo would be an act . . . unprecedented in naval warfare."[24] Wilson's reaction prompted William II, on 15 February, to order U-boat commanders to spare all neutral ships in the designated war zone. Bethmann Hollweg followed, on the 17th, with a note to the president suggesting that the submarine campaign would be stopped if the Americans could persuade the British to adhere to the Declaration of London in their blockade of Germany. Their conciliatory gestures only served to unify the feuding German admirals. Tirpitz condemned the "vacillating" of the emperor and chancellor and their "all too humble answer to America."[25] Pohl likewise lamented that "the people in Berlin" had developed "cold feet," reflected in their decision to "give way to the American threat."[26] From that day onward, Tirpitz and Bachmann joined Pohl in arguing that unrestricted submarine warfare, "once it had been announced to the world . . . must be stood by at all costs."[27]

The navy began the war with thirty-six U-boats and added nine more by February 1915, including the first two *UB* coastal submarines, but during the same months it lost eleven boats, relegating the oldest four (*U1–U4*) to training duties while seven others succumbed to enemy action or accidents. One sinking in particular demonstrated just how dangerous early undersea warfare could be. On 21 January, off the Dutch coast, *U 22* (*Kapitänleutnant* Bruno Hoppe) tracked down and sank what he thought was a British submarine, then cruised to the spot, on the surface, to rescue a lone survivor who, much to Hoppe's horror, was a sailor from *U 7*. Fortunately for the German navy, *U 7* and her twenty-four dead would be the war's only casualties of U-boat "friendly fire." The other six submarines lost in the war's first six months succumbed to the conventional hazards that would claim more U-boats in the months and years to come: two were rammed by British vessels, two struck mines, and the remaining two were also likely mine victims.[28]

Of the thirty-four U-boats in commission at the start of the campaign, some were too small for the cruises required to participate in unrestricted submarine warfare. The largest submarines available by the spring of 1915, *U 43* (launched September 1914) and *U 44* (October 1914), displaced 725 tons, measuring 213 feet long by 12 feet deep, with a beam of 20 feet (65 × 3.7 × 6.2 m). They were manned by four officers and a crew of thirty-two. The smallest submarines Germany considered oceangoing, the seven remaining from the dozen numbered *U 5* through *U 16*, had been launched in 1910–11. They had nearly the same draft and beam as the newest models but, at just under 190 feet (58 m) in length, were considerably shorter. Each displaced approximately five hundred tons and typically carried between two and four officers and a crew of around twenty-five. The navy's *UB* boats were even more limited. Designed to operate in shallow coastal waters, they had a surfaced displacement of 127 tons and measured 92 feet long by 10 feet deep, with a beam of just over 10 feet (28 × 3 × 3.2 m). They were manned by one officer and a crew of thirteen. The smallest oceangoing submarines carried enough fuel for a surfaced range of 1,800–2,100 nautical miles (3,330–3,890 km), but their electric batteries allowed them just 80–90 nautical miles (148–167 km) submerged. The first *UB* boats had an even shorter operational range, just 1,500 nautical miles (2,780 km) surfaced and 45 nautical miles (83 km) submerged. Only fifteen of the German submarines on hand when the campaign began (those numbered *U 19* and above, burning diesel fuel rather than kerosene) could operate at sea for up to three weeks at a time. They carried six torpedoes (compared to two for the *UB* boats), which they saved for attacks on warships, on merchantmen when enemy warships or aircraft were nearby, or in other dangerous circumstances. The need to ration torpedoes made the deck gun the weapon of choice for attacks when U-boats were surfaced, but the smallest dozen boats were not built with deck guns and had to be retrofitted with them, in each case with a single two-inch (5 cm) gun on the foredeck, a process not completed until May 1915. For all submarines of the First World War, but especially those operational in 1914–15, lack of speed relative to surface warships was the greatest liability. The oceangoing boats had a top speed of 13–15 knots surfaced, several knots slower than battleships (or ocean liners), which could simply outrun them when they were aware of their presence. Smaller warships such as destroyers and torpedo boats moved twice as fast as submarines and posed a considerable danger to them. The first *UB* boats, with a surfaced speed of just 6–7 knots, were even more vulnerable to enemy vessels.[29]

Despite their limitations, U-boats had continued to demonstrate their effectiveness throughout the weeks of debate over whether and when to launch the unrestricted campaign. Following a quiet month of December, during which the German undersea force sank no enemy ships, in the predawn hours of New Year's Day, Schneider's *U 24* claimed the largest victim to date, torpedoing the 15,000-ton British pre-dreadnought battleship *Formidable* in the Channel off Portland. The attack, at point-blank range (110 yards, or 100 m) in heavy seas, left 547 dead and resulted in the sacking of the squadron commander, Vice Admiral Sir Lewis Bayly, ironically an early advocate for greater vigilance against the U-boat threat. Bayly's subsequent assignment to the remote post of Queenstown (Cobh), Ireland, ultimately put him in a position to play a central role in antisubmarine warfare after the unrestricted campaign began.[30] In the meantime, on 21 January, *U 19* (*Kapitänleutnant* Constantin Kolbe) claimed the first merchantman in two months, sinking the 1,301-ton British steamer *Durward* off the Belgian coast. Then, on 30 January, six British steamers were destroyed in a single day, three off Liverpool by Hersing's *U 21*, totaling 3,917 tons, and three in the Channel off Le Havre by *U 20* (now under *Kapitänleutnant* Walther Schwieger), totaling 11,908 tons. While Hersing's men boarded and scuttled their victims, allowing the crews to be saved, Schwieger torpedoed his targets without warning, the first such cases in the war thus far. The crews of two of the three ships *U 20* sank managed to save themselves despite the surprise, but the 1,489-ton steamer *Oriole* went under with all hands (21 dead). In February, *U 16* (*Kapitänleutnant* Claus Hansen) sortied after Pohl's declaration of unrestricted submarine warfare but before the 18 February deadline, and followed *U 20*'s course to Le Havre. On the 15th, Hansen torpedoed the British-flagged *Dulwich* (2 dead) but captured and scuttled the French *Ville de Lille* after giving those aboard ten minutes to abandon ship. In contrast to Schwieger's as yet unauthorized coldbloodedness, Hansen reported that he did not torpedo the *Ville de Lille*, the first non-British merchantman sunk in the U-boat war, because he had seen women and children on its deck.[31]

U 16 went on to deliver the first two blows of unrestricted submarine warfare, albeit without sinking either ship. On 18 February, off Dieppe, Hansen targeted the French collier *Dinorah*, but the damaged steamer made it to port at Dunkirk without sinking. The following day, off Folkestone, he torpedoed the 7,020-ton Norwegian oil tanker *Belridge*, bound for Amsterdam from

New Orleans, which limped safely into Thames Haven. The targeting of the *Belridge*—a vessel flying the flag of a neutral country, en route from one neutral country to another—provided an early example of how difficult it would be to adhere to William II's directive to spare neutral vessels in an otherwise unrestricted campaign in which U-boats were not required to stop and identify potential victims before acting. The first sinkings of the campaign came the following day, in the Irish Sea, where *U 30* (*Kapitänleutnant* Erich von Rosenberg-Gruszcyski) torpedoed the 3,112-ton British freighter *Cambank*, bound for Liverpool with a cargo of Spanish copper ore, then stopped and scuttled a second, much smaller steamer hours later. On 23–24 February, *U 8* (*Kapitänleutnant* Alfred Stoss) sank five British merchantmen totaling just over 15,000 tons, all off Beachy Head, accounting for most of the 18,500 tons sunk in the campaign's truncated first month.[32]

Counting *U 16*'s two victims claimed prior to the 18 February deadline, for the month U-boats sank nine Allied ships, with a total reported loss of life of nine British merchant seamen. In addition to Hansen's chivalrous treatment of the *Ville de Lille*, some combination of calm weather and proximity to the coast or to other vessels facilitated the rescue of all aboard in five of the other eight sinkings. The specter of unprecedented ruthlessness, the negative publicity abroad, and the strained relations with neutral powers did not square with the initial reality of the campaign, as the potential brutality against civilians was tempered not just by the small number of U-boats available, but by the scruples of individual captains along with the navy's persistence in pursuing enemy warships, at far greater risk, along with enemy merchantmen. A clear example of these issues came after Otto Weddigen exchanged command of *U 9* for the newer and larger *U 29*. After calling at Ostend in occupied Belgium on 10 March, Weddigen proceeded down the Channel to the Devon coast where, on the 11th, he stopped and scuttled the French steamer *Auguste Conseil*, allowing the crew to be saved by an approaching Danish merchantman; the steamer's captain reported to *Le Figaro* that Weddigen was "very courteous" and "expressed his regrets" at having to sink his ship.[33] Cruising off the tip of Cornwall on the 12th, *U 29* sank three British merchantmen, then remained surfaced for hours, towing their lifeboats until Weddigen stopped a French sailing ship which took the castaways aboard. After claiming these four victims, totaling nearly 13,000 tons, with no loss of life, *U 29* broke off commerce raiding and set a course for the Grand Fleet's base at Scapa Flow. On 18 March, in Pentland Firth, Weddigen's boat was rammed and sunk by HMS *Dreadnought*, shortly after firing a torpedo that missed the nearby dreadnought *Neptune*. It sank with all hands, taking the life of the navy's first U-boat hero before he could play much of a role in unrestricted submarine warfare.[34]

Eight other U-boats joined *U 20* in registering sinkings during March, totaling 89,500 tons; two of these boats, joined by another thirteen, claimed victims in April totaling 38,600 tons.[35] By early May, twenty-four German submarines had sunk merchant ships. Aside from a Russian steamer torpedoed by Berckheim's *U 26* in the Baltic off the Aaland Islands, all of the sinkings came in the zone around the British Isles designated in Pohl's declaration of 18 February. As the weeks passed, William II's order to spare neutral ships within the zone was relaxed to exclude those obviously trading with Britain. During March, *U 28* (*Kapitänleutnant* Georg-Günther von Forstner) seized two Dutch vessels and sank a third; then, during April, six U-boats sank or seized a dozen neutral ships, with Norwegian, Danish, Swedish, and Greek vessels joining the Dutch among the victims. Forstner reflected the view of many U-boat commanders in doubting the identity of ships flying neutral flags, because "the deceptions practiced by the English" included having their merchantmen use false flags as a defensive measure. With antisubmarine warfare in its infancy, most attacks were carried out by U-boats operating on the surface, in coastal waters, and in daylight, a combination of factors that continued to limit casualties. Indeed, during March and April, less than a third of all sinkings caused a confirmed loss of life. The deadliest incident came on 28 March, when Forstner's *U 28* torpedoed and sank the 4,806-ton British passenger steamer *Falaba*, outbound from Liverpool to Sierra Leone (104 dead). Meanwhile, the continuing effort to sink British warships yielded only the 5,950-ton armed merchant cruiser *Bayano*, a former banana boat fitted with two six-inch guns, torpedoed by Wegener's *U 27* in the waters between Ulster and Scotland just before dawn on 11 March, with the loss of most of its crew (196 dead).[36]

Reflecting British opinion that the unrestricted campaign was an illegitimate form of warfare, Churchill directed the Admiralty to treat captured U-boat personnel as war criminals rather than prisoners of war. The policy received its first test early in the campaign, when two U-boats lost shortly before Weddigen's *U 29* both had survivors who fell into British hands. On 4 March, in the Straits of Dover, Stoss's *U 8* was forced to scuttle, under fire from two destroyers, after becoming entangled in an antisubmarine net. Six days later, *U 12* (now under *Kapitänleutnant* Hans Kratzsch) likewise had to surface and scuttle after being rammed by a destroyer off Fife Ness. The thirty-nine German prisoners (twenty-nine from *U 8*, ten from *U 12*) were held in naval detention, in spartan conditions, while their fate prompted a lively public debate in which the British press, politicians, and scholars alike offered opinions. The German government raised the stakes by transferring the same number of British prisoners to a similar special detention, and for maximum effect selected their thirty-nine "criminals" from among captured BEF officers with family ties to leading politicians or the aristocracy. The impasse continued as long as Churchill remained at the Admiralty. Meanwhile, the German army's introduction of poison gas at the Second Battle of Ypres in April and the first zeppelin raids on London in May expanded the war crimes debate beyond the issue of submarine warfare and laid the foundation for postwar trials to become part of the Allied agenda.[37]

In the last weeks of 1914, after the stabilization of the western front had left most of Belgium under German occupation, the navy began to build a forward base in Flanders, centered on Bruges (Brugge) six miles (10 km) inland and linked by existing canals to the ports of Ostend and Zeebrugge. By the spring of 1915 it had become home to a group of small *UB* boats, disassembled and shipped by rail from Germany, reassembled at Antwerp, and then sent to Bruges via inland canals. *UB 10* (*Oberleutnant* Otto Steinbrinck) was the first submarine to operate out of the new base, starting in late March. After May, when *UB 2* (*Oberleutnant* Werner Fürbringer) demonstrated that the passage from Germany could be made safely by sea, the navy began sending submarines directly to the Flanders base, where torpedo boats and destroyers soon joined them. The Straits of Dover were 285 miles (460 km) from the westernmost submarine base in Germany, at Emden on the German-Dutch border, but just seventy miles (113 km) from Ostend and eighty miles (130 km) from Zeebrugge; thus, the Flanders deployment enabled Germany to keep more U-boats in the waters around the British Isles without wasting precious fuel and time on the journey to and from their hunting grounds. Because of the special challenges of operating out of Flanders, submariners who were successful at it tended to remain there; these included Steinbrinck, who would end the war ranked first among U-boat commanders in numbers of ships sunk and fourth in total tonnage destroyed. His modest start included twenty-seven ships (13,382 tons) sunk during 1915. Further complicating its decentralized organizational structure, the navy made *Kapitänleutnant* Karl Bartenbach, prewar commander of *U 1*, head of a separate Flanders Flotilla equal in status to submarine commands created in August 1914 for the North Sea (under the High Sea Fleet) and in October 1914 for the Baltic.[38]

"HEINRICH"

In March 1915, the same month that U-boats began to operate out of Flanders, Austria-Hungary facilitated the expansion of submarine warfare into southern European waters by agreeing to allow German U-boats to operate out of its ports in the Adriatic, an effort it soon augmented with U-boats of its own. The Dual Monarchy entered the war with seven submarines, of which five were capable of offensive action. By December 1914 these were forward-deployed from Pola down the Adriatic to Cattaro (Kotor), at the southern tip of Dalmatia, within range of the blockade line the Allies had imposed in August at the mouth of the Adriatic, across the Straits of Otranto. In the first months of the war, the French navy maintained the blockade with only nominal British support, occasionally sending warships into the Adriatic to shell the Dalmatian coastline or to escort supply shipments to Montenegro and to landlocked Serbia via the Montenegrin port of Antivari (Bar). Vastly outnumbered in their surface strength, the Austrians remained on the defensive but could take heart in two successes late in the year. On 20 December, torpedo boats and shore batteries at Pola sank the French submarine *Curie*, foiling its attempt to enter the harbor to attack the Austrian dreadnoughts anchored there. Then, on the 21st, *U 12* (*Linienschiffsleutnant* Egon Lerch) torpedoed the 23,400-ton French dreadnought *Jean Bart* off the coast of Montenegro, where it was covering a shipment of supplies to Antivari. The *Jean Bart* survived but remained out of action for several months while being repaired at Malta; more significant to the course of the war, the French ended their convoys to Montenegro and never again sent a battleship into the Adriatic. Early in the new year, the Allied blockade line at the mouth of the Adriatic was pulled farther to the south, to a parallel some two hundred miles (320 km) below Cattaro, where the warships maintaining it would be safer from Austrian submarines. The Allied withdrawal left Montenegro's coastal trade undefended, and when Austria-Hungary joined the submarine war on commerce, its first victims were Montenegrin sailing vessels taken as prizes by Lerch's *U 12*, two on 22 March and four more on the 31st.[39]

The onset of unrestricted submarine warfare, and Germany's desire for access to Austrian bases for Mediterranean U-boat operations, provided the two navies with a welcome basis for cooperation that had been lacking up to that point. As with the Flanders Flotilla, the Germans established their first submarine presence in the Adriatic by sending small *UB* boats by rail to be assembled on site. *UB 7*, *UB 8*, and *UB 14* arrived at Pola in March, followed by *UB 3* in April; after they were launched, all were manned by German crews likewise sent overland. They were followed by Hersing's *U 21*, which cruised directly from Wilhelmshaven to Cattaro via the Straits of Gibraltar, making the voyage in eighteen days (25 April–13 May), refueling along the way in neutral Spanish waters. On 27 April, while Hersing was en route, the Austrian *U 5* (*Linienschiffsleutnant* Georg von Trapp) sank the 12,500-ton French armored cruiser *Léon Gambetta* off Cape Santa Maria di Leuca in the Italian boot heel (684 dead), prompting the Allies to pull their blockade line farther south, to the parallel of Cephalonia in the Ionian Islands. Thus, when *U 21* arrived it had no difficulty transiting the Straits of Otranto into the Adriatic. On the day Hersing left Wilhelmshaven, the Allies landed troops at Gallipoli, prompting Berlin to change his mission; after refueling at Cattaro, *U 21* left the Adriatic in search of Allied naval targets off the Dardanelles. While *UB 14* remained stationed at Pola temporarily as a training boat, during May, *UB 3*, *UB 7*, and *UB 8* were towed by Austrian warships into the Ionian Sea, then released to follow Hersing to the Turkish straits. *UB 3* disappeared en route without a trace, but the remaining two boats soon joined *U 21* in the coastal waters of Asia Minor.[40]

Hersing sank two British pre-dreadnoughts off Gallipoli shortly after his arrival, the 11,985-ton *Triumph* on 25 May and the 14,900-ton *Majestic* on the 27th. The attacks came in daylight close to the shore while the ships were providing fire support for Allied troops, allowing all but 113 of the men aboard them to be saved, but because the two sinkings led to a number of false U-boat sightings that disrupted such fire support in the weeks that followed, indirectly *U 21* caused countless casualties among Allied troops attacking the Turkish lines on the peninsula. Hersing's only subsequent unarmed victim, the 5,601-ton French troopship *Carthage*, was empty when sunk off Cape Helles on 4 July. After an uneventful summer patrol in the Black Sea, *U 21* returned to the Adriatic in the autumn to operate out of Austrian bases the following year.[41] The smaller submarines that followed Hersing were less successful. On 30 May, near the mouth of the Dardanelles, *UB 8* (*Oberleutnant* Ernst von Voigt) sank the 19,580-ton *Merion*, a heavily ballasted empty passenger liner masquerading as HMS *Tiger*, a battle cruiser actually stationed in the North Sea. Thereafter, Voigt operated out of Constantinople but claimed no further victims, and after Bulgaria joined the Central Powers (6 September 1915), his boat was transferred to the Bulgarian navy. Meanwhile, *UB 7* (*Oberleutnant* Wilhelm Werner), likewise operating out of Constantinople, sank the 6,011-ton British freighter *Patagonia* off Odessa on 15 September, then registered no further successes before being lost to a Russian mine off the Bulgarian coast a year later. Ironically, when it came to sinking unarmed vessels, Allied submarines operating in the vicinity of the straits took a greater toll than German U-boats. By the end of the Gallipoli campaign, the British navy's *E 11* (Lieutenant Commander Martin Nasmith) and other submarines that followed it through the Dardanelles minefields claimed a total of 29,000 tons of Turkish shipping in the Sea of Marmara, where they also sank a Turkish pre-dreadnought, a destroyer, and five gunboats.[42]

During May 1915 the Germans strengthened Austria-Hungary's small submarine force by shipping *UB 1* and *UB 15* by rail to Pola, where they were recommissioned as Austrian *U 10* and *U 11*. In June the Austrians added another U-boat when the French *Curie*, raised and repaired after being sunk in Pola harbor, entered service as *U 14*. By then, Italy had declared war against Austria-Hungary (23 May 1915) but waited another fifteen months to declare war on Germany; in the meantime, the Germans decided not to force the issue by declaring war on the Italians. During the intervening period, German U-boats operating in the Mediterranean were double-numbered as Austrian U-boats (for example, Hersing's *U 21* as Austrian *U 36*) to ensure their freedom of action against Italian-flagged targets. They carried a second false set of papers and, when possible, an Austrian aboard as one of the junior officers. The boats sent overland from Germany but commissioned by Austria-Hungary likewise included a mixture of personnel, at least for their Adriatic training cruises. This proved confusing not just for the Allies at the time, when attempting to determine the identity of attacking submarines, but for historians years later when attempting to credit tonnage sunk to individual U-boats and commanders. For example, *Oberleutnant* Heino von Heimburg, eventually a vice admiral in the Third Reich, commanded the training cruise of German *UB 15* (actually Austrian *U 11*), during which it sank the Italian submarine *Medusa* on 10 June, but he returned to his regular post commanding Austrian *U 26* (actually German *UB 14*) in time to sink the 9,800-ton Italian armored cruiser *Amalfi* off Venice on 7 July. A week later, Heimberg's boat left the Adriatic for Constantinople. On 13 August, operating as a German submarine, *UB 14* registered the deadliest sinking of a troopship thus far, torpedoing the 11,117-ton *Royal Edward* (866 dead) en route to Gallipoli, but it had less luck in the Black Sea, where Heimberg claimed just three smaller victims later in the year. Even after Germany was at war with Italy, the inconsistency of declarations of war against the Central Powers by other countries (most notably the United States against Germany in April 1917 but not against Austria-Hungary until December 1917) led to the continuation of double numbering all German submarines operating in the Mediterranean for the duration of the war. Ultimately, of the fifty-six German U-boats to receive Austrian numbers, only *U 10* (ex-*UB 1*) and *U 11* (ex-*UB 15*) were actually in the Austrian navy from the time of their arrival; *U 43* (ex-*UB 43*) and *U 47* (ex-*UB 47*) were transferred later, to replace Austrian submarines lost in action.[43] By the end of 1915, the sheer number of German U-boats in the Mediterranean made their presence there an open secret, fueling a quirky camaraderie among the Germans stationed at Austrian bases who, officially, were not there, or at least not German. *Oberleutnant* Martin Niemöller credited Hersing and his subalterns in *U 21* with starting the custom that German officers ashore "irrespective of rank and real name" addressed each other as "Heinrich."[44]

The rapid growth of a submarine presence in a theater detached from all other German naval operations led to the creation of a fourth U-boat command for the boats based in the Adriatic and a fifth for those based at Constantinople. The larger Pola-Cattaro command initially was under *Kapitänleutnant* Hans Adam, who served as the primary liaison with Austrian naval officials. From the start of their cooperation in submarine warfare, the relationship between the navies of the Central Powers featured a great degree of mutual respect. Hersing later recalled that he "was received in Pola and in Cattaro . . . with the greatest warmth and kindness," and the support the Austrians offered him left nothing to be desired. "Every request . . . was fulfilled immediately, whether it was for the accommodation of the crew, or delivery of food, or to assist in the repair of the boat, either at the arsenal in Pola or the depot ship *Gäa* in Cattaro." He harked back fondly to "the days that we were allowed to spend together with our Austrian U-boat comrades on the island of Brioni in Pola harbor, a small paradise" where visitors "could temporarily forget the severity of the war."[45] The Germans also admired the professionalism of the Austrians and envied their traditions. *Kapitänleutnant* Max Valentiner, who spent much of the war operating U-boats out of Austrian bases, recalled that "the naval officer corps impressed me a great deal. I would describe it as exemplary. The officers were all well-mannered" and "the old naval tradition was important to them. There were many officers whose father or grandfather had fought in 1866 under Admiral Tegetthoff at the Battle of Lissa and helped him to defeat the Italians." He considered "the training of the Austrian naval officers" to have been "outstanding." Like Hersing, Valentiner remembered the Austrians as good hosts, generous with their food and drink in the officers' mess of the

Gäa. The "friendly warmth of all Austrian comrades" made a lasting impression on German submariners stationed in the Adriatic.[46]

THE SINKING OF THE *LUSITANIA*

The climax of the first phase of unrestricted submarine warfare came on 7 May 1915, when Walther Schwieger's *U 20* torpedoed and sank the 30,400-ton British passenger liner *Lusitania* off the southern coast of Ireland. The ship had served the Cunard Line on the Liverpool–New York route since 1907, logging over two hundred Atlantic crossings. Designed with deck gun mountings and turbine engines capable of 25 knots, the *Lusitania* was requisitioned by the Admiralty in August 1914 but soon returned to civilian passenger service because its high rate of coal consumption and large crew made it too expensive to operate as an armed merchant cruiser. Thereafter, the *Lusitania* remained profitable in a wartime market that featured far fewer travelers but also fewer travel options, because so many other large liners had been converted to troopships or hospital ships. The liner was in New

FIGURE 2.2.
Walther Schwieger
(German Federal Archives)

York when unrestricted submarine warfare began; it made the crossing to Liverpool and back to New York without incident, even though its captain rebuffed the Admiralty's offer of destroyer escorts through the blockade zone. On 22 April, nine days before its next scheduled departure for Liverpool, the German embassy placed warnings in American newspapers alerting those considering the voyage that "vessels flying the flag of Great Britain, or any of her allies, are liable to destruction in those waters and that travelers sailing in the war zone on the ships of Great Britain or her allies do so at their own risk."[47] In some New York papers, the German warnings appeared alongside Cunard advertisements for the *Lusitania*, but amid the overall decline in demand for transatlantic passage, their impact remains a matter of speculation. Nevertheless, the total number of persons aboard for the ship's final crossing totaled just under two thousand, including roughly one hundred fewer crew and eight hundred fewer passengers than the peacetime norm.

As the *Lusitania* made its way across the Atlantic for the last time, German U-boats registered the most destructive week of the campaign thus far. Between 1 May and 6 May, six submarines sank thirty-one ships of various sizes, twenty-five of them British. Schwieger's *U 20* claimed the two largest of the lot, the 5,858-ton *Candidate*, shelled on the morning of 6 May, and the 5,495-ton *Centurion*, torpedoed on the afternoon of the same day, both off the coast of County Wexford, Ireland. In each case, the crew made it to the lifeboats and there were no casualties.[48] The two sinkings led to numerous warnings of U-boat activity in the general area, including one known to have been received by the *Lusitania*'s captain around noon on 7 May, some two hours before his own ship was sunk. Schwieger first sighted the big Cunard liner around 13:20 on the afternoon of the 7th, in clear weather, around eleven miles (18 km) off Old Head of Kinsale on the southern Irish coast. *U 20* closed quickly and at 14:10 fired a lone torpedo that struck its target at the waterline starboard, below the bridge. An immediate explosion was soon followed by a second blast farther astern, leading to the British contention (maintained for decades) that the U-boat had fired two torpedoes at the *Lusitania* rather than one. Within six minutes the ship's bow was awash, and it sank completely in just eighteen minutes.[49]

In terms of tonnage, the *Lusitania* was twice as large as any ship, naval or civilian, sunk by a submarine up to that point. In terms of lives lost, the 1,198 dead (against 764 survivors) were more than eleven times as many as had perished six weeks earlier in the *Falaba*, the campaign's previous most deadly sinking of a civilian vessel. Indeed, the torpedoing of the *Lusitania* caused more noncombatant deaths than any other recorded single act of war in any war to date. Though it was not an American ship and just 128 of the casualties were US citizens, the incident marked a turning point in American opinion on the war.[50] On 13 May President Wilson responded with a formal protest to Berlin, emphasizing broader principles rather than what he considered the finer point of which flag had been flying aboard the vessel in which American citizens had been attacked or killed. Citing "the sacred freedom of the seas," he asserted that "American citizens act within their indisputable rights . . . in traveling wherever their legitimate business calls them upon the high seas, and exercise those rights in what should be the well-justified confidence that their lives will not be endangered by acts done in clear violation of universally acknowledged international obligations." Wilson also condemned the warnings placed by the German embassy in the American press prior to the sinking of the *Lusitania*, on the grounds that "no warning that an unlawful and inhumane act will be committed can possibly be accepted as an excuse or palliation for that act or as an abatement of the responsibility for its commission."[51]

On 28 May, Foreign Secretary Jagow responded to Wilson's protest by arguing that the *Lusitania* was a legitimate target of war because it had "Canadian troops and munitions on board." The allegation regarding the troops proved to be false, but the ship's own manifest indicated that its cargo included 5,671 cases of cartridges and ammunition, along with 189 containers of unspecified "military goods." Aware that the detonation of these munitions might have caused the second explosion aboard the *Lusitania* and hastened its demise, British investigators subsequently coerced the ship's survivors to support the story that *U 20* had fired two torpedoes rather than one.[52] Yet widespread, fairly accurate reporting regarding the ship's military cargo made no difference to most Americans, who rejected the German position that the *Lusitania* was a legitimate target of war, as did virtually everyone in Britain. One recent analysis confirms that the issue of whether the ship "was carrying munitions . . . was absolutely beside the point" to the British public, which considered the sinking "the greatest single atrocity of the war."[53]

Wilson's initial protest following the *Lusitania* sinking also condemned three earlier German attacks involving American shipping or American loss of life: the sinking of the *Falaba* by *U 28* (28 March), in which the dead included one American; the targeting of the American tanker *Cushing* by bombs from a German plane off the Dutch coast (28 April); and the torpedoing of the American tanker *Gulflight* by Rosenberg-Gruszcyski's *U 30* off the coast of Cornwall (1 May), with the loss of three lives. While Jagow's letter of 28 May had defended the sinking of the *Falaba* along with the *Lusitania*, at Bethmann Hollweg's insistence the foreign secretary promised Wilson an investigation of the incidents involving the two American tankers. Jagow followed up on 1 June with an apology for the attacks on the tankers, citing mistaken identity in both cases, and promised to pay for damages incurred by the *Gulflight*, which had made it to port in Britain without sinking. Germany offered no restitution in the case of the *Cushing*, which incurred no damages after the bombs intended for it fell harmlessly into the sea.[54] The three casualties aboard the *Gulflight* would be the only American deaths caused by a U-boat in an attack against an American ship prior to the second round of unrestricted submarine warfare in 1917–18.

The American public generally approved of Wilson's response to the *Lusitania* sinking, which condemned German behavior without threatening war. The British ambassador in Washington, Sir Cecil Spring Rice, confirmed that Wilson's middle course reflected the sensibilities of most Americans. The embassy's own review of editorials in nearly a thousand newspapers from across the country published in the first three days after the sinking of the *Lusitania* could find only six calling for war with Germany. But the president could not satisfy his leading critics within or outside of his administration. William Jennings Bryan, the Democratic nominee for president in three of the four elections preceding Wilson's 1912 victory, as Wilson's secretary of state advocated a more evenhanded response, including criticism of the British blockade of Germany. Former president Theodore Roosevelt advocated a declaration of war and at least privately condemned Wilson's "cowardice and weakness."[55]

Evidence from the German side indicates that Wilson's position following the sinking of the *Lusitania* was strong enough to have a moderating effect on both William II and Bethmann Hollweg. The chancellor even informed German navy leaders that he "refused to be responsible for the campaign in its existing form." Public pressure had driven the chancellor to support unrestricted submarine warfare in the first place, and Tirpitz concluded that, at this stage, public opinion alone was keeping him from abandoning it. "He wanted to keep up the appearance" of continuing the campaign while at the same time introducing restrictions designed to avoid further offense to the Americans. Toward this end, Bethmann Hollweg persuaded William II to follow Jagow's apology for the attacks on the American tankers by renewing earlier orders against targeting neutral vessels; on 6 June, the emperor took the further step of banning attacks on large passenger liners, including those flying Allied flags. The new orders drew a sharp response from Tirpitz and Bachmann, who tendered their resignations in protest.[56] After William II compelled them to stay on and accept a submarine warfare that was far from unrestricted, they joined Bethmann Hollweg in urging the emperor to keep the new orders secret in order to preserve the credibility of the policy both domestically and internationally. He agreed, with fateful consequences for German-American relations. On 8 June, the pacifist Bryan resigned from Wilson's cabinet rather than support a policy he considered ineffective and likely to lead the United States to war with Germany. His successor as American secretary of state, Robert Lansing, soon became the cabinet's leading voice for intervention on the side of the Allies.[57]

German-American relations were further poisoned by the depiction of the sinking of the *Lusitania* on postcards and commemorative medals within Germany, though British propaganda alleging widespread celebration of the sinking had no basis in fact. Indeed, the British themselves struck many more copies of the relatively small number of original German medals and circulated them for propaganda purposes. Such efforts ensured that the sinking would cause irreparable harm to the public image of Germany in the United States. For his part, Schwieger did not enjoy the same status or acclaim accorded the war's first U-boat hero, Weddigen, in the wake of the sinking of the *Aboukir*, *Hogue*, and *Cressy*. While Weddigen had not hesitated to sink enemy warships regardless of the loss of life, he had taken a well-documented chivalrous approach to the sinking of civilian vessels. Schwieger, in contrast, from the start had been more coldblooded than most of his peers and, as a consequence, more effective than most of them. Even before 7 May his *U 20* had already sunk 33,000 tons of Allied shipping; the *Lusitania* nearly doubled that total, and a successful spring and summer would increase it further to 111,330 tons by the end of the first phase of unrestricted submarine warfare in September, a total that made him the war's early leader among U-boat commanders. Yet the German government deliberately did not honor Schwieger for sinking the *Lusitania*, or at any time during 1915, instead making him wait over a year to receive his next war decoration.[58]

On 9 June, still unaware of the impact of his first *Lusitania* note, Wilson sent a second note to Berlin, responding to Jagow's communications of 28 May and 1 June. He expressed "gratification" at Germany's apology for the attacks on the American tankers *Gulflight* and *Cushing* but rejected the justification of the sinking of the British *Falaba* and *Lusitania*. He dismissed German allegations that munitions had been aboard the *Lusitania* as "irrelevant to the question of the legality of the methods used by the German naval authorities in sinking the vessel."[59] Jagow waited until 8 July to respond, then merely repeated the contents of his previous note of 28 May. Wilson's third *Lusitania* note, dated 21 July, was the harshest of all, warning that the United States would uphold the maritime rights of neutrals "at any cost" and view "as deliberately unfriendly . . . repetition by the commanders of German naval vessels of acts in contravention of those rights." Nevertheless, he acknowledged the apparent (though still secret) changes in the rules of engagement for U-boat commanders, which had resulted in fewer attacks on neutral vessels over the past two months, and none on large passenger liners. The president even expressed confidence that "it is possible and practicable to conduct [German] submarine operations . . . in substantial accord with the accepted practices of regulated warfare."[60]

While the ultimate responsibility for the sinking of the *Lusitania*, of course, rested with the Germans, it was the Admiralty's cynical calculation that Britain had nothing to lose by shipping war materiel aboard civilian liners. Most of these shipments would make it through, and every passenger vessel sunk by a U-boat brought the United States closer to entering the war on the side of the Allies. The suggestion that Churchill, in his role as First Lord of the Admiralty, had orchestrated the disaster to provoke an American declaration of war on Germany aroused conspiracy theorists at the time and has continued to do so ever since. Churchill eventually fanned the flames by writing, on the eve of the next world war, that "in spite of all its horror, we must regard the sinking of the *Lusitania* as an event most important and favorable to the Allies."[61] In any event, the sinking reinforced the British conviction regarding the absolute illegitimacy of unrestricted submarine warfare and their intention, eventually, to treat German submariners as war criminals. Ironically, the impasse over the captured men of *U 8* and *U 12* ended less than a month later, after the ongoing debacle at the Dardanelles and Gallipoli forced Churchill to resign his post. The new First Lord, former prime minister Arthur Balfour, announced on 4 June that the thirty-nine captive German submariners and any subsequent survivors of sunken U-boats would be treated the same as any other prisoners of war, with "the general question of personal responsibility" for war crimes "reserved until the end of the war."[62]

FROM THE *LUSITANIA* TO THE *ARABIC* PLEDGE

By making sure that the *Lusitania* remained an exception in loss of civilian life, the Germans at least momentarily were able to inflict damage on Allied shipping without further alienating the Americans. The total tonnage claimed (not counting enemy warships sunk) was impressive enough. The figure for May, 126,900 tons, nearly surpassed March and April combined and was followed by 115,900 tons in June, 98,005 in July, and 182,770 in August.[63] During the summer, as in the spring, the typical vessel destroyed was relatively small and was sunk by a surfaced U-boat using its deck gun after the crew had been allowed to abandon ship. In cases where lives were lost, the casualties almost always numbered less than ten. In the three and a half months after the sinking of the *Lusitania*, the single most destructive incident (in terms of tonnage, cargo, and lives lost) occurred off the coast of Cornwall on 28 June, when Schneider's *U 24* torpedoed the 8,825-ton *Armenian*, a British steamer inbound from Hampton Roads with 1,400 mules aboard. Even though the crew was given time to abandon ship, twenty-nine men drowned in the sinking, many of them African American muleteers who refused to leave their animals.[64] Meanwhile, from May until the suspension of the unrestricted campaign, U-boats rarely went looking for Allied warships to sink. Other than the vessels torpedoed by Hersing and Heimberg, the most significant sinking occurred on 18 July off the Dalmatian coast, where Austrian *U 4* (*Linienschiffsleutnant* Rudolf Singule) torpedoed the 7,235-ton Italian armored cruiser *Giuseppe Garibaldi* (53 dead).[65]

While German submariners established a presence at Pola, Cattaro, and Constantinople, laying the foundation for future operations in the Mediterranean and Black Seas, during the same months they gradually expanded their range in northern waters as well, sinking targets beyond the blockade zone defined in Pohl's declaration of 4 February and also giving no quarter to the Scandinavian neutrals, especially Norway. Independent only since 1905, Norway had a large merchant marine registry but a negligible navy and, unlike Sweden and Denmark, traded more with Britain (its primary source of coal) than with Germany. The first Norwegian vessel was torpedoed on the second day of unrestricted submarine warfare, and U-boats went on to sink or capture a total of fifty over the next seven months, many of which were not in the blockade zone. The attacks escalated with the arrival of spring. During May, four different U-boats sank neutral ships in the central North Sea—two Norwegian, one Swedish, and one Danish—all north of Dogger Bank. The following month, likewise outside of the zone, Max Valentiner's *U 38* sank six British drifters (small deep-sea fishing vessels) on the same day, 23 June, all in waters north and east of the Shetland Islands, one of them above 61° N latitude. In late July *Kapitänleutnant* Hansen, having exchanged *U 16* for the newer and larger *U 41*, sank a Norwegian steamer bound for Bergen from New York, likewise above 61° N, at a point halfway between the Shetlands and the Faroe Islands.[66] The attacks became so frequent that Norwegian shipowners ultimately could assemble crews only by promising bonuses to survivors of vessels sunk by U-boats.[67]

In the spring and summer of 1915, a major eastern offensive of the Central Powers drove the Russians out of Poland. Concerned for the first time about Russia's long-term ability to stay in the war, Britain began to send supplies to its ally via the port of Archangel. To disrupt this effort, the navy sent Hoppe's *U 22* far beyond the blockade zone into the Arctic Sea, above 69° N, where on 8 August it sank the 7,940-ton British armed merchant cruiser *India* (160 dead) and, four days later, the British freighter *Grodno*. Meanwhile, the Russian army's retreat enabled the German navy to move the base of its Baltic submarine flotilla from Danzig to Libau (Liepaja) in occupied Latvia, 165 miles (265 km) closer to Petrograd. Berckheim's *U 26* remained the most successful of the Baltic U-boats, sinking two more Russian merchantmen and the 3,600-ton minelayer *Yenisei* before disappearing without a trace after 30 August, likely the victim of a mine. The Russian navy had been a leader in mine development since the Russo-Turkish War of 1877–78, and at least in 1914–15 its mines were still considered the most lethal. Ernst Hashagen, one of the most successful submarine commanders later in the war, noted that "no U-boat captain . . . willingly entered the Gulf of Finland," and "everyone who had any say in the matter steered clear of Russian operations."[68] Fortunately for German submariners, the dearth of enemy shipping in the Baltic gave the navy no reason to expand the U-boat force there.

Amid extensive minelaying conducted by both sides, the German navy began to supplement its oceangoing *U* and coastal *UB* boats with *UC* minelayers. The first fifteen *UC* boats, built by AG Vulcan of Hamburg and AG Weser of Bremen, were launched between April and August 1915. They were only slightly larger than the original *UB* coastal submarines, with a surfaced displacement of just under 170 tons. Like the first *UB* boats, they were manned by one officer and a crew of thirteen and had a surfaced speed of just 6–7 knots. Their only armament consisted of a dozen mines, two in each of six vertical launching chutes located under the foredeck, from which the weighted mines were dropped out of the bottom of the boat. The British first became aware of their existence on 2 July in the waters off Great Yarmouth when a coastal steamer ran over the submerged remains of *UC 2*, the apparent victim of an accident involving one of its own mines that had killed all hands.

The loss of *UC 2* was the first of five confirmed cases of a *UC* boat blowing itself up, most likely when a mine's weight chain had broken or fouled during deployment, causing the mine to bob upward and detonate against the boat's bottom. The first great success by a minelaying submarine came on 15 August off the coast of Finland, where *UC 4* (*Oberleutnant* Karl Vesper) mined and sank the 6,136-ton Russian minelayer *Ladoga* (ex-*Minin*). For the remainder of the war the greatest number of *UC* boats were assigned to the Flanders Flotilla, but some ended up in the Baltic, Adriatic, and Black Seas.[69]

The respite in diplomatic tension that followed Wilson's third *Lusitania* note ended on 19 August when Schneider's *U 24* torpedoed and sank the 15,800-ton British passenger liner *Arabic*. The attack occurred off the Irish coast south of Old Head of Kinsale, roughly forty miles (64 km) from the spot where the *Lusitania* had been sunk. The Germans could offer little justification for sinking the *Arabic*, which was outbound from Liverpool to New York and could not have been carrying supplies for the Allied war effort. The liner was half the size of the *Lusitania*, with a fraction of the number of passengers aboard, just forty-four of whom perished in the sinking, but two of the dead were American citizens. The deaths of Americans aboard a large passenger liner torpedoed by a U-boat put Wilson in a position of having to respond in a manner consistent with the warning included in his note of 21 July. His personal advisor, Colonel Edward House, joined Secretary of State Lansing in advising him that the United States should break diplomatic relations with Germany and prepare for war, but before taking such measures, the president wanted to give the Germans the opportunity to disavow the sinking. Lansing, who favored war on the spot, recast Wilson's response as a warning to the German ambassador, Count Johann von Bernstorff, that Germany could avoid war with the United States only by ending unrestricted submarine warfare.[70]

With most of the action on land in 1915 taking place in the east, William II and his entourage spent the summer at Schloss Pless in Silesia, the German army's eastern front headquarters. In a meeting there on 26 August, a week after the sinking of the *Arabic*, Bethmann Hollweg informed Tirpitz and Bachmann of his intention to promise Wilson that henceforth, "submarine commanders had definite orders not to torpedo passenger steamers without warning, and without opportunity being given for the rescue of passengers and crews." The capitulation was certain to carry a price domestically, since German public and political opinion had remained enthusiastic about unrestricted submarine warfare. Indeed, as recently as

15 August, Jagow had boasted to a Reichstag committee that Germany "would not allow its submarine policy to be influenced by America." The chancellor minimized the backlash by withholding announcement of the change in policy until after the end of the Reichstag's summer session the following day, 27 August, a decision that made it easier for the emperor to keep Bethmann Hollweg and Jagow in their posts, but the breach between the political and naval leadership could not be mended. Tirpitz and Bachmann rejected the chancellor's response to Wilson, soon to be known as the "*Arabic* pledge," as tantamount to an admission "that the submarine campaign was unlawful" and submitted their resignations once again. Pohl likewise asked to be relieved of command of the High Sea Fleet. The emperor insisted that Tirpitz and Pohl remain at their posts but decided to let Bachmann go, on 5 September calling Admiral Henning von Holtzendorff out of retirement to replace him as chief of the *Admiralstab*. Holtzendorff was an old rival of Tirpitz, and his appointment signaled the end of the state secretary's long tenure as Germany's most influential admiral. William II assured Tirpitz that he would still seek his advice "on all important questions of naval policy," but thereafter he would reside in Berlin rather than at headquarters and be in no position to function in an advisory role.[71]

Holtzendorff soon formed a common front with Bethmann Hollweg and the chief of the army High Command, General Erich von Falkenhayn, in favor of a more definitive, unambiguous end to unrestricted submarine warfare that would require U-boats to conform to traditional cruiser rules in their approach to unarmed ships. Such orders were deemed necessary because the continued aggressiveness of some U-boat commanders threatened to make the *Arabic* pledge a dead letter. The worst case had occurred on 4 September, when Schwieger's *U 20* torpedoed the 10,920-ton British liner *Hesperian*, outbound from Liverpool to Montreal, without warning. The incident would have had major repercussions if the ship had not taken two days to sink while under tow for Queenstown, finally going under in the vicinity of the wrecks of the *Lusitania* and *Arabic*. There were just thirty-two casualties, none of them American, all lost when a lifeboat capsized. Keen to avoid another international incident, William II issued the requisite orders returning the German undersea force to cruiser rules, effective 18 September.[72]

Germany abandoned its experiment with unrestricted submarine warfare exactly seven months after announcing it, even though the most recent and current months (August, with 182,770 tons sunk, and September, which would end with 136,050) were the most successful thus far.[73] During the course of the campaign, forty-nine U-boats (including thirteen *UB* boats and seven *UC* minelayers) sank ships totaling roughly three-quarters of a million tons. Fourteen U-boats were lost, seven with all hands. Ten commanders were killed and four taken prisoner after surviving the loss of their boats. The dead included two of the most successful commanders, Weddigen and Wegener. On a positive note for the Germans, the thirty-eight commanders who sank ships during the campaign and survived unscathed would put their experience to good use, sinking a total of just over 3.3 million tons of shipping plus three dozen warships of various sizes by the end of the war.

Because Britain had entered the war with over twenty-one million tons of merchant shipping capacity, the destruction of less than a million tons, not all of it from the British registry, had a negligible impact on the Allied war effort. In the end, Bachmann proved to be correct in his prediction that an unrestricted campaign undertaken with inadequate resources and inconsistent support from the political leadership would have "no effect in securing the ultimate victory of the German people" but "enough to create incidents and quarrels with the Americans."[74] The *Arabic* pledge promised to defuse diplomatic tensions with the United States, and despite the discord it caused between German political and naval leaders, it remained to be seen how much practical impact the change from unrestricted to restricted submarine warfare would have. During the past seven months, only in rare cases had German submarine commanders destroyed targets without warning or without regard to civilian casualties. Most victims of the unrestricted campaign had been sunk by surfaced U-boats using their deck guns after those aboard had been allowed to abandon ship. That would still be the case after 18 September. Two developments during the campaign also created lasting ambiguities that would enable U-boats to continue to take a considerable toll at no cost to German-American relations. The *UC* boats introduced a new element to undersea warfare, a submarine that sank its victims with mines rather than torpedoes or a deck gun, leaving the Allies and Americans unable to definitively attribute the sinkings to U-boat activity. At the same time, the double numbering of German U-boats as Austrian allowed the expansion of submarine warfare into the Mediterranean, leaving the Allies and Americans unable to attribute the sinkings there to the Germans even when U-boats obviously were to blame. Indeed, the decision to end the unrestricted campaign coincided with the September deployment of some of the most successful U-boats and commanders to the Mediterranean in anticipation of having them operate there throughout the autumn and winter in a relatively undefended environment using

Austria-Hungary's Adriatic bases. These included *U 33* (*Kapitänleutnant* Konrad Gansser), *U 34* (*Kapitänleutnant* Claus Rücker), *U 35* (*Kapitänleutnant* Waldemar Kophamel), and *U 39* (*Kapitänleutnant* Walter Forstmann), followed in November by *U 38* (*Kapitänleutnant* Max Valentiner). These five officers, by war's end, ranked among the seventeen most successful U-boat commanders in terms of tonnage sunk. Along with Hersing's *U 21*, redeployed from the Black Sea back to the Adriatic for 1916, they helped to ensure that the interlude between the end of unrestricted submarine warfare and its ultimate resumption would remain eventful.

Less than nine months passed between the publication of Tirpitz's interview with Wiegand and the end of Germany's initial unrestricted campaign, but in that time the war had changed profoundly, and with it the world had changed forever. The sinking of the *Lusitania* caused the greatest sensation at the time and became history's most shocking example of unrestricted submarine warfare. Along with the coinciding first use of poison gas on the battlefield and first air raids on cities, it signaled that the First World War would break new ground in man's inhumanity toward man. While such practices made war far deadlier, they also made it easier for the belligerents to mobilize their populations for an unprecedented total war, with the caveat that, once they gave their wholehearted support, they were disinclined to accept compromise. The Second Reich experienced this phenomenon early on. The extent of the German public's support for unrestricted submarine warfare as a response to the British blockade, its callous reaction to the *Lusitania* and other sinkings, and its disappointment at the campaign's suspension all serve as examples of the extent to which 1915 marked a turning point in a long process of desensitization that made the brutality of modern total war an accepted part of the human experience.[75]

NOTES

1. Tirpitz to Marie von Tirpitz, 28 September 1914, text in Tirpitz, *My Memoirs*, 2:242.

2. Tirpitz, *Ohnmachtspolitik*, 623; Francis W. Halsey, *The Literary Digest History of the World War*, 10 vols. (1919; reprint New York: Cosimo Classics, 2009), 9:235.

3. Tirpitz to Marie von Tirpitz, 21 November 1914, text in Tirpitz, *My Memoirs*, 2:272.

4. Zacher, *Scripps Newspapers*, 52.

5. Tirpitz, *Ohnmachtspolitik*, 623–27, reproduces the entire German text of the interview; Halsey, *Literary Digest History*, 9:235–36, quotes extensively from the English text.

6. Halsey, *Literary Digest History*, 9:236. The original German text says "one or two" rather than "several" merchant ships; see Tirpitz, *Ohnmachtspolitik*, 627.

7. Zacher, *Scripps Newspapers*, 238n125.

8. Sampling of American press, 22–24 December 1914, from http://newspaperarchive
.com. Halsey, *Literary Digest History*, 9:235, indicates the interview first appeared in the
New York World on 8 December, but all other sources have the *World* publishing it on
23 December.

9. Avner Offer, *The First World War: An Agrarian Interpretation* (Oxford: Clarendon
Press, 1989), 336.

10. Ibid., 54.

11. Theobald von Bethmann Hollweg, *Betrachtungen zum Weltkriege*, 2 vols. (Berlin:
Hobbing, 1919–21), 2:121.

12. Pohl to Ella von Pohl, 22 December 1914, text in Hugo von Pohl, *Aus Aufzeichnungen und Briefen während der Kriegszeit* (Berlin: Karl Siegismund, 1920), 93.

13. Pohl to Ella von Pohl, 23 December 1914, text in ibid., 94.

14. Bethmann Hollweg, *Betrachtungen*, 2:121.

15. Pohl to Ella von Pohl, 24 November 1914, text in Pohl, *Aufzeichnungen*, 90. See also
Raffael Scheck, *Alfred von Tirpitz and German Right-Wing Politics* (Atlantic Highlands,
NJ: Humanities Press, 1998), 35–36.

16. Tirpitz, *Ohnmachtspolitik*, 623; Halsey, *Literary Digest History*, 9:235.

17. Tirpitz to Pohl, 16 December 1914, text in Tirpitz, *My Memoirs*, 2:141–42.

18. Memorandum of *Korvettenkapitän* Mann, 3 January 1915, text in Tirpitz, *Ohnmachtspolitik*, 295.

19. Holger H. Herwig, "Total Rhetoric, Limited War: Germany's U-Boat Campaign
1917–1918," *Journal of Military and Strategic Studies* 1, no. 1 (1998), http://jmss.org/jmss/
index.php/jmss/article/view/19/18.

20. Sondhaus, *The Great War at Sea*, 123–27.

21. Tirpitz, *My Memoirs*, 2:143, 145.

22. "German Declaration of Naval Blockade against Shipping to Britain," Berlin, 4 February 1915, http://www.firstworldwar.com/source/pohl_uboatwar1915.htm.

23. Tirpitz, *My Memoirs*, 2:144.

24. "Text of U.S. 'Strict Accountability' Warning to Germany," 10 February 1915,
http://firstworldwar.com/source/wilsonwarningfeb1915.htm.

25. Tirpitz, *My Memoirs*, 2:149.

26. Pohl to Ella von Pohl, 15 February 1915, text in Pohl, *Aufzeichnungen*, 111; Pohl to
Ella von Pohl, 16 February 1915, text in ibid., 112.

27. Tirpitz, *My Memoirs*, 2:152.

28. Lowell Thomas, *Raiders of the Deep* (1928; reprint Penzance, UK: Periscope Publishing, 2002), 170–72; Robert M. Grant, *U-Boats Destroyed: The Effect of Anti-Submarine
Warfare, 1914–1918* (London: Putnam, 1964), 151.

29. Gröner, *Die deutschen Kriegsschiffe*, 3:26–34, 48–49; *Conway 1906–21*, 175–76, 180,
and http://uboat.net/wwi/types.

30. Nikolaus Jaud, "Christmas and New Year, 1914–1915, on *U 24*," in *U-Boat Stories: Narratives of German U-Boat Sailors*, ed. Karl Neureuther and Claus Bergen, trans.
Eric Sutton (London: Constable, 1931), 68; Lewis Bayly, *Pull Together! The Memoirs of
Admiral Sir Lewis Bayly* (London: George G. Harrap, 1939), 175–76, 181; http://uboat
.net/wwi/ships_hit.

31. Gibson and Prendergast, *The German Submarine War*, 17, 20–21; see also http://www.archeosousmarine.net/villedelille.html; http://uboat.net/wwi/ships_hit.

32. http://uboat.net/wwi/ships_hit.

33. "Sur Mer: Comment 'Auguste-Conseil' fut coulé," *Le Figaro*, 16 March 1915, clipping at http://www.wrecksite.eu/doc/wrecks/auguste_conseil_l_f_.jpg.

34. Kirchhoff, *Weddigen*, 44–47; Paul Kemp, *U-Boats Destroyed: German Submarine Losses in the Two World Wars* (Annapolis, MD: Naval Institute Press, 1997), 12.

35. These are the most widely cited figures, totaling 128,100 for the two months combined. Detailed data at http://uboat.net/wwi total up to 128,089 for the two months combined, but with 70,195 tons for March and 57,894 for April.

36. Forstner, *Journal*, 62; http://uboat.net/wwi/ships_hit.

37. James F. Willis, *Prologue to Nuremberg: The Politics and Diplomacy of Punishing War Criminals of the First World War* (Westport, CT: Greenwood, 1982), 17–21; Kemp, *U-Boats Destroyed*, 11–12.

38. Werner Fürbringer, *Fips: Legendary U-Boat Commander, 1915–1918*, trans. Geoffrey Brooks (1933; reprint Annapolis, MD: Naval Institute Press, 1999), 11–14; http://uboat.net/wwi/men/commanders/343.html.

39. Sondhaus, *The Naval Policy of Austria-Hungary*, 264–65; http://uboat.net/wwi/boats/successes/kuk12.html.

40. Sondhaus, *The Naval Policy of Austria-Hungary*, 268; Paul G. Halpern, *The Naval War in the Mediterranean* (Annapolis, MD: Naval Institute Press, 1987), 110–11, 116.

41. Hersing, *U 21 rettet die Dardanellen*, 51–77.

42. Bernd Langensiepen, Dirk Nottelmann, and Jochen Krüsmann, *Halbmond und Kaiseradler: Goeben und Breslau am Bosporus, 1914–1918* (Hamburg: Verlag E. S. Mittler & Sohn, 1999), 64–94 passim; Halpern, *The Naval War in the Mediterranean*, 161, 189.

43. Sondhaus, *The Naval Policy of Austria-Hungary*, 268, 279–80; Halpern, *The Naval War in the Mediterranean*, 154; Heino von Heimburg, *U-Boot gegen U-Boot* (Berlin: Druck und Verlag August Scherl, 1917), 28–35.

44. Martin Niemöller, *From U-Boat to Pulpit*, trans. D. Hastie Smith (Chicago: Willett, Clark, 1937), 84.

45. Hersing, *U 21 rettet die Dardanellen*, 78–79.

46. Max Valentiner, *Der Schrecken der Meere: Meine U-Boot-Abenteuer* (Leipzig: Amalthea-Verlag, 1931), 118–19.

47. Text in Diana Preston, *Lusitania: An Epic Tragedy* (New York: Walker Publishing, 2002), 91.

48. http://uboat.net/wwi/ships_hit/losses_year.html?date=1915-05&string=May+1915.

49. Preston, *Lusitania*, 190–244 passim.

50. While all sources agree on the number of dead, the number of Americans lost ranges from 123 to 128, depending upon whom one counts as "American." Figures for the number of survivors vary more widely, owing to discrepancies between the passenger list and persons actually aboard. One hundred eighty-eight passengers had some claim to American citizenship.

51. "U.S. Protest over the Sinking of the *Lusitania*," Washington, DC, 13 May 1915, http://www.firstworldwar.com/source/bryanlusitaniaprotest.htm. This source attributes

the protest note to Secretary of State William Jennings Bryan, but Justus D. Doenecke, *Nothing Less Than War: A New History of America's Entry into World War I* (Lexington: University Press of Kentucky, 2011), 77, is the most recent of many historians to identify Wilson as the author.

52. "The Sinking of the *Lusitania*—Official German Response by Foreign Minister Gottlieb von Jagow," Berlin, 28 May 1915, http://www.firstworldwar.com/source/lu sitania_germanresponse.htm. On the British investigation and invention of the "second torpedo" theory, see Preston, *Lusitania*, 402–4.

53. Adrian Gregory, *The Last Great War: British Society and the First World War* (Cambridge: Cambridge University Press, 2008), 61.

54. Doenecke, *Nothing Less Than War*, 69–70.

55. Ibid., 73, 78–79.

56. Tirpitz, *My Memoirs*, 2:156–58.

57. Doenecke, *Nothing Less Than War*, 79–84.

58. http://uboat.net/wwi/men/commanders/322.html.

59. "Second U.S. Protest over the Sinking of the *Lusitania*," Washington, DC, May [*sic*—9 June] 1915, http://www.firstworldwar.com/source/lusitania_2ndusprotest.htm.

60. "Third U.S. Protest over the Sinking of the *Lusitania*," Washington, 21 July 1915, http://www.firstworldwar.com/source/lusitania_3rdusprotest.htm.

61. Quoted in Preston, *Lusitania*, 5.

62. Quoted in Willis, *Prologue to Nuremberg*, 21.

63. These are the most widely cited figures; http://uboat.net/wwi lists ships totaling 127,650 tons for May, 115,879 for June, 101,510 for July, and 188,155 for August.

64. Nikolaus Jaud, "The Sinking of the *Armenia*," in *U-Boat Stories: Narratives of German U-Boat Sailors*, ed. Karl Neureuther and Claus Bergen, trans. Eric Sutton (London: Constable & Company, 1931), 146–50; http://uboat.net/wwi/ships_hit/451.html.

65. Sondhaus, *The Naval Policy of Austria-Hungary*, 280–81.

66. http://uboat.net/wwi/ships_hit/losses_year.html?date=1915-05&string=May+1915; http://uboat.net/wwi/ships_hit/losses_year.html?date=1915-05&string=June+1915; http:// uboat.net/wwi/ships_hit/losses_year.html?date=1915-05&string=July+1915.

67. Thomas, *Raiders of the Deep*, 274.

68. http://uboat.net/wwi/boats/successes/u22.html; http://uboat.net/wwi/boats/index .html?boat=26; Ernst Hashagen, *U-Boats Westward*, trans. Vesey Ross (New York: Putnam, 1931), 112.

69. Gröner, *Die deutschen Kriegsschiffe*, 3:57; Robert M. Grant, *U-Boat Intelligence, 1914–1918* (Hamden, CT: Archon, 1969), 13–14; Gibson and Prendergast, *The German Submarine War*, 50; http://uboat.net/wwi/boats/successes/uc4.html.

70. Doenecke, *Nothing Less Than War*, 116–18.

71. Tirpitz, *My Memoirs*, 2:161–67; Pohl to Ella von Pohl, 3 September 1915, text in Pohl, *Aufzeichnungen*, 146; see also Patrick J. Kelly, *Tirpitz and the Imperial German Navy* (Bloomington: Indiana University Press, 2011), 400, 403–4.

72. Tirpitz, *My Memoirs*, 2:169–70. See also http://www.rmslusitania.info/related -ships/hesperian/#attack.

73. The most generally quoted figure for September is 136,050 tons; http://uboat.net/wwi lists ships totaling 143,564 tons, including 85,987 taken through 18 September and 57,577 after.

74. Tirpitz, *My Memoirs*, 2:151.

75. Lawrence Sondhaus, *World War One: The Global Revolution* (Cambridge: Cambridge University Press, 2011), 4–5. See also Diana Preston, *A Higher Form of Killing: Six Weeks in World War I That Forever Changed the Nature of Warfare* (New York: Bloomsbury, 2015).

3

Interlude

Kapitänleutnant Max Valentiner had been in the Mediterranean for less than a week but already found it very much to his liking. After passing Gibraltar on 3 November 1915, his *U 38* made its way eastward along the North African coast, sinking a dozen Allied vessels totaling 33,096 tons; except for the French troopship *Calvados*, torpedoed on the 4th off Oran (740 dead), all were merchantmen destroyed under cruiser rules. He encountered his first passenger liner on the morning of 7 November while cruising west of Sicily. Valentiner sighted the Italian-flagged *Ancona* at 11:40, just as a heavy fog was lifting. The 8,210-ton ship, outbound from Naples to New York, with 572 passengers and crew aboard, did not heed his initial signal to stop, ultimately complying only after a ten-minute pursuit and sixteen shots from *U 38*'s deck gun. Curiously, during the chase, six of the *Ancona*'s lifeboats were lowered, full, yet when the ship finally stopped, there appeared to be much confusion on its deck and few of the remaining boats were deployed. "I could not believe that the crew would have left . . . the passengers to fend for themselves," Valentiner recalled later, but that, indeed, had been the case: the men in the six lifeboats had been the *Ancona*'s crew, abandoning the passengers to their fate even while the ship was still underway. Under the restrictions in effect since 18 September, Valentiner remained surfaced for forty-five minutes to give those aboard the opportunity to save themselves, but with smoke on the horizon indicating the approach of other ships, he could not afford to linger much longer before deciding to sink or spare the *Ancona*. At 12:35, standing off at 800 meters, he "shot a torpedo aimed at the bow of the steamer, to not sink it suddenly, but slowly, in order to give the people time to take to the lifeboats." The *Ancona* finally disappeared beneath the waves at 13:20, and given the additional time to abandon ship, all but 27 passengers ultimately survived. Valentiner had shown restraint under considerable pressure, but in the United States the Wilson administration considered the sinking yet another instance of a submarine torpedoing a passenger liner and killing innocent civilians, the dead in this case including nine Americans. Press reports that the *Ancona* had been torpedoed without warning, resulting in two or three hundred deaths, many of them women and children, only made matters worse. In the days that followed, the sinking of the *Ancona* very nearly led to a rupture in diplomatic relations—not between the United States and Germany, but between the United States and Austria-Hungary.[1]

Under the arrangement the Central Powers had made earlier in the year, Valentiner's boat had become Austrian when it passed through the Straits of Gibraltar. When he stopped the *Ancona*, *U 38* was flying the Austrian flag. Thus the subsequent American protests were directed not to Berlin but to Vienna, where the Austrian foreign minister, Count István Burián, defended the actions of *U 38* as if it were an Austrian submarine. Wilson's inner circle revisited their debate that had followed the sinking of the *Arabic* three months earlier, with Lansing and House again pushing the president to the brink of war; this time, however, they were frustrated by the absence

FIGURE 3.1. *U 38* in the Mediterranean

of hard evidence implicating Germany. Lansing, in particular, suspected that *U 38* was a German submarine, a view shared by much of the American press, but Burián maintained the ruse that the boat was Austrian, so Lansing had to as well. In his quest for a satisfactory outcome, Lansing found that threatening war over the sinking of the *Ancona* rang hollow because it was extremely unlikely that the United States would go to war with Austria-Hungary but not also Germany. In the American ultimatum to Vienna, dated 6 December, the secretary of state demanded a disavowal of the sinking, an indemnity, and punishment for the U-boat's commander. After several tense exchanges, on 29 December Burián gave Lansing his final response. He did not disavow the actions of *U 38* but agreed to pay an indemnity and indicated that the commander had been "punished . . . for exceeding his instructions." Burián also promised that Austria-Hungary henceforth would forbid its U-boat commanders from sinking merchantmen without giving those aboard the opportunity to save themselves, thus echoing Bethmann Hollweg's *Arabic* pledge. The outcome satisfied Wilson and was hailed in the press as a victory for American diplomacy. The crisis passed.[2]

Valentiner, of course, had remained on duty and was not punished. Between the sinking of the *Ancona* and the end of 1915, he claimed four more victims, increasing his total to seventeen ships sunk (68,972 tons) in just two months since entering the Mediterranean. The *Ancona* affair did not cause him to shy away from controversy. Hunting for targets off Crete on 30 December, the day after Burián's final statement to the Americans, Valentiner torpedoed and sank the 7,950-ton British liner *Persia* without warning. The 334 dead included two Americans, but the US consulate in Egypt soon confirmed the Austrian contention that the *Persia* had mounted a 4.7-inch (12 cm) gun, thus justifying Valentiner's decision to treat it as an auxiliary cruiser rather than a passenger ship.[3]

During the autumn of 1915, other German submarines in the Mediterranean, operating, like *U 38*, as Austrian submarines of the same numbers, also posted per-month totals of tonnage sunk that were greater than those registered in the unrestricted campaign. Gansser's *U 33* led the way, sinking twenty-eight ships (88,389 tons), followed by Valentiner's *U 38*, then Forstmann's *U 39* with twenty-one victims (65,002 tons). Kophamel's *U 35* added another sixteen (59,997 tons), while Rücker's *U 34* sank ten ships (37,218 tons). Thus, within the span of four months, just five German submarines sank nearly 320,000 tons of Allied shipping in the Mediterranean alone, all while operating under the restriction of cruiser rules. The total tonnage equaled over a third of the amount destroyed by all forty-nine U-boats that had registered successes during the preceding seven months of unrestricted submarine warfare. And thanks to their double numbering, their ninety-two victims included thirteen ships registered to Italy, an Allied country with which Germany was not yet at war.

While these U-boats exploited the ambiguities of the Mediterranean to Germany's advantage, closer to home the deployment of *UC* minelayers also worked as planned, likewise sinking Allied shipping at no cost to German-American relations. Between 18 September and the end of 1915, the mines sown by just six *UC* boats sank fifty-one merchant vessels (71,326 tons) along Britain's North Sea coast, plus a British destroyer and a submarine. In the wake of the abandonment of unrestricted submarine warfare, German leaders celebrated the success of the *UC* minelayers and of the U-boats sent to the Mediterranean, but their mood was tempered by sharp disagreement over the significance of it all. For Bethmann Hollweg and most of the civilian ministers, the results showed that unrestricted submarine warfare was unnecessary, while for Tirpitz and his allies, the demonstration of what could be accomplished with restricted submarine warfare led to speculation about just how devastating a properly prepared and supported unrestricted campaign would be.

TIRPITZ'S LAST STAND

After his fall from grace in September 1915, Tirpitz remained the leading proponent of unrestricted submarine warfare. Still officially in office in Berlin but exiled from the wartime decision-making circle around William II, he waited impatiently for events to turn his way. The break finally came from an unlikely source, the army High Command. Falkenhayn had focused German resources on the eastern front during 1915, hoping to knock Russia out of the war, but despite the massive casualties the Russian army had suffered in losing Poland to the Central Powers, Tsar Nicholas II rejected German overtures for a separate peace. Falkenhayn took little consolation in the conquest of Serbia, accomplished in the autumn after Bulgaria joined the Central Powers, since the liquidation of the Balkan front did little other than offset the Allies' establishment of the Italian front months earlier. As Tirpitz recalled in his memoirs, "the fighting fronts had stiffened, and a decision of the war had become still more difficult to achieve. It was . . . under . . . these circumstances that the army command requested a conference on the question of the submarine campaign."[4]

In a series of meetings held between 30 December and 5 January at the War Ministry in Berlin, Tirpitz made his case for the resumption of unrestricted submarine warfare, this time with a much larger undersea force capable of inflicting real damage on Britain. To wage such a campaign successfully, Germany had to plan for the very short service lives of its submarines and consider their officers and crews expendable; hundreds of U-boats would have to be built and hundreds of officers trained, along with thousands of men for their crews. Truly decisive submarine warfare would require not just the redeployment of the navy's human resources but significantly more money. Indeed, the largest U-boats constructed in 1917, after the resumption of unrestricted submarine warfare, would have a per-ton cost 40 percent greater than the German capital ships commissioned that year, and in order to afford the U-boats it needed, the navy would have to abandon the dreadnought and battle cruiser projects still under construction in the shipyards. After Tirpitz presented this calculus to the leading generals, Falkenhayn recognized its logical compatibility with the campaign of attrition he planned to unleash against France in 1916. Holtzendorff, also present for the meetings, joined Falkenhayn in changing his view. Tirpitz later recalled that his old rival considered the resumption of unrestricted submarine warfare "the salvation of the navy," especially in light of the inactivity of the High Sea Fleet since Pohl had assumed command in Wilhelmshaven ten months earlier. Holtzendorff advocated starting a new unrestricted campaign sooner rather than later, and Tirpitz, notwithstanding all he had just said about preparation, agreed to propose 1 March 1916 as the start date. Falkenhayn, planning to open the new western offensive at Verdun in February, likewise agreed to the date.[5]

In the aftermath of the meetings, Holtzendorff had the *Admiralstab* prepare a series of memoranda justifying the more aggressive course. Germany had fifty-four U-boats in service at the beginning of 1916, twenty more than had been available in February 1915 when the first unrestricted campaign began. This number (including fourteen *UB* boats and eleven *UC* minelayers) remained far short of Tirpitz's ideal, but by the end of winter another 149 U-boats of various types were under construction in German shipyards. The initial memorandum, issued on 7 January, "confidently assumed . . . English resistance would be broken in at most six months."[6] They had yet to share their plans with Pohl before he left his flagship on 8 January because of an illness soon diagnosed as liver cancer, which caused his death just weeks later. William II elevated Vice Admiral Reinhard Scheer, one of Pohl's squadron chiefs, to succeed him as commander of the High

Sea Fleet. Scheer, younger (at fifty-two) and far more aggressive than Pohl, soon persuaded the emperor to allow the High Sea Fleet to resume regular sorties into the North Sea. Tirpitz thought highly of Scheer, who had served under him years earlier in the Torpedo Inspection and held similar views on submarine warfare. During the first week of February, on Scheer's first visit to Berlin, Holtzendorff confided in him that "Falkenhayn . . . had given up his previous scruples concerning unrestricted U-boat warfare." He returned to the fleet expecting the campaign to be resumed on 1 March.[7] Alongside his own effort to bring the Grand Fleet to battle, coinciding with the unprecedented bloodletting Falkenhayn planned to unleash at Verdun, the renewal of unrestricted submarine warfare gave Scheer reason to hope that 1916 would be the year Germany won the war.

The admirals soon sought to broaden their circle of support. An *Admiralstab* memorandum dated 12 February was "submitted to a large number of economic experts," with Tirpitz contending that "all expressed their agreement with it." The state secretary also mobilized his considerable network of political and industrial connections, including industrialist Hugo Stinnes, to pressure the emperor and chancellor to support the campaign. Much to the chagrin of Bethmann Hollweg, Tirpitz's political allies soon spoke confidently of a German undersea force of two hundred boats, spinning together the figures of 54 in service and 149 under construction, as if all of the latter were near completion, with officers and crew ready to man them. Tirpitz's old friend Erzberger observed with dismay that advocates of unrestricted submarine warfare labeled anyone urging caution an "enemy of the Fatherland," an "antinationalist," or worse, and took too lightly the implications of the United States joining the Allies. Finally, on 29 February, anticipating the approval of the emperor and chancellor, Holtzendorff issued orders for an "intensified" submarine campaign, in effect a period preparatory to an unrestricted campaign. But their best efforts failed to sway William II or Bethmann Hollweg, and indeed they backfired. The emperor, exasperated by years of being cajoled and manipulated by Tirpitz, signaled his intentions by deliberately excluding the state secretary from a meeting on 4 March at which he was expected to make the decision. The meeting concluded with William II agreeing with Bethmann Hollweg, over the objections of Falkenhayn and Holtzendorff, that unrestricted submarine warfare should be "postponed indefinitely." Tirpitz submitted his resignation on 12 March, and this time the emperor accepted it, replacing him as state secretary with Admiral Eduard von Capelle.[8]

Meanwhile, Holtzendorff's "intensified" campaign remained in effect, at least for a few more weeks. *UC* minelayers operating out of Flanders had been joined in the waters around Britain by *U* and *UB* boats from Emden, Helgoland, and Wilhelmshaven, some sent around Scotland to the western approaches to the Channel, waters not visited since the end of the unrestricted campaign six months earlier. Commanders grew increasingly aggressive, though under the order of 29 February only armed Allied merchantmen were supposed to be attacked without warning. Victims included the 13,911-ton Dutch passenger liner *Tubantia*, torpedoed by *UB 13* (*Oberleutnant* Arthur Metz) on 16 March, shortly after leaving Amsterdam for Buenos Aires. Hard pressed to explain the inexplicable sinking, the Germans initially blamed it on a British mine, then on a faulty German torpedo they alleged had been in the water for several days before being struck by the Dutch liner. Though the ship went under slowly and all aboard were saved, the *Tubantia* was the largest neutral vessel sunk during the war, and the incident seriously strained German-Dutch relations.[9] These tensions came at an inopportune time for the Germans, who just one week earlier (9 March) had declared war on Portugal after the Portuguese government honored a British request to seize three dozen German and Austrian merchantmen that had sought refuge in Lisbon after the outbreak of the war.

In the midst of the "intensified" campaign, the navy agreed to spare one U-boat to transport a special passenger on a secret mission. On 21 April, three days before Irish nationalists were to launch the Easter Rising against Britain, *U 19* (now under *Oberleutnant* Raimund Weisbach) landed Irish revolutionary leader Sir Roger Casement and two associates at Tralee Bay in County Kerry, on the southwest coast of Ireland. They were arrested the same day, the British crushed the rising, and Casement was eventually hanged for treason. Despite the outcome, an independent Ireland recognized the mission on its fiftieth anniversary by hosting Weisbach, then eighty years old, during ceremonies in Dublin commemorating the Easter Rising.[10] The failure in Ireland did not deter the Germans from making similar use of U-boats the following year, in the wake of the Russian revolution, to transport nationalist leaders home to Finland and Georgia.

The suppression of the Easter Rising caused a bubble of anti-British sentiment in the United States, temporarily eclipsing American concerns over the "intensified" campaign that had grown after *UB 29* (*Oberleutnant* Herbert Pustkuchen) torpedoed the French ferry *Sussex* in the Channel on 24 March. Its passengers included two dozen Americans, and though none were killed, on 18 April Wilson demanded "an abandonment of [Germany's] present methods of warfare against passenger and freight-carrying vessels." Facing a return to the strict observance of cruiser rules promised by Bethmann Hollweg in the *Arabic* pledge, Scheer recalled all *U* and *UB* boats for service in fleet operations on the argument that traditional cruiser restrictions made commerce raiding too risky for U-boats. He also felt he could make better use of Germany's submarines against the Grand Fleet, especially since his first two fleet sorties (5–6 March and 24–25 April), using Hipper's battle cruiser squadron as bait, had failed to lure British capital ships into an engagement with the High Sea Fleet. On 4 May the foreign secretary, Jagow, informed Lansing of the change in policy. As with the *Arabic* pledge of the previous September, in the wake of the *Sussex* pledge at least one U-boat commander— Walther Schwieger—was slow to respond to new orders. On 8 May, in the waters south of Ireland, his *U 20* sank the 13,370-ton *Cymric*, an old White Star liner bound for Liverpool from New York. Fortunately for German-American relations, the ship was carrying cargo but few passengers, and the five dead included no US citizens.[11]

The *Sussex* pledge held, at least until February 1917, but the relationship between Germany and the United States continued to deteriorate in the months after Tirpitz left office. While Wilson took no action against the British blockade, Britain and the other Allied powers became increasingly dependent on American capital and supplies to sustain their war effort, giving the United States a considerable stake in an eventual Allied victory. In the thirty-two months between the outbreak of the war and American intervention in it, the Allies raised $2.6 billion on the US bond market and another $2 billion by liquidating prewar investments in American securities. Thanks to orders from the Allied countries, in 1916 the value of American munitions exports reached nearly $1.3 billion (up from $40 million in 1914), and the overall value of exported manufactured goods rose to $5.5 billion, or 12 percent of the gross national product (up from $2.4 billion, or 6 percent of GNP in 1914).[12] Following the suspension of unrestricted submarine warfare, the Germans attempted to stem the flow of American munitions and supplies via acts of sabotage within the United States. The operation was coordinated through the German embassy in Washington by the military attaché, Franz von Papen, and naval attaché, *Fregattenkapitän* Karl Boy-Ed. Papen, future German chancellor and a key figure in bringing Hitler to power in 1933, was deported in December 1915 after being linked to a plot to blow up American railway bridges; Boy-Ed avoided detection and remained at the embassy until it was closed in 1917. The most significant successful act of sabotage occurred on Sunday, 30 July 1916, at Black Tom Island in New York harbor, the primary shipping point for American munitions exports, where a series of fires starting at 02:00 that morning destroyed one thousand tons of munitions and caused $20 million in damage. The climactic explosion, equaling an earthquake of 5.0 on the Richter scale, shattered most windows in Lower Manhattan, seriously damaged the nearby Statue of Liberty, and was felt one hundred miles (160 km) away. The timing of the predawn Sunday blast limited casualties to seven killed, but several hundred workers and firefighters were injured. While government officials initially sought to focus the investigation on the alleged negligence of companies operating on Black Tom Island, sabotage was suspected from the start. Within hours of the explosion, the *New York Times* speculated that "the destruction of so large a quantity of Allied war material must prove cheering news to Berlin and Vienna."[13]

THE MEDITERRANEAN (1916)

In the aftermath of the *Sussex* pledge and Scheer's decision to use U-boats to support the operations of the High Sea Fleet, the focus of the submarine war shifted to the Mediterranean, where the boats and captains deployed in the autumn of 1915 had continued their run of success into the new year. During 1916, Valentiner's *U 38* went on to claim another fifty-three ships (114,067 tons), including six merchantmen (10,504 tons) and a French gunboat sunk during a brief sortie to Madeira, which served notice that, with Portugal now among the Allies, Germany intended to take the war to the Portuguese Atlantic islands. Meanwhile, Rücker's *U 34* also sank fifty-three ships (102,616 tons), and Forstmann's *U 39* added sixty-eight more (75,370 tons). After leading his peers in Mediterranean tonnage sunk in the autumn of 1915, Gansser was reassigned to the Black Sea for a wasted 1916, during which his *U 33* sank just eight ships (6,327 tons). Meanwhile, Hersing's *U 21* returned to the Mediterranean from the Black Sea for 1916 to sink ten ships (16,248 tons) as Austrian *U 36*. The most successful of all, *U 35*, sank a remarkable 124 ships (265,649 tons) during 1916, ironically after its initial commander, Kophamel, succeeded Hans Adam as head of the flotilla and turned over the boat to a novice, *Kapitänleutnant* Lothar von Arnauld de la Perière.

Great-grandson of a French artillery officer who had emigrated to Frederick the Great's Prussia, Arnauld entered the navy at age seventeen as the youngest member of Crew 03. After impressing his superiors for a decade, in 1913 he became an adjutant to Pohl on the *Admiralstab* and appeared

FIGURE 3.2.
Lothar von Arnauld de la Perière
(Berlin State Library)

destined, in the long run, for higher leadership. When Pohl became commander of the High Sea Fleet in February 1915, Arnauld remained with the
Admiralstab under Bachmann while seeking a post that would get him closer
to the action. The prospects for independent command for someone of his
age and rank (newly promoted to *Kapitänleutnant*, effective December 1914)
were limited to the airship division (*Marine-Luftschiff-Abteilung*) and the
submarine service; zeppelins were his first choice, but with unrestricted submarine warfare just starting, U-boats offered greater opportunity. Arnauld
transferred to the submarine service on 1 April 1915 and went to Kiel to join
the host of other junior officers then in training for it. He was assigned to
U 35 in mid-November, after Kophamel had captained the boat to the Adriatic via Gibraltar, then commanded it on its first Mediterranean sorties. Arnauld traveled by rail to Pola, where *U 35* was refitting in anticipation of its
next cruise in January 1916.[14]

While some U-boat commanders chafed at the limits imposed by cruiser
rules, Arnauld had no problem with restricted submarine warfare. As he

recalled later in an extended postwar interview with American journalist Lowell Thomas, "the restriction about torpedoing . . . made little difference to me, because . . . I much preferred the method of giving warning and doing my sinking with gunfire or by placing explosives aboard. In that way I saved torpedoes and, besides, I could accost the lifeboats, look over the ship's papers, and get its name and tonnage." This approach, he conceded, had much to do with his eventual success and celebrity: "Before a commander had a ship officially placed on his record he had to give its name as proof of sinking," and many U-boat commanders were shortchanged in the accounting "because of their inability to produce names and verification. The fact that I nearly always gave warning may explain why my record ran so high."[15] Indeed, there was a practical explanation for all of the survivors' stories about U-boats surfacing next to lifeboats and German officers demanding, at gunpoint, specifics about a sunken ship's identity.[16]

By using his torpedoes only as a last resort, Arnauld also avoided a problem that plagued many U-boat commanders throughout the war: the need to cut short what otherwise might have been a promising cruise after running out of torpedoes. In contrast, Arnauld noted, "My cruises were not gauged by the length of time my torpedoes lasted. I stayed out as long as I had shells and food left."[17] It was not unusual for him to bring his boat back to port with torpedoes left, but few shells. For example, on his record cruise of 26 July–20 August 1916, during which U 35 sank fifty-four ships (90,350 tons), he expended nine hundred shells but just four torpedoes. The same cruise was also typical in that the impressive tonnage total was built on volume rather than on the sinking of a smaller number of larger ships; of fifty-four victims, the largest was the first one sunk, the 4,977-ton Italian steamer *Dandolo*, and most of the rest were barely half that size.[18] The lack of larger targets, or of those sunk under dangerous circumstances, combined with Arnauld's modesty to make his story a dull one, even when relating his greatest triumph: "My record cruise was quite tame and humdrum," he conceded. "When U 35 put into port at Pola with fifty-four pennants flying, the harbor went wild. Yet we had encountered no spectacular adventures. It was ordinary routine. We stopped ships. The crews took to the boats. We examined the ship's papers, gave sailing instructions to the nearest land, and then sank the captured prizes."[19]

When it came to audacity, the cruise before Arnauld's record-breaking sortie made a far greater splash. On 21 June 1916 the Germans used their budding U-boat star for what amounted to an international publicity stunt, in which he took U 35 into Cartagena, docked, and hand-delivered to Spanish authorities a signed letter from William II to Alfonso XIII, thanking the king for his government's kind treatment of Germans stranded or interned in Spain. Arnauld extended his visit to the neutral port to the maximum twenty-four hours allowed to belligerent vessels under international law; photographs taken of *U 35* during the visit appeared in the press worldwide, further enhancing his reputation. By the autumn of 1916, if not earlier, Arnauld had achieved the status of national hero. On 11 October he received the *Pour le Mérite*, the highest Prussian decoration, in recognition of his record cruise and having reached the top of the table in tonnage sunk, after just nine months as a U-boat commander. During the following year, before Arnauld left *U 35*, further recognition of his exalted status came when he was entrusted with a special junior officer, "with orders to see that he got all the experience possible" aboard a U-boat: Prince Sigismund, son of Admiral Prince Henry of Prussia and nephew of William II.[20]

The submarines commanded by Arnauld, Valentiner, Rücker, Forstmann, and Gansser were identical sister boats of Type *U 31*, a 685-ton design manned by three officers and a crew of thirty-two, considered spacious by the standards of the time. In place of the hammocks of earlier U-boats, their crews slept in shifts on mattresses in tiered bunks. The galley even had a small electric oven for the cook to bake fresh bread, a luxury the navy justified as offsetting the cost of the dental problems that had been caused by making everyone eat hardtack. The larger boat allowed some social separation between the officers and the crew; the commander, his two lieutenants, and the chief engineer ate their meals at a small table set up in the bow cabin where the officers slept, served by one of the sailors who acted as their steward.[21] Such accommodations notwithstanding, life remained far more egalitarian than aboard even a medium-sized surface ship of the German navy, where the same four people would have dined in three different places, all with even greater separation from the crew. Predictably, when larger U-boats were constructed, designers persisted in their effort to facilitate proper social divisions. The Type *U 51* class, six 715-ton boats commissioned during the first half of 1916, had a small forward cabin where the commander slept and could eat his meals alone, separate from a wardroom shared by the rest of the officers, which featured bunks upholstered in leather; the upper berths folded down to create facing sofas, making the space no less comfortable than the standard compartment of a railway coach.[22] But amid the incremental increases in amenities for the officers, everyone aboard a U-boat still shared most of the same conditions and hardships. Operating in isolation, commanders enjoyed great latitude in enforcing regulations; because the nature of service undersea

added a life-or-death urgency to the proper execution of even the most routine functions, the obvious need for every man to do his job conscientiously
made rigid discipline unnecessary. Most commanders recognized the importance of maintaining a strong camaraderie, and throughout the war U-boat
crews typically enjoyed far better morale than the crews of larger warships.

During 1916 the number of German submarines based at Pola and Cattaro increased from eight to twenty-five, and at Constantinople, from five
to ten. The latter represented a peak, for only eleven U-boats were based in
the Black Sea during the entire war, and collectively they sank just 117,093
tons; meanwhile, of the five U-boats lost there, all succumbed by the end
of 1916. Acknowledging the high cost and low benefit of operating in the
Black Sea, early in 1917 the navy subordinated the small Constantinople
force to the Pola-Cattaro Mediterranean command. Additional U-boats sent
via Gibraltar late in 1916 included *U 52* (*Kapitänleutnant* Hans Walther),
which sank the 12,750-ton French pre-dreadnought *Suffren* (648 dead) on 25
November while en route to the Mediterranean and *U 32* (*Kapitänleutnant*
Kurt Hartwig), whose victims before the resumption of unrestricted submarine warfare included the 14,000-ton British pre-dreadnought *Cornwallis* (15
dead), sunk off Malta on 9 January 1917. Hartwig already had a remarkable
career before taking over *U 32*, having survived the Battle of the Falklands in
December 1914 aboard the light cruiser *Dresden*, then escaped internment
in neutral Chile to make his way home and into the submarine service. He
remained in the Mediterranean for the rest of the war, eventually becoming
one of the senior U-boat commanders there.[23]

To supplement the larger submarines sent directly from home waters,
the Germans continued to ship dismantled *UB* boats by rail to Pola to be
reassembled and commissioned in the Adriatic. The most successful of those
deployed during 1916 was *UB 47* (*Oberleutnant* Wolfgang Steinbauer), also
known as Austrian *U 47*, which sank the 18,510-ton British troopship *Franconia* (running empty, 12 dead) on 4 October, the 11,100-ton French pre-
dreadnought *Gaulois* (no casualties) on 27 December, and the 14,278-ton
British troopship *Ivernia* (125 dead) on 1 January 1917. Other Allied troop
transports and larger warships lost in the Mediterranean U-boat war during
1916 included the 4,750-ton French armored cruiser *Amiral Charner* (427
dead), sunk on 8 February by Hersing's *U 21*; the 13,753-ton French troopship *Provence* (990 dead), torpedoed on 25 February by Arnauld's *U 35*; the
7,930-ton Italian troopship *Principe Umberto* (1,926 dead), sunk on 8 June by
Austrian *U 5* (*Linienschiffsleutnant* Friedrich Schlosser); and the 14,966-ton

French troopship *Gallia* (1,338 dead), torpedoed on 4 October by Arnauld's *U 35*. Aside from the *Lusitania*, the latter three sinkings were the costliest in terms of lives lost of the entire war, with the sinking of the *Principe Umberto* being the deadliest overall by a wide margin.[24]

The deployment of additional *UC* minelayers to the Adriatic and Mediterranean during 1916 led to further Allied losses in lives, warships, and shipping tonnage (see section below). It was all the more vexing for the Allies, and gratifying for the Central Powers, that the heavy losses inflicted by U-boats in the Mediterranean came at almost no cost to the force deployed there. The twenty-two submarines Germany lost during 1916 included only two in the Mediterranean: *UC 12* (*Oberleutnant* Eberhard Fröhner), destroyed by one of its own mines on 16 March while sowing a minefield off Taranto, and *UB 44* (*Oberleutnant* Franz Wäger), which disappeared on 4 August while en route from Cattaro to Constantinople.[25]

MORE MINELAYERS

The Mediterranean-and-minelayers strategy that served the German navy so well in the last months of 1915 continued through 1916 for the latter as well as the former. Nearly half of the 149 U-boats under construction when Tirpitz left office were minelayers, most of them from Type *UC II* (also known as Type *UC 16*), one of the war's largest classes of U-boats, with a total of sixty-four units (*UC 16* through *UC 79*) launched between February and August of 1916. At 417 tons displacement, they were more than twice the size of the first fifteen *UC* boats, requiring three officers and a crew of twenty-three. Despite the accidents that had claimed some of the initial class of German minelayers, their design was essentially the same, with six vertical chutes under the foredeck that released weighted mines below the boat. Unlike their predecessors, however, they carried eighteen mines (instead of twelve) and were also equipped with seven torpedoes and a 3.45-inch (8.8 cm) deck gun, features that allowed them to function like any other submarine when not laying mines. Type *UE I* (also known as Type *U 71*), developed concurrently, with ten units numbered *U 71* through *U 80* launched between October 1915 and April 1916, was distinctive in combining the size and features of an oceangoing boat with the ability to lay mines. The type displaced 755 tons and was manned by four officers and a crew of twenty-eight. They carried the same 3.45-inch (8.8 cm) deck gun as Type *UC II* and just four torpedoes, but a remarkable thirty-four mines, deployable from two large stern tubes, a structural feature that made them far safer to operate than the

UC designs. The weight of the mines aboard them made the *UC II* and *UE I* boats slower than conventional submarines of similar displacement, but still a great improvement over the 6–7 knots surfaced and 5 submerged of the first *UC* boats. Type *UC II* was capable of 11–12 knots surfaced and 7 submerged, Type *UE I* of 10–11 knots surfaced and 8 knots submerged. With greater size and capability came greater cost; whereas the *UC II* boats ranged in price from 1.7 to 2.1 million Marks apiece, each *UE I* boat cost 3.1 million, similar to a non-minelaying boat of the same size.[26]

Shipping along the North Sea and Channel coasts of England certainly felt the impact of so many new *UC* boats hitting the water in such a short period of time. After sinking fifty-seven vessels of various sizes between the suspension of unrestricted submarine warfare and the end of 1915, the initial cohort of *UC* boats sank another ninety-nine during the first eight months of 1916. The new *UC II* boats registered their first successes in September, and over the last four months of 1916 the *UC*s collectively sank another 176, including 66 in November and 76 in December. Most of the vessels sunk in northern waters were small—for example, the eleven British trawlers destroyed by *UC 16* (*Oberleutnant* Egon von Werner) on a single day, 23 September—but victims included the 12,431-ton British steamer *Maloja*, mined by *UC 6* (*Oberleutnant* Count Matthias von Schmettow) off Dover on 27 February (155 dead), and the 13,405-ton British steamer *Alaunia*, mined by Werner's *UC 16* in the Channel off Hastings on 19 October (2 dead).[27] Meanwhile, the first *UE* boats, entering service after the *Sussex* pledge, were either assigned to the Mediterranean or to serve with the High Sea Fleet. In the latter capacity, *U 75* (*Kapitänleutnant* Curt Beitzen) registered arguably the war's greatest success of a minelaying U-boat on 5 June off the Orkneys when one of its mines sank the 10,850-ton armored cruiser *Hampshire* (643 dead), a ship bound for Archangel carrying Britain's war minister, Lord Kitchener, on a mission to the beleaguered Russian government. Kitchener became the highest-ranking officer or official of any country to die as a result of a U-boat's actions. Ironically, the mine struck by the *Hampshire* had been one of many sown near Scapa Flow during the High Sea Fleet sortie that resulted in the Battle of Jutland (31 May–1 June), in a fruitless attempt to sink capital ships of the Grand Fleet leaving and returning to their base.[28]

In a year in which the undersea war was dominated by action in the Mediterranean and by minelayers, it was only fitting that some of the greatest successes were registered by minelaying U-boats operating in the Mediterranean. Foremost among these was *U 73* (*Kapitänleutnant* Gustav Siess), sent to the Mediterranean via the Straits of Gibraltar, which mined the 14,000-ton British pre-dreadnought *Russell* on 27 April in Malta harbor (124 dead), then in autumn laid a minefield across the Zea Channel in the Greek islands that claimed two large victims running empty, the 12,009-ton French troopship *Burdigala* (1 dead) on 14 November and the 48,158-ton British hospital ship *Britannic* (30 dead) on 21 November. The latter, a sister ship of the *Titanic*, was the largest vessel sunk by submarine action in the entire war. Siess's *U 73* claimed another warship just after the first of the year, on 2 January off the Mediterranean outlet of the Suez Canal, when it mined the 13,500-ton *Peresviet*, a Russian pre-dreadnought attempting a roundabout voyage to Archangel from Vladivostok (where it had just been returned to the Russians by the Japanese, who had captured it in the war of 1904–5). Meanwhile, the 14,317-ton British troopship *Minnewaska* became 1916's largest Mediterranean victim of a *UC* boat when it was mined by *UC 23* (*Oberleutnant* Johannes Kirchner) off Crete on 29 November. The *Minnewaska*'s captain managed to beach his ship before it sank, saving the lives of all two thousand men aboard. The following month, *UC 14* (*Oberleutnant* Franz Becker) claimed the largest Allied warship sunk by a U-boat during 1916 when it mined the 13,427-ton Italian pre-dreadnought *Regina Margherita* (675 dead) on 12 December off Valona (Vlorë), Albania.[29] Prior to the end of 1916, Hersing's 650-ton *U 21* was the smallest submarine sent directly from home waters via Gibraltar to the Mediterranean, but in December the navy deployed the 417-ton *UC 34* (*Oberleutnant* Robert Sprenger) via the same route, its successful arrival in Pola in January 1917 attesting to the flexibility and value of the *UC* type, their size notwithstanding.

During 1915–16, the German navy learned lessons from its *UC* program that would become more generally applicable during 1917–18, after the resumption of unrestricted submarine warfare, in the acceptance of Tirpitz's argument that U-boats needed to be mass-produced and also considered expendable. On the mass-production side, the *UC II* class consisted of sixty-four virtually identical boats, launched within six months after the orders were dispersed among the Danzig navy yard and four private shipyards (Blohm & Voss and AG Vulcan of Hamburg, AG Weser of Bremen, and Germania of Kiel). On the operational side, the navy recognized that minelayers would be more likely to suffer catastrophic accidents and accepted that *UC* boats would have a higher loss rate (ultimately 50 of 79 for the entire war, or 63 percent) than the larger, less vulnerable *U* and *UB* boats (128 of 256, or 50 percent). Thus, they had the dubious distinction of being Germany's first expendable U-boats.

ANTISUBMARINE WARFARE: DETECTION, DESTRUCTION, CONTAINMENT
The wireless radio technology that had revolutionized ship-to-shore and
ship-to-ship communication in the years preceding 1914 was, of course,
crucial to wartime naval operations. As early as November 1914 British naval intelligence had the ability to read German naval wireless messages after
the Admiralty's Room 40 secured possession of three codebooks that had
fallen into Allied hands in the first months of the war: one from a German
merchant steamer seized in Australia at the beginning of the war; a second,
via the Russian navy, from the light cruiser *Magdeburg*, which ran aground
off the Estonian coast in August; and the third from the wreckage of one of
the destroyers sunk at Texel Island in October, in a chest netted by a British
trawler.[30] This breakthrough paid immediate dividends in enabling the British to locate and destroy Spee's squadron at the Falklands (8 December) and
to deploy the Grand Fleet in anticipation of the High Sea Fleet's second sortie
into the North Sea (16 December). In the latter case the British also used
"directional finding" or directional wireless stations recently established on
their North Sea coast, whose macro-level data interception proved useful in
tracking enemy forces at sea in real time by following the volume and location
of their wireless traffic, without decoding individual messages.[31]

By the end of 1914 the British were using code decryption and directional
wireless to determine the location of U-boats and to warn naval and mercantile vessels of their presence in a particular area. The German navy unwittingly
facilitated these efforts with the high number of wireless messages its submarines generated. Standing orders required U-boat commanders to check in via
wireless whenever they sank an enemy merchantman, encountered an enemy
warship, or were approaching home and needed to pass through a German
minefield. In northern waters all of these signals gave away U-boat positions
to British directional wireless, accurate to within fifty miles (80 km) in the Atlantic and twenty miles (32 km) in the North Sea. Even after they were aware
that they were being tracked, the Germans considered the transmissions worth
the risk. After developing their own directional wireless, they built stations on
the island of Helgoland, at Sylt and Borkum in the Frisian Islands, near Cuxhaven at Nordholz, and at Bruges in occupied Belgium, supplemented later by
additional facilities at Tondern in Schleswig and at Cleves in Westphalia. But
in the technological race, the British navy enjoyed a geographical edge as well
as the advantage of having directional wireless first. While the British could
scan the seas for enemy ship signals in every direction around the British Isles,
the Germans were blocked by the British Isles from receiving signals emitted

by ships farther west, limiting the usefulness of their directional wireless to the North Sea. Meanwhile, German naval intelligence opened its first crypto-graphic center at Bruges in July 1915; it became a regional station, covering the English Channel, when a new headquarters for decryption efforts was es-tablished at Neumünster, in Holstein, the following February. Other regional cryptographic stations were opened at Tondern (for the North Sea); Libau, in occupied Latvia (for the Baltic); Skopje, in occupied Macedonia (for the Medi-terranean); and the main Austrian base at Pola (for the Adriatic). After the war the Germans claimed that Neumünster could decrypt two-thirds of inter-cepted British messages at least partially, but they never succeeded in breaking the Grand Fleet's code. In his postwar memoirs, Scheer praised German naval intelligence for intercepting and deciphering British wireless messages but assumed that the British were unable to do the same and were receiving their intelligence of German ship movements from "agents or from submarines in the North Sea." Throughout the war, the German navy remained overconfi-dent in the security of its own codes and was slow to introduce new ones even when faced with evidence that old codes had been compromised. For example, in February 1915, the first unrestricted submarine warfare campaign opened with U-boats still communicating in a code (known as HVB) developed before the war for German overseas cruisers and merchantmen, even though its se-curity had been suspect since November 1914. It was finally replaced by a new code (known as FVB) in the summer of 1915.[32]

While the use of code decryption and directional wireless to locate U-boats enabled the Admiralty to warn ships away from them, the same technological ability could also serve efforts to hunt down and destroy them. Holtzendorff's "intensified" campaign order of 29 February 1916, authorizing the sinking of armed merchant ships without warning, and Scheer's conclusion in the wake of the *Sussex* pledge that cruiser rules, at least in the waters around the British Isles, were too risky for U-boats to follow both reflected the German reaction to the British navy's initial attempt at sinking submarines: the deployment of merchant cruisers with concealed deck guns, pretending to be helpless freighters, sent into the sea-lanes to attract enemy submarines. Known as "Q-ships" after a numbering system introduced by the Admiralty late in 1916, they were potentially the most formidable of the former civilian vessels com-missioned in the Auxiliary Patrol of the British navy.[33]

The first Q-ship was the former freighter *Vittoria*, sent out on patrol at the end of November 1914, six weeks after *U 17* made the *Glitra* the first merchantman sunk by a German submarine. After the *Vittoria* registered no successes in two months of service, the Admiralty repeated the experiment with a second Q-ship, the *Antwerp*, captained by a former submariner, Lieutenant Commander Godfrey Herbert, on the reasoning that "a submarine officer would naturally in his stalking be able to realize at once the limitations and possibilities of his opponent."[34] The *Antwerp*, commissioned in January 1915, likewise was paid off without sinking a U-boat, bringing a lull in the program before the sinking of the *Lusitania* inspired a renewal of experimentation with antisubmarine "mystery" ships. Finally, on 24 July 1915, the newly commissioned former collier *Prince Charles* (Lieutenant Mark Wardlaw) registered the first Q-ship success, sinking *U 36* (*Kapitänleutnant* Ernst Graeff) off remote North Rona Island, about fifty-five miles (90 km) north of the northern tip of Scotland. Wardlaw enticed *U 36* to surface, then opened fire and sank it before its crew could man its deck gun to launch an attack. Graeff and fourteen of his men survived the sinking and became prisoners of war, but eighteen of the crew perished.[35] On 15 August, a much smaller Q-ship, the converted fishing smack *Inverlyon*, used similar tactics in an attack off Yarmouth that sank *UB 4* (*Oberleutnant* Karl Gross) with all hands (15 dead).[36]

Shortly after the loss of *UB 4*, the former submariner Herbert, commanding the new Q-ship *Baralong*, launched a more controversial attack. On 19 August, coincidentally the same day that *U 24* sank the *Arabic*, the *Baralong* encountered *Kapitänleutnant* Wegener's *U 27* some seventy miles (115 km) off the southern coast of Ireland. *U 27* had surfaced to stop the British freighter *Nicosian*, and Wegener, like so many U-boat commanders during the initial unrestricted campaign, allowed the crew to abandon ship, even though his orders did not require him to do so. He was not alarmed when the *Baralong*, flying the American flag, closed on the scene, apparently to rescue the *Nicosian*'s survivors. But once the *Baralong* had reached point-blank range, Herbert ran up the British flag, revealed his previously hidden guns, and opened fire, sinking *U 27*. In contrast to Wardlaw's conduct with *U 36*, Herbert made no attempt to save the survivors and took no prisoners; Wegener and at least eleven of his crew were shot trying to surrender. Americans among the *Nicosian*'s crew eventually reported the incident, but the United States did not lodge a protest, even though the *Baralong* had closed on *U 27* under cover of the American flag. In subsequent correspondence, Wilson called the incident "horrible" and Lansing "shocking," yet their inaction only confirmed the double standard they had already adopted in their reactions to coldblooded behavior at sea.[37]

After changing names and captains, the *Baralong*, as the *Wyandra* (Lieutenant Commander A. Wilmot-Smith), was also responsible for the summer's third sinking of a U-boat. On 24 September, roughly 145 miles (235 km) off the western tip of Cornwall, the Q-ship approached *Kapitänleutnant* Hansen's *U 41* shortly after it had torpedoed the 6,651-ton British steamer *Urbino*, which it had stopped under cruiser rules as required under the emperor's orders of 18 September in the wake of the *Arabic* pledge. Wilmot-Smith, like Herbert, used the American flag and the apparent mission of rescuing survivors to cover its attack. Two of the thirty-seven men aboard *U 41* survived to be taken prisoner, including an officer eventually repatriated to Germany via a prisoner exchange who published his story.[38] The *Urbino* was the twenty-eighth and largest of the ships Hansen's *U 41* had sunk, totaling 58,648 tons, and the loss of such an experienced commander and crew certainly hurt the German undersea effort. Wegener's *U 27* likewise had ranked among the most successful U-boats of 1914–15, sinking a British seaplane carrier, a submarine, and ten merchant ships totaling 31,120 tons.

The most successful Q-ship captain, Lieutenant Commander Gordon Campbell, took command of the *Farnborough* (ex-*Loderer*) in October 1915, at the close of the initial campaign of unrestricted submarine warfare, and had to wait until Germany's brief "intensified" campaign the following spring to claim his first victim, *U 68* (*Kapitänleutnant* Ludwig Güntzel), sunk on 22 March 1916 off the western coast of Ireland with all hands (38 dead). Campbell developed tactics later used by most Q-ships, including dispatching a "panic party" in a lifeboat after sighting a U-boat, to more accurately simulate a freighter's reaction to an approaching submarine, while remaining aboard ship with the rest of his crew, manning their hidden guns. His *Farnborough* was also the first ship to use a new invention, the depth charge, in antisubmarine warfare.[39] Q-ships under Campbell's command sank two more U-boats after the resumption of unrestricted submarine warfare. By war's end the British navy employed over 180 "mystery ships of all sorts" which claimed eleven confirmed U-boat victims, raising the question of whether their value justified their cost.[40] After 1915, fewer experienced captains, such as Wegener and Hansen, were likely to be fooled by a Q-ship; *U 68*'s Güntzel, who had not yet sunk a ship before being sunk by the *Farnborough*, became more typical of the Q-ship victims. Of course one never knows what kind of commander Güntzel would have become with experience. Indeed, in January 1916 another novice commander very nearly fell victim to a Q-ship, the *Margit*, in the Mediterranean: Lothar Arnauld de la Perière, on his first cruise with

U 35. Arnauld ended up sinking 193 ships, 189 of them as commander of *U 35*, while the *Margit* paid off without ever sinking a U-boat.[41]

Critics of Q-ships within the British navy pointed not only to their very low success rate, but also to their problematic influence on U-boat commanders. During the periods of unrestricted submarine warfare, the presence of such "mystery ships" in the sea-lanes arguably compelled German submariners to take a more aggressive "shoot first, ask questions later" approach to any potential target, making them a mixed blessing for the Allied merchant fleet. They posed the greatest threat to submariners during restricted submarine warfare (September 1915 to February 1917), because, as Arnauld later recalled, during those months "we had to warn all ships before sinking them—that is, we had to approach on the surface and take a chance with a craft that might be an armory of concealed guns."[42]

Ultimately much more effort and money were expended on measures to contain U-boats rather than destroy them, through the deployment of antisubmarine barrages at the Straits of Dover and Otranto, and later along the North Sea blockade line between Scotland and Norway. From the start of the war, the British navy's Auxiliary Patrol included hundreds of fishing vessels, mostly manned by their civilian crews, the trawlers adapted primarily for minesweeping and the drifters, designed to drag deep-sea nets, instead dragging underwater barriers for enemy submarines. The first antisubmarine drifters were assembled at Dover in January 1915, and by June over 130 were in service there. They patrolled the straits dragging steel nets constructed in mesh patterns of ten-foot (3 m) squares, with the typical drifter trailing one thousand yards (900 m) of nets extending to a depth of 120 feet (36 m). Because the straits were just twenty-one miles (34 km) wide at their narrowest point and 180 feet (55 m) deep at their deepest, but with a mean depth of 108 feet (33 m), theoretically a line of three dozen drifters could block the entire passage. This goal remained theoretical thanks to the forces of nature; indeed, even in calm weather the tides and current posed tremendous challenges for the operation of such small boats. The drifters typically displaced 150–200 tons and were armed with nothing heavier than single six-pounder guns, and sometimes only a heavy machine gun, more for the psychological benefit of those aboard than for any practical purpose. Defenseless against even the smallest enemy warships, they had to be protected by destroyers or armed auxiliary steamers. Aside from their vulnerability, the use of drifters in antisubmarine warfare, along with the requisitioning of trawlers for minesweeping, had the unintended consequence of turning drifters and trawlers actually engaged in fishing into targets for U-boats, which earlier would not have bothered to sink a fishing vessel.[43]

Proponents of the Dover barrage claimed a number of successes based on circumstantial evidence, but German records indicate that the one confirmed case of a U-boat caught there during the first round of unrestricted submarine warfare was indeed the only U-boat lost in the straits during 1915 or 1916: *Kapitänleutnant* Stoss's *U 8*, scuttled on 4 March 1915 after becoming entangled in the nets.[44] Despite the meager early results in catching U-boats, the effort at Dover made operations far more challenging for the Flanders Flotilla and led to a unique genre of bow art for its U-boats. After *Oberleutnant* Fürbringer had black, white, and red aircraft-style roundels painted on "each side of the bow" of *UB 2*, "to serve as an identification symbol," his fellow commanders had similar "eyes" of various designs painted on their own boats as good luck charms to help them "see" their way through the barrage.[45] Such behavior reflected the reality that, at least for the time being, the Dover barrage arguably had greater effect as a psychological barrier than as an actual physical obstacle. Submariner superstitions common in all German flotillas were strongest at the Flanders base, where the bad luck generally assumed to haunt any boat that sortied on a Friday was considered especially applicable to one attempting to transit the Straits of Dover on that day of the week.[46] In any event, for the larger U-boats serving in the flotillas under the High Sea Fleet, the Dover barrage sufficed to compel more of those cruising to and from the Atlantic to expend time and fuel taking the longer route around the north of Scotland, reducing the number of days they could spend stalking the western approaches to the British Isles. Thus skeptics at the Admiralty were persuaded that the barrage of drifters was worth maintaining and strengthening. Meanwhile, the French navy allowed the British to handle the barrage at the Straits of Dover and deployed their own dragged nets only for harbor defense, in particular at Le Havre, where *UB 26* (*Oberleutnant* Wilhelm Smiths) was caught on 5 April 1916 and scuttled by its crew, all of whom survived to be taken prisoner. The French later raised and repaired *UB 26* and recommissioned it under the name *Roland Morillot* in honor of the commander of the submarine *Monge*, who had been killed when his boat was sunk on 28 December 1915 by Austrian destroyers operating out of Cattaro.[47]

In late May 1915, shortly after Italy entered the war, the British proposed sealing the mouth of the Adriatic with a drifter barrage across the Straits of Otranto. The Italians initially declined the offer but changed their mind about the magnitude of the undersea threat after submarines sank two of their armored cruisers, the *Amalfi* (7 July) and *Giuseppe Garibaldi* (18 July). By that time, on the British side, suspicion that German U-boats were using Austrian bases in the Adriatic had made the Otranto barrage project a priority. In September, sixty British drifters were deployed to Brindisi, where they fell under the command of Rear Admiral Cecil Thursby, head of the British Adriatic Squadron. Thursby's efforts suffered almost immediately from the detachment of several of the drifters to help escort transports evacuating Serbs from neutral Albania, where they had sought refuge after the Central Powers defeated and occupied Serbia in the autumn of 1915. Over the winter of 1915–16 the Allies evacuated 133,000 Serbian troops and nearly as many civilian refugees from the Italian-occupied ports of Durazzo (Durrës) and Valona to Corfu. The following spring the troops moved on to Salonika (Thessaloniki), where they joined British and French divisions, some evacuated from Gallipoli after the fighting ended there, with the goal of opening up a new Balkan front centered on Macedonia. The initial evacuation to Corfu took two months and involved nearly 250 individual steamer passages, well within range of the U-boats based at Cattaro, yet just four of the transports were sunk, all by mines. Morillot's *Monge* and a second French submarine, likewise sunk during December by Austrian destroyers, were the only Allied warships lost escorting the operation. The Central Powers also failed to sink a single transport during the redeployment of the Serbian army to Salonika, to which Thursby contributed two dozen drifters as escorts. On 13 May 1916, before all of his boats were finally returned, the Otranto drifters registered their only confirmed catch of the war when Austrian *U 6* (*Linienschiffsleutnant* Hugo von Falkhausen) became entangled in their nets and was abandoned by its crew, all of whom survived to be taken prisoner.[48] Meanwhile, the U-boats based in the Adriatic continued to pass through the porous barrier to rest and resupply at Pola and Cattaro between their destructive Mediterranean cruises.

After the submarines of the Central Powers failed to disrupt the transport of Serbian troops to Salonika, Arnauld's sinking of the French troopships *Provence* and *Gallia* and the Austrian *U 5*'s sinking of the Italian troopship *Principe Umberto* took the lives of over four thousand troops destined for the new Balkan front. Because these losses came at the hands of U-boats obviously operating out of the Adriatic, the Allies redoubled their efforts to seal the Straits of Otranto, but the geographic circumstances there made the project to construct a drifter barrage far more ambitious and problematic than at Dover. The mouth of the Adriatic was forty-five miles (72 km) wide at its narrowest point and 2,600 feet (800 m) deep at its deepest; by comparison, the Straits of Dover were less than half as wide and dramatically shallower. The currents were also much stronger, enough to open gaps of ten miles (16 km) in the drifter line during the course of a single night. To make matters worse for the Allies, after the loss of *U 6*, Austrian surface ships based at Cattaro (light cruisers, destroyers, and torpedo boats) increased the frequency of raids against the Otranto barrage, sinking one drifter on the night of 31 May–1 June and two on 8–9 July. Because the drifters were British and the warships assigned to protect them were mostly French and Italian, the issue of defending the barrage strained inter-Allied relations. Rear Admiral Mark Kerr, who succeeded Thursby in May 1916, increased the number of drifters to ninety-six by September and also made them more secure from Austrian attack by moving the barrage farther south, to a line between Cape Santa Maria di Leuca and Corfu. Fortunately for the Central Powers, the new line was even less effective, because the straits were much wider there, roughly eighty miles (130 km) across, and Kerr did not have enough drifters to cover such a distance. Indeed, he estimated that three hundred drifters would be needed to block the straits at that latitude.[49]

During the interlude in unrestricted submarine warfare, the Allies determined that mines suspended underwater were needed to supplement the drifter netting in the Dover and Otranto barrages, a conclusion that followed logically from the demonstrated effectiveness of minefields in blocking the passage of surface ships. Rear Admiral Reginald Bacon, commander of the Dover Patrol from 1915 to 1917, advocated the construction of a "vertical wall of mines" across the Straits of Dover, but the relative calm in northern waters during 1916 postponed serious planning for it until after the resumption of unrestricted submarine warfare the following year.[50] As the German navy began its preparations for a renewal of the unrestricted campaign, the Allies likewise prepared to supplement the Otranto barrage with mines in an attempt to limit the effectiveness of Arnauld, Valentiner, and the other U-boat commanders sent to the Mediterranean.

NOTES

1. Valentiner, *Der Schrecken der Meere*, 109–13, quoted 110 and 111; Doenecke, *Nothing Less Than War*, 127–28. The Austrian version of the sinking is given in Burián to Lansing, Vienna, 29 December 1915, *Papers Relating to the Foreign Relations of the United States, 1915*, Supplement, *The World War*, Document 873, https://history.state.gov/his toricaldocuments/frus1915Supp/d873. Valentiner's account, published sixteen years later, is essentially the same as the account given in this dispatch. The reports of a high death

toll likely stem from roughly half of the survivors being taken by Italian vessels to Sardinia and half by French vessels to Tunisia, with officials in each place concluding that the survivors they saw were the only ones. Many English-language sources still repeat as factual the allegations printed in the press immediately after the sinking of the *Ancona*, placing the death toll at two hundred or more.

2. Doenecke, *Nothing Less Than War*, 128. Burián quoted in Burián to Lansing, Vienna, 29 December 1915.

3. Ibid., 128.

4. Tirpitz, *My Memoirs*, 2:171.

5. Ibid., 2:171–72.

6. Ibid., 2:172; Grant, *U-Boats Destroyed*, 29.

7. Reinhard Scheer, *Germany's High Sea Fleet in the World War* (London: Cassell, 1920), 105.

8. Matthias Erzberger, *Erlebnisse im Weltkrieg* (Stuttgart: Deutsche Verlags-Anstalt, 1920), 214; Tirpitz, *My Memoirs*, 2:173–76; Kelly, *Tirpitz*, 408–9.

9. Marc Frey, *Der Erste Weltkrieg und die Niederlande: Ein neutrales land im politischen und wirtschaftlichen Kalkül der Kriegsgegner* (Berlin: Akademie Verlag, 1998), 76; George Grafton Wilson, "Report of the International Commission of Inquiry in the Loss of the Dutch Steamer Tubantia," *American Journal of International Law* 16 (1922): 432. After the Netherlands rejected Germany's offer to pay an indemnity of £300,000, equal to the original cost of the *Tubantia*, the two countries agreed to submit the case to arbitration after the war, a process which resulted, in 1922, in an award of £830,000 to the ship's owners, the Royal Holland Lloyd.

10. Karl Wiedemann, "Sir Roger Casement's Last Voyage," in *U-Boat Stories: Narratives of German U-Boat Sailors*, ed. Karl Neureuther and Claus Bergen, trans. Eric Sutton (London: Constable, 1931), 108–10; Weisbach obituary in the *Irish Times*, 28 July 1970, 10. Wiedemann indicates that the Germans initially gave Walther Schwieger the mission to transport Casement, but mechanical problems aboard *U 20* forced a last-minute change to Weisbach's *U 19*.

11. Doenecke, *Nothing Less Than War*, 167–72; Scheer, *Germany's High Sea Fleet*, 129–30. Wilson quoted from speech to US Congress, 19 April 1916, United States, 64th Cong., 1st Session, House Document 1034, text at http://wwi.lib.byu.edu/index.php/Wilson_on_the_Sussex_Case. See also http://www.whitestarhistory.com/cymric.

12. Sondhaus, *World War One*, 310.

13. *New York Times*, 31 July 1916, 1.

14. Gray, *The U-Boat War, 1914–1918*, 208, alleges that Arnauld "never forgot the bitter disappointment he experienced when he was rejected for flying duties" in the airship division, but gives no reason for the rejection. Thomas, *Raiders of the Deep*, 127, says he went to the submarine service because "no zeppelin command was available." Pohl to Ella von Pohl, Wilhelmshaven, 13 February 1915, text in Pohl, *Aufzeichnungen*, 110, indicates that Arnauld was still with the *Admiralstab* as of that date, barely six weeks before he reported for submarine officer training.

15. Quoted in Thomas, *Raiders of the Deep*, 146–47.

16. Gray, *The U-Boat War*, 172, includes one such story, without offering a context.

17. Quoted in Thomas, *Raiders of the Deep*, 147.

18. Gray, *The U-Boat War*, 210; http://uboat.net/wwi/boats/successes/u35.html.

19. Quoted in Thomas, *Raiders of the Deep*, 150–51.

20. Quoted in ibid., 154. See also Gray, *The U-Boat War*, 210; http://uboat.net/wwi/men/decorations/2.html.

21. Hans Fechter, *In der Alarmkoje von U 35* (Berlin-Wien: Ullstein, 1918), 45–47.

22. Claus Bergen, "My U-Boat Voyage," in *U-Boat Stories: Narratives of German U-Boat Sailors*, ed. Karl Neureuther and Claus Bergen, trans. Eric Sutton (London: Constable, 1931), 14–15.

23. Thomas, *Raiders of the Deep*, 163–67.

24. Hersing, *U 21 rettet die Dardanellen*, 81–84; http://uboat.net/wwi/boats/successes/ub47.html; http://uboat.net/wwi/ships_hit/greatest_loss_of_life.html.

25. Grant, *U-Boat Intelligence*, 183–84.

26. Gröner, *Die deutschen Kriegsschiffe*, 3:36, 58–59; *Conway 1906–21*, 181–82.

27. http://uboat.net/wwi/ships_hit/largest.html.

28. Scheer, *Germany's High Sea Fleet*, 200; *Conway, 1906–21*, 12.

29. http://uboat.net/wwi/ships_hit/largest.html.

30. Paul G. Halpern, *A Naval History of World War I* (Annapolis, MD: Naval Institute Press, 1994), 36–37.

31. Sondhaus, *The Great War at Sea*, 30–34, 79, 120–21.

32. Daniel R. Headrick, *The Invisible Weapon: Telecommunications and International Politics, 1851–1945* (Oxford: Oxford University Press, 1991), 164–66. Scheer quoted in *Germany's High Sea Fleet*, 123.

33. E. Keble Chatterton, *Q-Ships and Their Story* (London: Sidgwick & Jackson, 1922), 7; Gordon Campbell, *My Mystery Ships* (Garden City, NY: Doubleday, Doran & Company, 1929), 7.

34. Chatterton, *Q-Ships and Their Story*, 8.

35. Ibid., 14–16; Grant, *U-Boats Destroyed*, 27. Graeff's decision, just hours before *U 36* was sunk, to make a prize of the three-masted windjammer *Pass of Balmaha*, spared his second in command, an ensign who captained the sailing ship back to Germany, where it was later armed and sent to the South Pacific on a quixotic raiding voyage commanded by the "Sea Devil," Count Felix von Luckner.

36. Some sources, e.g., Kemp, *U-Boats Destroyed*, 14, characterize the *Inverlyon* as an armed trawler rather than a Q-ship.

37. Chatterton, *Q-Ships and Their Story*, 20–23; Doenecke, *Nothing Less Than War*, 122.

38. Iwan Crompton, *Englands Verbrechen an U 41: Der zweite "Baralong"-Fall im Weltkrieg*, ed. Werner von Langsdorff (Gütersloh: C. Bertelsmann, 1941), 105–23; Chatterton, *Q-Ships and Their Story*, 26–30.

39. Chatterton, *Q-Ships and Their Story*, 40–42.

40. Campbell, *My Mystery Ships*, 302. Most sources agree that there were eleven Q-ship victims, but owing to disagreements over what constituted a Q-ship (e.g., note 36 above) and how certain U-boats were sunk, fifteen different U-boats appear on one list or another.

41. Thomas, *Raiders of the Deep*, 145–46; Gray, *The U-Boat War*, 208–9.

42. Arnauld quoted in Thomas, *Raiders of the Deep*, 146.

43. Reginald Bacon, *The Dover Patrol, 1915–1917*, 2 vols. (New York: George H. Doran, 1919), 2:105–8; Gray, *The U-Boat War*, 140.

44. Grant, *U-Boats Destroyed*, 22.

45. Fürbringer, *Fips*, 15. Many of the Flanders boats were eventually painted with "mouths" too, and their bow art became as diverse as the fuselage art on American bombers in the Second World War. The navy did not discourage the practice, but it never caught on in any other U-boat flotilla.

46. On the Friday superstition, see Robert Moraht, *Die Versenkung des "Danton": meine U-Boots-Erlebnisse von der Ostsee bis zum Mittelmeer* (Berlin: Hutten Verlag, 1917), 94; Wilhelm Marschall, *Torpedo Achtung! Los! Erlebnisse im U-Bootkrieg 1917/18* (Berlin: Im Deutschen Verlag, 1938), 183; "Information Obtained from Survivors of *U 93*," ADM 137/3872/2. Marschall refers to *UB 105* leaving Cattaro at 00:05 on a Saturday morning to avoid a Friday departure. Edgar von Spiegel of *U 93* notes that his crew also considered the 13th day of the month unlucky for a sortie but, paradoxically, accepted a departure on Friday the 13th on the grounds that the bad luck of Friday canceled out the bad luck of the 13th.

47. Grant, *U-Boats Destroyed*, 32; http://uboat.net/wwi/boats/index.html?boat=UB+26.

48. Halpern, *The Naval War in the Mediterranean*, 163–64, 215–19, 278–79.

49. Ibid., 279–85.

50. Bacon, *The Dover Patrol*, 1:106.

4

Preparation

On 4 July 1916, Vice Admiral Reinhard Scheer finally gave William II his formal report of the Battle of Jutland. Five weeks earlier, he took the High Sea Fleet out on its third sortie of the year, from Wilhelmshaven up the Jutland coast of Denmark. As before, Hipper's battle cruisers led the way, and on the afternoon of 31 May they were the first to encounter British forces, the battle cruisers of Beatty's squadron, roughly one hundred miles (160 km) west of the Danish mainland. Their engagement soon drew in the rest of the two fleets. In the long-anticipated North Sea encounter, lasting into the predawn hours of 1 June, the Germans clearly inflicted more damage than they suffered. The British lost three battle cruisers, three armored cruisers, one flotilla leader, and seven destroyers, while the Germans lost one battle cruiser, one pre-dreadnought battleship, four light cruisers, and five destroyers of their own. The British also suffered far higher casualties, including 6,097 dead compared to 2,551 for the Germans. In the immediate aftermath, the Germans celebrated what was no more than a tactical victory, while the British were deeply disappointed at having failed to achieve a modern-day Trafalgar, even though, by preserving the status quo against the best effort the High Sea Fleet could reasonably offer, they had emerged victorious on a strategic level.

For most of his report, Scheer sounded like a battleship admiral defending the battle fleet that had been built at such great cost under Tirpitz's direction: "The battle has proved that in the enlargement of our fleet . . . we have been guided by the right strategical and tactical ideas. . . . The big ship, battleship and battle cruiser, is . . . and will be, the main strength of naval power." Nevertheless, reflecting his realization that Jutland had accomplished nothing, Scheer concluded that the battle fleet could have no further effect on the outcome of the war: "Even the most successful result from a high-sea battle will not compel England to make peace" or "make us masters of the blockade inflicted on us." Like Tirpitz, he pinned his hopes on Germany's submarines, arguing that "a victorious end to the war at not too distant a date can only be looked for by the crushing of English economic life through U-boat action against English commerce." Consistent with his earlier rejection of restricted submarine warfare for the U-boats under his control, Scheer cited his "convictions of duty" in so openly dissenting from the emperor's decision of 4 March and the subsequent *Sussex* pledge of 4 May. He advised against "too lenient a form of procedure" in undersea warfare, in which "the risk of the boats would be out of all proportion to the expected gain." Instead, he called for Germany to "act with the greatest severity" in pursuing a renewed unrestricted campaign.[1]

SCHEER, U-BOATS, AND THE SHIFT IN GERMAN STRATEGY

Given the considerable sums of money expended over the past twenty years to build the High Sea Fleet, it had to remain the central focus of Germany's effort at sea until after Jutland demonstrated, to the fleet's own commander, that even in a big battle in which it inflicted more damage than it absorbed, it could not change the overall strategic situation. Scheer's opinion mattered a great deal to William II, but in the circumstances of the first week of July 1916, a change in policy was out of the question. Just four months earlier, in the meeting precipitating Tirpitz's resignation, the emperor had decided that unrestricted submarine warfare should be "postponed indefinitely." The *Sussex* pledge had confirmed that decision, satisfying the Americans. Meanwhile, thanks to the number of U-boats now in service, restricted submarine warfare was causing more damage to Allied shipping than the earlier unrestricted campaign, and the Mediterranean and minelaying strategies enabled U-boats to do harm to the enemy without angering the United States. On land, Falkenhayn's Verdun strategy appeared to be taxing the French to the limit, while the Austrians threatened Italy with a significant (though much smaller) offensive in the Alps. Divisions redeployed for the offensives at Verdun and in the Alps had seriously weakened the eastern front, leading the Russians to launch a counterattack in Ukraine early in June, but the outcome of their offensive remained in doubt. Likewise, just three days before

Scheer's memorandum, the British had launched an attack along the Somme, apparently in an effort to distract the Germans from Verdun, but the scope and significance of their effort remained unclear. All things considered, the time did not appear right for William II to heed Scheer's advice and resume unrestricted submarine warfare.

Thus, for the moment, Scheer kept the *U* and *UB* boats that were under his control assigned to support fleet operations, as they had been during the sortie that resulted in the Battle of Jutland. In Jellicoe's account of the battle, the British admiral reported that U-boats had been actively engaged, and he claimed the "certain" sinking of one submarine and the "probable" sinking of three others. Scheer, who read Jellicoe's memoir before writing his own, confirmed that "with regard to the submarines he was totally mistaken, as none took part in the battle."[2] Indeed, the general failure of Scheer's plans to involve U-boats in the Jutland operation was one of his biggest disappointments, though the collateral success, days after the fact, of one of *U 75*'s mines sinking HMS *Hampshire* with Lord Kitchener aboard provided some consolation. While the *UB* and *UC* boats of the Flanders Flotilla continued to take the submarine war into British coastal waters, during June and July the U-boats under Scheer's command were limited to patrols of the North Sea, where they sank the occasional merchantman or navy trawler but no warships. In early August, Scheer sent two Type *UE I* boats on extended missions that likewise yielded meager results. Beitzen's *U 75* cruised north of the Arctic Circle to lay mines at the mouth of the White Sea but claimed just one victim, a British navy trawler deployed to help guard the approaches to Archangel, while *Kapitänleutnant* Dröscher, in *U 78*, sowed mines off the western coast of Scotland that also sank just one ship, a Norwegian freighter.[3]

As Scheer resigned himself to continuing regular sorties with the surface fleet until the leadership heeded his advice on the submarine war, he also resolved to make better use of his U-boats in conjunction with those sorties. The next time the High Sea Fleet went out, on 18–19 August, he again sent Hipper's squadron ahead to lure out the Grand Fleet and followed with the main body under his own command. Rather than taking a path up the Jutland coast of Denmark, this time he struck out across Dogger Bank, intending to have Hipper bombard Sunderland, on the coast of northeast England, as a provocation. The main difference came in Scheer's inclusion of U-boats, directed by a submarine officer aboard one of his battleships, which were to serve as pickets protecting the flanks of the German column on the outbound voyage, then deploy to ambush pursuing British capital ships when the High

Sea Fleet turned for home after the attack on Sunderland. The boats of the Flanders Flotilla were assigned to interdict British forces from the Channel and cruisers based at Harwich if they attempted to join the battle. Ironically, a British submarine, *E 23* (Lieutenant Commander R. R. Turner), intervened to throw off Scheer's plan, torpedoing the last dreadnought in his column, the *Westfalen*, on the morning of 19 August and damaging it badly enough to force its return to Wilhemshaven. Scheer proceeded toward Sunderland until early afternoon, when reports of British forces approaching from the south as well as the north prompted him to abandon his course and turn for home; by early evening, the British likewise had returned to their bases. While Scheer's U-boats failed to target any enemy capital ships, those guarding his flanks claimed two of the enemy light cruisers sent out to monitor his movements. First, Walther's *U 52* (which would sink the French battleship *Suffren* while en route to the Mediterranean later in the year) torpedoed and sank the 5,400-ton *Nottingham* on the morning of the 19th. Then, on the afternoon of the same day, a torpedo from *U 66* (*Kapitänleutnant* Thorwald von Bothmer) seriously damaged the 5,250-ton *Falmouth*, which was finished off on the 20th by *U 63* (*Kapitänleutnant* Otto Schultze) while being towed back to port.[4]

The loss of the *Nottingham* and *Falmouth* had a sobering effect on Jellicoe, leading to a fresh cost-benefit analysis of British sweeps of the North Sea to search for the High Sea Fleet. Jellicoe later confirmed that "the ease with which the enemy could lay a submarine trap for the fleet had been demonstrated on the 19th of August," causing him to conclude that "risks which we could afford to run earlier in the war were now unjustifiable." Beatty concurred, and in a letter to Jellicoe on 6 September, he quoted the adage, "When you are winning, risk nothing." By mid-September the two admirals had agreed not to send British dreadnoughts and battle cruisers south of 55°30' N, a line stretching across the North Sea from Newcastle to the German-Danish border. Thus, U-boats had finally played a role in fleet operations, but only to reinforce a caution in Jellicoe and Beatty that kept the Grand Fleet out of range of the High Sea Fleet and made it far less likely that the two fleets would ever come to blows again.[5]

Scheer planned another sortie for September, but storms postponed it. During the delay, a shakeup in the German military leadership resulted in his U-boats being detached from the fleet once again. On 29 August, William II made the fateful decision to entrust the High Command to Field Marshal Paul von Hindenburg and his chief of staff, Erich Ludendorff, in response to a series of events that began to unfold shortly after Scheer's Jutland memorandum. The British attack at the Somme had turned out to be a major offensive, and it had soon become clear that Falkenhayn would only be able to contain it by pulling significant resources away from the effort at Verdun. At the same time, the Russian offensive in Ukraine temporarily broke the Austrian sector of the eastern front, forcing the Austrians to end their Alpine offensive against the Italians in order to deal with the threat. Heartened by the Russian advance, neutral Romania entered the war on the side of the Allies and on 27 August invaded Austria-Hungary along its practically undefended Transylvanian border. To stave off the collapse of their principal ally, the Germans had to take divisions away from the west to shore up the front against the Russians and create a new one against the Romanians, leaving a stalemate as the best possible outcome at Verdun and the Somme. Germany faced a crisis, the most serious crisis it would face until August 1918. William II concluded that Falkenhayn was not the man to handle it and that sweeping changes were needed to avert disaster.

On the strength of their victorious record on the eastern front, Hindenburg and Ludendorff were entrusted not just with command of the army, but the navy as well, and were given sweeping powers on the home front under a militarization of war industries that became known as the Hindenburg Program. Consolidating their power during the month of September, they also gained ultimate authority over the armed forces of the other Central Powers, exercised in the name of William II, whom Germany's allies agreed to make titular supreme allied commander. When it came to naval matters, the views of Hindenburg and Ludendorff reflected those of Tirpitz, who had been trying hard to influence them ever since his retirement in March. Six weeks before Hindenburg assumed command, Tirpitz sent him a long letter detailing the virtues of unrestricted submarine warfare, closing with the flattering assertion that "the greater part of our people look upon Your Excellency as the only man who can save us."[6] Such sentiments were not new. As early as January 1915, Tirpitz asserted privately that "Hindenburg must be endowed with absolute power," and in subsequent correspondence he speculated about the field marshal becoming a dictatorial chancellor or even regent of Germany, exercising the monarchical power for William II.[7]

In a meeting at Schloss Pless, the army's eastern front headquarters, on 31 August, two days after the change in command, Holtzendorff echoed Scheer's arguments of 4 July in pressing for a resumption of unrestricted submarine warfare. To the chief of the *Admiralstab*, it seemed a logical component of a redoubled effort to win the war under the direction of

Hindenburg and Ludendorff, though he no doubt did not help his case by arguing, fancifully, that U-boats could defeat Britain by the end of 1916. Bethmann Hollweg and Jagow had the opposite reaction. Deeply shaken by the military setbacks that had necessitated the changes at headquarters, the foreign secretary, in particular, feared that an unrestricted campaign would make a negotiated peace impossible and would very likely push the European neutrals, along with the United States, into the arms of the Allies. Hindenburg and Ludendorff favored unrestricted submarine warfare but first wanted to defeat the Romanians.[8] Their reasoning (correct, as it turned out) held that decisive action against Romania would deter any other neutral country within Germany's reach from joining the Allies. Holtzendorff came away with an understanding that the High Command would revisit the question of resuming the unrestricted campaign after Romania was defeated; meanwhile, with the endorsement of the generals, he ordered the universal application of restricted submarine warfare as a necessary prerequisite for it. Scheer, dismayed at what he considered a half measure, thus returned the U-boats that had been with the High Sea Fleet since the *Sussex* pledge of May to commerce raiding under cruiser rules.

FIGURE 4.1. *U 53* at Newport (San Diego Air & Space Museum Archives)

In a series of cruises begun or planned by the end of September, *U 57* (*Kapitänleutnant* Carl-Siegfried von Georg) was the most successful, recording two dozen victims in just over a month, ranging in size from the 10,320-ton British steamer *Rowanmore*, torpedoed on 26 October off the western coast of Ireland, to a number of trawlers, plus one British navy sloop.[9] Others ranked as more significant in serving notice that the range of U-boats had increased dramatically. On 7 October, *U 53* (*Kapitänleutnant* Hans Rose) surfaced at Newport, Rhode Island, after a twenty-day voyage across the Atlantic. Rose spent six hours in the port, allowing his boat and its crew to be photographed for the newspapers, then on the following day returned to international waters off Nantucket, where he stopped and sank five ships—three British, one Dutch, and one Norwegian—totaling 20,691 tons, then set a course for home. The presence of an active U-boat off the coast of the United States caused a panic on Wall Street and a spike in maritime insurance rates, but President Wilson (in the last month of a close reelection campaign, waged on the slogan "He Kept Us Out of War") downplayed the episode. None of the ships Rose sank was American and no American lives were lost; the US Navy, which scrambled a flotilla of destroyers to rescue those cast adrift in *U 53*'s wake, concluded that the sinkings had not violated international law or Germany's specific pledges to restrict U-boat warfare.[10] Another sobering example of U-boat capabilities came in the Arctic, where Britain had increased its efforts to send supplies to Russia via the northern route. The Type *UE I* minelayers *U 75* and *U 76* were joined there in September and October by no less than four conventional submarines, which in the span of five weeks sank nine ships (24,296 tons) bound for Archangel. The northernmost sinking was registered on 11 October by *U 46* (*Kapitänleutnant* Leo Hillebrand), which torpedoed the 3,903-ton British collier *Iola* at 72°50' N latitude, 153 miles (283 km) due north of North Cape.[11]

The forty-one-day transatlantic voyage of *U 53*, a boat with a surfaced displacement of just 715 tons, was made possible only by storing additional diesel fuel in two of the diving tanks and additional fresh water in some of the torpedo tubes, ingenious modifications that, of course, affected the boat's mobility and fighting ability.[12] The longer cruises attempted in the autumn of 1916 confirmed that, aside from fuel capacity, the weight and space taken up by fresh water was the most important factor in limiting the time a U-boat could remain at sea. Arnauld, whose *U 35* displaced 685 tons, lamented that "there was never room to carry enough water" for the monthlong patrols that became the norm for the Mediterranean U-boats during 1916. "The bathing allowance was a few cupfuls doled out every Sunday morning. We cleaned up once a week, and then we did not get halfway clean."[13] *U 35*'s chief engineer, Hans Fechter, remembered only the officers and the cook being allowed the luxury of washing their hands on a daily basis, using a basin in which the water was changed every three days.[14] U-boats deploying to the Mediterranean from home waters faced even stricter water rationing on the long outbound voyage; a crew member on one such cruise, aboard *UB 50*, recalled that by the time they neared their destination, the ban on shaving had led to "both officers and men . . . growing wild and woolly beards," while "faces and hands had gradually grown so black that not a patch of bright skin was visible."[15] On the last day of a cruise, Arnauld followed the common practice of "order[ing] the last of the water supply to be divided" among the crew so that they would look presentable for their arrival.[16] For the long Arctic patrols, the problems of fuel and water supply were joined by the challenges of operating in extreme cold. The air inside a submarine was as hot or as cold as the air or water outside, affected only by the heat generated by the engines, making cruises to higher latitudes particularly uncomfortable. Even far south of the Arctic Circle, for U-boats passing to and from the North Atlantic via the safe route around Scotland, icing on the conning tower in the winter months made life miserable not only for the man on watch but for anyone else seeking a bit of fresh air, and seriously limited operations if it were severe enough to cause the hatch to freeze open or shut.

With his U-boats reassigned to restricted submarine warfare, Scheer filled their role with destroyers when he took out the High Sea Fleet for its next sortie, on 18–19 October. He did not venture north of the "risk nothing" line Jellicoe and Beatty had adopted a month earlier and thus did not encounter the Grand Fleet. Afterward, Scheer concluded that his destroyers would be of more use against British antisubmarine defenses at the eastern approach to the Channel and redeployed two of the High Sea Fleet's torpedo flotillas to Zeebrugge, where a half-flotilla had been sent earlier to support the U-boats of the Flanders Flotilla. On the night of 26–27 October, this combined force attacked the Dover barrage, sinking ten drifters, two destroyers, and one transport steamer without losing any of its own ships.[17] The weakening of the defenses at the straits made the Channel more easily accessible to submarines for the remainder of the year, allowing the newly expanded force of *UC* boats in the Flanders Flotilla to extend their minelaying through the Channel to its western approaches, north to the southern coast of Ireland, and south all the way into the Bay of Biscay. The dramatic record of success by *UC* boats late in 1916 (sixty-six ships sunk in November, seventy-six in December) would not have been possible without it.

While these smaller boats transited the Channel to their hunting grounds, Georg's *U 57* and other larger submarines made their way to the western approaches to the British Isles via the longer, safer route around the north of Scotland. Those registering disappointing results on their first sorties of the autumn included Schwieger's *U 20*, which sank just four ships (8,825 tons), and *U 30* (now under *Kapitänleutnant* Franz Grünert), which sank just two (2,913 tons), before taking center stage in a drama that unfolded on their way home. The crisis escalated quickly after Grünert, on the morning of 3 November, reported engine trouble while off the coast of Norway, near Bergen. Schwieger's *U 20* picked up the distress signal and soon met the crippled boat to escort it the rest of the way to Wilhelmshaven. British naval intelligence, reading German wireless traffic, became aware of their situation during the day on the 3rd and alerted Jellicoe, who dispatched light cruisers and destroyers from Scapa Flow on sweeps of the Norwegian and Danish coasts to intercept them. *U 20* accompanied *U 30* across the Skagerrak to the Danish coast where, in the early evening of 4 November, both boats ran aground in a fog north of Horns Reef. If the stranded U-boats and their crews were found first by the British, they would be captured; if they survived to be found by the Danes, they would be interned for the duration of the war. *U 30* soon managed to work itself free of the sand but was too damaged to risk submerging, and in any event Grünert refused to leave the scene while *U 20* remained aground. Shortly after 22:00, news of their predicament reached Wilhelmshaven, prompting Scheer to dispatch a half-flotilla of destroyers on a rescue mission, covered by an impromptu sortie of the High Sea Fleet including half of his available capital ships.[18]

Scheer's sixth and final sortie of 1916 included eight dreadnoughts and the battle cruiser *Moltke*, and though it appeared to be a massive overreaction to the situation at hand, it reflected his concern for the fate of the two submarines, especially *U 20*, which had torpedoed the *Lusitania* eighteen months earlier and was still commanded by the same officer, Schwieger. The boat ranked among the war's most successful, with 145,830 tons sunk thus far, and its commander was known for an aggressiveness that at times got the better of him (for example, torpedoing a passenger liner after the *Arabic* pledge, and doing the same again days after the *Sussex* pledge). The enigmatic Schwieger also ranked among the navy's most beloved officers. As one of his subordinates aboard *U 20* later noted, "he was the soul of kindness toward the officers and men under him. . . . He had the gifts to command both respect and liking, and was a general favorite in the German navy."[19] But to the Allies, he was a war criminal. The German destroyers reached the scene shortly after 07:00 on 5 November and for four hours tried to pull *U 20* free, giving up only after high tide passed with the boat still stranded. *Moltke* and the dreadnoughts continued to stand guard while Schwieger and the crew of *U 20* were rescued, *U 30* was taken under tow, and *U 20* was rendered useless by detonating a torpedo in one of its forward tubes. The operation proceeded without interruption until 13:00, when the British submarine *J 1* (Lieutenant Commander Noel Laurence) arrived to torpedo the dreadnoughts *Grosser Kurfürst* and *Kronprinz*. Laurence, the star among Britain's submariners, had already torpedoed the *Moltke* in August 1915 in the Baltic while commanding *E 1*; on that occasion, without even sinking the battle cruiser, he had prompted the withdrawal of units of the High Sea Fleet that were covering a failed attempt to take Riga from the Russians. This time, too, neither German capital ship was badly damaged and each ultimately made it to port under its own power, but the incident called into question the wisdom of putting the largest vessels of the fleet in play for a peripheral operation.[20]

Indeed, the realization that two dreadnoughts might have been lost for the sake of saving two U-boats infuriated William II, who forbade Scheer to

FIGURE 4.2. *U 20* aground at Horns Reef (Library of Congress)

take such a risk in the future. On 22 November the admiral was summoned to headquarters at Schloss Pless, where he went beyond merely explaining himself in defending the sortie. During an audience with the emperor, Scheer took the opportunity to prepare William II for similar operations in the future. Once unrestricted submarine warfare resumed, he explained, "the fleet will have to devote itself to one task, to get the U-boats safely out to sea and bring them safely home again." Scheer concluded, "Every U-boat is of such importance that it is worth risking the whole available fleet to afford it assistance and support." While such sentiments contrasted sharply with Tirpitz's earlier conclusion that U-boats and their crews must be considered expendable, this glaring logical inconsistency failed to slow the momentum toward Germany's ultimate leap of faith. While at Schloss Pless, Scheer had his first meetings with Hindenburg and Ludendorff and was pleased to find that they had a "complete understanding of the circumstances and conditions of our naval warfare." The generals agreed that "if the war should drag on for so long, February 1, 1917, was the latest date at which to start the unrestricted U-boat campaign."[21]

By the time of Germany's decision to resume unrestricted submarine warfare, the restricted undersea campaign had already taken a heavy toll on Allied shipping, claiming 231,573 tons in September, 341,363 in October, and 326,689 in November. German submarines went on to sink another 307,847 tons in December, then 328,391 in January 1917. Even though their orders required operation under cruiser rules, U-boats were able to inflict more damage than during the first round of unrestricted submarine warfare because so many more of them were now in service. By the end of January they had sunk roughly twice the tonnage in five months that had been taken in the seven months of unrestricted submarine warfare in 1915. Remarkably, during these same months, Germany lost just eleven U-boats, four of which were sunk by the Russians in the Black Sea.[22] Early in the new year, the German submarine force for the first time topped one hundred boats, which the navy began to reassign in preparation for the upcoming campaign. The headquarters of the Baltic Flotilla was moved from Libau to Bremerhaven, but most of its boats went to Flanders, where the growing force was subdivided into two flotillas. The skeleton flotilla at Bremerhaven would be abandoned in the spring, its remaining U-boats dispersed among the flotillas of the High Sea Fleet.

U-BOAT CONSTRUCTION (1915–17)

The Central Powers would be much better prepared for unrestricted submarine warfare in 1917 than they had been in 1915. At the end of 1916,

Germany had 133 U-boats (including twenty-eight *UB* boats and fifty-four *UC* minelayers), to which Austria-Hungary could add twenty more. The capabilities of the submarines at their disposal also differed dramatically from those deployed two years earlier. They included the first of the class of Type *U 151* U-cruisers (*U-kreuzer*), more than twice the size of the largest U-boats of February 1915 and, at 5.7 million Marks apiece, also twice as expensive. They had a surfaced displacement of just over 1,500 tons and dimensions of 213 feet in length, 17 feet deep, and 29 feet across the beam (65 × 5.3 × 8.9 m). The U-cruisers were laid down as cargo submarines for a propaganda exercise demonstrating a blockaded Germany's ability to trade with the United States. Their large fuel tanks gave them a surfaced range of twenty-five thousand nautical miles (46,300 km), more than enough to reach American or equatorial waters and return home to Germany without refueling. The first boat completed, the *Deutschland*, crossed the Atlantic twice as a merchantman during 1916, but the second, named *Bremen*, disappeared on its outbound voyage. As hostilities with the United States became more likely, the *Deutschland* and the remaining six boats of the class were either refitted or completed as warships, numbered *U 151* through *U 157*. Each of the U-cruisers required a complement of six officers and a crew of fifty, and they had room for a prize crew of twenty (including another two officers) to seize vessels deemed too valuable to sink. Owing to their size, their speed (12 knots surfaced, 5 knots submerged) was similar to smaller submarines, but their firepower far surpassed that of their predecessors. Their armament included two 5.9-inch (15 cm) deck guns along with eighteen torpedoes, and they could also lay specially shaped mines discharged through their torpedo tubes. Four of the U-cruisers (*U 151–154*) had two additional 3.45-inch (8.8 cm) deck guns, and some were fitted with external cable-cutting equipment to enable them to sever undersea telegraph cables. Of the seven, only *U 155* (ex-*Deutschland*) was ready for service by February 1917, but the rest were in commission by the end of the year.[23]

The U-cruisers reflected the quest for a more lethal U-boat with larger fuel tanks, greater freshwater storage capacity, and more livable conditions for the crew, all essential to long-range missions. For the duration of the war, German submarine builders remained torn between experimenting with similar larger designs and acting on Tirpitz's logic that submarines had to be considered expendable, a logic that called for a greater number of smaller boats that did not require such large crews. Of the designs making their debut in time for the resumption of unrestricted submarine warfare, the most suc-

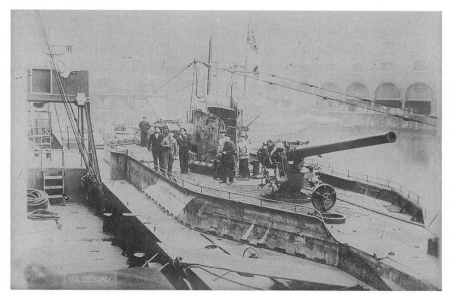

FIGURE 4.3.   *U 155* after installation of 15-cm deck guns (Library of Congress)

cessful were the twenty-two of Type *U 93*, the first of which was launched in December 1916, followed by two more in January 1917. They displaced approximately 840 tons surfaced, measuring 235 feet long by 13 feet deep, with a beam of 21 feet (71.6 × 3.9 × 6.3 m), and were manned by three officers and a crew of thirty-six. They were faster surfaced (with a top speed of nearly 17 knots) and submerged (8–9 knots) than earlier submarines, and their sixteen torpedoes plus a 4.1-inch (10.5 cm) deck gun gave them much more firepower. They carried enough fuel for a surfaced range of 8,300 nautical miles (15,370 km), but their batteries allowed them just over 50 nautical miles (93 km) submerged. Though barely half the size of the U-cruisers, the Type *U 93* boats cost 4.4 million Marks apiece, making them the most expensive German submarines yet built, other than the U-cruisers, and with a far higher per-ton cost. At the same time, the navy still built *UB* coastal submarines and *UC* minelayers, but by 1917 the newest of these types exceeded the displacement of the oceangoing U-boats of 1914–15. Thus the navy did not save money by continuing to build large numbers of smaller U-boats, in part because "small" was much larger than it used to be, and in part because of wartime inflation. Whereas the initial 127-ton *UB* boats cost just over 700,000 Marks apiece, for the thirty 263-ton boats of Type *UB II* commissioned in 1915–16 the price nearly doubled to 1.3 million Marks. The first of eighty-nine 516-ton boats of Type *UB III*, launched in January 1917, cost 3.3 million Marks, and for those commissioned late in the war the figure rose above 3.7 million.[24]

The impressive operational range of the Type *U 93* boats and the U-cruisers would have been irrelevant if not for wartime improvements in German long-wave wireless telegraphy, which allowed submarines to communicate at ever-greater distances. Transmitters at Nauen near Berlin, at Eilvese near Hanover, and at Bruges in Flanders were used to direct U-boats in northern and Atlantic waters, while transmitters at Pola and Damascus facilitated submarine communications (for Austrian as well as German boats) in the Mediterranean, Adriatic, and Black Seas. An increase in Nauen's power to four hundred thousand watts, in effect in time for the resumption of unrestricted submarine warfare in 1917, enabled U-boats to pick up its signal in the Cape Verde Islands, a distance of roughly 3,200 miles (5,200 km). Submarines were also able to receive the stronger signal underwater at depths approaching one hundred feet (30 m). The more powerful wireless sets installed aboard U-boats likewise enabled them to transmit their own messages at greater distances. The five-hundred-watt unit standard for 1914–16 allowed German submarines to send signals up to three hundred miles (500 km), but the one-kilowatt unit standard by 1917–18 allowed transmissions home from the Canary Islands (2,100 miles, or 3,400 km). Without these wartime advances in wireless technology, the increased range of the newer, larger U-boats would have had little relevance, and the second round of unrestricted submarine warfare would have been as limited, geographically, as the first.[25]

Of course, in order to sustain a successful unrestricted campaign, Germany needed not just more capable U-boats, but greater numbers of them, to enable the navy to expand its undersea reach and to replace the anticipated heavier losses in submarines destroyed by the enemy. Concurrent with the restricted campaign of autumn 1916 and the debate among the leadership over when to resume unrestricted submarine warfare, the steps taken to mobilize labor under the Hindenburg Program promised to give the shipyards the workforce needed to sustain the effort. Shortly after Scheer's visit to Schloss Pless, the Reichstag passed the Patriotic Auxiliary Service Law (2 December 1916), making employment compulsory for all males aged seventeen to sixty not already in the armed forces. Bethmann Hollweg secured the support of workers by recognizing their right to maintain unions in the expanded war industries and mandating arbitration of labor disputes. The chancellor also left out some of Ludendorff's more extreme ideas, such as lowering the minimum working age to fifteen, applying the law to women as well as men, allowing only those in "productive" employment to have access to rationed food, and closing the universities except for war-related scientific research. When the parties most chancellors since Bismarck had used as the basis for their Reichstag majorities (the Conservatives and the center-right National Liberals) balked at Beth-mann Hollweg's concessions to the workers and their unions, he turned to the parties most comfortable with those concessions (the SPD, the Catholic Center Party, and the Progressive People's Party) to secure passage of the law, by the rather odd vote of 235 in favor, 19 opposed, and 143 abstaining. Amendments soon made the law palatable to more Germans by exempting farmers, students, and some white-collar workers; as a result, in the first five months after the law passed, the 120,000 new war workers included just 36,000 compelled to work because of it. Ultimately the Hindenburg Program got the labor force it needed only by expanding a program giving leave to skilled workers serving in the army. By September 1916 the war ministry had already exempted 1.2 million workers from military service; by the following summer, the Hindenburg Program added another seven hundred thousand. German farmers, though exempted from war work, were freed to seek factory jobs after six hundred thousand Poles and roughly twice as many Russian prisoners of war were employed as agricultural labor.

It is difficult to assess the outcome of the Hindenburg Program because, as one historian has noted, so much of it reflected the "smoke and mirrors" of domestic propaganda.[26] Nevertheless, several points remain beyond dis-pute. A year after its implementation, the Central Powers had a surplus in most weapons, and two years later, when they lost the war, it was not be-cause of a shortage of materiel. The High Command used the Hindenburg Program to expand its own power on all levels. German industrialists reaped huge profits, but workers also saw their wages rise thanks to Bethmann Holl-weg's concessions to them, and unions experienced a revival in membership and influence. Unfortunately for the German war effort, the labor force of newly empowered unionized workers, rural transplants, women, and foreign deportees was less productive—by one estimate 20 percent less productive—than the prewar industrial workforce.[27] The same factors that affected war industries in general could be seen in German shipyards, in particular those building U-boats. The two largest shipyards in Germany, the navy yards at Wilhelmshaven and Kiel, served the needs of the surface fleet exclusively, but the next four in size, all private firms, experienced considerable wartime growth because of the submarine program. The workforce at Blohm & Voss of Hamburg, the largest prewar private builder, grew by 22 percent and topped 12,500 by war's end. Germania of Kiel, AG Weser of Bremen, and AG Vulcan of Hamburg expanded by 57 percent, 57 percent, and 153 percent, respectively, until each employed just over ten thousand workers. The navy's torpedo factory at Friedrichsort near Kiel likewise expanded dramatically, by 132 percent, to employ over 5,500 workers by 1918. For these firms, the shortage of skilled shipyard labor became acute during the first unrestricted campaign in 1915, when the navy ordered unprecedented numbers of submarines.[28] The rapidly expanding shipyards also lacked sufficient numbers of competent managers and experienced foremen. The navy intervened to secure the release of skilled shipyard workers who had been called up for service in the army; especially after the onset of the Hindenburg Program, these veterans were joined in the shipyards by "younger workers [and] to a lesser extent, women and prisoners of war."[29] The physical demands of the work led to very high attrition among those new to the shipyards and an overall high turnover rate; for example, Blohm & Voss added 12,173 workers in the twelve months after October 1916 but, during the same period, lost 10,026 while maintaining an average workforce of roughly twelve thousand. The influx of men released from the army under the Hindenburg Program stabilized the situation somewhat, as they were better able to handle the work. Management also had the authority to send those considered slackers or malcontents back to the front, and they did not hesitate to use the "threat of the trenches" to inspire harder work with fewer complaints.[30]

To build the U-cruisers and Type *U 93* boats, the navy doubled the number of shipyards involved in U-boat construction from five to ten. Though Germania of Kiel handled their conversion to (or completion as) warships, the seven U-cruisers, owing to their initial conceptualization as cargo submarines, were the product of four smaller shipyards that had served the merchant marine before the war: Reiherstiegwerft of Hamburg built three of them, Flensburger Schiffbau two, and Atlaswerke of Bremen and H. C. Stülcken & Sohn of Hamburg one apiece. None had ever constructed a submarine before or would again afterward. The eight Type *U 93* contracts not awarded to Germania likewise went to a shipyard otherwise not used for U-boat construction, Bremer Vulcan of Vegesack. Especially in the case of the U-cruisers, it made more sense to employ firms otherwise not involved in U-boat construction than to have shipyards already set up to build smaller designs stop doing so in order to reconfigure slips and retrain workers for significantly different projects. The navy followed the same logic throughout the war in distributing contracts among the shipyards it used the most. Counting all boats completed before the war ended (including those never activated), Blohm & Voss built eighty-nine, Germania eighty-four, AG Weser eighty-one, AG Vulcan sixty-nine, and the Danzig navy yard forty-six. Oceangoing U-boats accounted for most of those built by Germania (sixty-two, compared to twenty-two UB or UC boats) and by the Danzig navy yard (thirty-nine, compared to seven UC and UE minelayers). In contrast, AG Weser built sixty-nine UB or UC boats and just a dozen of the larger types, while Blohm & Voss and AG Vulcan specialized in UB, UC, and UE boats and built no conventional oceangoing U-boats at all.[31] Of the 125 oceangoing boats with diesel engines (U-boats numbered U 19 and above, plus UE minelayers), eighty-three had machinery from MAN, thirty-two from Germania, six from Körting, and four from Benz. Engine contracts for the 241 UB and UC boats were divided among MAN, Körting, Daimler, Benz, and AEG.[32] The wartime program of submarine construction thus expanded the German naval-industrial complex, disbursing lucrative contracts to far more firms than had been involved in building the capital ships of the High Sea Fleet or producing the engines, armor plate, and heavy artillery they required.

THE DECISION

During Scheer's meeting with the emperor and his generals at Schloss Pless on 22 November 1916, both Hindenburg and Ludendorff reiterated their earlier position that unrestricted submarine warfare should not be resumed until after the Central Powers had defeated Romania. Scheer also found the generals concerned that the Dutch might join the Allies when the unrestricted campaign resumed, based on a "definite assurance" from the German ambassador to the Netherlands that this would be the case. The two issues were connected because, at least until after the defeat of Romania, the German army could not cover the contingency of a declaration of war by the Netherlands. Though fears of the Dutch abandoning their neutrality proved to be unfounded, they were grounded in the realization that the Netherlands had lost more ships to U-boat activity than any neutral country other than Norway. After sinking just three Dutch-flagged vessels during 1915, German submarines were responsible for the loss of twenty-eight more during 1916, of which the 13,911-ton *Tubantia* (16 March) had been the largest. While most of the increase was attributable to UC minelayers, which had no control over who would run into their mines once they were laid, German-Dutch relations suffered all the same.[33]

After German troops took Bucharest on 6 December, the Romanian army retreated into Moldavia, where it held the southern flank of Russia's eastern front for another year. Romania finally concluded an armistice with the Central Powers when Russia did, after the Bolshevik Revolution, but the fall of the Romanian capital marked the end of the campaign as far as Hindenburg and Ludendorff were concerned. Recognizing that the German army could not survive a repeat of the bloody battles of 1916, they resolved to adopt a defensive posture for 1917 while keeping troops poised to exploit any opportunities that arose on the eastern and Italian fronts. The only movement planned for the western front was a controlled withdrawal to the so-called Hindenburg Line, a fortified front constructed from Lille to Verdun, in some places thirty miles (50 km) behind the former front, bearing witness to the intention to stand on the defensive. Thus, the High Command had nothing to lose by supporting Holtzendorff and giving the U-boats a chance to show how decisive they could be.

On 8 December, Hindenburg raised the issue of unrestricted submarine warfare with William II, only to find the path blocked by Bethmann Hollweg, who had secured the emperor's consent to a peace overture, delivered to the Allies via the United States on 12 December. The delay frustrated the generals and admirals, but Scheer conceded the wisdom of the move. Even though the proposals "had little prospect of finding success with our enemies . . . the fact that they had been made would tend to simplify the situation and, in case of refusal, to rouse the will of the people to strain themselves to the uttermost for the final conflict."[34] Wilson, hoping to act as mediator, on 18 December asked the belligerents for their terms. Bethmann Hollweg, who had never renounced the expansionist war aims he had articulated for Germany in September 1914, issued a vague response on behalf of the Central Powers, then asked the emperor for more time to let diplomacy work, even after it became clear, by 31 December, that none of the Allies would accept a negotiated peace. In the first days of the new year, the daily meetings at Schloss Pless assumed an increasingly stormy character. On 8 January, Holtzendorff joined Hindenburg and Ludendorff in demanding a return to unrestricted submarine warfare, urging William II to sack Bethmann Hollweg if he refused to support it. The chancellor folded the following day, agreeing to the demands of the High Command, and the emperor issued the orders to resume the unrestricted campaign on 1 February.[35]

In the meeting of 9 January, Holtzendorff and the generals brushed aside the concerns of the emperor and chancellor regarding American intervention.

For the contingency that the United States might try to mobilize and ship an army to the western front, Ludendorff later recalled that the calculation was "to reduce enemy tonnage [so] that the quick transport of the new American armies was out of the question." In any case, it would be difficult for the Wilson administration to sustain an intervention after "a certain proportion of the transports had been sunk. The navy counted upon being able to do this."[36] In this regard Holtzendorff reflected the views of Scheer, Hipper, and other leading admirals. In a detailed memorandum to Hindenburg dated 22 December, the chief of the *Admiralstab* had calculated that if U-boats sank an average of six hundred thousand tons of Allied shipping per month for five months, Britain would have to sue for peace. He justified "the risk of war with America, so long as the U-boat campaign is begun early enough to ensure peace before the next harvest, that is, before August 1," a target date that allowed an extra, sixth month for the U-boats to do their work. He concluded that "an unrestricted U-boat campaign, begun soon, is the right means to bring the war to a victorious end for us. Moreover, it is the only means to that end."[37] To facilitate the construction of the additional submarines needed to pursue the campaign to a successful conclusion, Holtzendorff agreed to take steps first advocated by Tirpitz twelve months earlier, abandoning two dreadnoughts and five battle cruisers, then at various stages of completion, to free shipyard personnel and resources to build U-boats.

Holtzendorff's memorandum shaped not just the assumptions underlying the decisions made on 9 January but also the circumstances of their implementation. The admiral had cautioned Hindenburg that "the declaration and commencement of the unrestricted U-boat war should be simultaneous, so that there is no time for negotiations."[38] In the days that followed, the resumption of unrestricted submarine warfare remained a closely guarded secret. The Foreign Office, under Arthur Zimmermann since Jagow's resignation in late November, waited until 19 January to inform the German ambassador in Washington, Count Bernstorff. Even Tirpitz did not learn of the decision until the 25th.[39] The High Command still did not trust Bethmann Hollweg, even after he agreed to support the policy, and on the 10th asked the emperor, once again, to replace him. That same day, however, the Allies unwittingly vindicated the chancellor's peace strategy by responding to Wilson's mediation effort with terms similar to what they would eventually give themselves in the Versailles Treaty two and a half years later, ensuring that no talks could have occurred. By appearing willing to discuss peace while the Allies were not, Bethmann Hollweg had seized the moral high ground for

Germany as it prepared to reintroduce unrestricted submarine warfare. As much as this mattered within Germany, it would be of no consequence in the court of international public opinion after the U-boats were unleashed.[40]

Once the decision to resume the unrestricted campaign had been made, Germany's next step was to secure the participation and support of Austria-Hungary, a quest made easier by the statement of Allied war aims on 10 January. Beyond the evacuation and restitution of territories the Central Powers had conquered since 1914 (plus Alsace-Lorraine), the Allies demanded that Austria-Hungary grant freedom to its Italian, Romanian, and Slavic minorities, steps that would require the dismemberment of the Habsburg state. On 12 January the Austrian foreign minister, Count Ottokar Czernin, sent a note to Washington formally denouncing the Allied response and blaming the Allied powers for the continuation of the war. One week later, Zimmermann went to Vienna, accompanied by Holtzendorff, for a conference with the political and military leaders of Austria-Hungary. At their meeting, held on the 20th, they benefited from the endorsement of the commander of the Austrian navy, Admiral Anton Haus, whose enthusiasm for the change in policy contrasted sharply with the skepticism of Czernin and of Emperor Charles, who had inherited the Habsburg throne from Francis Joseph the previous November. After Holtzendorff admitted that German U-boat commanders had already received their orders, they accepted the fait accompli. On 26 January, Charles accompanied Haus to Germany for more detailed discussions at Schloss Pless, during which they pledged to disarm aging cruisers at Cattaro to free up the manpower needed to facilitate the increase in German submarine traffic there. They also promised to deploy their own submarines in the central Mediterranean against Allied shipping operating between Malta and Salonika. But the campaign soon lost its most ardent Austrian supporter when Haus, then sixty-five, succumbed to pneumonia on the trip home from Germany. He died on 8 February, shortly after returning to his flagship at Pola. Charles remained convinced, at heart, that the decision to resume unrestricted submarine warfare was a mistake and soon concluded that Austria-Hungary could be saved only via a separate peace with the Allies. Within weeks he opened a secret channel to France using his brother-in-law, Prince Sixtus of Bourbon-Parma, as an intermediary. Meanwhile, Austria-Hungary remained formally committed to its alliance with Germany and to the unrestricted campaign, pursued under the direction of Haus's successor, Admiral Maximilian Njegovan. Even Czernin remained unaware of the "Sixtus Affair" until the French government made it public in the spring of 1918.[41]

Recent British measures to tighten the blockade ensured that the German public would welcome the renewal of the unrestricted campaign. In February 1916 the British government had consolidated its economic warfare initiatives under a new Ministry of Blockade; then, in July, it abrogated the Declaration of London and began to assert the legitimacy of the blockade under international law. That same month, the Netherlands bowed to British pressure and signed a trade treaty promising half of all Dutch agricultural exports to Britain; thereafter, the British navy deployed destroyers from Harwich to escort weekly convoys from Dutch ports to the Thames, carrying food that otherwise would have gone to the German home front. Food imports to Germany from, or through, its other neutral neighbors, Denmark and Switzerland, also declined owing to the concerns those countries had about maintaining their own food supplies. As early as the summer of 1916, the poor quality and insufficient quantity of food available to shipyard workers caused strikes at Germania and AG Weser. Then, making matters worse, the German grain harvest of 1916 yielded just 21.8 million tons, down from 30.3 million in 1913 and far short of the total needed to offset yet another year without the Russian grain imports that had helped feed the Reich before the war. By the end of September 1916, Berlin alone had eleven publicly run kitchens, plus seventy-seven centers to distribute food. During the "turnip winter" of 1916–17, named for the readily available vegetable that became ever more prominent in the average diet, the reduction in rations left the average German civilian with just over 1,300 calories per day, significantly less than the prewar peacetime average of nearly 2,300. Inflation also became a serious problem, with the increase in wages trailing far behind the increase in the prices of food and other essentials.[42]

Given these harsh realities, and with the British—after December 1916 under the charismatic leadership of David Lloyd George—preparing to tighten the screws further, Germany's political, military, and naval leaders united behind unrestricted submarine warfare to an extent not possible earlier in the war. In addition to being pursued with greater resources than those available in 1915, the upcoming campaign would never be clouded by the same degree of indecision or doubt that had plagued the previous effort. Indeed, even those harboring misgivings about provoking American intervention accepted the argument that the prevailing circumstances presented no alternative. Unrestricted submarine warfare would remain Germany's policy as long as it held any hope of winning the war.

NOTES

1. Scheer to William II, Wilhelmshaven, 4 July 1916, text in Scheer, *Germany's High Sea Fleet*, 168–69.

2. John Rushworth Jellicoe, *The Grand Fleet, 1914–1916: Its Creation, Development, and Work* (New York: George H. Doran, 1919), 489; Scheer, *Germany's High Sea Fleet*, 168.

3. http://uboat.net/wwi/boats/successes/u75.html; http://uboat.net/wwi/boats/successes/u78.html.

4. Jellicoe, *The Grand Fleet*, 434–42; Scheer, *Germany's High Sea Fleet*, 180–84.

5. Jellicoe, *The Grand Fleet*, 443; Beatty to Jellicoe, 6 September 1916, quoted in Halpern, *A Naval History of World War I*, 331.

6. Tirpitz to Hindenburg, Berlin, 16 July 1916, text in Tirpitz, *Ohnmachtspolitik*, 562–66.

7. Tirpitz to Marie von Tirpitz, 20 January 1915, text in Tirpitz, *My Memoirs*, 2:294, and in six more letters, passim, down to Tirpitz to Marie von Tirpitz, 21 April 1915, text in ibid., 2:344. See also Kelly, *Tirpitz*, 416.

8. Doenecke, *Nothing Less Than War*, 218.

9. http://uboat.net/wwi/boats/successes/u57.html.

10. Doenecke, *Nothing Less Than War*, 218–19; http://uboat.net/wwi/boats/successes/u53.html. Hans Rose, *Auftauchen! Kriegsfahrten von "U 53"* (Essen: Essener Verlagsanstalt, 1939), 66–120, provides a detailed account of *U 53*'s voyage to Newport and back.

11. http://uboat.net/wwi/ships_hit/3048.html.

12. Rose, *Auftauchen!*, 60–63.

13. Quoted in Thomas, *Raiders of the Deep*, 155.

14. Fechter, *In der Alarmkoje von U 35*, 46.

15. Wireless Operator Ruhland, "From Kiel to Cattaro," in *U-Boat Stories: Narratives of German U-Boat Sailors*, ed. Karl Neureuther and Claus Bergen, trans. Eric Sutton (London: Constable, 1931), 180–82.

16. Quoted in Thomas, *Raiders of the Deep*, 155.

17. Scheer, *Germany's High Sea Fleet*, 186–89. The account of the raid of 26–27 October in Bacon, *The Dover Patrol*, 2:25–30, claims that six drifters were sunk, three drifters and a trawler damaged.

18. Scheer, *Germany's High Sea Fleet*, 191; Jellicoe, *The Grand Fleet*, 456; http://uboat.net/wwi/boats/successes/u20.html; http://uboat.net/wwi/boats/successes/u30.html.

19. Scheer, *Germany's High Sea Fleet*, 193; *Leutnant* Rudolf Zentner, quoted in Thomas, *Raiders of the Deep*, 91.

20. Scheer, *Germany's High Sea Fleet*, 192; Jellicoe, *The Grand Fleet*, 456–57.

21. Scheer, *Germany's High Sea Fleet*, 193–94, quoted 194.

22. http://uboat.net/wwi/fates/losses.html.

23. Grant, *U-Boats Destroyed*, 40; Eberhard Rössler, *Die deutschen U-Kreuzer und Transport-U-Boote* (Bonn: Bernard & Graefe Verlag, 2003), 74–77; Gröner, *Die deutschen Kriegsschiffe*, 3:47; *Conway 1906–21*, 180. See also König, *Voyage of the Deutschland*, passim. König, a reserve naval officer, commanded the submarine on its two merchant cruises (to Baltimore, June–August 1916, and to New London, CT, October–December 1916) but

not after its commissioning as *U 155*. The *Bremen* disappeared in September 1916 while on a cruise to Norfolk, VA.

24. Gröner, *Die deutschen Kriegsschiffe*, 3:38, 48, 50, 52; *Conway 1906–21*, 178, 181.

25. Headrick, *The Invisible Weapon*, 164.

26. Holger H. Herwig, *The First World War: Germany and Austria-Hungary, 1914–1918* (London: Arnold, 1997), 263.

27. See Albrecht Ritschl, "The Pity of Peace: Germany's Economy at War, 1914–1918 and Beyond," in *The Economics of World War I*, ed. Stephen Broadberry and Mark Harrison (Cambridge: Cambridge University Press, 2005), 47.

28. Volker Ullrich, "Die Januarstreik 1918 in Hamburg, Kiel und Bremen: Eine vergleichende Studie zur Geschichte der Streikbewegungen im Ersten Weltkrieg," *Zeitschrift des Vereins für Hamburgische Geschichte* 71 (1985): 47.

29. Ibid., 48.

30. Ibid., 48–49.

31. See links available from http://uboat.net/wwi/types/shipyards.html.

32. *Conway 1906–21*, 176–82.

33. Scheer, *Germany's High Sea Fleet*, 194. See also Frey, *Der Erste Weltkrieg und die Niederlande*, 81–83; http://uboat.net/wwi/ships_hit/search.php, search "nl."

34. Scheer, *Germany's High Sea Fleet*, 195.

35. Donecke, *Nothing Less Than War*, 228–39; Scheck, *Tirpitz and German Right-Wing Politics*, 56–57.

36. Erich Ludendorff, *Ludendorff's Own Story*, 2 vols. (New York: Harper, 1919), 2:20.

37. Holtzendorff to Hindenburg, 22 December 1916, text in Scheer, *Germany's High Sea Fleet*, 248–52.

38. Holtzendorff to Hindenburg, 22 December 1916, text in ibid., 251.

39. Donecke, *Nothing Less Than War*, 239; Scheck, *Tirpitz and German Right-Wing Politics*, 57.

40. Scheck, *Tirpitz and German Right-Wing Politics*, 57.

41. Béla Kiraly, Peter Pastor, and Ivan Sanders, eds., *Essays on World War I: Total War and Peacemaking* (New York: Brooklyn College Press, 1982), 229; Sondhaus, *The Naval Policy of Austria-Hungary*, 293–94, 302, 332–33.

42. Eric W. Osborne, *Britain's Economic Blockade of Germany, 1914–1919* (London: Frank Cass, 2004), 127–45, 153, 159–61; Keith Allen, "Food and the German Home Front: Evidence from Berlin," in *Evidence, History and the Great War: Historians and the Impact of 1914–18*, ed. Gail Braybon, 172–97 (New York: Berghahn Books, 2003); Gibson and Prendergast, *The German Submarine War*, 175; Ullrich, "Die Januarstreik," 53.

5

The Sharpest Weapon

Ever since November 1914, when the late Admiral Pohl first proposed unrestricted submarine warfare, Bethmann Hollweg had been opposed to it more often than not. Thus, it was no small irony that it fell to the chancellor to make the public announcement of its resumption. In a speech to the Reichstag on 31 January, he reassured the assembled representatives of something he did not truly believe: that it was the right decision, at the right time, and very likely to succeed. He noted that "the bad wheat harvest of the world" in 1916 "already confronts England, France and Italy with serious difficulties," making them more dependent on overseas sources for food. He cited the "firm conviction" of the naval leadership "that Great Britain will be brought to peace by arms" and noted that "our allies agree with our views. . . . Just as we lay a blockaded area around Great Britain and the west coast of France . . . Austria-Hungary declares a blockaded area around Italy." Bethmann Hollweg shared with the Reichstag Hindenburg's recent assessment that "our front stands firm on all sides. We have . . . the requisite reserves. The spirit of the troops is good and confident." Alluding to the risk of the United States declaring war on Germany, he cited the field marshal's conclusion that "the military situation, as a whole, permits us to accept all consequences which an unrestricted U-boat war may bring about." The chancellor left no doubt about "the seriousness of the step which we are taking," closing with the observation that "in now deciding to employ the best and sharpest weapon, we are guided . . . by a sober consideration of all the circumstances that come

FIGURE 5.1.
Theobald von Bethmann Hollweg
(Bibliothèque nationale de France)

into question." He made a point of emphasizing "the most important fact of all . . . that the number of our submarines has very considerably increased as compared with last spring, and thereby a firm basis has been created for success." The preparation likewise had not been lacking; indeed, "as regards all that human strength can do to enforce success for the Fatherland, you may be assured, gentlemen, that nothing has been neglected."[1]

Because the Germans made no secret of the conditions on their home front during the "turnip winter," President Wilson feared they might again resort to unrestricted submarine warfare unless the war ended soon and thus had attached great importance to Bethmann Hollweg's apparent willingness to negotiate peace. But in a speech before the US Senate on 22 January, urging both sides to accept a "peace without victory," the president once again revealed his bias against the Central Powers, observing that the German response to his request of 18 December, for both sides to state their terms, had been less than helpful, "stat[ing] merely that they were ready to meet their antagonists in conference to discuss terms of peace." In contrast,

Wilson characterized the more specific Allied response of 10 January, out-lining a victor's terms that made peace talks impossible, as having brought the world "that much nearer the definite discussion of the peace which shall end the present war."[2] Thus, Wilson was taken aback when the Ger-man ambassador in Washington, Count Bernstorff, gave formal notice of the resumption of unrestricted submarine warfare, framed as a response to the "peace without victory" speech. The message, delivered within hours of Bethmann Hollweg's address to the Reichstag, began with a preamble that condemned Britain for "using her naval power for a criminal attempt to force Germany into submission by starvation." Bernstorff then informed the United States that "from February 1, 1917, sea traffic will be stopped with every available weapon and without further notice in the . . . blockade zones around Great Britain, France, Italy and in the Eastern Mediterra-nean," the boundaries of which were outlined specifically in the remainder of the document. Because the policy was changing with no advance warn-ing, Bernstorff promised that "neutral ships . . . will be spared during a suf-ficiently long period" to enable them to leave the designated zones, a grace period ultimately fixed at one month. Germany would allow the continua-tion of unmolested passenger travel between the United States and Britain, but under conditions so restrictive (one American-flagged liner each way per week, following a specific route, bearing markings prescribed by the Germans) that they were certain to be rejected.[3]

Wilson wasted no time in rejecting the change in German policy. Before a joint session of Congress on 3 February, he quoted at length from the text of Germany's *Sussex* pledge of 4 May 1916, issued in response to his own ultimatum of 18 April 1916 that Germany "abandon its present methods of submarine warfare" or else face a breach of diplomatic relations with the United States. Because those methods had resumed, Wilson announced the expulsion of Bernstorff from the United States and recalled the American ambassador from Germany. He also threatened war "if American ships and American lives should in fact be sacrificed by [German] naval commanders in heedless contravention of . . . international law and the obvious dictates of humanity."[4] Holtzendorff's orders to U-boat commanders, issued on 12 January, three days after the emperor's decision to resume the unrestricted campaign, increased the likelihood that this would happen: "From February 1, 1917 onward, every enemy merchantman met within the restricted zone is to be attacked without warning. For the intimidation of neutral shipping, an effect as strong as possible at the beginning will be of great significance."[5]

"AN EFFECT AS STRONG AS POSSIBLE"

Even if there had been no formal announcement of it, the sudden increase in German submarine activity would have signaled the change in policy. After seventeen U-boats sank thirty-nine ships of various sizes during the last week of January, twenty-eight U-boats claimed eighty-four victims during the first week of February. Nearly half of the vessels sunk were British (forty-one), but the French (twelve), Russians (five), Italians (three), and Belgians (one) also suffered losses. While many sinkings were still carried out by surfaced U-boats using their deck guns or explosive charges placed by demolition teams, in which cases the crews were allowed to abandon ship, the mandate to sink without warning resulted in deaths in at least one-third of all attacks. The costliest incident of the first week, in terms of lives lost, came on 7 February off the southern coast of Ireland, where *U 85* (*Kapitänleutnant* Willy Petz) torpedoed the 8,668-ton British passenger steamer *California* (43 dead). Not surprisingly, submarine commanders responded in different ways to the one-month grace period for neutral ships caught en route by the change in policy, since it contradicted the directive calling for "the intimidation of neutral shipping . . . at the beginning" of the campaign. A quarter of the ships sunk during the first week flew neutral flags, including fourteen from Norway, two from the Netherlands, and one each from Sweden, Peru, Spain, Denmark, Greece, and the United States. The 3,143-ton freighter *Housatonic* had the distinction of being the first American-flagged vessel deliberately sunk by a U-boat. On 3 February, the same day Wilson broke diplomatic relations with Germany, *U 53* encountered the *Housatonic* twenty miles (32 km) off the tip of Cornwall. The same boat with the same commander, Hans Rose, had made the war's only American port call by a U-boat the previous October, at Newport, and on this occasion Rose had the good sense to operate according to cruiser rules. He stopped the *Housatonic*, ascertained that its cargo—a shipment of grain, bound for London from Galveston—was clearly contraband, then allowed the crew to board their lifeboats before sinking the ship. Rose even towed the *Housatonic*'s boats for an hour and a half before leaving them in the care of a British trawler, ensuring that no lives were lost. His behavior on that day very likely postponed an American declaration of war.[6]

In the first weeks of the campaign, the leading commanders and crews more than met the expectations of their superiors by producing dramatic results. In the month of February, Arnauld's *U 35* sank sixteen ships (36,800 tons), topping the table in the Mediterranean; his victims included the American four-masted schooner *Lyman M. Law*, sunk on the 12th off Sardinia but, like the

Housatonic, after being stopped and with no loss of life. Meanwhile, Hersing's *U 21*, recalled from the Mediterranean, claimed thirteen victims (36,510 tons) in the Atlantic, including two off Portugal en route to new hunting grounds in the sea-lanes south of Ireland. New boats with veteran commanders also distinguished themselves, in particular *UC 65* (*Oberleutnant* Otto Steinbrinck) of the Flanders Flotilla, which sank 27,070 tons in February, then 19,320 more on 1 March. The month's two deadliest sinkings involved troopships in the Mediterranean. On 15 February, off Cape Matapan, Forstmann's *U 39* sank the 2,854-ton *Minas*, overloaded with Italian troops bound for Salonika (870 dead). Two days later, *U 65* (*Kapitänleutnant* Hermann von Fischel) sank the 12,644-ton *Athos* shortly after it exited the Suez Canal bound for Marseilles, with Chinese laborers from Hong Kong and French African troops embarked at a stop in Djibouti (754 dead). *U 50* (*Kapitänleutnant* Gerhard Berger) had the distinction of sinking the largest ship in the campaign's first month, torpedoing the 18,099-ton Cunard liner *Laconia* on 25 February without warning. Even though the attack occurred far out to sea in the Atlantic, 160 miles (257 km) west of Ireland, just 12 of the 292 passengers and crew perished, but the dead included Chicago socialite Mary Hoy and her daughter Elizabeth, friends of First Lady Edith Wilson.[7]

Addressing a joint session of Congress on 26 February, Wilson acknowledged the loss of the *Housatonic* and *Lyman M. Law* but conceded that, since both ships had been warned and evacuated before being sunk, neither incident constituted the sort of "overt act" that should trigger a declaration of war. Nevertheless, he acknowledged the chilling effect of unrestricted submarine warfare on American shipping lines and maritime insurance companies and proposed, as a solution, an "armed neutrality," including the installation of guns aboard American merchantmen and provision of public funds to insure them against loss. News of the demise of the *Laconia* reached Washington during Wilson's speech, but because the liner was British and armed, and the loss of life had been relatively insignificant (the well-connected Hoys notwithstanding), those who sought to turn the incident into a *Lusitania* of 1917 were disappointed.[8]

In any event, the loss of one ship or another was soon overshadowed by the publication of the sensational "Zimmermann telegram," a message from the German foreign minister sent to his ambassador in Mexico City, Heinrich von Eckhardt, on 19 January, informing him that unrestricted submarine warfare would resume on 1 February and instructing him on how to proceed in the event of an American declaration of war. Eckhardt was to promise the

Mexicans the return of the states of Texas, Arizona, and New Mexico in exchange for entering the war on Germany's side, and to enlist their help in getting Japan to abandon the Allies and join the Central Powers. The Admiralty's Room 40 intercepted and decoded Zimmermann's message, and on 19 February the British Foreign Office shared it with the US State Department. Wilson first learned of the telegram on the 25th but did not release it to the press until he was satisfied it was not a British forgery. It was published on 1 March, under sensational headlines nationwide.[9] Though the plan outlined in the "Zimmermann telegram" was ridiculed at the time as far fetched, traditionally it has been credited with turning American public opinion decisively against Germany. Recent scholarship, however, indicates that the telegram's primary significance was its effect on the president. While Wilson had held out hope for peace, majority opinion within his cabinet, Congress, and the American public already favored war. For the noninterventionist minority, generally suspicious of the British, the telegram likewise made little difference, owing to Britain's role in bringing it to light.[10] Zimmermann compounded the diplomatic damage and further strengthened the hand of the interventionists in the United States by acknowledging the authenticity of the telegram in a Reichstag speech later in March. By then, the fall of Tsar Nicholas II in the initial Russian revolution had eliminated a critical obstacle to American intervention, sparing Wilson from the ideological conundrum of entering a war against autocratic states allied with Europe's leading autocrat.[11]

After destroying an unprecedented 520,410 tons of shipping in February 1917, U-boats claimed another 564,500 tons in March.[12] Minelayers were responsible for the greatest individual successes, both against British steamers, when Steinbrinck's *UC 65* sank the 11,483-ton *Drina*, inbound from Buenos Aires, on 1 March and *UC 17* (*Oberleutnant* Ralph Wenninger) sank the 11,140-ton *Rotorua*, inbound from New Zealand, on the 22nd. Nearly four hundred vessels were destroyed during the month, a quarter of them neutral and just four flying the American flag, but each of these incidents brought the United States closer to war with Germany. On 12 March, *U 62* (*Kapitänleutnant* Ernst Hashagen) sank the 1,806-ton *Algonquin* sixty-five miles (105 km) west of the tip of Cornwall. Then, on 16–18 March, U-boats sank three American vessels on consecutive days. First, *U 70* (*Kapitänleutnant* Otto Wünsche) torpedoed the 4,115-ton *Vigilancia*, 145 miles (233 km) west of the tip of Cornwall. The following day, *UC 66* (*Oberleutnant* Herbert Pustkuchen) stopped the 5,252-ton *City of Memphis*, thirty-three miles (53 km) off the southern coast of Ireland, allowed its crew to abandon ship, and then sank it with shell fire. Finally, on the 18th, *UC 21* (*Oberleutnant* Reinhold Saltzwedel) stopped and scuttled the 5,225-ton oil tanker *Illinois* near the Channel Islands, also allowing the crew to board its lifeboats. Of the four ships, the *Vigilancia* was the only one sunk without warning and the only one to suffer fatalities (15 dead, including 6 American citizens), but the other three incidents demonstrated that the degree of chivalry shown in February by Rose, after sinking the *Housatonic*, was becoming a thing of the past. Hashagen, Pustkuchen, and Saltzwedel all refused to tow lifeboats closer to shore, and many of the survivors succumbed to illness from exposure.[13] The sinkings prompted Wilson, on 20 March, to meet at length with his cabinet, which endorsed war unanimously. The following day, the Navy Department issued secret mobilization orders to warship commanders, to be opened in the event of a declaration of war. Publicly, the president remained undecided, but three days later he called a special session of Congress, to convene on 2 April.[14]

APRIL 1917: AMERICAN INTERVENTION AND THE RECORD MONTH

On the afternoon of 8 December 1941, in response to the bombing of Pearl Harbor the previous day, President Franklin Roosevelt went to Capitol Hill to ask Congress for a declaration of war against Japan. After his brief address, just over seven minutes and barely five hundred words in length, the legislators granted his wish, unanimously in the Senate and with just one dissenting vote in the House of Representatives. The scene on the evening of 2 April 1917 could not have been more different. Lacking a sudden or deliberate action by Germany to justify a declaration of war, Wilson spoke for nearly forty-five minutes, delivering an address of over 2,700 words, framing his case with references to his previous speeches and actions and to Germany's repeated violations of its own pledges. As in most subsequent cases of American presidents asking Congress to approve military action (1941 being the notable exception), Wilson also universalized the cause as one of right versus wrong, of humanity versus an inhumane foe. "The present German submarine warfare against commerce is a warfare against mankind. It is a war against all nations. American ships have been sunk, American lives taken, in ways which [have] stirred us very deeply. . . . [T]he ships and people of other neutral and friendly nations have been sunk and overwhelmed in the waters in the same way. There has been no discrimination. The challenge is to all mankind." He asked "that the Congress declare the recent course of the Imperial German Government to be in fact nothing less than war against the government and people of the United States; that it formally accept the status of belligerent which has thus been thrust upon it; and that it take immediate steps . . . to bring the Government of the German Empire to terms and end the war."[15]

Wilson's remarks were punctuated by frequent applause, reflecting the general enthusiasm for war among the legislators. Ironically, those congratulating him afterward included the senior member of the Senate, Henry Cabot Lodge of Massachusetts, who just over two years later would lead the Republican opposition to ratifying the Versailles Treaty. Dissent came mostly from representatives of the midwestern states, where isolationist opinion crossed party lines. Opponents included the Senate Foreign Relations Committee chairman, Democrat William J. Stone of Missouri, but in the aftermath of the president's speech none was more vocal than Republican Robert La Follette of Wisconsin. La Follette was instrumental in delaying the Senate's war vote until 4 April, when he delivered a pointed four-hour rebuttal to Wilson's case for war, indicting the president along with the press for demonizing the U-boat while ignoring Britain's no-holds-barred tactics. "The public sees nothing, thinks of nothing but the wrongs committed by the German submarine," he argued, "and hears nothing, knows nothing of [the] wrongdoing of England that forced Germany to take the course she has taken or submit to the unlawful starving of her civilian population." Republican George Norris of Nebraska blamed Wall Street and big business for pushing the country to war and warned that "we are about to put a dollar sign on the American flag." Among Wilson's supporters, Senator John Sharp Williams of Mississippi was perhaps the most eloquent in rejecting La Follette's justification of German methods and Norris's populist attacks on big business. Refocusing the debate on the damage U-boats had done, Williams reminded the chamber that "Wall Street and the money power of the capitalists did not sink the *Lusitania*. . . . Wall Street did not sink the *Arabic*. Wall Street did not sink the *Sussex*. Wall Street did not sink the *Algonquin* with the American flag on her main staff, nor did Wall Street sink the last three American ships with flags flying that were sunk in the same way." Such arguments carried the day, ultimately by a landslide in both the Senate, later on 4 April (82–6), and in the House of Representatives on 6 April (373–50).[16]

Having failed in his quest to shape a lasting postwar peace as a neutral mediator, Wilson now sought to do so by making the United States the key contributor to an Allied victory. For this reason, he did not want to be bound by the territorial promises the Allies had made to each other since 1914. Thus, the United States did not conclude a treaty linking itself to the Triple

Entente (as, for example, Italy had in 1915), but instead joined the Allies as an "associated power." Wilson also wanted war with Germany alone, not the rest of the Central Powers; on 9 April, Austria-Hungary severed diplomatic relations with the United States in response to its declaration of war against Germany, but the United States did not declare war on the Dual Monarchy until 7 December, and it never went further than breaking diplomatic relations with Bulgaria and the Ottoman Empire. The American precedent of entering the war without joining the Entente proved popular especially in the Western Hemisphere. Starting with Cuba, on 7 April, eight Latin American countries also became "associated powers" of the Allies, while another four broke diplomatic relations with Germany but did not declare war. Of those joining the Allies, only Brazil eventually contributed armed forces, a naval division for Atlantic convoy duty. The rest supported the cause by following the example of the United States in seizing German merchant ships that had sought internment in their neutral ports in 1914–15. Once these vessels were refitted for Allied service, the tonnage helped to compensate for shipping lost to U-boats after the resumption of the unrestricted campaign.[17] The addition of the United States to the ranks of the belligerents also opened the way for neutral shipping to be requisitioned by the Allied powers for their wartime use. The Netherlands, with its large merchant marine, suffered the most from the loss of the United States as a champion of neutral rights at sea; indeed, the Americans eventually joined the British in seizing 132 Dutch ships totaling roughly 650,000 tons, over one-third of the entire Dutch merchant marine.[18]

After setting new records for tonnage sunk in February and again in March, German U-boats destroyed a remarkable 860,330 tons in April, a monthly total not topped even by Nazi Germany's much larger submarine force during the Second World War.[19] Within the month, eighty-seven German submarines (including nineteen *UB* and thirty-five *UC* boats) recorded at least one sinking. With very few passenger liners venturing out, once again the largest targets and deadliest attacks involved ships transporting troops, including the 8,939-ton *Arcadia* and 10,963-ton *Cameronia*, sunk on the same day, 15 April, in the Eastern Mediterranean while carrying reinforcements for the Gaza offensive of the Egyptian Expeditionary Force (EEF) against German-led Turkish forces holding Palestine. Despite being the smaller of the two ships, the *Arcadia* (279 dead), torpedoed by *UC 74* (*Kapitänleutnant* Wilhelm Marschall) while en route from Salonika to Alexandria, experienced a greater loss of life than the *Cameronia*, sunk by *U 33* (now under *Kapitänleutnant* Siess) while en route from Marseilles to Alexandria.[20] On 25 April, off the tip of Cornwall, *UB 32* (*Kapitänleutnant* Max Viebeg) torpedoed the 11,120-ton British troopship *Ballarat*, inbound from Australia, but all aboard were saved, in part because many of them were already on deck at the time of the sinking for an ANZAC Day memorial service. Aside from troopships, the largest vessel sunk during the month was the 12,350-ton British passenger liner *Medina*, by *UB 31* (*Oberleutnant* Thomas Bieber) on 28 April, off the coast of Devon (6 dead). The 7,924-ton freighter *Missourian*, sunk without loss of life on the 4th by *Kapitänleutnant* Walther's *U 52* shortly after leaving Genoa for New York, was the largest, by far, of the nine American ships destroyed in April. Other highlights of the record month included the operational debut of the Type *U 93* submarines, with the lead boat of the class, under *Kapitänleutnant* Edgar von Spiegel von und zu Peckelsheim, sinking nine ships (24,631 tons) in fifteen days during its outbound voyage from the North Sea to its assigned hunting grounds west of Ireland. The Austrians also started to send some of their own U-boats into the Eastern Mediterranean, where three of them sank five ships totaling 23,706 tons, of which the largest was the 8,173-ton British steamer *Mashobra* (8 dead), on 15 April, by *U 29* (*Linienschiffsleutnant* Leo Prásil).[21]

During the record month of April, Hersing's *U 21* (launched February 1913) was the oldest of the eighty-seven U-boats to sink a ship, and one of just five that had been in service when the war began. While the newer, larger U-boats, with more torpedoes (in some cases, more mines) and heavier-caliber deck guns, gave Germany a more lethal undersea force, the less cramped conditions aboard them for the first time made it feasible to take prisoners from the vessels they sank. In order to deny the Allies the services of experienced merchant captains, after the resumption of unrestricted submarine warfare, U-boats took dozens of them captive, in some cases along with their engineers and radio operators, to sit out the rest of the conflict in prisoner-of-war camps in Germany or Austria-Hungary. The conditions facing prisoners aboard a submarine typically were no harsher than those of the crew. Arnauld received no complaints after taking five British merchant captains aboard *U 35* during an April sortie via the Straits of Gibraltar into the Atlantic, despite the relatively tight conditions aboard his boat and the length of the cruise back to Cattaro. One of them left behind a note which became one of Arnauld's most prized mementos of the war, thanking him "for the kind and courteous treatment . . . at the hands of you, your officers, and . . . the whole of your crew, during the 23 days I have been prisoner of war on your vessel."[22] Unfortunately, U-boat commanders continued to receive little recognition for their humane treatment of the enemy, leaving fewer of them inclined to provide it, not just because their orders now gave them the option to sink without warning, but also because the circumstances of war or forces of nature often made humane gestures futile or irrelevant. For example, when *U 32* sank the 2,480-ton Italian cargo steamer *Porto di Rodi* in the Ionian Sea on 10 April, using the deck gun after allowing the crew of thirty-one to abandon ship, the commanding officer, *Kapitänleutnant* Hartwig, "took the lifeboats in tow" because the "shore was distant and the sea was rough." He released the boats once "the coast finally loomed in sight" and "the lifeboats only had a short pull before them. The Italians were grateful and we parted with a friendly leave-taking," but "a bare few minutes later a vicious storm hit us." Hartwig later learned from an Allied account of the sinking that none of the Italians had made it ashore. "The boats had been lost. Nothing was known of my provisions for the safety of the crew. It was thought that I had sunk the ship with all on board."[23]

The record month of April brought the total shipping sunk over the first three months of the campaign to more than 1.9 million tons, a pace slightly better than the 600,000 tons per month that Holtzendorff had calculated would bring peace before the next harvest. In the face of such results, the German High Command remained outwardly confident that the war would be over before the United States could send troops to the western front. Nevertheless, Hindenburg and Ludendorff considered it prudent to end the fighting on the eastern front as soon as possible to prepare for the contingency of focusing their resources on the west in 1918. Disappointed that the abdication of Nicholas II had not knocked Russia out of the war, they sought to destabilize the Provisional Government that replaced the tsarist regime by providing transportation home for Vladimir Ilyich Ulianov, better known as Lenin, and other exiled leaders of the Bolshevik party. A "sealed train" carrying Lenin and thirty comrades left Switzerland on 9 April, three days after the American declaration of war. He reached Petrograd on 16 April to a tumultuous welcome. Less than seven months later, the Bolshevik Revolution would make him master of Russia.[24]

THE UNITED STATES, BRITAIN, AND THE ALLIED CONVOY SYSTEM

More than any other wartime American president, Wilson allowed his generals and admirals to determine strategies and policies, requiring only that the United States must have a clear role in the Allied victory in order to ensure his own leading role in crafting the postwar peace settlement. British and French military and naval leaders who wanted US troops and ships committed piece-meal when they became available (to be amalgamated with their own forces, under their command) thus were at odds with their American counterparts, who could not square such demands with Wilson's expectations. The com-mander of the American Expeditionary Force (AEF), General John J. Persh-ing, insisted on deploying an American army on an American sector of the western front, even though a force of that size could not possibly be ready before the summer of 1918. Likewise, the commander of the US Atlantic Fleet, Admiral Henry T. Mayo, insisted that his forces had to stay together. In particular, Mayo rejected British appeals for American dreadnoughts to join the Grand Fleet as part of a series of battleship redeployments that would al-low deactivation of the oldest British pre-dreadnoughts, freeing manpower to serve on antisubmarine patrols in 119 new destroyers then nearing comple-tion. Mayo also declined to participate directly in the antisubmarine effort; in response to a request for the deployment to European waters of all available American destroyers, he promised a token force of just six of them.[25]

It was left to Rear Admiral William S. Sims, most recently head of the US Naval War College in Newport, to bridge the differences between the Ameri-can and British navies. Wilson ordered Sims to London in late March on a secret mission to the Admiralty; the declaration of war came while he was en route, and after his arrival the president made him commander of American naval forces in European waters. Sims was uniquely positioned for the task at hand. As a former destroyer flotilla commander, he understood destroyers and antisubmarine warfare. As a former naval attaché in Paris and St. Peters-burg, he was well suited to play a diplomatic role. His background was very similar to that of Admiral Sir Lewis Bayly (a fellow former war college head, destroyer flotilla commander, and naval attaché), with whom he would have to work closely to secure the Atlantic sea-lanes against the U-boat threat. Sims was also an old friend of Admiral Jellicoe, who had been appointed First Sea Lord in November 1916. They first met in 1900 in China, during the Boxer Rebellion, and Sims's periodic prewar visits to Britain enabled them to main-tain their relationship. A Canadian by birth, Sims was also the US Navy's leading anglophile. In his capacity as American naval commander in Europe, he would serve the Allied cause by persuading his own navy to deploy the types and numbers of ships that were needed most, and by mediating between Jellicoe and Bayly, who did not get along well with one another.[26]

To avoid alarming the public, the British government had kept the record losses in shipping in February and March a closely guarded secret. In his first meeting with Jellicoe, on 10 April, Sims received the sobering details of just how much tonnage had been sunk since the renewal of unrestricted submarine warfare, with projections of how much more the Allies were likely to lose that spring. The damage was much more significant than the Wilson administration had assumed, yet also not as great as the Germans thought it had been, owing to Holtzendorff's underestimation of how much tonnage the Allies had available to them and overestimation of how much they required to continue their war effort at current levels. At the start of 1917 the Allies needed 15.5 million tons of shipping to sustain themselves but had access to 21.5 million tons, for a surplus of six million; Holtzendorff had assumed their surplus was half as large, just three million tons, and thus considered the sinking of an average of six hundred thousand tons for five months sufficient to eliminate their margin of security. Nevertheless, in the first three months of the campaign, U-boats had destroyed nearly two million tons, and at that rate they would eliminate even the larger margin before the end of the year. When Sims asked if the Admiralty had a solution to the U-boat threat, Jellicoe replied that there was "absolutely none that we can see now." Sims found the "general belief in British naval circles that [Germany's] plan would succeed" to be particularly disheartening, yet "it was a matter of very simple arithmetic to determine the length of time the Allies could stand such a strain." U-boats would not bring the British to their knees by Holtzendorff's target date of 1 August, but if they maintained the pace of the campaign's first three months for another six months, Jellicoe believed "the limit of endurance would be reached around November 1, 1917."[27]

Britain's decision to adopt convoys as the primary countermeasure against the U-boat threat came shortly after the American declaration of war and the arrival of Sims in London. During his first two weeks of interaction with British naval and political leaders, the American admiral recognized that those advocating the change in policy had to overcome considerable obstacles. Prewar opponents of the use of convoys against commerce-raiding cruisers included the influential strategist Sir Julian Corbett, who believed any concentration of merchantmen only made it easier for the enemy to sink them.[28] Because submarines were much slower than cruisers, such sentiments grew stronger when the submarine superseded the cruiser threat. Indeed, most merchant captains would rather take their chances at outrunning U-boats than risk their ship in a convoy, which moved at the speed of the slowest ship. Senior British naval authorities even doubted that merchantmen were capable of steaming in formation. They did not view as precedents the convoys of troopships escorted by Allied warships since August 1914, because they involved requisitioned civilian ships under naval control, or the Dutch food convoys initiated in July 1916, whose short route placed little burden on the Harwich-based force that routinely conducted antisubmarine patrols in the same waters. Skeptics at the Admiralty were quick to point out that the convoy routes under consideration could not be covered similarly with forces already at hand. While a cruiser or two could defend a convoy against surface raiders, a much larger number of destroyers and other smaller warships would be needed to provide adequate defense against submarines.

Sims found Jellicoe siding with those skeptical of convoys, while Admiral Beatty, who had succeeded him as Grand Fleet commander, was among the few senior officers supporting them. The prime minister, Lloyd George, favored convoys but claimed to have gotten nowhere with Jellicoe. Commander Reginald Henderson and a circle of junior officers at the Admiralty favored convoys and mustered evidence to support their case, which Sims reviewed on 29 April while visiting Jellicoe at the Admiralty. On the 30th, Lloyd George likewise visited the Admiralty and, according to his own account, came away with a commitment from the First Sea Lord to attempt convoys at least on a trial basis. At a dinner later that evening, Lloyd George attributed the breakthrough to the influence of Sims. The American admiral took credit for prevailing upon Jellicoe to order Henderson and his colleagues to prepare the feasibility study on convoys but would go no further. Indeed, when questioned after the fact about his role, he remarked that "in the absence of an authorized statement from the Admiralty" or a very high-ranking officer serving within it, which he doubted would ever be issued, "it would be a mistake [to] claim that the influence of our officers was the determining factor in the adoption of the convoy."[29] British scholars writing on the convoy question have always been reluctant to give Sims the credit Lloyd George felt he deserved. One recent work also rejects the notion that the prime minister prompted the adoption of the convoy policy on 30 April, arguing instead for a gradual transformation from December 1916 onward, after the changes that brought Lloyd George to power and made Jellicoe the First Sea Lord. Nicholas Black (who minimizes the role of Henderson and does not mention Sims at all) credits Jellicoe with approving convoys of colliers to France on 16 January, seven weeks before the United States declared war, and convoys of Britain's Scandinavian trade on 21 April, a week and a half before the prime minister's visit to the Admiralty. The record also shows that on 26 April, likewise before Lloyd George's meeting with Jellicoe, the head of the Admiralty's

Anti-Submarine Division, Rear Admiral Alexander Duff, cited the success of the French coal convoys along with the American declaration of war as reasons to adopt a comprehensive convoy system. The idea of "trial convoys," too, was discussed long before 30 April.[30]

In any case, Sims undeniably played the key part in facilitating Anglo-American cooperation after the policy changed. On 4 May, the six destroyers initially conceded by Admiral Mayo joined Admiral Bayly's antisubmarine force at Queenstown, on Cork harbor, and within a month Sims managed to get him a dozen more. The Admiralty assumed responsibility for organizing convoys in the principal American ports but did not initially designate a chief convoy officer; Admiral Sir William Grant eventually assumed the role, along with command of the North American and West Indian station. After initially attempting to do his job while headquartered at Bermuda, Grant raised his flag aboard a converted yacht anchored in the Potomac River at Washington and became much more like a British counterpart to Sims in the United States. The Admiralty assigned local convoy officers to New York and Hampton Roads and, after 22 June, when the convoy system was extended to Canadian ports, to Halifax and Sydney in Nova Scotia. In contrast to the Second World War, when Allied convoys included both cargo ships and troopships, in the First World War the difference in speed between the fast ocean liners employed as troop transports and the average freighter, and the relative speed of both compared to that of a submarine, dictated that cargo convoys and troop convoys be kept separate. The US Navy used group numbers to identify convoys of American troopships bound for Europe, and the Admiralty used a combination of letters and numbers for all the rest: "H" or "O" depending upon whether they were "homeward" (inbound to Europe from overseas ports) or "outbound" (returning mostly empty ships), with a second letter distinguishing their port of origin, followed by a sequential number. Convoys from New York (HN), Hampton Roads (HH), and Sydney (HS) consisted exclusively of cargo ships, while the faster Halifax (HX) convoys included Canadian troopships, non-US troopships carrying American soldiers, and cargo ships capable of keeping up with them.[31]

The first transatlantic convoy, HH1, consisted of twelve ships that left Hampton Roads on 24 May; two stragglers were diverted to Halifax, but the remaining ten ships crossed safely and were dispersed to various British ports by 10 June. Meanwhile, Pershing and the AEF staff left New York aboard the White Star liner *Baltic* on 27 May, followed on 14–17 June by fourteen thousand troops of the US First Division, a token start for an American army that would have 2.1 million men on French soil at war's end. While the *Baltic* made the crossing unescorted, the First Division's convoy of seventeen ships (designated Groups 1–4) had the strongest protection of any in the war: four cruisers, a dozen destroyers, and two armed yachts, supplemented by another five destroyers from Queenstown for the last three days of the voyage into St. Nazaire, which they reached on 27 June. While the two armed yachts went on to form the nucleus of an American naval presence at Brest, six of the destroyers joined the Queenstown force, which by early July grew to include thirty-four American destroyers, enough to allow the transfer of the last of Bayly's British destroyers to other commands. Sims also eventually delivered the American dreadnoughts the British had requested, ultimately nine in all, facilitating the deactivation of their oldest pre-dreadnoughts and the reassignment of their crews to the expanding British destroyer force.[32]

On 20 July the Queenstown destroyers met their first cargo convoy, HS1, fifteen ships that had left Sydney ten days earlier, ending a temporary arrangement under which most inbound convoys had been met by British destroyers steaming all the way out from Devonport on Plymouth harbor. Once the Queenstown base was fully operational, its destroyers met convoys southwest of Ireland and escorted them to a second rendezvous point at the western approach to the Channel, where the Devonport destroyers took over all ships bound for British ports while the Queenstown destroyers continued on with those bound for Brest and other French Atlantic ports. The addition of convoys from New York, starting with the nineteen cargo ships of HN1 (14 July–30 July), promised to further strain the destroyer resources of Queenstown and Devonport, prompting a proactive decision to route all convoys bound for Liverpool, Glasgow, and other British "West Coast" destinations around the north of Ireland and into the Irish Sea via the North Channel (between Ulster and Scotland), with British destroyers based at Buncrana on Lough Swilly responsible for escorting them into port. After the first such convoy, the twenty-four ships of HH7 (6 July–24 July), reached its destinations with no losses, the general pattern called for transatlantic cargo convoys formed in Hampton Roads, New York, and Nova Scotia to be organized into separate "West Coast" and "East Coast" convoys (the latter bound for Channel ports, the Thames estuary, or France), with alternating departures. The Queenstown and Devonport destroyers maintained their shared responsibility, but only for the "East Coast" convoys, which continued to be routed south of Ireland and split at the western approach, with the American destroyers escorting ships into French ports and the British destroyers taking the rest into the Channel.[33]

Though Rose's *U 53* had demonstrated the previous year that a smaller U-boat could make a transatlantic voyage, the seven U-cruisers were the only submarines available to Germany in 1917 fully capable of operating in American waters. Recognizing this limitation, the Allies never repeated the extraordinary protection given to the First Division convoy. The American and British destroyers assigned to escort duties almost always limited their operations to the eastern Atlantic, where they picked up convoys that had been accompanied from the American and Canadian ports across the western and central Atlantic by a lone cruiser to guard against the remote possibility of attack by a German surface raider or long-range U-boat. For cargo convoys, American navy cruisers and British navy cruisers each shouldered roughly a third of this burden, with British armed merchant cruisers escorting the rest; for troopship convoys, only proper warships were used as escorts, with the French navy contributing a small number of cruisers to supplement the American and British effort. American cruisers escorted all American troopship convoys and most HN convoys, leaving the British responsible for almost all HH convoys in addition to the HX and HS formations. A convoy protection model developed under which the destroyers based at Queenstown and Buncrana would escort an outbound group of empty troopships or merchantmen to meet an inbound convoy and its cruiser; the cruiser would then turn to continue westward to the United States or Canada with the empty ships, while the destroyers turned to accompany the ships of the inbound convoy to their British or French destinations. This arrangement was always followed if the cruiser was American (or a French cruiser operating out of New York), but most British cruisers escorting convoys inbound to Britain remained with them all the way into port, even after the destroyers joined up. For "West Coast" convoys routed north of Ireland, the median rendezvous point was 55°50' N 12°40' W, roughly 220 miles (355 km) west-northwest of Buncrana, while for the "East Coast" convoys routed south of Ireland, it was 49°0' N 12°20' W, roughly 250 miles (400 km) southwest of Queenstown, but in both cases the points varied considerably depending on the weather. For example, on 22 September a group of Queenstown destroyers steamed 560 miles (900 km) to the west-southwest, to 49°29' N 17°13' W, to meet convoy HN8. At the opposite extreme, on the following 17 March, a group of Buncrana destroyers steamed just forty-seven miles (75 km) to 55°29' N 6°39' W to meet convoy

HS31 after it had already passed Lough Swilly and was entering the North Channel. In between, during the winter months, bad weather caused the destroyer escorts of at least six "West Coast" and three "East Coast" convoys to be canceled altogether, but at little risk to the ships involved, because seas too rough for destroyers were also too rough for U-boats.[34]

At least in theory, convoys were most vulnerable to attack during the ocean rendezvous, especially if an escorting American or French cruiser left them before the destroyers appeared. Because the American cruisers were under standing orders to turn west no later than 15° W and the median rendezvous point was closer to 12° W, many convoys went unescorted for a day or two before being picked up by their destroyers. Nevertheless, the priority given to protecting fully loaded convoys resulted in few eastbound cargo ships (and no troopships) ever being sunk on the high seas; indeed, ships were more likely to be sunk closer to their destinations, during or after the process of dispersing them to various ports. By the summer of 1917, convoys were leaving every four days from Hampton Roads and every eight days from New York, Sydney, and Halifax, resulting, on average, in twenty convoys crossing the North Atlantic per month. Destroyers on convoy duty soon became the war's busiest naval vessels, each spending five days at sea for every two or three in port, and on the average cruising six thousand miles (10,000 km) per month.[35]

Just as Germany, earlier in 1917, had altered its naval construction program in order to expand the U-boat force, Britain and the United States amended theirs to meet the needs of convoy escort and antisubmarine warfare. In the nineteen months after the American declaration of war, the US Navy added another ninety-eight destroyers, nearly tripling the number it had in commission, and at the end of the war had another 175 under construction. At the same time, the Americans doubled the size of their own submarine force, adding forty-nine boats to the fifty already in service at the beginning of 1917. Thanks to Sims's prior experience as a destroyer flotilla commander, he knew the best American destroyer captains and arranged to have them transferred to Bayly's force at Queenstown. These included William "Bull" Halsey and Frank Fletcher, admirals in the Second World War who experienced their first action at sea on North Atlantic convoy duty.[36]

While Anglo-American cooperation naturally focused on the transatlantic convoys, they were just part of a broader network created after the decisions made at the Admiralty in late April. Within a month, additional routes had been established between Norway and Scotland; between Gibraltar and various British ports; and, in the Mediterranean, between Malta and Alexandria.

By summer, convoys had been added from Freetown, Sierra Leone, to Britain and from Dakar, Senegal, to France. In the quest to protect all these convoy routes, the shortage of destroyers made somewhat smaller sloops more important than ever. Introduced in 1915 as a fleet minesweeper, the type was mass-produced for antisubmarine duty, with Britain building 112 sloops by 1917 (and another eight for France). On convoy duty they served both in lieu of destroyers and alongside them. Armed merchant cruisers, other auxiliary warships, and even armed trawlers and drifters supplemented destroyers and sloops, their weaknesses compromising the effectiveness of their protection, especially beyond the transatlantic routes. After the adoption of convoys, the British navy commissioned a number of "escort merchant ships," armed with up to six guns, none heavier than six-inch (15.2 cm) caliber. They were distinguished from other armed merchant cruisers not by their armament (which was more or less the same) but by their role, being used exclusively for convoy duty. For defensive purposes, many merchantmen employed in convoys were fitted with a single stern gun, in larger ships as heavy as six inches.[37]

HOPEFUL SPRING

Germany's U-boats never came close to repeating their record performance of April 1917, but the months of May, with 616,320 tons of shipping sunk, and June, with 696,725, were their third- and second-best of the war, keeping the pace above Holtzendorff's goal of destroying 600,000 tons per month. During the remaining spring months, the single most destructive sinking, in terms of tonnage and lives lost, came in the Gulf of Genoa on 4 May, when *Kapitänleutnant* Schultze's *U 63* torpedoed the 14,348-ton British troopship *Transylvania*, en route from Marseilles to Alexandria with more reinforcements for the EEF's Gaza offensive. The casualties (413 dead) would have been greater if not for the heroic rescue efforts of the two Japanese destroyers escorting the *Transylvania*, part of a flotilla of destroyers sent from Japan to Malta the previous month.[38] Another notably deadly sinking came one week later, off the coast of Catalonia, when *U 34* (now under *Kapitänleutnant* Johannes Klasing) torpedoed the overcrowded 1,918-ton French steamer *Medjerda* (344 dead). Other, larger U-boat victims were sunk with remarkably little loss of life, including the 8,271-ton British hospital ship *Dover Castle*, by *UC 67* (*Oberleutnant* Karl Neumann) on 26 May, while en route from Malta to Gibraltar (7 dead); the 11,899-ton British steamer *Southland*, by Wünsche's *U 70* on 4 June, 140 miles (225 km) northwest of Ireland (4 dead); and the 10,402-ton British steamer *Ultonia*, by Rose's *U 53* on 27 June, 190 miles (305 km) due west of Brest (1 dead). On 26 June, in the waters north of Ireland, *U 94* (*Kapitänleutnant* Alfred Saalwächter) torpedoed the 11,635-ton British steamer *Haverford*, but the ship remained afloat and was beached by its crew on the Donegal coast the following day (8 dead). Not surprisingly, Neumann's attack on the *Dover Castle* was the most controversial of these sinkings; he targeted it with one torpedo, then finished it off an hour later with another, a degree of premeditation that earned him a postwar indictment for war crimes, even though 834 patients, staff, and crew were saved by British destroyers between the two attacks. In geographic terms, the most remote operations of the spring were the Arctic sorties of *U 45* (*Kapitänleutnant* Erich Sittenfeld) in May and *U 28* (now under *Kapitänleutnant* Georg Schmidt) in June, which collectively sank six Allied steamships, three Russian and three British, on the route into Archangel.[39] The navy would wait until the summer to deploy the first of the U-cruisers on longer-range voyages. When they entered service, they were assigned to a separate group (*U-Kreuzer-Verband*) at Kiel, with a special status under Holtzendorff and the *Admiralstab*.[40]

In 1917, as in 1916, the Mediterranean remained the most fertile hunting ground for U-boats, and to help ensure that it remained so, during April the Austrian navy made plans for a major surface attack on the Otranto barrage, hoping for results similar to those achieved in the German destroyer attack against the Dover barrage the previous October, which for months afterward had made it easier for the U-boats of the Flanders Flotilla to transit the Channel. In the year after the Otranto barrage claimed its only confirmed victim, Austrian *U 6* in May 1916, the cruisers and destroyers based at Cattaro periodically raided the drifter line at the mouth of the Adriatic. Rear Admiral Kerr's decision to move the barrage farther south, to the parallel of Santa Maria di Leuca, the boot heel of Italy, two hundred miles (320 km) from the Austrian base, improved its security but not its effectiveness. Despite adding more drifters, the barrage registered no more confirmed successes, although Austrian *U 30* (*Linienschiffsleutnant* Friedrich Fähndrich) disappeared without a trace on 31 March 1917, en route to its first Mediterranean cruise, and may have been a victim of the barrage.

The plan of attack included an Austrian raiding force of three light cruisers, led by *Linienschiffskapitän* Miklós Horthy in the *Novara*, supplemented by a diversion on the coast of Albania by two destroyers, commanded by *Korvettenkapitän* Prince Johannes von und zu Liechtenstein, with the German *UC 25* (*Kapitänleutnant* Johannes Feldkirchner) and two Austrian U-boats staking out the Allied bases at Brindisi and Valona in order to torpedo warships attempting to respond to the raid. Their sortie, on the night of 14–15 May, escalated the following day into the Battle of the Otranto Straits, the war's most extensive high-sea action in the Adriatic.[41]

Following Horthy's predawn attack on the barrage line, which sank fourteen drifters and damaged four others, Liechtenstein's destroyers sank three ships in an Italian convoy off the Albanian coast, along with a destroyer escorting them. The U-boats failed to stop the Allies from deploying five cruisers and eighteen destroyers to search for the Austrian attackers, and for most of the morning of the 15th these Allied ships were between Horthy's and Liechtenstein's vessels and the safety of Cattaro. A three-hour running duel between Horthy's *Novara* and the larger, more heavily armed HMS *Dartmouth* left the Austrian cruiser badly damaged and its captain seriously wounded. Feldkirchner (whose career had been uneventful since registering the war's first sinking of an Allied merchantman, the *Glitra*, back in October 1914) on this day sealed the victory for the Austrians by torpedoing the *Dartmouth*, which survived the blow but had to be towed back to Brindisi; Horthy's *Novara* likewise had to be towed back to Cattaro after the battle. Liechtenstein's destroyers survived the action by taking refuge temporarily at Durazzo, in Austrian-occupied northern Albania, before rejoining Horthy's cruisers to make it safely home. On the afternoon of the 15th a French destroyer sank after striking a mine laid by *UC 25* during the morning action, bringing the total Allied losses in the battle to two destroyers, three merchantmen, and fourteen drifters, against no losses for the Austrians. Horthy's victory effectively neutralized the Otranto barrage well into the summer; indeed, for six weeks after the battle, Kerr did not even attempt to maintain the drifter line at night. The beneficiaries included Forstmann's *U 39*, which in the month of June alone sank fifteen vessels totaling 30,462 tons, more than any other German U-boat operating out of Austrian bases.[42]

While the German navy after 1916 no longer deliberately deployed submarines against larger Allied warships, during the first half of 1917 U-boats continued to register some significant successes against them. On 25 January, off the northern coast of Ireland, Type *UE* boat *U 80* (*Kapitänleutnant* Alfred von Glasenapp) mined the 14,852-ton British armed merchant cruiser *Laurentic*, resulting in the greatest loss of life ever caused by a ship striking a mine (345 dead). On 19 March, off Sardinia, *U 64* (*Kapitänleutnant* Robert Moraht) torpedoed the 18,320-ton French pre-dreadnought *Danton*, the largest warship sunk by a submarine during the war (296 dead). On 14 June, west of the Shetland Islands, *U 69* (*Kapitänleutnant* Ernst Wilhelms) torpedoed and damaged the 13,441-ton British armed merchant cruiser *Avenger*, which subsequently sank while under tow to Scapa Flow (1 dead). Finally, on 27 June, *UC 61* (*Oberleutnant* Georg Gerth) of the Flanders Flotilla mined the 7,578-ton French armored cruiser *Kléber* off Brest (42 dead). Such incidents served notice that the Allies had to continue to devote valuable resources to protecting their larger warships from the U-boat threat or else leave them in port.[43]

For the first five months of the campaign, February through June, German U-boats more than met Holtzendorff's goal of destroying 600,000 tons of shipping per month; they actually exceeded it by almost 10 percent, sinking nearly 3.3 million tons by 1 July. The destruction of 1,900 vessels of various sizes had come at the cost of just eighteen submarines lost, of which fourteen were small *UB* or *UC* boats. As in the past, the lost boats were more likely to have been under newer or less successful commanders; exceptions this time included Count von Schmettow, whose *UC 26* was rammed in the Straits of Dover on 8 May by a British destroyer, and Herbert Pustkuchen, whose *UC 66* was lost with all hands on 27 May in the Scilly Islands after being bombed by a Curtis flying boat of the Royal Naval Air Service. They would be sorely missed, for between them they had destroyed nearly a quarter of a million tons (Schmettow's 111,628 and Pustkuchen's 107,520, the latter including the controversial *Sussex* sinking in 1916).[44] Other notable losses included Bruno Hoppe of *U 83*, sunk by Gordon Campbell's Q-ship *Farnborough* on 17 February southwest of Ireland; Willy Petz of *U 85*, sunk by the Q-ship *Privet* on 12 March in the Channel;[45] and Edgar von Spiegel of *U 93*, captured by the Q-ship *Prize* on 30 April southwest of Ireland, in an attack his boat managed to survive. In the latter encounter, Spiegel was preparing to board the *Prize* when it revealed its guns and opened fire at point-blank range, knocking him from the deck of *U 93* into the water, after which he was rescued and taken prisoner, along with his navigator and one of his crew. Spiegel joined British eyewitnesses in confirming that *U 93* "suddenly sank" after the attack, amid "an explosion with black smoke." He spent the rest of the war in a POW camp assuming the boat had been lost, along with the remaining officers and crew, learning only after his postwar repatriation that his second in command (*Oberleutnant* Wilhelm Ziegner) had actually faked the explosion, submerged the damaged boat, and slipped away safely.[46]

As spring gave way to summer, the Germans thought they were on the verge of pushing the British to their breaking point. Because Holtzendorff had underestimated by half the surplus of enemy tonnage over absolute need, they were not as close as they thought they were; nevertheless, as Jellicoe had indicated to Sims in their first April conversation, the rate of shipping lost during the springtime months, if projected forward, would bring Britain to the "limit of endurance" all the same, only some three months later than the chief of the *Admiralstab* had calculated. A combination of Allied initiatives promised to add to their shipping tonnage—new construction, the refurbishing of German steamers interned in the United States and other countries now at war with Germany, and the requisitioning of neutral (mostly Dutch) merchant ships—but none would make much difference before the end of 1917. Thus, the pressure was on for the convoy system to prove its effectiveness in limiting the damage done by U-boats in order to buy time for these initiatives to work. Meanwhile, control of the seas around Europe remained very much in doubt, along with the ability of the Allies to continue their war effort.

NOTES

1. "Theobald von Bethmann-Hollweg's Speech to the Reichstag regarding Unrestricted Submarine Warfare," Berlin, 31 January 1917, http://www.firstworldwar.com/source/uboat_bethmann.htm.

2. "Address of President Woodrow Wilson to the U.S. Senate," Washington, 22 January 1917, http://www.firstworldwar.com/source/peacewithoutvictory.htm. See also Doenecke, *Nothing Less Than War*, 242–43.

3. "Germany's Policy of Unrestricted Submarine Warfare," Washington, 31 January 1917, http://www.firstworldwar.com/source/uboat_bernstorff.htm.

4. "President Wilson's Speech to Congress Regarding Unrestricted U-Boat Warfare," Washington, 3 February 1917, http://www.firstworldwar.com/source/uboat_wilson.htm.

5. Quoted in Doenecke, *Nothing Less Than War*, 239.

6. http://uboat.net/wwi/ships_hit/losses_year.html?date=1917-02&string=February +1917; Rose, *Auftauchen*, 141–45.

7. http://uboat.net/wwi/ships_hit/losses_year.html?date=1917-02&string=February +1917; Doenecke, *Nothing Less Than War*, 266.

8. Doenecke, *Nothing Less Than War*, 264–67.

9. Nicholas Black, *The British Naval Staff in the First World War* (Woodbridge: Boydell Press, 2009), 2; Doenecke, *Nothing Less Than War*, 263–64, 267.

10. See Thomas Boghardt, *The Zimmermann Telegram: Intelligence, Diplomacy, and America's Entry into World War I* (Annapolis, MD: Naval Institute Press, 2012).

11. "Arthur Zimmermann's Speech Regarding the Zimmermann Telegram," Berlin, 29 March 1917, http://www.firstworldwar.com/source/zimmermann_speech.htm; Doenecke, *Nothing Less Than War*, 283.

12. These are the most widely cited figures, totaling 1.085 million for the two months combined. Detailed data at http://uboat.net/wwi total up to just over 1.088 million (506,057 tons for February and 582,066 for March).

13. http://uboat.net/wwi/ships_hit/losses_year.html?date=1917-03&string=March +1917; Doenecke, *Nothing Less Than War*, 278–80.

14. Doenecke, *Nothing Less Than War*, 281–82; mobilization orders cited in Joseph K. Taussig, *The Queenstown Patrol, 1917: The Diary of Commander Joseph Knefler Taussig, U.S. Navy*, ed. William N. Still, Jr. (Newport, RI: Naval War College Press, 1996), 5.

15. "U.S. Declaration of War with Germany," Washington, 2 April 1917, http://www .firstworldwar.com/source/usawardeclaration.htm.

16. Doenecke, *Nothing Less Than War*, 290–96. Norris quoted in ibid., 292; La Follette quoted in *Congressional Record*, 65th Cong., 1917, 230; Williams quoted in ibid., 236.

17. Sondhaus, *World War One*, 312–15.

18. Frey, *Der Erste Weltkrieg und die Niederlande*, 272.

19. This is the most widely cited figure. Detailed data in http://uboat.net/wwi total up to 860,953 tons, not including warships sunk, unarmed ships seized rather than sunk, and ships sunk by Austrian U-boats.

20. Marschall, *Torpedo Achtung*, 36–42; http://uboat.net/wwi/ships_hit/greatest_loss_ of_life.html. Various sources give a wide variety of figures for the number of dead in the sinking of the *Cameronia*, ranging from a low of 11 to a high of 210.

21. http://uboat.net/wwi/ships_hit/losses_year.html?date=1917-04&string= April+1917.

22. William McLellan Hunter to Arnauld, Cattaro, 6 May 1917, reproduced in Thomas, *Raiders of the Deep*, 161.

23. Thomas, *Raiders of the Deep*, 165.

24. Sondhaus, *World War One*, 237–41.

25. Jerry W. Jones, *U.S. Battleship Operations in World War I* (Annapolis, MD: Naval Institute Press, 1998), 3, 9–12.

26. Elting E. Morison, *Admiral Sims and the Modern American Navy* (Boston: Houghton Mifflin, 1942), 280, 341–42, 377–81, and passim.

27. William Snowden Sims, *The Victory at Sea*, with Burton J. Hendrick (Garden City, NY: Doubleday, Page, 1920), 9–11.

28. Julian Stafford Corbett, *Some Principles of Naval Strategy* (London: Longmans, Green, 1911), 261–79.

29. Morison, *Admiral Sims*, 348–53; Sims quoted 352. Julian Stafford Corbett, *History of the Great War: Naval Operations*, 5 vols. (London: Longmans, Green, 1920–31), 4:324, credits Henderson with leading the officers at the Admiralty favoring convoys. David Lloyd George, *War Memoirs*, 6 vols. (Boston: Little, Brown, 1933–37), 3:105–7, acknowledges Sims but takes much of the credit for establishing the convoy system.

30. Black, *The British Naval Staff*, 173–83.

31. Benedict Crowell and Robert Forrest Wilson, *The Road to France*, vol. 2, *The Transportation of Troops and Military Supplies, 1917–1918* (New Haven, CT: Yale University Press, 1921), 467; Michael L. Hadley and Roger Sarty, *Tin-Pots and Pirate Ships: Canadian Naval Forces and German Sea Raiders, 1880–1918* (Montreal: McGill-Queen's University Press, 1991), 234; William Johnston, "The Royal Canadian Navy and the First World War," in *The Naval Service of Canada, 1910–2010: The Centennial Story*, ed. Richard H. Gimblett (Toronto: Dundurn Press, 2009), 34. Admiral Grant was appointed station commander and chief convoy officer in February 1918 and moved to Washington in March 1918.

32. United Kingdom, National Archives, Admiralty (hereafter ADM) 137/2656, HH1; Crowell and Wilson, *The Road to France*, 388–407, 603; Taussig, *Queenstown Patrol*, 66–71, 96, 192n136; Jones, *U.S. Battleship Operations*, 6, 16–18.

33. ADM 137/2656, HS1; ADM 137/2656, HN1; ADM 137/2656, HH7; ADM 137/2656, HH, HN, and HS précis of convoy reports.

34. Crowell and Wilson, *The Road to France*, 2:475; ADM 137/2656, HS31; ADM 137/2656, HN8. Macro-level data compiled from ADM 137/2656, HH, HN, and HS précis of convoy reports.

35. Thomas Hughes, "Learning to Fight: Bill Halsey and the Early American Destroyer Force," *Journal of Military History* 77, no. 1 (January 2013): 83–84; Walter S. Delany, *Bayly's Navy* (Washington, DC: Naval Historical Foundation, 1980), 12; Gibson and Prendergast, *The German Submarine War*, 175.

36. Hughes, "Learning to Fight," 73–76, 81–86; *Conway, 1906–21*, 123–31.

37. Gibson and Prendergast, *The German Submarine War*, 175–76; Halpern, *The Naval War in the Mediterranean*, 369; *Conway, 1906–21*, 94–95, 102.

38. Halpern, *The Naval War in the Mediterranean*, 344; http://uboat.net/wwi/ships_hit/6084.html.

39. http://uboat.net/wwi/ships_hit/losses_year.html?date=1917-05&string=May+1917; http://uboat.net/wwi/ships_hit/losses_year.html?date=1917-06&string=June+1917. On the sinking of the *Dover Castle*, see Gibson and Prendergast, *The German Submarine War*, 249–50, and Gary D. Solis, "Obedience of Orders and the Law of War: Judicial Application in American Forums," *American University International Law Review* 15, no. 2 (1999): 500.

40. Scheer, *Germany's High Sea Fleet*, 325.

41. This paragraph and the following paragraph are based on Paul G. Halpern, *The Battle of the Otranto Straits: Controlling the Gateway to the Adriatic in World War I* (Bloomington: Indiana University Press, 2004).

42. http://uboat.net/wwi/men/commanders/75.html.

43. http://uboat.net/wwi/ships_hit/largest.html; http://uboat.net/wwi/ships_hit/7100.html. On the sinking of the *Danton*, see Moraht, *Die Versenkung des "Danton,"* 116–23.

44. http://uboat.net/wwi/boats/index.html?boat=UC+26; http://uboat.net/wwi/boats/index.html?boat=UC+66. The latter cites wreckage found in 2009 to rebut the traditional explanation that *UC 66* was sunk by its own mines on 12 June after a depth-charge attack by the British navy trawler *Sea King*; researcher Innes McCartney concludes that the later sinking date "requires an excessively long patrol length" for *UC 66*'s final sortie.

45. Kemp, *U-Boats Destroyed*, 24–25.

46. "Information Obtained from Survivors of *U 93*," ADM 137/3872/2; see also Scheer, *Germany's High Sea Fleet*, 282.

6

Falling Short

"The *Admiralstab*'s six-month period, within which unrestricted submarine warfare would 'bring England to its knees,' was nearing an end," recalled Center Party leader Matthias Erzberger. "The widest circles of the German people believed in this political dogma unswervingly," and the High Command had also encouraged such optimism on the western front, where a leaflet was circulated in the trenches repeating the same assurance: "Our *Admiralstab* assumes full responsibility, that by the end of July or beginning of August England will ask us for peace."[1] The submariners embraced the challenge, along with the burden it placed upon them. Joachim Kramsta, watch officer aboard *U 66*, counted among those taking in stride the shorter time in port between patrols, because "if we can't bring down England before autumn, we have lost the war."[2] While Holtzendorff's specific tonnage calculations remained unknown to the public, the promise that unrestricted submarine warfare would achieve decisive results on or around 1 August 1917 had become an expectation.

But ominous signs of the strains wrought by three years of war tempered the general optimism. Every time the Reichstag reconvened to fulfill its constitutional duty of approving more war credits, more members of the traditionally pacifist SPD had broken ranks to vote no. After surviving the "turnip winter," workers newly empowered under the Patriotic Auxiliary Service Law of the previous December responded to an April 1917 reduction in rations with massive strikes that threatened war production, leaving Hindenburg and Ludendorff furious over the concessions Bethmann Hollweg had made to the unions. Additional strikes, in March at Germania in Kiel, AG Weser in Bremen, and the navy's torpedo factory in Friedrichsort, then in May at the Hamburg shipyards, had a direct effect on construction and arming of U-boats.[3] In the midst of the labor unrest, the growing antiwar Left of the SPD formed the Independent Social Democratic Party (USPD). On and after May Day, SPD and USPD speakers drew huge crowds, including sailors in Kiel and Wilhelmshaven. The German people faced yet another reduction in rations in the summer that left the average civilian with just 1,100 calories per day, less than half the prewar norm. In the High Sea Fleet, sailors endured not just reduced quantity but also poor quality of food, at a time when the typical officers' mess remained well stocked. On 6 June, the crew of the dreadnought *Prinzregent Luitpold* even resorted to a hunger strike to receive better food.[4]

Given the atmosphere of hope for an imminent peace mixed with despair over current conditions, Erzberger was "very disturbed" by the tone of a conversation he had on 10 June with Colonel Max Bauer, an officer widely

FIGURE 6.1.
Matthias Erzberger
(German Federal Archives)

regarded as "Ludendorff's right hand" at the High Command. Bauer, visiting the German capital from headquarters for the first time in several months, appeared "quite surprised to have found a downright irresponsible optimism in Berlin about the end of the war." Indeed, after reciting a list of reasons why the German people should not be optimistic about the war ending anytime soon, Bauer spoke of the need to prepare for "a new winter campaign" to start after the first of the year. Erzberger, deeply shaken, sought out a recent visitor to headquarters, a "leading industrialist," who corroborated what Bauer had said: "While Hindenburg and Ludendorff had assured him, just three weeks earlier, that England must ask for peace in August, they had told him a few days ago . . . that one must plan for a winter offensive."[5] Erzberger had always supported a strong navy and had been an important political ally of Tirpitz before the war. In November 1914 he helped arrange the fateful Wiegand interview, but he eventually concluded that, when it came to U-boats, no good could come from using them indiscriminately. He emerged as a leading voice against unrestricted submarine warfare early in 1916, when Tirpitz, before resigning his office as state secretary, last lobbied for its resumption. The Center Party leader believed, earlier than most Germans, that "if America enters the war, then the war is lost."[6] He counted among the skeptics in April 1917, when the record month of U-boat performance coincided with the declaration of war by the United States. Now, armed with what he considered confirmation that the resumption of unrestricted submarine warfare had done nothing but raise false hopes, he felt moved to action. The next opportunity to bring the matter to a head came in early July, when Bethmann Hollweg reconvened the Reichstag to fulfill, once again, its constitutional function of approving war credits.

THE PEACE RESOLUTION, THE NAVY, AND UNRESTRICTED SUBMARINE WARFARE

In December 1916, Erzberger had provided key assistance to Bethmann Hollweg in securing passage of the Patriotic Auxiliary Service Law by a coalition of the SPD, Center Party, and Progressive People's Party. Over the months that followed, the abdication of the tsar in Russia and the declaration of war by the United States drove many Reichstag members of these same three parties to view a negotiated end to the war as more realistic than the pursuit of a victorious peace under Hindenburg and Ludendorff. Starting on May Day, SPD members echoed the new USPD's criticism of German war aims, raising the possibility that most of the Reichstag's socialists might go into opposition

the next time Bethmann Hollweg called a vote on war credits, a scenario Erzberger felt would be devastating for national unity. As an alternative, he proposed that the SPD join his party and the Progressives in a public statement
for a negotiated peace. After selling the idea to the Center Party's Reichstag
delegation on 3 July, the following day he gave a speech critical of unrestricted
submarine warfare in which he "expressed the strongest doubts" that it would
work as promised. When Tirpitz's successor, Admiral Capelle, defended the
navy's position by citing Holtzendorff's tonnage projections, on 6 July Erzberger openly questioned the accuracy of his figures. While the exact totals for
June were still being tabulated (and, in any event, would be a closely guarded
secret), by 1 July U-boats already had sunk, in five months, 10 percent more
than the three million tons Holtzendorff had calculated would force Britain
to negotiate peace within six months, yet Britain's resolve appeared undi-
minished, casting doubt over the promise that the war would somehow end
before the home front had to face another hard winter.[7] On 7 July, Erzberger
and his political allies presented the Reichstag with the Peace Resolution, a
carefully worded document that began by reminding the world (and most
importantly, the German High Command) why Germany had said it was
going to war in the first place, quoting directly from William II's address on
the day hostilities began: "As on August 1, 1914, so also now on the verge of
a fourth year of war, the words of the speech from the throne still hold: 'We
are not impelled by the lust of conquest.'" The resolution asserted that "the
Reichstag strives for a peace of understanding and a lasting reconciliation of
peoples. Any violations of territory, and political, economic, and financial
persecutions are incompatible with such a peace." Goals included "freedom
of the seas" along with "the friendly association of peoples" and "the creation
of international organizations of justice." But the resolution also pledged defiance, "as long as the enemy governments . . . threaten Germany and her allies
with conquest and domination," and closed by expressing solidarity with the
troops, "the men who have fought with courage to protect the Fatherland."[8]

The introduction of the Peace Resolution touched off a crisis within the
German leadership. Hindenburg and Ludendorff blamed Bethmann Hollweg for mismanaging the politicians and hastened to Berlin from headquarters to limit the damage. On 12 July they threatened to resign unless the
chancellor was replaced. On their behalf, Colonel Bauer prevailed upon the
heir to the throne, Crown Prince William, to call an emergency meeting of
the heads of the major Reichstag parties to gauge their level of confidence
in Bethmann Hollweg. After receiving only lukewarm support from the SPD

and Progressive leaders and none at all from Erzberger and the others, the chancellor capitulated the following day, ending an eight-year run in office. The generals met with Erzberger and other politicians on the afternoon of the 13th, at which point they "voiced no objection to the resolution of the Reichstag" and focused instead on restoring calm. "Hindenburg and Ludendorff . . . assured [us] that the fronts would absolutely hold and that we could confidently face the future." When Erzberger questioned them about the specific premises of unrestricted submarine warfare, he "was surprised to learn that the whole calculation about the world tonnage was unknown to Ludendorff until that hour." The following day Erzberger "had another conversation with Ludendorff about the U-boat war" and again questioned him about Holtzendorff's tonnage calculations "without meeting with great understanding." He also observed that Ludendorff "now expressed more concerns about the resolution than the previous day."[9] Thus Erzberger was puzzled at how the High Command could have supported the unrestricted campaign, and indeed insisted upon it, without its leaders having a specific understanding of what it was supposed to accomplish; the opposite would have been easier to believe, that they had intimate knowledge of tonnage figures and were falsifying them. Both scenarios were disturbing. Either Ludendorff was lying, or the most fateful strategic decision of the war had been made in an astonishingly cavalier manner.

Erzberger never got an answer to his question of what had changed the High Command's position between the middle of May and the first week of June regarding the plausibility of the war ending on or around 1 August, but Ludendorff's responses seemed to rule out the notion that it had anything to do with tonnage figures or with unrestricted submarine warfare not working as expected. Bauer's biographer asserts that the colonel's pessimistic tone with Erzberger was deliberately calculated to undermine the Center Party leader's confidence in Bethmann Hollweg, whom the High Command had resolved to replace after the April strikes. To that extent, it worked, resulting in a "temporary tactical alliance" between the generals and Erzberger that forced the chancellor to resign. But Bauer's cynical ploy had a fateful unintended consequence, for by destroying what little faith Erzberger still had in Germany's ability to pursue the war to a successful conclusion, it led him to introduce the Peace Resolution. The change in behavior of the High Command as soon as Bethmann Hollweg resigned supports this thesis. Hindenburg and Ludendorff appeared calm and confident in their meeting with the politicians on 13 July, and afterward Bauer's correspondence with Erzberger was marked by an optimism that contrasted sharply with his pessimism in their crucial June meeting.[10]

There were, indeed, reasons for optimism, for by July 1917 Germany's problems paled in comparison with what the Allied powers had encountered in recent months. After surviving the ten-month bloodletting at Verdun in 1916, France suffered a serious breakdown in morale during and after the Nivelle offensive (16 April–9 May), including widespread mutinies. Russia likewise had endured one disaster after another from 1914 through 1916, only to experience the sudden collapse of the tsarist regime in March, followed by the return of Lenin in April and the subsequent emergence of the Bolsheviks as an antiwar alternative to the Provisional Government. With the French army a shambles and the Russians apparently on the verge of quitting the war, the High Command had good reason to assume that a knockout blow could be delivered against France in the winter months of the new year. But what about the centrality of defeating Britain, and U-boat warfare as the only means to accomplish it? By becoming ever more insistent about unrestricted submarine warfare post-Jutland, the admirals unwittingly had provided Hindenburg and Ludendorff with valuable cover should the army fail. The wording of the army's trench handbills in the spring of 1917 ("our *Admiralstab* assumes full responsibility, that by the end of July or beginning of August England will ask us for peace") and the language Ludendorff used to explain away the acceptance of the risk that American troops would tip the balance in the west ("the navy counted upon being able to [sink] a certain proportion of the transports") are but two indications that army leaders were setting up the navy to take the blame if Germany did not win the war. The admirals, self-conscious about the High Sea Fleet's failure to make a difference in the war, played right into their hands, and would continue to do so as the generals planned the army's final big push for early 1918.

Meanwhile, the assurances of Hindenburg and Ludendorff did nothing to deter Erzberger and his Reichstag allies from proceeding with the Peace Resolution, even after it became clear that the generals openly opposed it. In any event, the new chancellor, Georg Michaelis, a bureaucratic nonentity acceptable to the High Command, was powerless to stop it. The resolution passed on 19 July by a vote of 212–126, with 59 abstentions. In a true parliamentary monarchy (such as Britain), the government would have been compelled to respect the will of the majority or else resign, but under the quasi-parliamentary system of the Second Reich, a vote for peace in which barely 30 percent of the Reichstag supported the government carried all the weight of a nonbinding resolution. It had consequences all the same. William II's appointment of Michaelis created a vacuum at the Reich Chancellery that made Hindenburg and Ludendorff de facto dictators of Germany. Tirpitz, whose lingering hopes of becoming chancellor were dashed by the appointment of Michaelis, nevertheless welcomed the dictatorship of the generals and joined East Prussian politician Wolfgang Kapp in establishing the Fatherland Party. Less a conventional political party than a vehicle to rally the public behind the High Command, the Fatherland Party enabled Tirpitz, in retirement, to reinforce the official position that unrestricted submarine warfare was indispensable to the eventual German victory.[11] Not surprisingly, Erzberger soon lost the connections he once had at the High Command and also became a prime target of Fatherland Party attacks. As early as September, a speech he intended to give questioning the U-boat campaign was blocked by the censors, and he was denied a visa to travel to Austria-Hungary for a speaking engagement.[12] After the six-month anniversary of unrestricted submarine warfare passed without Britain suing for peace, the German people could take solace only in Hindenburg's vague assurance, conveyed by the war minister, General Hermann von Stein, during the debate over the Peace Resolution, that "we Germans will be victorious, so long as we hold out until the U-boat war can have its effect,"[13] a goal that had the added benefit, from the army's perspective, of keeping the public focused on the navy as the service responsible for winning the war.

In the meantime, the hunger strike aboard the *Prinzregent Luitpold* on 6 June proved to be a sign of things to come, as the summer food shortages led to the first widespread mutinies aboard the idle capital ships of the High Sea Fleet. Under the direction of Admiral Capelle, the Imperial Navy Office responded to the initial demonstration by authorizing the creation of "food committees" aboard all ships of the fleet, but few captains formed the committees until their crews forced them to. The situation deteriorated still more after the passage of the Peace Resolution. Unrest in the fleet became increasingly politicized, and during the months of July and August alone, an estimated five thousand sailors joined the antiwar USPD. The first half of August was particularly tense, with some sailors refusing all orders. The *Prinzregent Luitpold* was again at the center of the demonstrations, which spread to four other dreadnoughts and a light cruiser. The demands of the sailors included better food and more shore leave but also a "peace without annexations or indemnities," invoking not the Reichstag's Peace Resolution but the peace formula of the Petrograd Soviet, which had inspired the Socialist International to convene a peace conference at Stockholm attended by USPD leaders. Scheer reacted decisively in breaking the demonstrations, and courts-martial soon meted out a total of 360 years in prison terms to the mutineers. The proceedings ended on 5 September with the executions of two leaders of the mutiny, but Capelle did not share Scheer's optimism that "order was restored in the fleet."[14] Afterward, the fleet commander allowed the shipboard circulation of patriotic Fatherland Party propaganda while barring USPD newspapers and leaflets.[15] A similar effort occurred in the shipyards adjacent to naval installations, whose owners—longtime friends and supporters of Tirpitz—played a leading role in the Fatherland Party.[16] Scheer's insistence that USPD members be punished for inciting the mutiny ultimately led to a disastrous Reichstag speech by Capelle on 9 October, precipitating the resignation of Michaelis after barely three months in office in favor of veteran Bavarian politician Georg von Hertling, prewar leader of the Center Party in the Reichstag. Meanwhile, Scheer and the admirals concluded that action was the best antidote to the unrest in the fleet. On the day after the executions at Wilhelmshaven, Holtzendorff began planning with the army for an amphibious operation to secure the Gulf of Riga from the Russians. The successful campaign was completed in October, with the support of half of the High Sea Fleet, including the battle cruiser *Moltke* and ten dreadnoughts.[17]

Within all of the navies that succumbed to mutiny in 1917–18 (the German, Austrian, and Russian), the same trend could be seen: the smaller the warship, the better the morale and the later the vessel was likely to be involved in mutiny, if at all. Indeed, no German or Austrian U-boat crew ever rose up against its officers, even in the last days of the war. Scheer was not the only commanding officer to link activity with loyalty and idleness with mutiny; while the larger warships remained at anchor for months or even a year at a time, the light cruisers, destroyers, torpedo boats, and submarines of all navies saw action continuously, maintained higher morale, and experienced less trouble when times grew more difficult. Quality of shipboard command was as important as the question of activity versus idleness, and it also favored the smaller warships. Increasing numbers of the most highly regarded junior officers were given command of U-boats, and others went to the smaller surface vessels, leaving less capable men to take their places aboard the battleships and larger cruisers. In sharp contrast to the typical U-boat, where three or four junior officers lived at close quarters with a crew of two or three dozen men, sharing in all of their hardships, every larger warship was a microcosm of the society of the country it represented, and for the Central Powers—as for Russia—the differences were extreme.

During the last two years of the war, the inexperience or mediocrity of shipboard "middle management" exacerbated the problem of the social gulf between officers and common sailors, at a time when the relative inactivity of the big ships would have caused increased tensions in any event. Life in port also meant closer contact with the home front, making the sailors of Kiel and Wilhelmshaven, Pola and Cattaro, just as likely as those in Kronstadt and Sevastopol to see their own hardships in the broader context of conditions within their countries as a whole and to sympathize with politicians and parties that promised a better future.

Not surprisingly, U-boat commanders and crews returning from sorties at any time after July 1917 had great difficulty reconciling the clarity and simplicity of their own wartime experience with the increasingly complex social and political realities at naval bases and shipyards, and on the home front in general. Submariners commenting on the Peace Resolution or the USPD's influence among sailors and shipyard workers, either at the time or in their postwar memoirs, typically explained these developments in terms of disloyalty, treachery, or weakness. Hersing, of *U 21* fame, reflected the views of many of them in holding enemies on the home front responsible for snatching defeat from the jaws of victory, "whether it was the Reichstag with its Peace Resolution, or the strikes of munitions workers," which he alleged were "staged by foreigners."[18] But in addition to having less idle time and less contact with the politics of the home front, U-boat personnel also did not have to endure the short rations that were so corrosive to morale aboard larger warships that rarely left port.[19] They enjoyed the further benefit of being able to supplement their food supply with provisions from the ships they sank. During the leaner times that set in once the convoy system took effect, German submariners harked back fondly to the booty taken earlier in the war. For Rose's *U 53*, some of the happiest times were "when we took 5,000 cans of corned beef from the *Eptapyrgion*, and ten barrels of onions from the *Scalpa*, and Spanish apples from the *Algorta*."[20] Fürbringer recalled that after his *UB 39* captured three thousand eggs from the British steamer *Targus*, he had to allot each crew member "twelve to fourteen eggs daily" because in "the heat of the boat, they could not be stored."[21] In a similar vein, one of Arnauld's favorite stories was of *U 35*'s sinking of "an Italian steamer loaded with bananas," which were spread on the deck of the surfaced submarine "to ripen a bit in the hot Mediterranean sun," after which "we were fortunate . . . to gorge ourselves with bananas."[22] Thus, the shortage of food, the most basic underlying cause of the erosion of morale within the armed forces as well as on the home front, affected U-boat personnel less than most other Germans, leaving them in no position to understand the ultimate collapse of the Second Reich.

DIMINISHING RETURNS

Insulated though they were from the tensions in Berlin, by July 1917 many German submariners were just as uneasy as the politicians. Fürbringer remembered vividly the mood in the Flanders Flotilla as it became increasingly unlikely that "unrestricted submarine warfare . . . would achieve its objective within six months." Since the resumption of the campaign, "we sank ship after ship, a fantastic number, and yet it always seemed to us that we were failing to make an impression on the numbers of merchant vessels putting into enemy ports." Indeed, "in the high summer of 1917 . . . some of us began to suspect that we were not only faced with the task of destroying the merchant tonnage of the Entente nations, but that we were pitted in a gigantic battle against practically all the tonnage in the world." While "it was of course our duty to maintain the level of buoyant optimism which had been characteristic of unrestricted submarine warfare at the outset," Fürbringer recalled that "the first doubts had begun to emerge about the possibility of victory. . . . Only in the most intimate circles did these conversations take place, but they cast a long shadow."[23]

Over the last six months of 1917, such doubts only grew stronger. The German navy continued to deploy increasing numbers of U-boats and, among them, more of the new Type *U 93* boats, along with the first U-cruisers. The geographic scope of operations continued to reach northward above the Arctic Circle while also expanding farther out into the Atlantic, to the waters around the Azores, and down the western coast of Africa. Yet in every month from July through November, the number of ships sunk was less than the previous month, and with the exception of October, the tonnage sunk likewise fell every month. For both measures of success, an uptick in December provided the only hope that the decline could be reversed. While the tactics and technology of antisubmarine warfare improved in a variety of ways, the decline began in the first full month after the Allies introduced their comprehensive convoy system, the immediate impact of which can hardly be overstated. *Oberleutnant* Karl Dönitz, then a U-boat First Officer, decades later remembered the dramatic difference made by convoys. "The oceans at once became bare and empty; for long periods of time the U-boats, operating individually, would see nothing at all, and then suddenly up would loom a huge concourse of ships . . . surrounded by a strong escort of warships of all types.

The solitary U-boat, which most probably had sighted the convoy purely by chance, would then attack" and "might well sink one or two of the ships" before "the convoy would steam on . . . bringing a rich cargo of foodstuffs and raw materials safely to port."[24]

The clear difficulties U-boats encountered in intercepting convoys, especially those including troopships, soon became a source of great optimism on the Allied side and despair among the Germans. For the U-boats, finding a target amid the vastness of the ocean was not unlike locating a needle in a haystack; the convoy system, in effect, left them searching for far fewer, larger needles in the same haystack. Germany's geographic disadvantage vis-à-vis Britain in the use of directional wireless meant that the British could use theirs to help track U-boats that sortied around the British Isles into the Atlantic, while the Germans could not use theirs to track inbound convoys, because their stations were blocked by the British Isles from receiving signals from ships farther west. U-boat commanders were also frustrated that the routing and frequency of Allied convoys seemed to follow no discernible pattern. The Admiralty's designated convoy lanes were some sixty miles (100 km) wide; cargo convoys and troopship convoys steamed in parallel lanes but on different schedules, with the lanes changed every six or seven days. A special "diversion code" could also be used to further change the lanes on any day as needed.[25] Thus Dönitz did not exaggerate when he asserted that most convoys were found "purely by chance." Under normal circumstances, a U-boat commander stumbling onto a cargo lane might encounter a convoy consisting of ships slow enough for him to track down and target, but as soon as his presence became known, the Admiralty would issue a diversion code, after which the traffic would abruptly stop. Meanwhile, a commander encountering a troopship lane might see only one convoy in a week, consisting of ships too fast for him to catch unless he met them head-on, and then not see another convoy before the lanes were changed. U-boats cruising where they could reasonably expect inbound troopships ran a greater risk of going home with no successes to their credit, while those finding a cargo lane could claim more tonnage but only by sinking a greater number of smaller ships, and none carrying troops.[26]

Perhaps the most telling indicator of the success of convoys was the precipitous drop in the sinking of larger merchantmen, which were now much more difficult and dangerous for U-boats to approach. During the last half of 1917, they sank over 1,200 unarmed ships, of which just three displaced ten thousand tons or more. On 21 August, Rose's *U 53* sank the 10,435-ton

British steamer *Devonian* (2 dead) in an attack on an outbound convoy off the northern coast of Ireland.[27] Then, on 7 September, *U 48* (*Kapitänleutnant* Karl Edeling) sank the 13,714-ton British steamer *Minnehaha* (43 dead) off the southern coast of Ireland, likewise while in convoy.[28] The largest vessel sunk in the Mediterranean, the 11,477-ton Italian cargo ship *Milazzo*, by Georg von Trapp's *U 14* on 29 August, 250 miles (400 km) east of Malta, was also the largest merchantman sunk by an Austrian submarine in the entire war.[29]

Over the same months, U-boats had similar poor luck in targeting larger Allied warships. Dreadnoughts, battle cruisers, and even pre-dreadnought battleships rarely ventured into waters where they might be at risk, leaving obsolete older cruisers and armed merchantmen as the largest armed targets. On 23 July in the Hebrides, *UC 49* (*Kapitänleutnant* Karl Petri) sank the 12,077-ton armed merchant cruiser *Otway* (10 dead).[30] Three days later, off Beachy Head, Steinbrinck's *UC 65* mined the 11,000-ton protected cruiser *Ariadne* (38 dead).[31] On 2 October, off the northern coast of Ireland, *U 79* (*Kapitänleutnant* Otto Rohrbeck) attacked the ships of HH24 just as they dispersed, torpedoing the convoy's ocean escort, the 14,300-ton armored cruiser *Drake* (18 dead), then mining the freighter *Lugano* and one of the Buncrana destroyers.[32] On 19 October, 250 miles (400 km) west of Brest, Hashagen's *U 62* sank the 12,977-ton armed merchant cruiser *Orama* (5 dead), ocean escort of HD7, a convoy inbound from Dakar. Hashagen used his last torpedo in the attack, accomplished only after evading four American destroyers; he later recalled his relief that he and his men could "show our faces at home" after boosting their tonnage with such a large victim.[33]

Sinking multiple smaller ships from the same convoy proved to be even more difficult than targeting a single larger vessel, as no single Allied convoy of the First World War lost more than three ships to U-boat action, and only rarely to the same U-boat. On his last patrol before sinking the *Orama*, Hashagen was responsible for one such action, on 30 August, when *U 62* torpedoed and sank three British freighters (the *Eastern Prince*, *Grelhame*, and *Noya*), totaling nearly 11,000 tons, off the Channel coast of Cornwall. All were inbound from Hampton Roads in convoy HH16 but had been separated from their escorting destroyers by a storm the previous day.[34] When a convoy experienced as many as three losses, it was more typical for more than one U-boat to be involved. In one example, on 10–11 October, Rose's *U 53* initiated the action against HH25, another convoy inbound from Hampton Roads, at the western approach to the Channel by torpedoing the 5,736-ton escort merchant ship *Bostonian* (4 dead), which had served as the convoy's ocean escort. The next day, *UC 50* (*Kapitänleutnant* Rudolf Seuffer) followed the 3,700-ton tanker *Mira* up the Channel after the Devonport destroyers had left it, then mined it off Beachy Head, while hundreds of miles to the west, off the southeast coast of Ireland, *U 61* (*Kapitänleutnant* Victor Dieckmann) torpedoed and sank the 4,313-ton freighter *Rhodesia*, a straggler that had lost touch with HH25 during the crossing.[35]

Over the last half of 1917, the US Navy sought to reduce such breakdowns in protection at the western approach to the Channel by gradually increasing its presence at Brest. In addition to providing greater security for the ever-greater number of ships steaming directly for French ports, the growing force relieved the Queenstown destroyers of the burden of escorting them all the way from the ocean rendezvous point into Brest or St. Nazaire. In October, after Rear Admiral Henry B. Wilson was assigned to Brest as commander of American naval forces in France, Sims sent him five destroyers from Queenstown. More soon followed, transferred from Bayly's command or sent directly from the United States, providing a dramatic upgrade to the eight armed yachts that had been at Brest since July. By the end of the year, a revised routine for inbound "East Coast" convoys employed the Queenstown destroyers only until the convoys split at the western approach to the Channel; at that point the Brest escorts (the American destroyers and yachts, at times supplemented by French destroyers and patrol boats) assumed responsibility for the ships bound for the French Atlantic ports, while the Devonport destroyers continued to take the rest into the Channel. By war's end, the American force at Brest grew to include thirty-five destroyers, eighteen armed yachts, and five torpedo boats, supported by minesweepers, tugs, tenders, a repair ship, and a salvage vessel.[36] The rise in importance of the base at Brest brought a reduction at Queenstown, where Bayly's American destroyer force peaked at thirty-nine ships in April 1918 before shrinking to twenty-four at the Armistice. Nevertheless, of the eighty-five American destroyers sent to European waters in 1917–18, forty-seven served under Bayly at one time or another. The American contribution at Queenstown also included seven submarines, thirty small patrol-torpedo boats known as "submarine chasers," a minelayer, and the lone US Navy Q-ship *Santee*.[37] The latter reflected an American fascination with "mystery ships" as antisubmarine weapons, but it registered no successes after its deployment in November 1917 and barely made it back to Queenstown after being torpedoed on 27 December by Dieckmann's *U 61*.[38] Earlier the same month, the American navy lost its first warship in the U-boat war when Rose's *U 53* sank the USS *Jacob Jones*

(64 dead). The destroyer was torpedoed on 6 December off the Scilly Islands while returning to Queenstown after escorting an inbound convoy.[39]

After sinking the *Jacob Jones*, Rose radioed Queenstown before departing the scene, to give the location of the lifeboats.[40] Such gestures became increasingly rare in the war's last year, as German submariners, in turn, experienced less humane treatment at the hands of the Allies. Indeed, those fortunate enough to survive the sinking of a U-boat at any time after the resumption of unrestricted submarine warfare ran a greater risk of being shot in the water rather than rescued; such incidents were reported by survivors of *UC 55* (September 1917) and *UB 110* (July 1918). Other survivors experienced the indignity of being stripped for souvenirs by their captors, with uniform buttons and any other items bearing Imperial German insignia especially prized by British seamen. One survivor from *U 81* (May 1917) reported "corners, buttons, and pockets cut off greatcoat," with "one button cut off already when half dead on deck," moments after he was pulled out of the water.[41]

The overall decline in tonnage sunk continued even after the German cryptanalysts at Neumünster, in the autumn of 1917, succeeded in breaking the British convoy code. The inability of U-boats to capitalize on this intelligence breakthrough prompted Scheer to detach cruisers from the fleet to function as commerce raiders for the first time since 1914–15. A mid-October sortie by the light cruisers *Brummer* and *Bremse* targeted the Allied convoy route between Norway and Scotland, culminating on the 17th in an attack on a convoy of a dozen merchantmen, escorted by two destroyers and two armed trawlers. They sank nine of the merchantmen and both destroyers before returning to Wilhelmshaven. Scheer repeated the operation in mid-December with two half-flotillas of torpedo boats, which on 12 December sank four merchantmen, six navy trawlers, and a destroyer in a sweep of the same convoy route. The success of these raids prompted the British to employ more formidable escorts, ultimately capital ships, to protect the Norway–Scotland route. That they did so without undue fear of the U-boat threat attested to their growing level of confidence in their antisubmarine countermeasures.[42]

Amid the growing disappointment over the diminishing returns of unrestricted submarine warfare, the commanders and crews of the Type *U 93* boats experienced just as much frustration as their peers in older, smaller submarines. The number of boats in the class registering successes increased from three during July to seven during December, but the latter, in that month, collectively managed a total of just fourteen sinkings (37,447 tons). The most successful of the class, *U 105*, had the best of the year's novice commanders,

Kapitänleutnant Friedrich Strackerjan. His boat sank 31,873 tons in the last three months of 1917, including 19,680 tons in December alone, more than that month's combined total of its six most successful sister boats.[43] Many commanders making their debut amid the more difficult conditions prevailing after mid-1917 experienced little or no success even when entrusted with newer, more capable submarines. *U 106* (*Kapitänleutnant* Hans Hufnagel) served as a tragic counterpoint to *U 105*, sinking one British destroyer and no merchantmen on its only patrol, which ended on 7 October when it struck a mine off Terschelling on its way home, sinking with all hands.[44]

The deployment of the much larger U-cruisers ultimately proved to be no more decisive than the Type *U 93* boats, despite the considerable hopes attached to them. Four sortied before the end of 1917. Veteran Mediterranean commanders Gansser, formerly of *U 33*, and Valentiner, formerly of *U 38*, received *U 156* and *U 157*, respectively, but the navy made less obvious assignments for the remaining pair, giving *U 155* to *Kapitänleutnant* Karl Meusel, who had never commanded a submarine before, and *U 151* to Waldemar Kophamel, who preceded Arnauld in *U 35* but then spent nearly two years ashore in Pola and Cattaro as Mediterranean flotilla commander; now a *Korvettenkapitän*, he was the highest-ranking officer to command a German submarine during the war. *U 155* sortied in May, followed by *U 151* in August, then *U 156* and *U 157* in November. Kophamel's boat did not return to Kiel until December, setting a submarine record of 114 consecutive days at sea that was soon broken by Valentiner, whose *U 157* stayed out for 139 days. All four made their way to open waters via the same route, calculated to avoid the danger from Allied mines in the North Sea: from their base at Kiel via the Kattegat and Skagerrak, up the coast of Norway, then westward well north of Scotland, nearly to Iceland, before turning south.[45] They spent much of their time hunting in the waters around Madeira and the Azores, beyond the practical range of most other U-boats, and all but *U 155* also cruised along the western coast of Africa. When it came to the comfort of the crews, the combination of calmer seas but greater heat made tropical operations a mixed blessing. The engine room temperature of 53° C (127° F) once recorded aboard *U 155* was, unfortunately, not uncommon in the lower latitudes.[46]

Despite the inexperience of its commander, *U 155* had the most successful maiden voyage of the lot, sinking nineteen ships (52,387 tons) in just over nine weeks, along a path of destruction from the waters just south of Iceland to the sea-lanes between the Azores and Gibraltar. Kophamel's *U 151*, staying out much longer but also after convoys had been fully implemented, sank fourteen ships (37,760 tons), including the 4,437-ton British steamer *Gryfevale* on 21 October off Cape Blanco on the coast of Mauritania at 21° N latitude, the farthest south that a U-boat had claimed a victim thus far. Thereafter, the relative lack of success of Germany's largest submarines followed the overall pattern of diminishing returns. Gansser's *U 156* managed to destroy just nine ships (21,860 tons) on a voyage that extended to the coast of Western Sahara, and Valentiner's *U 157* did even worse, sinking just seven ships (10,333 tons) on its record-length cruise.[47] While the range of their 5.9-inch (15 cm) deck guns enabled the U-cruisers to stop or cripple potential victims at great distances, their lack of speed and poor handling qualities made them less than ideal as commerce raiders. Compared to the Type *U 93* boats, their dimensions were shorter, deeper, and wider, and they were nearly twice as heavy. *Oberleutnant* Martin Niemöller, Kophamel's second-in-command aboard *U 151*, blamed the boat's twenty-nine-foot (8.9 m) beam for its tendency to rock fore and aft in heavy seas, conditions under which "seasickness claim[ed] many victims" even among veterans. Valentiner had little good to say about *U 157* aside from its firepower. Its "laughably weak" engines caused it to move "more slowly than an ordinary steamer" on the surface; when submerged, it "was plump, not agile, and . . . even slower than above water."[48]

Perhaps more limiting than their technical and technological shortcomings, the U-cruisers suffered from being treated as assets their commanders should not expose to great risk. Successful U-boat commanders such as Valentiner, Gansser, and, earlier in the war, Kophamel were masters of the situational risk-reward calculation inherent in every encounter between a submarine and a potential target, but their talents were largely wasted on vessels the navy came to view as the undersea equivalent to the emperor's precious dreadnoughts. The U-cruisers, not surprisingly, also attracted greater attention from the enemy, making their commanders even more cautious. When *U 156* and *U 157* were scheduled to meet in the Canary Islands to take on a cargo of wolfram ore from a Spanish merchantman, Gansser twice canceled their rendezvous out of concern for their mutual safety, then had his fears validated when British submarine *E 48* (Lieutenant Frederick H. Taylor) showed up at their ultimate meeting point to fire several torpedoes at them, one of which hit *U 156*—fortunately for the Germans, a dud. The lack of success of *U 157* came despite Valentiner's ingenuity in seizing the 1,788-ton Norwegian freighter *Norefos* off the western coast of Africa, arming it with a single light cannon and using it as an auxiliary until it ran out of coal. It was the first time that a U-cruiser deployed its twenty-man prize crew, which, under the command of a reserve officer, joined the hostage Norwegians in operating the *Norefos* as a reconnaissance vessel for *U 157* and also, at times, a tow boat, enabling Valentiner to save diesel fuel and extend his time at sea. He ended up cruising all the way to the Gulf of Guinea, within sixty miles (96 km) of the Equator, at which point *U 157* was still within wireless range of the powerful transmitter at Nauen, outside of Berlin. The smallest ship Valentiner sank, the 129-ton Portuguese sailing vessel *Estrella Da Bissao*, off Freetown, Sierra Leone, on 17 February 1918, just above 8° N latitude, also had the distinction of being his southernmost victim.[49]

In addition to its disappointingly slight impact on enemy shipping, the record voyage of *U 157* also demonstrated the unforeseen negative consequences for the fitness of those assigned to such long cruises. After his return to Kiel, Valentiner was alarmed to find that he was "not in a condition to go longer distances by foot" and felt "like a very old man, who again and again had to stop for a while or sit on a bench to rest."[50] Germany's third-most-successful U-boat ace of the war, with nearly 300,000 tons to his credit, never commanded another submarine. In the Second World War and beyond, the world's navies would pay greater attention to maintaining the physical fitness of submarine personnel on extended deployments. In the short term, for the remainder of the First World War, the unanticipated side effects of the long U-cruiser voyages meant that the navy had to change their commanders and most of their crews from one sortie to the next, at a great cost to operational effectiveness. No doubt owing to the unique challenges of commanding a U-cruiser at sea, there is no record of an officer ever lamenting his reassignment away from one.

During the same months that the U-cruisers extended the campaign into the tropics, the navy continued to deploy smaller, older U-boats to the Arctic. Schmidt's *U 28* and Hillebrand's *U 46*, both veterans of previous Arctic cruises, hunted along the route into Archangel again during the summer and autumn of 1917; not surprisingly, in waters where the Allies had not bothered to form convoys, they were more successful than most U-boats operating elsewhere. In August and September, Schmidt sank five ships totaling 19,656 tons, while in October and November, Hillebrand sank another five totaling 14,943. *U 28* did not survive its last sinking, the 4,649-ton British steamer *Olive Branch*, torpedoed on 2 September, eighty-five miles (137 km) north of North Cape. After the steamer's crew abandoned ship with *U 28* still lurking nearby, the *Olive Branch* erupted in an ammunition explosion which damaged the U-boat badly enough that Schmidt surfaced to enable his men to save themselves. The survivors of the *Olive Branch* refused to take the survivors of *U 28* into their lifeboats, with the result that Schmidt and his entire crew perished while all but one member of the steamer's crew survived. *U 46* likewise recorded a fateful final Arctic sinking, but for no reason other than its timing: 7 November, the day the Bolsheviks seized power in Petrograd. Hillebrand's boat was the last deployed to interdict Allied shipments into Archangel, which stopped after 15 December when Lenin's government concluded an armistice with the Central Powers.[51]

ANTISUBMARINE WARFARE AND ESCALATING U-BOAT LOSSES

Germany commissioned another eighty-seven U-boats during 1917, as many as any one country had built in all the years before 1914 combined, but this barely sufficed to maintain the force at the size it had been on 1 February, when unrestricted submarine warfare resumed. Sixty-three U-boats were lost in action during the year, almost three times as many as in 1916, and all but two of them after 1 February. A variety of factors subtracted an additional fifteen boats from the active force: two were transferred to Austria-Hungary, eight were converted to training purposes, two were given up for internment in neutral countries, and three were lost in accidents. The net result was that Germany ended the year with 142 U-boats, including forty-nine coastal *UB* boats and thirty-two *UC* minelayers, just nine more than it had in December 1916.[52]

Of the sixty-three U-boats lost on active duty during 1917, forty-three were sunk from July onward, evidence of the success of the more effective antisubmarine warfare methods developed concurrently with the introduction of convoys. The Admiralty's new Intelligence Division 25 (ID 25) was responsible for tracking U-boats, using data from directional wireless stations built earlier in the war plus new ones constructed in Ireland. Combining the resources of Room 40 and the Enemy Submarine Section, ID 25 issued an increasing number of warnings about U-boat activity to Allied ships at sea, from 39 per month early in 1917 to 172 per month during the last year of the war. German submarines continued to maintain a greater presence on the airwaves than surface vessels, following standing orders that required them to check in via wireless whenever they sank an enemy merchantman or encountered an enemy warship, even though these signals, when picked up by British directional wireless stations, increased the likelihood that convoys would avoid them and destroyers would sink them. Foreshadowing the "wolf pack" tactics of the Second World War, during

1917 U-boats tried to counter the convoys by coordinating their operations, but these efforts only added to their wireless traffic and made them that much easier to avoid, or attack, as in the case of *U 156* and *U 157*, ambushed during their rendezvous in the Canary Islands.[53]

Even when off the airwaves, U-boats could not avoid detection by the underwater hydrophones deployed in increasing numbers by the British during 1917. Inspired by the *Titanic* disaster, Canadian inventor Reginald Fessenden developed the hydrophone (an acoustical echo ranging device) after 1912, originally to alert ships to icebergs and other unseen collision dangers. Following the first success of a hydrophone in locating a U-boat underwater, in April 1916 on the Dover barrage, the technology was deployed to aid in submarine detection around the British Isles, in seabed coastal sets hardwired to stations ashore as well as in portable units aboard surface vessels. Hydrophones were particularly valuable in foiling the work of minelaying submarines, because they could actually hear *UC* boats laying their mines, which were then that much easier to locate and sweep. Indeed, one *UC* boat commander commented on "the astounding promptness of the countermeasures" after he had laid a minefield, only to see it swept just two hours later. Hydrophones thus contributed to the German conclusion that minelaying around the British Isles was wasted effort and to the decision to scale back production of *UC* boats. After commissioning sixty-six of them in 1915–16, the German navy added just thirteen after resuming unrestricted submarine warfare in 1917, and it never deployed sixteen *UC III* boats completed during 1918. In the meantime, the British navy expanded its use of hydrophones to the Mediterranean in June 1917, and by the autumn, stations had been established at Malta, Otranto, and off Gallipoli.[54]

Shipboard hydrophones were particularly dangerous to U-boats once the vessels equipped with them were also armed with depth charges, drums of explosives detonated by the water pressure at a preselected depth. The most common depth charge of the war, known as Type D, was introduced in January 1916. Its three hundred pounds (140 kg) of TNT made it a formidable weapon, but as late as June 1917 it remained in such short supply that vessels on antisubmarine patrol—destroyers, sloops, and Q-ships—were sent to sea with just four of them. Thereafter, depth charges became a priority item in Allied war production, with so many being produced that by the following summer warships on convoy duty typically carried between thirty and fifty of them, enabling the British navy alone to drop a total of 16,451 by the end of the war. The first undisputed success of a depth-charge attack came on 13 December 1916, when the British destroyer *Landrail* sank *UB 29* (*Oberleutnant* Erich Platsch) off the southern coast of Ireland, with the loss of all hands. Eleven months later, on 17 November 1917, the destroyer USS *Fanning* became the first American warship to register a success against a U-boat when it used depth charges to sink *U 58* (*Kapitänleutnant* Gustav Amberger), also off the southern coast of Ireland. Even when a depth charge did not detonate close enough to a submarine to cause its immediate destruction, the underwater shock waves it produced popped rivets and induced leaks; if the latter appeared to be catastrophic, the commander always attempted to surface to enable the crew to save themselves before scuttling the boat. Such was the case in the sinking of *U 58*, which Amberger and most of his crew survived to be taken prisoner. Some damaged U-boats with catastrophic leaks were finished off by shell fire upon surfacing; thus, depth charges likely played some role in a number of U-boat losses attributed to other causes.[55]

While the British applied higher technology to make U-boats acoustically detectable, during the same months of 1916–17 most navies began to employ aircraft in antisubmarine warfare once it became clear that a submerged submarine invisible from the perspective of the surface could be seen from the air, especially when silhouetted against a sandy seabed. On 15 September 1916, the Austrian navy became the first to destroy a submarine in an air attack when a seaplane based at Cattaro bombed and sank the French *Foucault*. The British registered their first aerial antisubmarine success in May 1917 in the sinking of Pustkuchen's *UC 66* by a Curtis flying boat, then claimed a second on 22 September when another Curtis flying boat, operating from the Royal Naval Air Service's base at Dunkirk, bombed and sank *UB 32* (*Oberleutnant* Benno von Ditfurth) off the Dutch coast. While Britain ultimately deployed more aircraft in antisubmarine warfare than anyone else, these were the only submarines sunk by British planes unassisted by warships. Yet long before the end of the war, fear of attack by aircraft served as a deterrent to U-boat operations whenever they were known to be in the area, foreshadowing the Second World War, when aircraft surpassed destroyers and other smaller warships to become the submarine's most effective enemy.[56]

Though their successes, too, numbered in the single digits, Q-ships continued to sink more U-boats than aircraft, but with the negative side effect of encouraging many German submariners to be more ruthless when approaching any merchantman that appeared suspicious. Over half of the confirmed losses of U-boats to Q-ships occurred before the resumption of unrestricted submarine warfare, and the last for which the evidence has held up over time occurred on 7 June 1917, when Gordon Campbell, after exchanging the *Farnborough* for the *Pargust*, sank *UC 29* (*Oberleutnant* Ernst Rosenow) off the southern coast of Ireland. Various accounts attributing one or more of three subsequent U-boat losses to Q-ships have since been debunked. The Q-ship *Acton* supposedly sank *UC 72* (*Oberleutnant* Ernst Voigt) on 20 August in the Bay of Biscay, but in 2013 the wreck of *UC 72* was found in the Straits of Dover. The Q-ship *Stonecrop* was long credited with sinking *U 88*, commanded by *Kapitänleutnant* Schwieger, formerly of *U 20*, on 5 September, but *U 88* is now generally considered to have struck a mine off Terschelling (though, from the British perspective, a humble Q-ship killing the man responsible for sinking the *Lusitania* made a much better story). Finally, the veteran Q-ship *Privet* at one time was credited with sinking *Kapitänleutnant* Klasing's *U 34* just before the Armistice, apparently for no better reason than that it was stationed at Gibraltar when the war ended, and *U 34* disappeared after leaving Pola on 18 October 1918. In any case, the lack of effectiveness of Q-ships after the spring of 1917 reflected the new reality that the widespread Allied use of convoys made U-boat commanders all the more wary of approaching a lone "mystery ship."[57]

After the resumption of unrestricted submarine warfare, the Allies continued to invest in antisubmarine barrages despite meager results. The Austrian victory in the Battle of the Otranto Straits, by a badly outnumbered force, caused further recriminations in the already tense relationship between the British, French, and Italians, especially after the latter requested that the Allies contribute more resources to blockade the mouth of the Adriatic. The British responded, though not as the Italians wished. In a series of changes starting in August 1917, they upgraded their Eastern Mediterranean Squadron into a restored Mediterranean Fleet under Admiral Sir Somerset Gough-Calthorpe, but downgraded their Adriatic Squadron to the status of "Adriatic Force," with Commodore Sir Howard Kelly replacing Rear Admiral Kerr as its head. The British sent just one additional light cruiser to help protect the barrage, which remained porous long after Horthy's successful attack. In August, when Valentiner last took *U 38* through the Straits of Otranto before returning home to take command of *U 157*, he "did not find the slightest countermeasure" in place and "did not once see a drifter" during his passage.[58] But in a move that proved crucial in the long run, the British followed the deployment of hydrophones to Otranto by also opening a seaplane station there, reinforcing Allied air superiority over the straits for the remainder of the war. Britain and France refocused their aid to Italy after the German-supported

Austrian breakthrough at Caporetto (24 October–19 November) reduced by half the size of the Italian army, as the need to stabilize the Italian front clearly took precedence over sealing the mouth of the Adriatic. Meanwhile, coinciding with the more robust British presence in the Eastern Mediterranean, the Japanese contribution at Malta, which grew to include one cruiser and fourteen destroyers, helped protect convoys in the Western Mediterranean, as did American vessels sent to Gibraltar, where the Allies contemplated building yet another antisubmarine barrage.[59]

On the Dover barrage, the resumption of unrestricted submarine warfare provided Rear Admiral Bacon with the justification to carry out his plan for a multilayered underwater "vertical wall of mines," completed late in 1917.[60] The more formidable fixed barrage did not bring an end to the use of drifters, even though they continued to register few successes. Bacon credited them with catching Edeling's *U 48* on 24 November, forcing the boat to scuttle with the loss of the commander and half the crew, but the German account claimed the scuttling occurred after *U 48* ran aground on a sandbar and then lost a brief gun battle with a drifter.[61] Overall, the combination of fixed and dragged antisubmarine nets and mines claimed just six more confirmed successes during the remainder of the war, but several other U-boats were lost to minefields sown off the Dutch and Flemish coasts, or disappeared without a trace after leaving Ostend and Zeebrugge. German destroyers operating out of those bases had long posed a menace to vessels of the Auxiliary Patrol operating in the Straits of Dover, at much closer range than Cattaro to the Otranto Straits. During 1917, Bacon used coastal monitors to bombard both ports, with the heaviest shellings coming against Zeebrugge on the night of 11–12 May and Ostend on 4–5 June, but the canals linking both ports to Bruges remained open to the U-boats of the Flanders Flotilla and the destroyers protecting them.[62] German troops subsequently held western Flanders in the Third Battle of Ypres, better known as Passchendaele (31 July–10 November). In their bloodiest battle of the war other than the Somme, British and Imperial troops sustained nearly a quarter of a million casualties to move the front just five miles (8 km), after which it remained roughly sixty-five miles (105 km) to the west of the flotilla's bases.

In addition to adding mines to barrages, the British continued their heavy mining of the North Sea, repeatedly laying fresh fields just beyond the vast defensive arc of minefields the Germans themselves had sown from the Danish coast to the Dutch coast, centered on the island of Helgoland. During 1917, roughly twenty U-boats were sunk by these mines,[63] forcing Scheer to place a high priority on minesweeping in order to ensure that more of them made it safely out to open waters. His "convoy service for U-boats" included minesweepers to lead the way, escorted by destroyers, torpedo boats, or small armed auxiliary steamers to protect the minesweepers, followed by ballasted merchantmen known as *Sperrschiffe* (literally "barrier ships") to detonate any unswept mines. These elaborate processions, with U-boats in single file at the rear, snaked through corridors designated by color codes (for example, the "blue route" up the Jutland coast toward Horns Reef, and the "yellow route" along the West Frisians toward Terschelling). At times when British minelaying was so extensive and relentless that the Germans could not keep any of their North Sea routes clear, U-boats used the Kiel Canal across Schleswig-Holstein for a detour to the Baltic, then followed the same route to sea as the U-cruisers based at Kiel, via the Kattegat and Skagerrak, to avoid most of the mine danger.[64] After Beatty assumed command of the Grand Fleet, the British at times deployed light cruisers to attack German minesweepers, compelling Scheer to send out more powerful ships, even dreadnoughts, to protect them. On one occasion Beatty responded, in kind, with capital ships of his own, sending Vice Admiral T. W. D. Napier with the new battle cruisers *Courageous*, *Glorious*, and *Repulse* to support eight light cruisers and several destroyers disrupting a German attempt to clear a British minefield. The only sortie by British capital ships south of the 55°30' N "risk nothing" line established by Jellicoe and Beatty in September 1916 resulted in the Second Battle of Helgoland Bight (17 November 1917), an inconclusive action in which Napier's battle cruisers exchanged shots with the dreadnoughts *Kaiser* and *Kaiserin* before withdrawing.[65]

The sixty-three U-boats lost in action during 1917 took with them fifty-two submarine commanders, of whom Walther Schwieger, with 185,212 tons sunk, had been the most successful; indeed, the six commanders eventually passing his mark all survived the war. Other notable losses included Reinhold Saltzwedel, whose *UB 81* sank after it struck a mine in the Channel, off the Isle of Wight, on 2 December. *UB 81* was the sixth submarine Saltzwedel commanded during the war, all of them *UB* or *UC* boats in the Flanders Flotilla. In a career that spanned just twenty-one months, he sank a total of 172,824 tons, enough to place him tenth on the list of most successful U-boat commanders, the highest other than Schwieger not to survive the war. Ernst Wilhelms, whose 102,875 tons were all sunk with *U 69*, was lost during July 1917 when his submarine disappeared without a trace while cruising off the coast of Ireland. Another notable death did not involve the loss of a submarine: Rudolf Schneider, whose 142,727 tons included the controversial *Arabic* sinking of 1915, drowned on 13 October while in command of *U 87* after being washed overboard from the conning tower in a storm in the upper North Sea. *U 87* also did not survive the year, falling victim to a British destroyer in the Irish Sea on Christmas Day. The deaths of these officers, along with Herbert Pust-kuchen and Matthias von Schmettow in the spring of 1917, brought to six the number of U-boat commanders with over one hundred thousand tons sunk to perish during the year.[66]

Experienced officers were difficult to replace, as were the crews that perished with them. After just twenty-nine U-boats were sunk with no survivors in the first three years of the war, forty-one were lost with all hands during 1917 alone.[67] To make matters worse, for the survivors of near misses, the advent of depth-charge attacks introduced to undersea warfare a malady akin to the shell shock of the trenches. Weddigen's former first officer Johannes Spiess, who succeeded him in *U 9* and went on to command five different U-boats by 1918, once observed that "after a bad . . . depth-charge attack the daily practice dives were clumsily carried out, simply because the nerve of the crew had been badly shaken."[68] After the war, Arnauld recounted the story of his "petty officer of navigation" aboard *U 35*, "an old submarine man" with "what seemed to be nerves of steel," breaking down completely after a particularly harrowing patrol. "He was through. He refused to go on cruise again, and got himself transferred to shore duty."[69] In his memoirs, Valentiner cited the tragic example of his chief engineer aboard *U 38*, the "otherwise capable" *Herr* Kögler, who by early 1917 "was used up . . . finished, and completely apathetic (*teilnahmslos*) owing to his nerves." Like so many shell-shock victims in the army, Kögler subsequently was branded a "*Drückeberger* (shirker)," a status that changed only after Valen-tiner's intervention with his doctor. Kögler was sent to a sanatorium where he died "in complete mental derangement" just weeks after leaving *U 38*.[70] Such cases, combined with the greater number of boats being lost, made submarine duty less attractive for recruits, forcing the navy to abandon the volunteer character of the undersea service. As the unrestricted campaign continued, sailors were assigned to a U-boat as if it were any other naval vessel, with predictable consequences for efficiency as well as for morale.[71]

After reaching 696,725 tons for the month of June, the toll taken by unre-stricted submarine warfare fell to 555,510 tons in July, 472,370 tons in August, and 353,600 tons in September before rebounding to 466,540 tons in October. Germany did not force Britain to the breaking point by Holtzendorff's target date of 1 August, before another harvest could be brought to bear, or by 1 No-vember, the "limit of endurance" initially projected by Jellicoe to Sims. While the unrestricted campaign far surpassed its goal of destroying three million tons in six months and went on to claim just over five million tons in nine months, it fell short of sinking the six million tons actually needed to force a reduction in the Allied war effort. During November 1917 the tonnage sunk by U-boats fell to just 302,600, the lowest monthly total since September 1916, and it became clear that the campaign, on its own, would not force an end to the war on Germany's terms. From the first sign of trouble in July, Scheer lobbied for "a central organization for U-boats," which were still controlled through five different commands after the creation of the U-cruiser Group in 1917 offset the subordination of the Black Sea U-boats to the Mediterranean Flotilla. In December, his efforts led to the creation of a new U-boat Office under Vice Admiral Ernst von Mann-Tiechler, who reported to Capelle in the Imperial Navy Office.[72] The change did nothing to resolve command-and-control issues but promised to make construction, repair, and overall planning more efficient.

Such measures, of course, did nothing to alter the fundamental reality that the gamble on unrestricted submarine warfare had been nothing short of disastrous, failing to defeat Britain while adding another potentially powerful adversary, the United States, to the ranks of the enemy. Yet as 1917 drew to a close, developments elsewhere in the war raised the possibility that Germany might not have to pay for the grave miscalculation of its leaders. Every front line in Europe remained on Allied soil. While the German army had conserved its strength during the year, the British (at Passchendaele) had shed a great deal of blood for little gain, while the French (in the Nivelle offensive) and the Italians (at Caporetto) had suffered setbacks serious enough to call into question whether their armies would be capable of offensive action again. U-boats were not keeping the United States from sending troops to Europe, but just 175,000 had arrived by the end of the year, and American resistance to the piecemeal assignment of AEF divisions to the British and French armies delayed their deployment after they arrived. Meanwhile, the German decision to help Lenin leave his Swiss exile, just days after the American declaration of war, ultimately resulted in Russia suing for peace before the manpower of the United States could become a factor on the western front, creating a window of opportunity for Germany to win the war despite all that had gone wrong. As the Central Powers and Soviet Russia opened peace talks at Brest-Litovsk, the High Command anticipated a definitive end to hostilities in the east that would allow the transfer of German troops to the west for a final, successful push against Paris early in 1918. Unrestricted submarine warfare alone had not been decisive, but it remained a significant means of keeping the pressure on the Allies while Germany played its last cards in the war on land. The amount of shipping destroyed in December 1917 (411,770 tons) underscored the continued seriousness of the U-boat threat, and a month into the new year, on the first anniversary of the resumption of unrestricted submarine warfare, the overall shipping tonnage at the disposal of the Allies would still be decreasing. But the German and Austrian governments had asked a great deal of their people since 1914 and would continue to demand more, begging the question of whether the Central Powers could achieve a military victory before collapsing from exhaustion. The uneasy coexistence between hope and despair, so much in evidence as early as the spring of 1917, remained so as 1918 began.

NOTES

1. Erzberger, *Erlebnisse im Weltkrieg*, 251.

2. Joachim Kramsta, *Aus dem Logbuch des 1. Wachoffiziers U 66: Auszüge aus Briefen und Tagebuchblättern* (Bremen: Industrie- und Handelsverlag G.m.b.H., 1931), 16 June 1917, 165.

3. Ullrich, "Die Januarstreik 1918," 54–57.

4. Osborne, *Britain's Economic Blockade*, 161, 163; Sondhaus, *World War One*, 291; Sondhaus, *The Great War at Sea*, 287–88.

5. Erzberger, *Erlebnisse im Weltkrieg*, 252.

6. Ibid., 216.

7. Ibid., 252–58.

8. "German Reichstag Peace Resolution," 19 July 1917, http://www.firstworldwar .com/source/reichstagpeaceresolution.htm.

9. Erzberger, *Erlebnisse im Weltkrieg*, 264.

10. Adolf Vogt, *Oberst Max Bauer: Generalstabsoffizier im Zwielicht, 1869–1929* (Osnabrück: Biblio Verlag, 1974), 91–101.

11. Herwig, *The First World War: Germany and Austria-Hungary*, 374–75; Kelly, *Tirpitz*, 418–22.

12. Erzberger, *Erlebnisse im Weltkrieg*, 268.

13. Ibid., 257.

14. Daniel Horn, *The German Naval Mutinies of World War I* (New Brunswick, NJ: Rutgers University Press, 1969), 41–42, 65–66, 112–13, 132–63; Scheer quoted 163.

15. Herwig, *The First World War: Germany and Austria-Hungary*, 378.

16. Ullrich, "Die Januarstreik 1918," 52.

17. Sondhaus, *The Great War at Sea*, 290–303.

18. Hersing, *U 21 rettet die Dardanellen*, 131.

19. Gibson and Prendergast, *The German Submarine War*, 182.

20. Rose, *Auftauchen!*, 197.

21. Fürbringer, *Fips*, 54.

22. Quoted in Thomas, *Raiders of the Deep*, 148–49.

23. Fürbringer, *Fips*, 89–90.

24. Karl Dönitz, *Memoirs: Ten Years and Twenty Days*, trans. R. H. Stevens (New York: World Publishing Company, 1959), 4.

25. Crowell and Wilson, *The Road to France*, 2:475–76, 484.

26. Ibid., 2:489–90.

27. Rose, *Auftauchen!*, 160–65; http://uboat.net/wwi/ships_hit/1626.html.

28. http://www.atlantictransportline.us/content/31Minnehaha.htm; http://uboat.net/wwi/ships_hit/4168.html.

29. Sondhaus, *The Naval Policy of Austria-Hungary*, 311; http://uboat.net/wwi/ships_hit/4150.html.

30. http://www.uboat.net/wwi/ships_hit/4620.html.

31. http://www.uboat.net/wwi/ships_hit/439.html.

32. ADM 137/2656, HH24; http://www.uboat.net/wwi/boats/successes/u79.html.

33. Hashagen, *U-Boats Westward*, 188–92. United States Congress, Senate, *Naval Investigation: Hearings before the Subcommittee of the Committee on Naval Affairs*, 66th Cong., 2nd Session, 2462, includes a false report that the submarine responsible for sinking the *Orama* was sunk afterward by Allied destroyers.

34. ADM 137/2656, HH16; http://uboat.net/wwi/boats/successes/u62.html.

35. ADM 137/2656, HH25; http://uboat.net/wwi/ships_hit/losses_year.html?date=1917 -10&string=October+1917.

36. See Joseph Husband, *On the Coast of France: The Story of the United States Naval Forces in French Waters* (Chicago: A. C. McClurg, 1919).

37. Bayly, *Pull Together!*, 220; Taussig, *Queenstown Patrol*, 192n136.

38. http://uboat.net/wwi/ships_hit/5437.html. Taussig, *Queenstown Patrol*, 160, confirms there was no shortage of volunteers for duty aboard the *Santee*.

39. "*Jacob Jones I* (DD-61)," https://www.history.navy.mil/research/histories/ship -histories/danfs/j/jacob-jones-i.html.

40. Ibid.

41. Paul Kagelmann, *Unterseeboot-Minenleger im Weltkrieg: Wir von der I. U-Flottille, Kriegserlebnisse eines U-Boots-Deckoffiziers in der Hochseeflotte und auf Unterseebooten* (Bremen: Anker-Verlag, 1934), 115; Fürbringer, *Fips*, chapter 11; "U 81: Memorandum and Minute," ADM 137/3872/2, 144.

42. Headrick, *The Invisible Weapon*, 164–66; Scheer, *Germany's High Sea Fleet*, 309–14.

43. http://uboat.net/wwi/boats/successes/u105.html; http://uboat.net/wwi/ships_hit/ losses_year.html?date=1917-12&string=December+1917.

44. http://uboat.net/wwi/boats/index.html?boat=106.

45. Scheer, *Germany's High Sea Fleet*, 291.

46. König, *Voyage of the Deutschland*, 117. Heat was also a problem for summer operations in the Eastern Mediterranean, where *UB 105* once recorded an engine room temperature of 63° C (145° F), combined with 90 percent humidity. See Marschall, *Torpedo Achtung!*, 219.

47. Rössler, *Die deutschen U-Kreuzer*, 78–95; http://uboat.net/wwi/boats/successes/ u151.html; http://uboat.net/wwi/boats/successes/u155.html; http://uboat.net/wwi/boats/ successes/u156.html; http://uboat.net/wwi/boats/successes/u157.html.

48. Valentiner, *Der Schrecken der Meere*, 226–27; Niemöller, *From U-Boat to Pulpit*, 56.

49. Valentiner, *Der Schrecken der Meere*, 244–67, quoted 267; http://uboat.net/wwi/ships_hit/4436.html.

50. Valentiner, *Der Schrecken der Meere*, 267.

51. Gray, *The U-Boat War*, 205; http://uboat.net/wwi/boats/successes/u28.html; http://uboat.net/wwi/ships_hit/4436.html.

52. Grant, *U-Boats Destroyed*, 72.

53. Headrick, *The Invisible Weapon*, 164–65, 167; Black, *The British Naval Staff*, 187.

54. Gibson and Prendergast, *The German Submarine War*, 90, 148, 188, 255n, quoted 188. See also Grant, *U-Boats Destroyed*, 29, 40, 72, 140.

55. Fraser M. McKee, "An Explosive Story: The Rise and Fall of the Depth Charge," *Northern Mariner* 3 (1993): 49–50; Kemp, *U-Boats Destroyed*, 22, 38; http://uboat.net/wwi/boats/index.html?boat=UB+29; http://uboat.net/wwi/boats/index.html?boat=58.

56. Halpern, *The Naval War in the Mediterranean*, 277; John J. Abbatiello, *Anti-Submarine Warfare in World War I: British Naval Aviation and the Defeat of the U-Boats* (London: Routledge, 2006), 1–3. Until the recent (2009) reevaluation of the cause of *UC 66*'s demise, *UB 32* was considered the only submarine sunk from the air by a British plane. See chapter 5, note 44 above.

57. Chatterton, *Q-Ships and Their Story*, passim; Campbell, *My Mystery Ships*, passim; Grant, *U-Boats Destroyed*, 152–54; Kemp, *U-Boats Destroyed*, 29, 32, 34. Both Grant and Kemp list *UC 72* as the last Q-ship victim. On the location of the wreck of *UC 72* in 2013, see http://uboat.net/wwi/men/commanders/377.html. On the fate of *U 34*, see http://uboat.net/wwi/boats/index.html?boat=34. The fictional account of the sinking of *U 34* by HMS *Privet* in Thomas, *Raiders of the Deep*, 345, was considered authoritative for decades after its initial publication in 1928.

58. Valentiner, *Der Schrecken der Meere*, 214.

59. Sondhaus, *The Great War at Sea*, 268.

60. Bacon, *The Dover Patrol*, 1:106.

61. Ibid., 2:71; http://uboat.net/wwi/boats/index.html?boat=48.

62. Bacon, *The Dover Patrol*, 1:138–44.

63. Grant, *U-Boats Destroyed*, 152–54.

64. Scheer, *Germany's High Sea Fleet*, 288–91. The twenty-one Sperrschiffe employed by the navy during the First World War included six foreign merchantmen seized in German ports at the start of the war. See Gröner, *Die deutschen Kriegsschiffe*, 3:225–28.

65. Scheer, *Germany's High Sea Fleet*, 304–9.

66. http://uboat.net/wwi/men/commanders/most_successful.html.

67. Kemp, *U-Boats Destroyed*, 9–41. The yearly figures are four in 1914, nine in 1915, and sixteen in 1916, followed by forty-one in 1917. The Austrians also lost one boat with all hands in 1915 and one in 1917.

68. Gibson and Prendergast, *The German Submarine War*, 183.

69. Quoted in Thomas, *Raiders of the Deep*, 157.

70. Valentiner, *Der Schrecken der Meere*, 188.

71. Gibson and Prendergast, *The German Submarine War*, 183.

72. Scheer, *Germany's High Sea Fleet*, 328.

7

Anxious Months

While the High Command planned for, then launched, Germany's last great offensive in France, the navy shared the army's sense of grim determination, only with considerably less reason for optimism. Shortly after the war, Admiral Scheer recalled being "filled . . . with anxiety" throughout the winter and spring of 1918, owing to "the gradual decline in the monthly sinkings accomplished by the U-boats." The rate at which the Allies were sinking German submarines also declined, but still "many a U-boat with a splendid and experienced commander did not return." To make matters worse, "the new commanders had to gain experience under considerably less favorable conditions," with their positions ever more likely to be detected by directional wireless and hydrophones, after which ever-greater Allied resources were deployed to hunt them down. More extensive Allied mining operations made it still more challenging for U-boats to get out to sea and return home safely. Not surprisingly, their fate became the focal point of a navy whose most formidable surface ships remained idle. According to Scheer, "the commanders of the fleet noted down the positions of every single U-boat; its departure and return were followed with care and suspense." In the face of clear evidence that German submarines were failing to achieve their goals, "all our thoughts centered on finding ways and means to keep up the standard of their achievements and to increase them." For all their flaws and miscalculations, Germany's admirals approached the challenges of 1918 with a sense of duty and honor that contrasted sharply with the cynicism

FIGURE 7.1.
Reinhard Scheer
(The European Library)

of the generals. Indeed, long after the High Command had begun to plot
a way to shift blame to the navy if Germany failed to win the war, Scheer
and the admirals remained accountable for delivering a victorious peace via
unrestricted submarine warfare. "We felt that we were responsible for the
attainment of such an end to the war as had been promised to the German
people, and that we could achieve it by this means alone."[1]

A victorious end to the war, or indeed any outcome that ended the Allied blockade or reopened prewar sources of food, could not come too soon
for the Central Powers. Germany had another disastrous grain harvest in
1917, measuring just 14.9 million tons, less than half the prewar norm, and
the United States made the food shortage worse by following Britain's lead
in imposing an embargo on exports to Germany's neutral neighbors. The
food crisis had implications for the army as it prepared for the upcoming
offensive. Each of the 1.4 million men on the western front was rationed just
2,500 calories per day, more than twice the civilian average but still far below
the Allied norm. The army even segregated the most physically fit men into

"attack" divisions, assigning the rest to weaker "trench" divisions tasked with merely holding their sectors.[2] Food also factored into a chain of events that delayed the offensive and reduced the size of the army attempting it. The shortages helped fuel massive strikes in January 1918 in both Germany and Austria-Hungary, which inspired Soviet Russia to drag out the negotiations at Brest-Litovsk in the hope that the Central Powers would soon succumb to revolution. They responded by recognizing an independent Ukraine on 9 February, then deployed troops to secure its grain fields for their hungry home fronts. Lenin's government capitulated, only to have peace delayed by Ludendorff, who had long promoted the idea that resources from vassal states in the east could mitigate the effects of a blockade. Eastern operations continued for another two weeks until friendly local regimes had been installed not just in Ukraine but also in the Baltic states and Belarus. In the Treaty of Brest-Litovsk (3 March), Soviet Russia recognized the loss of these territories, which provided sanctuary for anti-Bolshevik "White" armies when the Russian Civil War broke out later that month. Amid the chaos, the High Command left troops all along the former front and sent others where none had been previously, enlisting the help of the navy to transport divisions to Finland in April and to Georgia in June. In both cases U-boats were used to prepare the way for German military intervention. During the autumn of 1917, the submarines of the Courland Flotilla, successor at Libau to the defunct Baltic Flotilla, transported to Finland, piecemeal, a Finnish rifle battalion that had been serving in the German army, along with munitions for the independence movement. On 18 November, the last of these missions ended in the loss of *UC 57* (*Kapitänleutnant* Friedrich Wissmann) to a Russian mine in the Gulf of Finland, after which the Germans ended all Baltic submarine operations. Meanwhile, at the opposite end of the front, the Germans began meddling in Georgia because of their strategic interest in the oil resources of neighboring Azerbaijan, and twice sent *UB 42* (*Oberleutnant* Kurt Schwarz) across the Black Sea from Constantinople on special missions to transport Georgian nationalist leaders home.[3]

These encroachments, undertaken with Russia temporarily paralyzed by revolution and civil war, foreshadowed (and likely inspired) the Third Reich's attempt to exploit the same lands a generation later, with far greater ruthlessness and brutality. In 1918, however, the High Command's eastern ambitions only robbed Germany of manpower desperately needed in the west. Ludendorff, even in defeat, would refuse to acknowledge that these troops could have tipped the balance in France, asserting instead that "not a man too many was left in the East."[4] But more than half of the divisions stationed on former Russian soil on 3 March (forty-three of seventy-six) remained there, leaving the thirty-three redeployed divisions to account for Germany's narrow advantage on the western front (192 divisions against 165 for the Allies).

THE TONNAGE WAR

In contrast to the Battle of the Atlantic during the Second World War, which shifted decisively in the spring of 1943 between March (when the Germans were still sinking Allied shipping faster than it could be replaced) and May (when the Allies started sinking U-boats faster than they could be replaced), the submarine campaign of the First World War had no distinct turning point. By November 1917 it became clear that the Allies had withstood the onslaught of unrestricted submarine warfare, but the Germans had fallen less than a million tons short of forcing a reduction in the Allied war effort, and when the amount of tonnage sunk rose again in December, to a level over 110,000 tons greater than the previous month, it naturally raised fears in Allied circles that the Germans had succeeded in arresting the decline of their U-boat campaign. While German submarines never caused Britain to experience anything like the sort of hunger than the British blockade inflicted on Germany, in January 1918 Lloyd George finally introduced food rationing. As of 1 February, the first anniversary of the resumption of unrestricted submarine warfare, shipping remained the Achilles' heel of the Allies. The overall tonnage at their disposal was still decreasing, at a time when nearly 90 percent of the American troops eventually deployed to Europe were still in the United States, and both Britain and France were more dependent than ever on the manpower and resources of their overseas empires. Thus, the last-ditch effort of the German army to win the war on land coincided with the last act of the tonnage war at sea, where victory hinged on the ability of U-boats to continue to sink Allied shipping faster than it could be replaced.

In the first months of 1918 the assignment of more U-boats against the northern convoy route, into Liverpool and other "West Coast" destinations via the North Channel, paid immediate dividends, including five major successes within a span of just seven weeks. On 27 January, in the North Channel, Hillebrand's *U 46* sank the 13,405-ton British steamer *Andania* (7 dead). On 4 February, off the western coast of Scotland, *UB 67* (*Kapitänleutnant* Gerhard Schulz) sank the 13,936-ton *Aurania* (8 dead), outbound to New York in ballast. The following evening, in the North Channel, off the island of Islay, *UB 77* (*Kapitänleutnant* Wilhelm Meyer) sank a British troopship inbound from Halifax in convoy HX20 with over two thousand US troops aboard, the 14,348-ton *Tuscania* (166 dead). On 1 March, also in the North Channel, one of the oldest submarines still in service, *Kapitänleutnant* Spiess's *U 19*, torpedoed and sank the ocean escort of inbound convoy HS29, the 12,515-ton British armed merchant cruiser *Calgarian* (49 dead). Two weeks later, off the northern coast of Ireland, *U 110* (*Korvettenkapitän* Carl Albrecht Kroll) sank the 10,037-ton British steamer *Amazon* (no casualties), but succumbed soon after to a depth-charge attack by two of the Buncrana destroyers, which killed Kroll and all but four of his crew of forty-two.[5]

The relatively light death tolls from most of the larger ships sunk while in convoy in the early months of 1918 attest to an important ancillary benefit of the system: the vast majority of those aboard a sinking ship were now rescued by the escorting vessels. The same was true amid the heavier loss of life in the sinking of the *Tuscania*, in which most of the dead came from among those first off the ship, whose lifeboats were wrecked or capsized on a dark, stormy night. After the convoy's destroyer escorts dropped depth charges and were satisfied that the attacking U-boat had left the scene, they pulled alongside the sinking ship and took off everyone who had remained aboard without further incident.[6] In the First World War, as in the Second, the escorting warships could never place an entire convoy at risk for the sake of saving the survivors of a single sunken ship, but as long as U-boats operated individually, escorts were able to shift to rescue operations relatively quickly, as soon as an area was deemed secure. In the Second World War, the use of "wolf pack" tactics in convoy attacks would make such operations a luxury, as escorts could rarely be confident that additional U-boats were not nearby.

While registering their string of successes against larger targets at the end of the northern route of the "West Coast" convoys, U-boats continued to have their best luck against "East Coast" convoys by attacking them as they dispersed to the Channel and French ports, despite the addition of the formidable Allied destroyer presence at Brest to complement those at Queenstown and Devonport. In mid-February, ships of HN43, an "East Coast" convoy, endured two attacks after splitting at the western approach to the Channel, first on the 11th by Rose's *U 53*, which sank the 4,327-ton British freighter *Merton Hall* (57 dead) off Ushant while it was under escort by the Brest destroyers, then on the 14th by *UB 57* (*Oberleutnant* Johannes Lohs), which sank the 4,325-ton British freighter *Carlisle Castle* (1 dead) off Dungeness after its care had passed from the Devonport destroyers to local patrol boats. The next "East Coast" convoy out of New York, HN45, likewise lost two ships, both British steamers, torpedoed by Hans Adam's *U 82* in the Channel south of Cornwall on 19 February, just after the split at the western approach: the 5,165-ton *Philadelphian* (4 dead) and the 5,117-ton *Glencarron* (no casualties).[7] Two months passed before any other inbound formations suffered as much, in both cases "West Coast" convoys that had approached the British Isles via the northern route. On 11 April, *UB 73* (*Kapitänleutnant* Karl Neureuther) and *UB 64* (*Kapitänleutnant* Otto von Schrader) both attacked HH48 in the North Channel, the former sinking the 3,741-ton British steamer *Myrtle Branch* (15 dead) just hours before the latter sank the 2,045-ton American steamer *Lakemoor* (46 dead). Later the same month, after most of convoy HN62 put in safely at Liverpool, two ships continuing on to Bristol were torpedoed and sunk by *U 91* (*Kapitänleutnant* Alfred von Glasenapp) in the predawn hours of 28 April off the coast of Wales: the 8,075-ton British steamer *Oronsa* (3 dead) and the 5,668-ton Portuguese steamer *Damao* (no casualties).[8] Unfortunately for the Germans, such breakdowns in protection occurred too infrequently. At the anniversary of the first transatlantic convoy, 90 percent of HN convoys (sixty-three of seventy) had made the crossing without losing a single ship to U-boat action, and the figures were almost as impressive for the HS route (83 percent, or thirty-four of forty-one) and HH route (79 percent, or forty-four of fifty-six). HN and HS convoys of thirty-five ships had crossed completely unscathed, along with HH convoys of thirty ships. On all convoy routes, the Allies had lost many more ships to storms and mechanical failures than to German submarines.[9]

British-flagged ships ultimately carried 49 percent of all US troops departing for Europe, American-flagged ships 45 percent; Liverpool welcomed the greatest share of them, at just over 40 percent, surpassing Brest (38 percent) and St. Nazaire (10 percent).[10] In the first months of 1918, as the sheer number of US troops making the crossing in the fast HX convoys far surpassed the number of Canadians, so many of the ships were loading at New York that it no longer made sense to the Admiralty to have the convoys assemble at Halifax, their official port of origin. From April through the end of the war, all HX convoys originated in New York, still departing every eight days, alternating with the HN cargo convoys, which also left for Europe every eight days. Admiral Grant subsequently placated Canadian authorities (and preempted even greater congestion at New York) by starting a new Halifax convoy series in May, designated HC, consisting of slightly slower ships. Like the HX convoys, they departed every eight days and included cargo ships as well as troopships, with most of the latter now loading at Montreal, which was more readily accessible than Halifax for Canadian and American troop trains. The HC convoys, like the earlier HX convoys, ultimately also included some American troopships originating in New York.[11]

During the spring and summer months of 1918, many U-boat commanders sought to reverse their declining fortunes by attacking outbound rather than inbound convoys, reasoning that sinking a transport or cargo ship hurt the Allied war effort regardless of whether it was full or empty; the Germans assumed, correctly, that convoys of empty ships might be less carefully protected.[12] Because the cruisers from the North American ports and the destroyers coming out of Queenstown or Brest were all under orders to give priority to fully loaded eastbound ships, empty westbound ships were especially vulnerable in the event of a gap in coverage during the ocean rendezvous. One such case, on 31 May, resulted in *U 90* (*Kapitänleutnant* Walter Remy) sinking the 18,170-ton *President Lincoln* some three hundred miles (480 km) west of Brest, just after its escorting destroyers had turned to protect HN69, an inbound convoy of twenty-nine ships from New York. It was the largest American troopship sunk in the war but, being empty at the time, just twenty-six lives were lost.[13] In a similar attack on 1 July, one hundred miles (160 km) west of Brest, *U 86* (*Oberleutnant* Helmut Patzig) sank the 16,339-ton American troopship *Covington* (6 dead). Another attack on an outbound convoy, on 17 July, southwest of Ireland, by *U 55* (*Kapitänleutnant* Wilhelm Werner), claimed the 13,603-ton British steamer *Carpathia* (5 dead), a ship famous for having rescued the *Titanic*'s survivors in 1912. Two days later, off the northern coast of Ireland, Schrader's *UB 64* torpedoed the 32,234-ton British liner *Justicia*, outbound from Liverpool to New York via the northern route; the damaged ship remained afloat, only to be torpedoed and sunk by *UB 124* (*Oberleutnant* Hans Oscar Wutsdorff) on 20 July while under tow (10 dead). After circling around to the south of Ireland, on 23 July Schrader's *UB 64* claimed another victim, sinking the 10,509-ton British armed merchant cruiser *Marmora* (10 dead), an escort in a convoy outbound to Dakar.[14]

The action in the Mediterranean early in the year included two significant sinkings by commanders already decorated for torpedoing Allied battleships. On 30 January, *Kapitänleutnant* Moraht's *U 64*, which had torpedoed the French battleship *Danton* in 1917, sank the 13,528-ton British steamer *Minnetonka* (4 dead) off Malta. Then, on 26 March, *Kapitänleutnant* Franz Becker, whose *UC 14* had mined the Italian battleship *Regina Margherita* in 1916, commanded *UB 50* in the sinking of the 11,495-ton Italian steamer *Volturno* (no reported casualties) off the coast of Algeria.[15] In another notable action, on 29 April, Wolfgang Steinbauer, now a *Kapitänleutnant* in command of *UB 48*, launched a daring nighttime raid on Carloforte, Sardinia, entering the port surfaced to sink the 6,564-ton British steamer *Kingstonian* with shell fire.[16] Shortly thereafter, the two deadliest submarine actions of 1918 occurred on the same day, 11 May, both against troopships, both in the Mediterranean. First, in the predawn hours off the coast of Tunisia, *UC 54* (*Kapitänleutnant* Heinrich XXXVII Prinz Reuß zu Köstritz) torpedoed and sank a French troopship bound for Salonika, the 9,350-ton *Sant Anna* (605 dead). Hours later, in the Strait of Messina, *UC 52* (*Oberleutnant* Hellmuth von Doemming) sank an Italian troopship bound for Tripoli, the 8,261-ton *Verona* (880 dead). Another deadly Mediterranean sinking followed two months later, on 15 July, when *Kapitänleutnant* Marschall, now in command of *UB 105*, attacked a Malta-to-Alexandria convoy off the Libyan coast near Benghazi and sank three ships within a matter of hours, including a French transport with Moroccan troops aboard, the 3,716-ton *Djemmah* (442 dead).[17]

In the Atlantic or in northern waters, ships carrying so many troops or civilian passengers enjoyed much better protection and, if attacked, suffered far fewer losses. Against the backdrop of relatively low death tolls in most U-boat attacks on larger targets after the adoption of convoys, the most shocking sinking of the spring and summer months of 1918 came on 27 June, when Patzig's *U 86* torpedoed the 11,423-ton Canadian hospital ship *Llandovery Castle*, inbound from Halifax, 116 miles (187 km) west of the tip of Cornwall. The ship was unescorted but clearly marked, and the dead numbered 234, many of them killed when their lifeboats succumbed to fire from *U 86*'s deck gun after Patzig apparently had second thoughts about the sinking and sought to destroy all evidence of it. One lifeboat escaped with twenty-four survivors, whose testimony led to postwar war crimes indictments for Patzig and his two lieutenants.[18] A total of seventeen Allied hospital ships were sunk during the war, of which fourteen were torpedoed by U-boats and three mined; the Allied navies, in turn, sank four hospital ships, of which one was torpedoed, two mined, and one sunk by gunfire. None surpassed the *Llandovery Castle* in loss of life.

After four U-cruisers were deployed to the tropics during the second half of 1917, all seven sortied during 1918, including six that were at sea before the end of spring. Having entrusted the novice *Kapitänleutnant* Meusel with *U 155* on its successful first sortie in 1917, the navy made the questionable decision to assign six of the seven boats to officers who had never commanded a submarine at sea before. The logic of propriety over pragmatism dictated that U-cruisers, being larger and more significant than other U-boats, should be commanded by officers with greater seniority, regardless of their lack of undersea experience. *Kapitänleutnant* Constantin Kolbe, who had commanded *U 19* earlier in the war (albeit without great distinction), at thirty-three was the youngest of the U-cruiser commanders of 1918 and the only veteran submariner of the group. The rest had entered submarine school during 1917 after serving in a variety of capacities earlier in the war. *Korvettenkapitän* Erich Eckelmann, at thirty-eight the oldest of the group, had been second-in-command of the pre-dreadnought *Preussen*. *Korvettenkapitän* Heinrich von Nostitz und Jänckendorff and *Korvettenkapitän* Ortwin Rave had been artillery officers aboard dreadnoughts, in the case of Nostitz, on Scheer's flagship *Friedrich der Grosse*. *Korvettenkapitän* Gernot Goetting and *Kapitänleutnant* Richard Feldt both had served aboard light cruisers, while *Korvettenkapitän* Hermann Gercke had spent the entire war in the Baltic command on the staff of the emperor's brother, Admiral Prince Henry. No doubt, in some of their cases connections meant as much as aptitude in securing their ultimate assignments.[19]

The first four U-cruiser patrols of 1918 followed the same outbound course as the four sorties of 1917, heading south after reaching the open ocean between Scotland and Iceland. *U 152*, under Kolbe, left Kiel in late December for a maiden voyage that lasted until mid-April. Kolbe hunted off the coast of Portugal before cruising down the western coast of Africa as far as 15° N latitude. The seventeen ships he destroyed were mostly small (totaling 30,660 tons) and included five Spanish steamers, one of them sunk between Dakar and the Cape Verde Islands. Eckelmann, after taking over *U 155* from Meusel, followed the same outbound course in mid-January but did not cruise as far south, sinking sixteen ships (50,522 tons) in an area bounded by the Azores, Madeira, Gibraltar, and Lisbon before returning home in early May. He sank his largest victim on 7 April, the 9,500-ton armed Italian freighter *Sterope*, after a surface battle using *U 155*'s two 15-cm deck guns. The first cruise of *U 153*, under Goetting's command, met with far less success. In a patrol that lasted from mid-February until early June, he followed Kolbe's earlier course to the latitude of Dakar but managed to sink just four ships (12,742 tons). The maiden voyage of *U 154*, under the command of Gercke, also began in mid-February, just days after that of *U 153*, and followed a parallel course much of the way, allowing the two boats to rendezvous frequently. Gercke cruised as far south as 6° N latitude, to the coast of Liberia, but with even less success than Goetting. He sank just five small ships (8,132 tons) and in one attack suffered an accident with one of his deck guns that killed eight of his crew. The ill-fated cruise of *U 154* came to an abrupt end on 11 May, during its homeward voyage, when one of Gercke's wireless messages was intercepted at Gibraltar, giving away his location to the enemy. Within hours, British submarine *E 35* (Lieutenant Guy D'Oyly Hughes) tracked down and torpedoed *U 154* in the waters between Cape St. Vincent and Madeira, where it was lost with all hands (77 dead). Goetting's *U 153* was just four miles (7 km) away at the time of *U 154*'s demise, and Hashagen's *U 62* was even closer. Indeed, Hashagen was close enough to see the fatal explosion, having arranged a rendezvous to take Gercke's unused torpedoes and some diesel fuel aboard his own boat to allow him to stay out longer. Hashagen attributed *U 62*'s survival to his own change of course away from the designated meeting spot, thanks to a school of whales whose breaching he mistook for the surfacing of one or both of the U-cruisers.[20]

The last two U-cruiser sorties of the spring both went west rather than south. After succeeding Kophamel as commander of *U 151*, Nostitz left Kiel in mid-April and headed for the eastern coast of the United States. He claimed his first victim, the three-masted schooner *Hattie Dunn*, on the 25th, at 75° W longitude off the Delmarva Peninsula. *U 151* lingered in the waters off the mid-Atlantic states for nearly two weeks and sank another eight American vessels, torpedoing the largest of the lot, the 5,093-ton passenger steamer *Carolina* (13 dead), on 2 June, 125 miles (200 km) southeast of Sandy Hook, New Jersey. On 18 June, while on his homeward voyage, Nostitz sank the 8,173-ton *Dwinsk* (23 dead), one of a number of Russian steamers seized by the British after the Bolshevik Revolution; at the time of its demise, the ship was some four hundred miles (645 km) northeast of Bermuda, en route back to Hampton Roads from France, steaming unescorted in waters the Allies had considered safe from the U-boat threat. *U 151*'s destruction of twenty ships (50,635 tons) made its voyage the most successful by a U-cruiser in 1918.[21] Intending to keep the pressure on the United States and Canada, the German navy timed the next U-cruiser's arrival in American waters to coincide with Nostitz's departure for home. *U 156*, now under Richard Feldt, arrived off the North American coast in late June and remained until late August. While on station, Feldt sank thirty-five mercantile and fishing vessels of various sizes, totaling 28,611 tons, and also laid a minefield off Long Island that, on 19 July, claimed the 13,680-ton armored cruiser *San Diego* (6 dead), the largest US Navy ship sunk during the war. Two days after the demise of the *San Diego*, *U 156*'s two 15-cm deck guns fired the only enemy shells to land on US soil during the war, in the course of an attack that sank four barges just three miles (5 km) off the town of Orleans on Cape Cod. Moving on to the waters off Nova Scotia, on 20 August Feldt seized the 239-ton Canadian trawler *Triumph* and armed it with his prize crew. Over the next week the *Triumph* functioned as an auxiliary to *U 156*, sinking another six fishing vessels before Feldt ordered it scuttled after it ran out of coal.[22]

Neither *U 151* nor *U 156* encountered a convoy bound for Europe, but their presence along the American coast prompted the assignment of additional protection to the formations leaving Hampton Roads and New York, including submarine chasers for the first day of the voyage and additional cruisers for up to three days.[23] These deployments left even fewer vessels for antisubmarine patrols along the coast: just eighteen older American destroyers for the entire Atlantic seaboard of the United States and Canada, backed by submarine chasers, obsolete gunboats, and auxiliaries, to which the Canadians eventually added their own makeshift force including one sloop, one armed yacht, and over one hundred trawlers and drifters. On the same day that Feldt sank the barges off Cape Cod, Admiral Grant's concern for the security of the western Atlantic prompted him to request that newly commissioned American destroyers be held back from European waters to strengthen the "present inadequate antisubmarine forces on this side," the weakness of which could "no longer be justified" in light of the U-cruiser threat. His suggestion brought a firm rebuke from the Admiralty.[24]

The U-cruisers of 1918 foreshadowed the action in the Battle of the Atlantic during the Second World War, in that they demonstrated to the American and Canadian public that Germany could bring the war to their shores. But they sank too few enemy merchantmen to have a practical impact on the tonnage war, and their modest record vindicated the Allied decision to continue to focus on protecting convoys closer to their final approaches into European ports and not be distracted by the deployment of a U-boat or two to the North American coast. The persistence of the antisubmarine effort paid clear dividends. Even though the Germans maintained a consistent number of submarines at sea, most of which were larger and more powerful than those deployed earlier in the war, the overall volume of tonnage sunk by U-boats per month remained flat for the first eight months of 1918, averaging just over three hundred thousand tons, roughly equivalent to the worst month (November) of 1917. The totals included 295,630 tons in January, 335,200 in February, 368,750 in March, 300,070 in April, 296,560 in May, 268,505 in June, 280,820 in July, and 310,180 in August,[25] ultimately far too little to counter the additional tonnage the Allies were able to deploy, which was subject only to the limits of how fast shipyards, especially in the United States, could work to build or refurbish ships. In 1917–18 the Americans recommissioned 109 interned German ships totaling 629,000 tons, none more significant than the 54,280-ton *Leviathan* (ex-*Vaterland*), formerly of the Hamburg–Amerika Line, which made its first crossing in December 1917 and ultimately transported more American troops to Europe than any other single ship. The Allied requisition of Dutch merchantmen, completed in March 1918, included eighty-seven seized in American ports and forty-five in ports of the British Empire, some 650,000 tons in all. Taking into account its share of these requisitions, Britain's registry, in May 1918, finally gained more tonnage than it lost, for the first month since the resumption of unrestricted submarine warfare. Two sources alone—the expropriation of German ships in the United States and the requisition of Dutch ships worldwide—each added the equivalent of what U-boats were sinking in two months at their reduced success rate of 1918. German tonnage seized in the various Latin American countries that had joined the Allies after the US declaration of war, when added to new construction, promised to tip the balance still more.[26] The Emergency Fleet Corporation, established by the US Congress in April 1917, ultimately claimed credit for launching 507 ships totaling 2.8 million tons, including 151 built from the keel up and 356 requisitioned from among vessels already under construction.[27]

The Germans might have come closer to winning the tonnage war if they had been able to increase the size of their submarine fleet, but their number of U-boats deployed (like the amount of tonnage they sank) remained flat, despite the best efforts of Vice Admiral Mann-Tiechler and his staff in the new U-boat Office. The German navy started 1918 with 142 U-boats and added 69 more (including 47 *UB* boats) between New Year's Day and the Armistice. Another sixteen *UC* minelayers, 474-ton units of Type *UC III*, were completed but never activated. But against these additions, sixty-nine were sunk, five converted to training boats, and three interned in neutral countries.[28] Throughout the year, labor problems threatened both submarine construction and the navy's torpedo supply, as well as the repair of U-boats deployed to the Mediterranean. As in the wave of unrest that swept Germany in the spring of 1917, in the strikes of January 1918 the workers at Germania in Kiel and the torpedo factory in Friedrichsort were the first to walk out, followed by those of the Hamburg shipyards, then AG Weser in Bremen. In Kiel, local authorities kept the shipyards under civilian control, but in Hamburg

and Bremen the army took over, giving idled workers the choice of returning to their jobs or reporting for military duty. The strikes were broken and,
by mid-February, military control of shipyards ended, but throughout the
spring and summer, workers remained disgruntled and, consequently, less
productive. Meanwhile, in Austria-Hungary, seven hundred thousand workers struck during the January unrest, including technicians from Germany
repairing U-boats in the Pola Arsenal, who walked out in solidarity with local
Slavic laborers. Admiral Njegovan maintained order in the fleet at Pola but,
just days later, had to suppress a serious mutiny at the base in Cattaro (1–3
February). Emperor Charles responded to the crisis by sacking Njegovan
and promoting forty-nine-year-old Miklós Horthy to rear admiral and fleet
commander, an extraordinary move that forced the twenty-eight officers who
outranked Horthy to retire or transfer to posts ashore.[29]

Amid growing concerns for the future of its Austrian-based operations,
the German navy took some consolation that the monthly rate of loss of
U-boats eased: after forty-three were sunk in the last five months of 1917,
sixty-nine were sunk during the ten and a half months of action in 1918.
Unfortunately, the rate of catastrophic loss increased, as fifty of the sixty-
nine were lost with all hands, compared to forty-one with no survivors in
all of 1917. While there was no clear turning point in the tonnage war of
1917–18, the balance sheet of Allied tonnage sunk versus German submarines lost clearly tipped from favoring the Germans in 1917 (6.15 million
tons at a cost of sixty-three U-boats) to favoring the Allies in 1918 (2.75
million tons at a cost of sixty-nine U-boats).

THE FINAL ALLIED COUNTERATTACK: CONVOYS, COUNTERMEASURES, AND BARRAGES

After so few U-boats recorded significant successes in attacking convoys
during the last months of 1917, the German navy revised the regimen of the
U-boat school at Eckernförde, on the Baltic, to include stalking simulated
convoys of ships assembled for daily cruises.[30] The additional tactical training
did nothing to remedy the biggest problem, which remained simply locating
convoys to attack. According to one postwar American assessment, "the U-
boats not only seldom attempted to sink a loaded American troopship, but
seldom even saw one." Even after the Neumünster cryptanalysts broke the
British convoy code, the complexity of the Allied scheme of scheduling separate cargo and troop convoys, staggering their departures, and changing their
sea-lanes left the Germans unable to discern a pattern in where or when to

expect targets to appear. Of course, as the same American assessment explained, for the convoys into France, "all lanes at sea converged into one lane outside Brest or St. Nazaire, and the U-boat needed only to lie in wait on this lane to encounter everything that came along, whether cargo carrier or trooper." But in those shallow waters, the submarine commander knew "he could be seen by observers aloft in airplanes or balloons, and when their signals had brought the destroyers, he had no defense except to lie quietly on the bottom sands and hope that the depth charges would miss."[31]

Indeed, whether on the high seas or in coastal waters, most U-boat commanders considered the main convoy routes too dangerous because of the presence of so many escorting warships armed with depth charges. These were not idle fears, for depth charges alone sank at least twenty-two U-boats during 1918, nearly a third of those lost in the war's last year.[32] Perhaps more than any other antisubmarine countermeasure, this one weapon inverted the premises of the U-boat war against Allied shipping. As early as the Wiegand interview of 1914, Tirpitz had assumed that the credible threat of sinking ships would accomplish the same goal as actually sinking them, frightening the Allies into submission. He could not have foreseen that credible antisubmarine countermeasures, culminating by 1918 in the extensive use of depth charges, would accomplish the same goal as actually sinking U-boats, frightening German submariners into avoiding the very targets they most needed to sink.

U-boat commanders reluctant to attack convoys found far fewer significant targets steaming alone or unescorted. Those dispensing with escorts were simply too fast to catch, most notably the largest prize of all, the *Leviathan*. As the German *Vaterland*, the giant liner had an advertised prewar speed of 22 knots, but on its American shakedown cruise in the autumn of 1917 it did even better, making 23.5 knots between New York and Guantanamo Bay. Allied merchantmen had to be able to make 12 knots, fully loaded, to be considered for troopship duty, and many were capable of little more; thus it made no sense to run a ship as fast as the *Leviathan* at half speed for the sake of keeping it in convoy, especially when it was twice as fast as the average surfaced U-boat and three times faster than one submerged. At a time when the average troop convoy took twelve to fourteen days to make the Atlantic crossing, the *Leviathan* typically took eight days (and four times did it in seven), enabling the Allies to make greater use of their largest transport by running it independently. The *Leviathan* made ten crossings to France between December 1917 and October 1918, the first six unescorted, before being accompanied on three of its last four by destroyers of the new *Wickes* class, the only US Navy warships that could match its speed for the entire voyage. The only troopships ever to accompany the *Leviathan* were the Pacific coast railway steamers *Great Northern* and *Northern Pacific*, which in peacetime had carried passengers between San Francisco and Seattle, the western terminus of the transcontinental railways for which they were named. At just 8,255 and 9,708 tons, respectively, they had nothing in common with the *Leviathan* other than their 23-knot speed, which enabled each to make six unescorted crossings in 1918.[33] In addition to being too fast for U-boats to catch or target, the largest troopships featured a combination of size and speed that made them a danger to any U-boat that wandered into their lane. One such example came during the night of 11–12 May off the western approach to the Channel, when *U 103* (*Kapitänleutnant* Claus Rücker) found itself squarely in the path of the 46,358-ton British liner *Olympic*, sister of the ill-fated *Titanic* and *Britannic*, bound for Cherbourg from New York with a full load of American troops. The *Olympic* normally made 21–22 knots but was steaming at 24 when it ran down *U 103*, closing too fast for Rücker to get off a shot. He dove at the last minute to avoid a collision, only to have his boat sucked into the big liner's propellers as it passed overhead. The resulting damage forced Rücker to surface and scuttle, after which one of the two American destroyers escorting the *Olympic* rescued him along with most of his crew.[34]

By 1918 the improvements in Allied surveillance and countermeasures left the typical U-boat more often in the role of the hunted rather than the hunter. An increasing number of U-boat cruises met with little or no success before ending in disaster, a problem especially acute for boats with inexperienced commanders. Of the sixty-nine U-boats that were sunk during 1918, nine were commanded by officers who had yet to sink a ship before losing their own boats. Another seven had claimed just one victim, and a total of twenty-four had sunk five ships or less.[35] In some cases veteran commanders performed no better than their less experienced colleagues, especially when facing the greater challenges of the war's last year in new boats manned by newly drafted crews. Rücker stands out as the most dramatic example of this phenomenon. After ranking with Arnauld, Forstmann, and Valentiner as one of the leading Mediterranean U-boat aces earlier in the war, claiming 159,188 tons with *U 34* in 1915–16, he managed to sink just 15,467 tons on five patrols with *U 103* in 1917–18. Survivors of *U 103*'s collision with the *Olympic*, most of whom had not served with Rücker earlier, characterized him as "an overcautious commander" with an "irritable, nervous condition," whose "anxiety was . . . infectious," resulting in mistakes and miscalculations by the other officers and members of the crew. Their fourth patrol, in March 1918, had been especially difficult, as "between 50 and 60 depth charges were dropped in the neighborhood of *U 103* within the course of a few days." Rücker persevered, according to his subordinates, for purely personal reasons, hoping to sink enough tonnage to be awarded the *Pour le Mérite*. He remained in command of *U 103* for what turned out to be its final patrol even though "the state of his nerves appeared to have been well known."[36] Despite losing his boat and spending the rest of the war in captivity, Rücker placed ninth among all U-boat commanders on the final list of tonnage sunk, but he had the dubious distinction of being the most successful German submarine commander (and the only one among the top sixteen) not to receive the *Pour le Mérite*.

With so many U-boats having little or no success, Scheer again decided to deploy surface warships against Allied shipping. In April 1918 he attempted to repeat, in much greater force, the earlier successful raids against the convoy route between Norway and Scotland, undertaken in October 1917 by the light cruisers *Brummer* and *Bremse*, then in December 1917 by torpedo boats. In response to intelligence that the British were now using dreadnoughts and battle cruisers to escort merchantmen on the Norway–Scotland route, Scheer decided to sortie with every available capital ship of the High Sea Fleet, leaving out only three older dreadnoughts still not back from supporting the army's deployment of the German division to Finland that same month. Hipper's five battle cruisers led Scheer's main force of sixteen dreadnoughts out of Wilhelmshaven late on 22 April, heading up the Danish coast on the same general course that had resulted in the Battle of Jutland nearly two years earlier. Scheer took along a scouting group of light cruisers and four flotillas of destroyers and instructed the U-boats that were in the North Sea at the time to screen for British warships between the fleet and the coast of Scotland (they encountered none); otherwise, U-boats were limited to a reconnaissance role (in which the only notable report turned out to be false). On the morning of the 24th, as the lead ships of the German column closed to within forty miles (64 km) of the Norwegian coast at Stavanger, one of Hipper's battle cruisers, the *Moltke*, lost a propeller in a mechanical mishap that damaged its hull and flooded its engine room. Hipper forged ahead to the convoy lanes with his four remaining battle cruisers but missed by one day a westbound convoy, whose escort included four British battle cruisers, and was too early to intercept the next eastbound convoy, escorted by a division of American dreadnoughts. Hipper carried the search to the latitude of 60° N, almost all the way to Bergen, before turning back to rejoin Scheer and the main body of the fleet. Meanwhile, the increase in German wireless activity after the *Moltke*'s accident alerted the British that the High Sea Fleet had sortied. Earlier in April, Beatty had moved the main body of the Grand Fleet from Scapa Flow to the battle cruiser base at Rosyth, 250 miles (400 km) closer to Wilhelmshaven, putting it in a better position to intercept the High Sea Fleet should it come out, but on the 24th he left port too late to catch Scheer on his run home. The first sortie by the entire German battle fleet since October 1916 would also be its last. In the end, the only submarine to come close to playing an important role during the operation was British rather than German: on the evening of 25 April, as the *Moltke* limped toward Helgoland and the safety of the German defense perimeter, *E 42* (Lieutenant C. H. Allen) torpedoed it. Fortunately for Scheer, who had left the crippled ship to steam the last leg of the voyage into Wilhelmshaven under its own power, the blow added little to the hull damage suffered in the earlier accident, and the *Moltke* made it into port without sinking.[37]

The British took almost thirty-six hours to react to the High Sea Fleet sortie of 22 April, and for good reason: they were preoccupied with an operation of their own against the Flanders Flotilla's bases at Zeebrugge and Ostend, coincidentally timed to start on the evening of the 22nd. Over the preceding months Vice Admiral Sir Roger Keyes, Bacon's successor as head of the Dover Patrol, had revived and refined his predecessor's earlier proposal for raids to close the two Belgian ports to U-boats, focusing on blocking the mouths of the two canals connecting Zeebrugge and Ostend to Bruges. For the attack on Zeebrugge, Keyes ultimately decided to land commandos in the old light cruiser *Vindictive* to neutralize shore batteries, wreck two old submarines packed with explosives at key points in the harbor, and block the canal with three old cruisers filled with cement. The complex operation, prepared under great secrecy, went awry from the start. The commandos were landed but suffered such high casualties that they were unable to complete their mission. One of the submarines struck its target as planned, but the other broke its tow line en route to Zeebrugge and had to be abandoned. Finally, one of the three blockships was sunk in the wrong place and the other two failed to completely close the canal mouth. The British initially celebrated the operation as a great victory, but it closed Zeebrugge for only a few days. A concurrent attack on Ostend on the night of 22–23 April failed completely when the old cruisers destined to be sunk as blockships across the mouth of the canal there were grounded harmlessly on nearby sandbars. A second attack on Ostend, on the night of 9–10 May, included a preliminary bombing raid by the Royal Air Force (RAF)—formed one month earlier by the merger of the Royal Naval Air Service and the army's Royal Flying Corps—after which the *Vindictive*, heavily damaged in the Zeebrugge raid, and another old cruiser were sunk as blockships at the mouth of the canal. The operation effectively closed Ostend, but because Zeebrugge remained open, the Flanders Flotilla remained viable until early October, when the final Allied offensive on the western front forced the navy to abandon its Belgian base.[38]

The British launched the raids on Zeebrugge and Ostend only after failing to shut down the Flanders Flotilla using more conventional means. Following the completion of their improvements to the nearby Dover barrage, they constructed another barrage in a semicircle from the shallows at the mouth of the Scheldt to a point eighteen miles (29 km) out to sea from Zeebrugge, then inshore to the shallows off Dunkirk, thirty-five miles (56 km) west-southwest down the coastline from the Scheldt. This great arc of "mine-studded nets and patrol boats" did not close the base, but the additional barrier made every sortie that much more dangerous; indeed, Flanders-based U-boats accounted for half (twenty-seven of fifty-four) of all German submarines lost between January and August 1918. During the same months, the increased frequency of air raids from southeastern England made life in Zeebrugge and Ostend only marginally safer than at sea, prompting the Germans to construct submarine pens with reinforced concrete roofs six feet (2 m) thick, foreshadowing those built for Hitler's U-boats on the Atlantic coast of France during the Second World War. Though admittedly an extreme example, the Flanders Flotilla ultimately became emblematic of the German undersea force as a whole. Interviewing survivors of the navy's Belgian-based submarine effort a decade after the war, Lowell Thomas concluded that "the history of the Flanders Flotilla is a tale of contending against imperfect defenses that gradually became more and more perfect."[39]

No other antisubmarine barrage equaled those constructed at Dover and off Flanders, but by the war's last summer, the one across the Straits of Otranto had taken on a much more formidable character, albeit while also remaining relatively easy for a careful U-boat commander to get through. Martin Niemöller, returning to the Adriatic for the first time in two years to take command of *UC 67* for a mission to lay mines off Marseilles, in July 1918 took his new boat through the straits, avoiding a "stout steel net . . . between the coast of Italy at Santa Maria di Leuca and the northern extremity of Corfu" that had not been there in 1916. To enable surface vessels to pass overhead, the top of the net was "a fathom" underwater, while the bottom edge extended "a good two hundred feet under water," certainly an inconvenience but hardly a barrier, as the straits were 2,600 feet (800 m) deep at their deepest point. The planes of the British air station at Otranto gave German and Austrian submarines transiting the straits another good reason to dive deeper. In his July sortie Niemöller avoided that threat, only to fall victim to an attack days later by a British plane operating out of Malta, which damaged *UC 67* badly enough to force him to abandon his mission and return to his Adriatic base.[40]

Before leaving his command at the Dover Patrol, Bacon had proposed the most ambitious antisubmarine barrage of all, the so-called Northern Barrage, to close the "safe route" for U-boats around the north of Scotland into the open Atlantic. The project involved assembling nets and sowing seventy thousand mines along the 325 miles (525 km) between the Orkney Islands and the coast of Norway, a line four times longer than the Otranto barrage in its final version. The Admiralty approved the project in September 1917, and work began in March 1918, with the United States assuming most of the cost and US Navy personnel joining the British in its construction. *U 62*'s Hashagen considered the Northern Barrage proof that "the Americans . . . could tackle an almost insoluble problem with enormous and inexhaustible optimism." Yet he "went through the middle of it three times" without incident, leaving him to doubt the American claim that it sank twenty U-boats, believing the number to be no more than "two or three at the outside."[41] Scheer contended that "the great depth of the water in this part of the North Sea made it possible for U-boats to avoid the barrier by travelling at a sufficient depth below the surface. So far as we could ascertain, we suffered no losses in U-boats from these mines."[42] While Scheer is certainly wrong in claiming the Northern Barrage sank no German submarines at all, it very likely did not sink more than six of them. While it is perhaps unfair to judge too harshly a project ultimately completed just one month before the Armistice, the results of the Northern Barrage hardly justified the effort and the cost, estimated to have reached $40 million in 1918 dollars. Measured in terms of cost per U-boat destroyed, it was, by far, the most expensive antisubmarine measure attempted by the Allies in the entire war.[43]

By 1918 the Allies also had intensified their antisubmarine efforts at the Straits of Gibraltar, though contemporary accounts, and historians writing after the fact, disagree over whether the measures put in place there warranted the label of "barrage." The straits were a mere 8.9 miles (14.3 km) across at their narrowest point, less than half as wide as the Straits of Dover, but had a depth ranging from 980 to 2,950 feet (300 to 900 m), nine times deeper at their shallowest point than the mean depth at Dover. Thus, while they were much easier to block at or near the surface, their depth allowed submarines plenty of room to dive beneath any nets or mines. Arnauld, who took *U 35* past Gibraltar on two occasions, in April and October of 1917, recalled that "the British had the straits protected with nets, mines, and patrols of destroyers. I always preferred to go through on the surface at night rather than take a chance with nets and submerged bombs. The searchlights played across the entire width of the neck of water, but it was possible to sneak through by hugging the African coast."[44] Antisubmarine assets deployed to Gibraltar in 1918 included an American contribution of destroyers, coast guard cutters, submarine chasers, and armed yachts, supplementing British forces that included the Q-ship *Privet*. The US Navy at the time referred to this makeshift Gibraltar squadron as the "Gibraltar Barrage," contributing to the subsequent confusion over whether a proper barrage had existed at the straits.[45] Some Americans also used the term "barrage" in the generally accepted sense, for example, a US Navy mechanic who arrived at Gibraltar just weeks before the Armistice, recalling that "we arrived there just in time to finish the Gibraltar barrage" and claiming that "our division sunk [*sic*] three submarines."[46] But according to a US Navy strategic assessment of the straits published shortly after the war, a proper barrage never existed, and for good reason: "Aside from the deep water and the very strong currents in the Straits of Gibraltar, the advantages to be gained by a barrage in this position were not deemed to be of sufficient importance to demand the development of the special [deepwater] mine which would have been required for this purpose."[47] Historian Paul Halpern, author of the definitive account of the First World War in the Mediterranean, notes that the Allies discussed a Gibraltar barrage but that the traffic of U-boats through the straits was far less than at Dover or Otranto and did not justify the cost or the effort. Most of the boats sent from Germany to the Mediterranean stayed there for the duration of the war and did not attempt to transit the straits to return home until days before the Armistice.[48] Valentiner's 1916 cruise to Madeira in *U 38* and Arnauld's two 1917 sorties in *U 35* were rare exceptions to the general rule that German U-boats based in the Adriatic did not venture all the way out into the Atlantic. Thus, the "barrage" ultimately deployed at Gibraltar was limited to aggressive surface patrols and powerful searchlights to discourage U-boats from attempting the passage at night, and did not include the nets and mines Arnauld and other German submariners assumed were there.

FIGURE 7.2.   Hindenburg and Ludendorff with William II (US National Archives and Records Administration)

THE NAVY AND THE TURNING POINT IN THE WAR ON LAND

The offensive that began on 21 March 1918 was the German army's greatest effort on the western front since August 1914, and from the start it had the air of a desperate last gamble. In numbers of divisions, the Germans enjoyed an advantage over the Allies, but their headcount of 1.4 million men (for 192 divisions) revealed that their average division was operating at half strength. The Hindenburg Program had left them reasonably well equipped but still marginally inferior to the Allies in artillery and aircraft, and dramatically so in tanks, the Anglo-French innovation of 1916–17 which Germany had not seriously tried to copy. The spirit of the troops remained good as long as they continued to advance, but even in the more physically fit "attack" divisions, hungry soldiers supplemented their short rations with food and wine found in the trenches they captured, an indulgence that compromised discipline and slowed their progress. Breaches of discipline were frequent enough, overall, to prompt reminders from superiors of the obligation to maintain proper military bearing. Ludendorff's plan of attack focused initially on the ground of the Somme battlefield of 1916, at the junction of the sectors covered by the British and French armies. One week into the offensive the Germans nearly succeeded in breaking the Allied front there, shaking the confidence of the British so much that they agreed to form a common Supreme Allied Command under Marshal Ferdinand Foch. In April the main German thrust came against British and Imperial forces in western Flanders, retaking ground lost at Passchendaele the previous autumn and pushing the front a bit farther away from Zeebrugge and Ostend. The following month and into early June, the Germans focused on the French army and advanced to the River Marne, where they established a foothold at Chateau-Thierry, just fifty-six miles (90 km) from Paris.

During May, General Pershing agreed to assign AEF divisions to the other Allied armies as an emergency measure; they soon saw action in counterattacks at Cantigny (28 May) and Belleau Wood (1–26 June). Thereafter, significant British and Imperial reinforcements joined the ever-increasing number of Americans to push the total Allied strength to 203 divisions by the time the Germans launched the final phase of their offensive, resulting in the Second Battle of the Marne (15 July–6 August). At the start of the climactic battle the Germans, on paper, still had the larger force, increased to 209 divisions by the arrival of another seventeen from Russia, but 641,000 battle casualties over the first four months of the offensive had reduced many German divisions to mere shells. After the first day of Second Marne, German troops stood closer to Paris than at any time since September 1914, yet within three days the Allies had stabilized their lines, enabling Foch to coordinate a counterattack at Chateau-Thierry, where fresh American divisions played a prominent role. The tide had clearly turned. Chancellor Hertling recalled later that "on the 18th even the most optimistic among us knew that all was lost."[49] The Germans withdrew north of the Marne, but not before giving up twenty-nine thousand prisoners, an unusually large number for them. Hindenburg and Ludendorff did not have the luxury of analyzing their failure before the next crisis. At the Battle of Amiens (8–11 August), British and Imperial forces achieved a stunning breakthrough along the Somme, after which German troops seemed to lack the strength and will to counterattack. The Allies took thirty-three thousand prisoners at Amiens, including sixteen thousand on the battle's first day, confirming fears that the spirit of the army was breaking. Indeed, Ludendorff called 8 August "the black day of the German army."[50]

Even before the defeat at Amiens, the clear implications of the army's failure at Second Marne demoralized the principal advocates of unrestricted submarine warfare. By the end of July, Holtzendorff had submitted his resignation, citing failing health, while Tirpitz had retired to his country home at Sankt Blasien in the Black Forest, without formally resigning his leadership of the Fatherland Party. Ludendorff praised Scheer for being "an unusually clear-thinking man" at this most anxious time, yet the High Sea Fleet commander could think of little other than how to exploit the situation to consolidate his own power over the navy. After Scheer persuaded William II that both Holtzendorff and Capelle had lost the confidence of the officer corps, the emperor accepted the resignation of the former and sacked the latter, and he agreed to make Scheer head of a new Naval High Command (*Seekriegsleitung*) vested with administrative as well as operational authority. The change necessitated Scheer's relocation from Wilhelmshaven to western front headquarters at Spa in Belgium, where he succeeded Holtzendorff as the navy's principal representative. At Wilhelmshaven, Hipper took over as commander of the High Sea Fleet but remained subordinate to Scheer, while in Berlin, Vice Admiral Paul Behncke, commander of one of Scheer's dreadnought squadrons, succeeded Capelle as state secretary of the Imperial Navy Office. The changes took effect on 11 August, just as the army's debacle at Amiens was coming to a close. Scheer arrived at Spa the next day.[51]

NOTES

1. Scheer, *Germany's High Sea Fleet*, 330.

2. Sondhaus, *World War One*, 360–61, 406–7. The Italian army was the least well-fed Allied force, with an ideal ration of four thousand calories per day but a reality of just over three thousand.

3. Sondhaus, *The Great War at Sea*, 322, 327; http://uboat.net/wwi/boats/index.html ?boat=UC+57; http://uboat.net/wwi/boats/index.html?boat=UB+42.

4. Ludendorff, *Ludendorff's Own Story*, 2:411.

5. http://uboat.net/wwi/ships_hit/largest.html; ADM 137/2656, HN29. On the loss of *U 110*, see Kemp, *U-Boats Destroyed*, 45.

6. There is no consensus on the *Tuscania* death toll. "S. S. Tuscania: Details of Disaster," *Melbourne Argus*, 9 February 1918, at http://trove.nla.gov.au/newspaper/article/1638596, gives figures of 2,397 on board, with 2,011 soldiers, 141 crew, and 35 "others" rescued, and 210 missing. "The Sinking of the Tuscania," http://www.worldwar1.com/dbc/tuscania .htm, says 230 of the 2,397 on board died, including 201 US soldiers. The shipwrecks website http://www.wrecksite.eu/wreck.aspx?10317 gives figures of 2,235 on board, including 2,030 US Army, 2 US Navy, 6 passengers, and 197 crew, of whom 166 died. The site http:// uboat.net/wwi/ships_hit/6169.html likewise gives the figure of 166 dead. An Island of Islay history website, http://islayhistory.blogspot.com/2012/08/tusciana-burials.html, confirms at least 85 American soldiers were buried there after the disaster.

7. ADM 137/2656, HN43; ADM 137/2656, HN45; http://www.uboat.net/wwi/ships_ hit/losses_year.html?date=1918-02&string=February+1918.

8. ADM 137/2656, HH48; ADM 137/2656, HN62; http://www.uboat.net/wwi/ships_ hit/losses_year.html?date=1918-04&string=April+1918.

9. Data compiled from ADM 137/2656, HH, HN, and HS précis of convoy reports.

10. Walter Kudlick, "Sealift for the AEF," http://www.worldwar1.com/dbc/sealift .htm#a; see also data in Leonard P. Ayres, *War with Germany: A Statistical Summary* (Washington, DC: US Government Printing Office, 1919).

11. Hadley and Sarty, *Tin-Pots and Pirate Ships*, 233–34.

12. Gibson and Prendergast, *The German Submarine War*, 176.

13. ADM 137/2656, HN69; http://www.uboat.net/wwi/ships_hit/4905.html.

14. http://uboat.net/wwi/ships_hit/largest.html. Wireless Operator Haidt, "The Sinking of the *Justitia*," in *U-Boat Stories: Narratives of German U-Boat Sailors*, ed. Karl Neureuther and Claus Bergen, trans. Eric Sutton (London: Constable, 1931), 166–71, claims that *U 54* (*Oberleutnant* Hellmuth von Ruckteschell) sank the *Justicia*, not *UB 124*.

15. http://uboat.net/wwi/ships_hit/largest.html.

16. Boatswain's Mate Seidel, "Raid on the Sardinian Port of Carloforte," in *U-Boat Stories: Narratives of German U-Boat Sailors*, ed. Karl Neureuther and Claus Bergen, trans. Eric Sutton (London: Constable, 1931), 183–87; http://www.uboat.net/wwi/ships_ hit/3337.html.

17. Marschall, *Torpedo Achtung!*, 205–16; http://www.uboat.net/wwi/ships_hit/great est_loss_of_life.html.

18. Gibson and Prendergast, *The German Submarine War*, 311–12.

19. See biographical sketches in Yves Dufeil, *Dictionnaire biografique des commandants de la Marine Impériale allemande* (N.p.: Histomar Publications, 2016), http://en.calameo .com/read/000802552841bc1ae847e, passim.

20. Rössler, *Die deutschen U-Kreuzer*, 96–102; Compton-Hall, *Submarines and the War at Sea*, 283–86; Hashagen, *U-Boats Westward*, 173–75; http://uboat.net/wwi/men/ commanders/146.html; http://uboat.net/wwi/men/commanders/58.html; http://uboat .net/wwi/men/commanders/94.html; http://uboat.net/wwi/men/commanders/86.html.

21. Rössler, *Die deutschen U-Kreuzer*, 105–7; http://uboat.net/wwi/men/commanders/ 231.html.

22. Rössler, *Die deutschen U-Kreuzer*, 107–8; http://uboat.net/wwi/men/commanders/ 69.html; Jake Klim, *Attack on Orleans: The World War I Submarine Raid on Cape Cod* (Charleston, SC: History Press, 2014); Hadley and Sarty, *Tin-Pots and Pirate Ships*, 263–67.

23. E.g., ADM 137/2656, HH 62 (departed 13 July), ADM 137/2656, HN 87 (departed 8 October).

24. Hadley and Sarty, *Tin-Pots and Pirate Ships*, 250, 291; Grant quoted 250.

25. These are the round numbers cited most often. Data from http://uboat.net total as follows: 316,926 tons for January, 323,192 for February, 379,406 for March, 293,584 for April, 310,188 for May, 253,236 for June, 298,218 for July, and 301,139 for August. Most discrepancies stem from when and whether to count armed merchantmen as warships.

26. Figures from William C. King, ed., *King's Complete History of the World War* (Springfield, MA: History Associates, 1922), 294; Frey, *Der Erste Weltkrieg und die Nieder-lande*, 272; Halpern, *A Naval History of World War I*, 423.

27. United States Congress, Senate, Committee on Commerce, *United States Shipping Board Emergency Fleet Corporation: Hearings before the Committee on Commerce*, 65th Cong., 2nd and 3rd Sessions, on S.Res. 170, part 3, 56–57.

28. Grant, *U-Boats Destroyed*, 140.

29. Ullrich, "Die Januarstreik 1918," 59–74; Sondhaus, *The Naval Policy of Austria-Hungary*, 317–28.

30. Valentiner, *Der Schrecken der Meere*, 269–70.

31. Crowell and Wilson, *The Road to France*, 2:487, 2:427–28.

32. McKee, "An Explosive Story," 49–50; Grant, *U-Boats Destroyed*, 39, 152, 159, 164.

33. Crowell and Wilson, *The Road to France*, 2:333, 418, 487–88, 604–20. The *Leviathan* emerged from the war unscathed even though the Germans placed a high priority on sinking it, reflected in the premature announcement in the German press that it had, indeed, been sunk on 20 July, when the victim, instead, was the 32,234-ton British troopship *Justicia*.

34. "*U 103*: Interrogation of Survivors," June 1918, ADM 137/3872/2; Kemp, *U-Boats Destroyed*, 49.

35. Data compiled from http://uboat.net/wwi/men/commanders/listing.html.

36. "*U 103*: Interrogation of Survivors," June 1918, ADM 137/3872/2, especially Part III.

37. Scheer, *Germany's High Sea Fleet*, 318–23.

38. See Charles Sanford Terry, *Ostend and Zeebrugge, April 23–May 19, 1918: The dispatches of Vice-Admiral Sir Roger Keyes and Other Narratives of the Operations* (London: Oxford University Press, 1919).

39. Thomas, *Raiders of the Deep*, 230–34, quoted 230; Grant, *U-Boats Destroyed*, 155–57. While the Flanders Flotilla indeed suffered disproportionately high losses, the assertion in Thomas (230) that "one day in February of 1918 eighteen German undersea raiders left Zeebrugge" but "only two returned" is completely fanciful.

40. Niemöller, *From U-Boat to Pulpit*, 87–97, quoted 88.

41. Hashagen, *U-Boats Westward*, 115.

42. Scheer, *Germany's High Sea Fleet*, 293.

43. Grant, *U-Boats Destroyed*, 157–58, lists *U 156* (in September) and *UB 123* (in October) as certain casualties of the Northern Barrage, with *U 92*, *U 102*, *UB 104*, and *UB 127* (all in September) as likely victims. Kemp, *U-Boats Destroyed*, 56–58, attributes only *U 102*, *U 156*, and *UB 123* to the Northern Barrage but has *U 92* and *UB 127* succumbing to mines in the Fair Isle Passage, which was covered by the western end of the Northern Barrage. See also Black, *The British Naval Staff*, 171.

44. Quoted in Thomas, *Raiders of the Deep*, 157–58.

45. E.g. Alex R. Larzelere, *The Coast Guard in World War I: An Untold Story* (Annapolis, MD: Naval Institute Press, 2003), 117, who asserts that "the barrage was a squadron of vessels assigned to the Strait of Gibraltar for the purpose of intercepting and destroying German submarines."

46. Master Mechanic Earl Dow Greer, USN, quoted at WorldWar1Vets.com, "Submarine Warfare in WW1," http://www.wwvets.com/Submarines.html.

47. United States Navy Department, *The Northern Barrage and Other Mining Activities* (Washington: US Government Printing Service, 1920), 135.

48. Halpern, *The Naval War in the Mediterranean*, 381.

49. Quoted in Robert H. Zieger, *America's Great War: World War I and the American Experience* (Lanham, MD: Rowman & Littlefield, 2000), 98.

50. Ludendorff, *Ludendorff's Own Story*, 2:326.

51. Scheer, *Germany's High Sea Fleet*, 330; Kelly, *Tirpitz*, 422; Sondhaus, *The Great War at Sea*, 335.

8

Defeat

Scheer had interacted with Hindenburg and Ludendorff on several occasions since their first meeting at Schloss Pless in November 1916, yet he felt the need to hurry to headquarters ahead of his staff "to introduce myself . . . in my new capacity," as head of the Naval High Command. He found the generals "much impressed with the gravity of the events" of recent days, "which . . . had placed our war on land definitely on the defensive." With the failure of the army appearing more likely than ever, Hindenburg and Ludendorff did not miss the opportunity to again emphasize that "the main hope of a favorable end to the war lay in a successful offensive of the U-boats." In contrast to the generals, Scheer did not shirk responsibility for bringing Germany victory, but he did need the High Command's help to build more submarines and bring them into commission faster. He recalled that "General Ludendorff promised . . . to do his utmost" to provide the navy with more, and better, shipyard workers.[1] For his part, Ludendorff was not impressed with Scheer's new office or the pretensions the admiral attached to it; in his own memoirs, published just a year later, he referred to Scheer having merely succeeded Holtzendorff as chief of the *Admiralstab*. He also had a different memory of his promise regarding the additional workers, in which he "explained that General Headquarters was not in a position to supply them, and could agree to release only a certain number of specially trained engineers and skilled hands. This involved only a few men." Ludendorff also recalled advising Scheer, on 12 August, that "the evacuation of our submarine base at Bruges might soon become necessary."[2] Scheer did not remember discussing the fate of the Flanders Flotilla on that occasion, and with good reason. The front in Flanders at the time was still in the vicinity of Ypres, roughly seventy miles (115 km) west of Zeebrugge, very close to where it had been ever since the end of 1914. If Ludendorff indeed expressed concern about the Flanders naval base at that stage, it was a telling reflection of what little faith he had in the army's ability to hold the front.

THE SCHEER PROGRAM: REALITY OR FANTASY?

The workers Scheer requested of Ludendorff would be essential to the success of the plan soon known as the Scheer Program. Drafted by Vice Admiral Behncke and announced by the Imperial Navy Office on 18 September, the Scheer Program appeared to be a belated naval complement to the Hindenburg Program of 1916, calling for a dramatic increase in U-boat construction. The same shipyards that ultimately completed eighty-five boats during 1918 were already expected to double production during 1919, but the Scheer Program nearly quadrupled the goal, to 333 boats, and added another seventy-nine to be completed during 1920.[3] Direct oversight of the program fell to Vice Admiral Mann-Tiechler, soon promoted from head of the U-boat Office to succeed Behncke in the role of state secretary, but it included no provisions for procuring the materials or assembling and feeding the labor force. The forty-eight thousand additional workers needed to meet the plan's goals for 1919 would have more than doubled the headcount at the four shipyards that built the overwhelming majority of German submarines—Blohm & Voss of Hamburg, AG Weser of Bremen, Germania of Kiel, and AG Vulcan of Hamburg—each of which had already expanded dramatically since 1914. For an industry suffering since 1915 from a shortage of skilled, competent workers, such an increase in the size of the labor force was unrealistic if not impossible. Problems emerging after the onset of the Hindenburg Program and the passage of the Patriotic Auxiliary Service Law had never been resolved. Younger workers, female workers, and workers from rural areas (whose places in agriculture had been taken by prisoners of war) remained considerably less productive than the prewar force of shipyard labor. The high attrition and turnover rate among workers introduced to the shipyards during the war never improved. For the shipyards, as for so many factories, the release and return of experienced workers from the army often did more harm than good, for the presence in the workplace of eyewitnesses from the trenches tended to increase antiwar sentiment and political radicalism. A study by the Imperial

Navy Office completed shortly before the end of the war blamed the lack of productivity on the "physical weakness" of workers from the time of the "turnip winter" of 1916–17 onward, compounded by a general unwillingness to work and decreasing discipline over the last two years of the war.[4]

The Scheer Program also hinged on the navy being able to train the officers and seamen to operate the expanded undersea force, a task even more problematic than assembling the workforce to build it. Even without the additional hundreds of boats envisioned for the future, the shortage of commanders was already acute. In the last half of the war the navy gave submarine commands to twenty reserve officers (half of whom never sank a ship) and also opened the U-boat school at Eckernförde to members of Crew 12 and Crew 13. Seven officers from Crew 12 were given their own boats late in the war, along with one from Crew 13, *Leutnant* Rudolf Haagen, who received command of *U 79* on 27 August 1918, the day after his twenty-third birthday.[5] By 1918 the Germans had learned just how important a talented, experienced commander could be to the survival of his boat and its crew; while the six most successful U-boat commanders were all destined to survive the war, as were fourteen of the top eighteen, new commanders with recently commissioned U-boats and newly assembled crews experienced relatively high loss rates. For this reason, the navy refused to cut short the curriculum of the U-boat school, where officers and seamen in submarine training continued to log the requisite number of hours on cruises in the Baltic before being deployed in an active U-boat. The 224 German submarines under construction at the Armistice included over two dozen that could have been commissioned had trained personnel been available. Thus, even without the additional U-boats proposed under the Scheer Program, the Germans already had demonstrated that they could build U-boats faster than they could prepare people to man them. In the Second World War the German navy would find again that this dilemma had no solution, given the challenges of operating a smaller warship type under circumstances in which even the most routine moves could become life threatening.

Its fantastic aspects notwithstanding, the Scheer Program had real consequences. Combined with the creation of the Naval High Command, it had the negative impact of being responsible, directly or indirectly, for the transfer of 48 percent of the fleet's warship commanders and 45 percent of first officers between August and October of 1918.[6] The wholesale reassignment of command personnel placed more of the best senior and mid-career officers in posts on land at the same time that the submarine service continued to take the best junior officers. The effects would be seen in the final mutiny of the High Sea Fleet, during which the breakdown of order and authority was accelerated by too many mediocre men being caught in leadership roles that demanded more than they could deliver.

Because the Scheer Program was divorced from the reality Germany faced in the autumn of 1918, historians have been at a loss to explain why it was drafted in the first place. Paul Halpern has concluded that "Scheer . . . might have pushed it more for psychological reasons." In a similar vein, Holger Herwig has speculated that the Scheer Program was little more than "a massive propaganda effort designed to have an effect at home and abroad." At the time, Ludendorff accepted at face value Scheer's apparent conviction "that submarine building could be speeded up and a better result obtained," but when it came to the High Command's capacity to release workers to the shipyards, "discussions lasted into October," by which time Germany's "exceedingly grave" situation made their labor arrangements, and the entire plan, completely meaningless.[7]

THE END OF THE WAR IN THE ATLANTIC

The labor discussions with Ludendorff were not the only meaningless conversations Scheer engaged in. Over the summer of 1918, in the weeks prior to the creation of the Naval High Command, he had a protracted, largely rhetorical exchange with the *Admiralstab* and the Foreign Office over whether a zone of unrestricted submarine warfare should be designated off the eastern coast of the United States. Nostitz's *U 151* and Feldt's *U 156* (and, before them, Rose's *U 53* in 1916) had followed cruiser rules on their sorties into American waters, allowing the crews of each vessel they destroyed to abandon ship, but according to Scheer, Holtzendorff's staff had "urgently recommended the declaration of a blockade of the American coast" to enable U-boats to attack, without warning, "the troopships [and] the immense supplies that went from America to the Western theatre of war." The Foreign Office "made strong objection to the declaration of this blockade" on the grounds that it would drive Chile and Argentina to join the Allies, after which "Spain would follow." The *Admiralstab*'s proposal that U-boats should attack the transatlantic convoys at their source came in response to the general failure to intercept them upon their approach to European waters, but in a meeting at Spa on 28 July, Scheer finally brought an end to the discussion by opposing a formal extension of unrestricted submarine warfare to the American coast, on the grounds that "we could not count on stationing more than three boats there until the end of the year," making any declaration little more than bluff. Instead, he argued, "We should more quickly attain our end with the U-boat campaign by keeping the blockaded area around England and the coast of France under the greatest possible pressure, than by extending the blockaded area to include the American coast."[8] He may have been stating the obvious, in geographic terms, but his conclusion also directed more U-boats to focus on the waters where Allied detection and countermeasures were the strongest, and where their own losses had been the greatest.

While Scheer thus did not consider long-distance patrols to be of central importance, submarines continued to be sent on such missions during the last months of the war. Of the navy's six remaining Type *U 151* U-cruisers, two were at sea when he became head of the Naval High Command, and another two sortied by early September. *Kapitänleutnant* Feldt's *U 156*, on patrol off the northeastern United States and the Canadian Maritime provinces since late June, finally left for home in late August. Meanwhile, in late July, *Korvettenkapitän* Rave succeeded Valentiner as commander of *U 157* and, rather than head for American waters, followed the course of the springtime cruise of Eckelmann's *U 155* to hunting grounds bordered by the Azores, Madeira, Gibraltar, and Lisbon. A month before his arrival in the area, the Allies had begun detaching ships from HH, HN, and HS convoys in mid-ocean to proceed, unescorted, via Gibraltar to Marseilles and various Italian ports; over one hundred ships took this route between July and the Armistice, steaming on routes right past the Azores, but Rave failed to sink any of them. Indeed, the second sortie of *U 157* was the least successful of the thirteen undertaken by U-cruisers in 1917–18, resulting in the destruction of just eight small vessels (5,572 tons) in a 111-day patrol that was still in progress when all U-boats were called home. Rave ultimately sought refuge in Norwegian waters, where *U 157* was interned two days before the Armistice; he was repatriated to Germany with his crew before the end of the year. *U 156* was not so lucky. Feldt's U-cruiser was lost with all hands (77 dead) on the final leg of its homeward voyage from the North American coast after last radioing home on 24 September from the vicinity of the Northern Barrage.[9]

By the time of its demise, *U 156*'s place off the American coast had been taken by *U 155*, which left in mid-August for its third cruise, under *Korvettenkapitän* Ferdinand Studt, its third novice commander and, at age thirty-nine (from Crew 98), the navy's oldest officer to take a submarine to sea in the entire war. *U 155* sank eight ships (17,525 tons), of which the largest was the 6,744-ton American steamer *Lucia*, a requisitioned Austrian ship fitted with experimental "buoyancy boxes" that supposedly rendered her unsinkable. Convoy authorities were confident enough in the invention to allow the ship to steam for France unescorted, in the company of another freighter. Studt stalked the two ships for days before torpedoing the *Lucia* at dusk on 17 October, some 1,200 miles (1,930 km) off the eastern United States; four men were killed in the explosion, the rest rescued the following day when an American cruiser and destroyer finally reached the scene. *U 155* sank the *Lucia* on its own homeward voyage, just days before all U-boats were recalled to Germany, and did not reach Kiel until two days after the Armistice.[10] The sinking was the final German success in the open waters of the Atlantic, even though *U 155* was not the last U-cruiser to sortie during 1918. *U 152*, now under *Kapitänleutnant* Adolf Franz, another novice commander, left Kiel after *U 155*, in early September, and claimed its last victim, the unescorted Norwegian sailing bark *Stifinder*, on 15 October, not far from where *U 155* would sink the *Lucia* two days later. *U 152*'s greatest success had come two weeks earlier, on 29–30 September, in a surface attack on an outbound American convoy northwest of the Azores. In the course of a long pursuit, Franz used his two big deck guns to damage an empty oil tanker, the 6,936-ton *George G. Henry*, and sink the 5,130-ton freighter *Ticonderoga* (213 dead). The latter, aside from the *Stifinder*, was the only ship Franz managed to sink before all U-boats were called home, giving him a meager 6,870 tons for his entire mission. Rave, Studt, and Franz were all on their homeward voyages when a final sortie by Nostitz's *U 151*, begun on 17 October, was cut short by the recall order before the boat made it beyond the North Sea.[11]

In the last months of the war, the German navy deployed the first two boats of a new class of U-cruisers built from the keel up as warships. *U 139* and *U 140* were even larger than the Type *U 151* U-cruisers and, at 10.8 million Marks apiece, nearly twice as expensive. Named for the lead boat of the class, the Type *U 139* design had a surfaced displacement of 1,930 tons and dimensions of 302 feet long by 17 feet deep, with a beam of 30 feet (92 × 5.3 × 9.1 m), essentially the same size in cross section as Type *U 151*, only significantly longer and thus 430 tons heavier. It required an additional six crew to operate, for a total of fifty-six, and like its predecessors it carried six officers along with a prize crew of twenty to seize vessels too valuable to sink. It carried a deck armament of two 5.9-inch (15 cm) guns along with twenty-four torpedoes, six more than Type *U 151*, but could not lay mines. Improvements included armor 3.5 inches (9 cm) thick on the conning tower, making it feasible to engage in a surface duel with an armed merchantman or even a cruiser, and a thicker pressurized hull that allowed a diving depth of 245 feet (75 m). Most significant of all, the speed of the Type *U 139* boat (nearly 16 knots surfaced, nearly 8 knots submerged) topped the U-cruiser by a full 4 knots surfaced and 3 knots submerged, the gain resulting in part because of its greater length and overall sleeker shape, and in part because less weight was budgeted for fuel tanks, giving the design a surfaced range of 17,750 nautical miles (32,870 km), only about two-thirds that of a Type *U 151* boat, but still more than enough to reach American or equatorial waters and return home without refueling.[12]

The Type *U 139* boats were built in Kiel by Germania. *U 140* was commissioned first, in March 1918, and given to Kophamel, most recently of *U 151*, the only senior submarine officer who also had extensive command experience. *U 139* followed in May and was given to Arnauld, recalled from the Mediterranean after sinking a remarkable 449,081 tons on fifteen patrols over a period of twenty-six months as commander of *U 35*. They were the only German submarines to receive names, *Kapitänleutnant Schwieger* for *U 139* and *Kapitänleutnant Weddigen* for *U 140*, but this gesture honoring U-boat commanders killed in action failed to catch on, and throughout their brief service lives both boats were commonly referred to by their numbers. A third unit of the class, *U 141*, was commissioned in June 1918 and given to Kolbe, most recently of *U 152*, but did not sortie before the war ended. The lead unit of a modified 2,158-ton version of the same design, *U 142*, intended for *U 155*'s Eckelmann, was commissioned the day before the Armistice and left Kiel only to go to the breakers. Another thirty-two boats of the class were under construction at war's end, seven of which were at least 70 percent complete; these included *U 144*, promised to *U 53*'s Hans Rose, which would have been the first of the class capable of stowing a small seaplane.[13]

The Type *U 139* boats were the most expensive submarines built to date, and not just because of their size and operational attributes. Onboard aesthetics and amenities were intended to make them more comfortable during their long voyages and continued the design trend of providing greater social separation between officers and the crew when space permitted; indeed, the accommodations for officers aboard Imperial Germany's last submarines were luxurious when compared to those aboard any other type of U-boat. Lowell Thomas, interviewing Arnauld at his home in Wilhelmshaven in the late 1920s, found remnants of *U 139* all around him. The "fine, satiny maple" of the boat's interior paneling and trim had been "ripped out of the submarine . . . before she was turned over to the Allies following Germany's defeat" and recycled by Arnauld to craft the "doors and moldings and panels in the house." Arnauld had also salvaged "much of the furniture of the house" from *U 139*, including the desk he used in his study.[14]

Size, cost, and capabilities notwithstanding, the performance of *U 139* and *U 140* was little better than the least successful of the Type *U 151* U-cruisers. Kophamel's *U 140* left Kiel first, in early July, and headed to the eastern coast of North America to supplement the efforts of Feldt's *U 156*. After stopping and scuttling a Portuguese sailing vessel en route, Kophamel cruised from Cape Hatteras up the coast to the waters southeast of Nantucket, sinking another six ships along the way, including an empty American tanker returning from Britain, the 10,829-ton *O. B. Jennings* (2 dead), torpedoed on 4 August roughly one hundred miles (160 km) east of the Delmarva peninsula. *U 140*'s modest tally of seven vessels sunk (30,594 tons) surpassed the yield of every other U-cruiser patrol of 1918 except those of *U 151* and *U 155* and also topped *U 139*. Kophamel would have had even greater success had he caught up with convoy HS53, which he followed across the North Atlantic on his way home, ultimately closing to within sixty miles (96 km) of it by the time its ships met the Buncrana destroyer escort.[15] After weeks of frustrating delays, Arnauld finally put to sea in mid-September for what turned out to be an ill-fated cruise. *U 139* was scheduled to follow *U 140* to American waters, but a stormy passage from the North Sea into the North Atlantic affected the boat's handling and left it in danger of capsizing. Arnauld restored *U 139*'s stability by redistributing the weight of the diesel fuel, pumping some of it into two of the diving tanks, but in the process he lost 15 percent of his fuel supply and no longer had enough for an American cruise. Redirected to the Canary Islands via the Azores, on 1 October he attacked an inbound convoy northwest of Cape Finisterre, only to have one of the two small steamers he torpedoed sink on top of the diving *U 139*, leaving its "upper works . . . hopelessly ruined" and the main periscope destroyed. Arnauld proceeded with his "rather crippled specimen of a U-boat" to the Azores, where his final victim was a Portuguese navy trawler, sunk in a gun battle on 14 October. Despite being limited to fighting on the surface, Arnauld continued on his revised course for another week, until he received the general recall order. History's most successful submarine commander managed to destroy just four ships (6,788 tons) on the last patrol of his career.[16]

The last U-boats deployed to the Atlantic also included large minelayers of the new type *UE II*, of which nine (numbered *U 117* through *U 120* and *U 122* through *U 126*) were commissioned between March and October of

1918. Like the *UE I* boats that had entered service in 1916, they combined the size and features of an oceangoing submarine with the ability to lay mines, but in a much larger and more heavily armed design. The type displaced 1,164 tons (compared to 755 for the *UE I*) and was manned by four officers and a crew of thirty-six. They deployed their forty-two mines from two large stern tubes, carried fourteen torpedoes, and were fitted with one 5.9-inch (15 cm) deck gun. More powerful engines and larger fuel tanks gave them a greater speed (14–15 knots surfaced, 7 submerged) and much greater range (13,900 nautical miles, or 25,740 km) than the *UE I* boats. At 6.1 million Marks apiece, they also cost roughly twice as much. The cruise of *U 117*, under the veteran *Kapitänleutnant* Otto Dröscher, paralleled that of Kophamel's *U 140*, leaving Kiel in July and returning in September. Dröscher sank twenty ships (27,459 tons) along the Atlantic coast of North America between Cape Hatteras and the waters south of Newfoundland. He recorded most of his successes during August, but the 18,000-ton pre-dreadnought USS *Minnesota* was damaged by one of his mines on 29 September, off Ocean City, Maryland, a week after *U 117* was safely back in Kiel. Dröscher's boat was one of just four of the *UE II* type to sortie before the Armistice. The other three (*U 118*, *U 119*, and *U 122*) did not venture past the western approaches to the British Isles and collectively sank just three ships (10,717 tons). The five that were commissioned but never left port included *U 124*, commanded by *Kapitänleutnant* Rolf Carls, future admiral of the Third Reich.[17] Even though the voyage of *U 117* must be considered a success by 1918 standards, its cruise was plagued by the sort of mechanical failures and breakdowns that became all too common for German submarines launched during the last two years of the war. Of a long list of problems, the most serious was a persistent oil leak that threatened to give away Dröscher's location and ultimately nearly left him stranded on the way home. *U 117* made it back to Kiel only because it was able to rendezvous with *U 140* on 12–13 September in the Faroe Islands, Danish possessions two hundred miles (320 km) north of Scotland, and take aboard diesel fuel that Kophamel's men siphoned into seventy-five empty shell cases repurposed as miniature oil drums. Dröscher also had problems with his torpedoes; one remained stuck, temporarily, in its tube when he tried to fire it, and five others were duds that failed to detonate when striking their targets. Given the scope and frequency of labor unrest at the navy's Friedrichsort torpedo factory and in the shipyards that built U-boats, such failures of machinery and weaponry no doubt led some to blame sabotage, but poor materials and shoddy workmanship were a more likely cause.[18]

The Atlantic patrols may not have been valued by Scheer, yet the four long-range submarines at sea during August (*U 117*, *U 140*, *U 156*, and *U 157*) still combined to sink fifty-six vessels of various sizes, one-third of the total of 169 claimed that month by the entire undersea force. For the four that sank ships between September and the Armistice (*U 139*, *U 152*, *U 155*, and *U 157*), the share of the destruction dropped to less than one-tenth of the total, just 16 of 198 ships. *U 117* also received credit for three ships that sank in October and November after striking mines it had laid earlier.[19]

THE END OF THE WAR IN EUROPEAN WATERS

Scheer's stated preference for "keeping the blockaded area around England and the coast of France under the greatest possible pressure" failed to yield the desired results, owing to the continued improvements the Allies were making in detecting U-boats and in antisubmarine countermeasures. They also expanded their use of convoys into coastal areas on a daily basis, most notably for the eastern coast of Great Britain, where Germany's shorter-range *UB* and *UC* boats had long registered most of their successes. The largest coastal convoy of 1918, between the Humber and the Tyne, included seventy-three ships protected by eighteen escorts.[20] Amid the continued decline in tonnage destroyed, fewer and fewer larger ships were sunk. Of the 282 mercantile vessels sunk in European waters by U-boats after July 1918, only one displaced over ten thousand tons.

While the navy's largest submarines ranged as far as the coasts of North America and equatorial Africa, those operating in European waters rarely sortied far enough into the Atlantic to exploit gaps in convoy coverage between the cruisers based in North America and destroyers from Queenstown or Brest. Fewer still ventured far enough to encounter a cruiser escorting an Allied convoy. An exception to this general rule came on 7 August, when one of the most successful U-boats of 1917–18, Hashagen's *U 62*, sank the 9,517-ton French armored cruiser *Dupetit-Thouars* with two torpedo hits some five hundred miles (800 km) west of Brest. Six American destroyers steaming out of Brest to meet the convoy that the *Dupetit-Thouars* had escorted from New York came upon its lifeboats the next day, and all but thirteen of the crew of 566 were saved.[21] In a less daring attack a month later on the same convoy route, *U 82* (*Kapitänleutnant* Heinrich Middendorff) targeted the empty 18,372-ton American troopship *Mount Vernon* (ex-*Kronprinzessin Cecilie*) on its outbound voyage, two hundred miles (320 km) west of Brest. The action, on 5 September, damaged the former North German Lloyd liner with a single torpedo, but the four

American destroyers escorting it used depth charges to drive off *U 82* before Middendorff could fire another. The *Mount Vernon* lost thirty-six of its crew but remained afloat; it turned back to Brest, which it reached under its own power, and thus avoided becoming the largest American-flagged ship sunk during the war. Other outbound ships torpedoed by U-boats in the same general area included the 7,323-ton British transport *Milwaukee*, sunk with just one fatality on 31 August by Strackerjan's *U 105*, some 375 miles (600 km) west of Brest. By the summer and autumn of 1918, such instances of a U-boat sinking or damaging a larger vessel did nothing to affect Allied operations. By the time the transatlantic convoy system ended on the day after the Armistice, 6,061 ships had been escorted from the United States and Canada to Europe over the preceding eighteen months, with the peak coming in October 1918, when convoys including 511 ships made the crossing.[22]

Against all odds, U-boat commanders bold enough to attack convoys still managed to register the occasional significant sinking in the waters around the British Isles. *Kapitänleutnant* Kurt Siewert of *U 107*—the most successful of the reserve officers to command a U-boat, with 45,456 tons destroyed in 1917–18—claimed his largest victim, the 9,291-ton British steamer *Flavia*, on 23 August, thirty miles (48 km) off County Donegal on the northern coast of Ireland, in an attack on convoy HS51. The *Flavia* was also the largest unarmed ship sunk in European waters during August, but, to put the accomplishment in perspective, the other thirty-seven ships in HS51 reached port safely. On 9 September, fifty-two miles (84 km) off the southern coast of Ireland, *Kapitänleutnant* Petri, now in command of *UB 87*, attacked a convoy outbound from Liverpool to New York and sank the 12,469-ton British steamer *Missanabie* (45 dead), the largest Allied victim of that month. On 4 October, two hundred miles (320 km) south of Ireland, *UB 91* (*Kapitänleutnant* Wolf Hans Hertwig) torpedoed the 7,936-ton Japanese passenger liner *Hirano Maru*, steaming in a convoy outbound from Liverpool to West Africa but with the ultimate destination of Yokohama. The ship went under with 292 of its passengers, becoming the largest Allied vessel sunk during October. It would have been the deadliest sinking, too, if not for a daring raid into the Irish Sea days later by *UB 123* (*Oberleutnant* Robert Ramm). On 10 October, just outside Dublin harbor, Ramm torpedoed and sank the 2,646-ton *Leinster*, a British steamer bound for Holyhead, crowded with troops, nurses, and civilian passengers (501 dead). It was the only ship *UB 123* ever sank; on its homeward voyage a week later, the boat disappeared shortly after Ramm radioed for advice on the best route through the Northern Barrage.[23]

For much of the war, U-boats had been disproportionately successful in the Mediterranean, but by the late summer of 1918 the German submariners operating out of Austria-Hungary's Adriatic bases led an increasingly precarious existence. Their flotilla had grown to include twenty-five boats by the end of 1916 and was maintained at that level thereafter, with additional submarines sent to make good any losses; as of October 1918, the German boats were supplemented by nineteen surviving Austrian submarines. The Germans had been shaken by the Cattaro mutiny of February 1918, but they admired Horthy and applauded his subsequent efforts to revive the Austrian navy; Valentiner, who later dedicated his memoirs to Horthy, was among those who wished their own emperor would be bold enough to turn over command of the German navy to a dynamic younger admiral. Horthy soon hinged the fate of his fleet on repeating his May 1917 raid on the Otranto barrage, this time using Austria-Hungary's four dreadnoughts, in an operation scheduled for 10 June. When one of his big battleships, the *Szent István*, was sunk in the Dalmatian islands by an Italian motor torpedo boat, the operation was canceled and morale plummeted. By then, the German commanders who were once the scourge of the Mediterranean had all been reassigned elsewhere, including the officers destined to finish the war as the navy's top three U-boat aces. In the autumn of 1917, Valentiner left *U 38* for the U-cruiser *U 157*, while Walter Forstmann left *U 39* to take command of the III U-boat Flotilla at Emden. Arnauld stayed on the longest, until March 1918, before giving up *U 35* for *U 139*, leaving Wolfgang Steinbauer as the most successful commander still operating out of Pola or Cattaro. First in *UB 47*, then *UB 48*, Steinbauer sank almost all of his fifty victims (181,571 tons) in the Mediterranean, a total sufficient to place him eighth on the overall list, yet he finished the war lamenting the one that got away: on 18 October, while hunting in the Cervi Channel off the island of Milos, his *UB 48* scored two torpedo hits on the 18,400-ton French pre-dreadnought *Voltaire* but failed to sink it. Other veteran commanders still in the Mediterranean at war's end included Gustav Siess and Kurt Hartwig. Siess sank fifty-three ships (159,545 tons) and two pre-dreadnought battleships while commanding *U 33* and *U 73*, while Hartwig sank forty-four ships (153,082 tons) with *U 32* and *U 63*. Hartwig's last victim, the 5,875-ton British steamer *War Council*, torpedoed eighty-five miles (137 km) southwest of Cape Matapan on 16 October, was also the largest ship sunk in the Mediterranean during the last weeks of the campaign there.[24]

Younger commanders shouldering the burden in the Mediterranean late in the war included three men destined to be significant figures in the Third Reich. Wilhelm Canaris, head of German intelligence (*Abwehr*) before being executed in 1945 for his role in the anti-Nazi resistance, as a thirty-year-old *Kapitänleutnant* succeeded Valentiner in command of *U 38*, then during 1918 sank four ships (23,592 tons) as commander of *U 34* and *UB 128*. Canaris, like Hartwig, had survived the Battle of the Falklands in December 1914 aboard the light cruiser *Dresden*, then escaped internment in neutral Chile to make his way home and into the submarine service. Martin Niemöller, more famous for his second career as a Protestant clergyman and leader of the Christian anti-Nazi resistance, survived eight years in concentration camps under the Third Reich. As a twenty-six-year-old *Oberleutnant*, Niemöller received command of *UC 67* after serving under Kophamel aboard *U 151* and sank three ships (9,903 tons) before the end of the war. Finally, Karl Dönitz, commander of Hitler's U-boats and, ultimately, the entire Nazi German navy, as a twenty-six-year-old *Oberleutnant* commanded both *UC 25* and *UB 68*, sinking five ships (16,598 tons) during 1918. Dönitz was captured by the British on 4 October when mechanical problems forced *UB 68* to surface after it sank the 3,883-ton steamer *Oopack* in a convoy 150 miles (240 km) east of Malta. He had planned to attack the convoy in tandem with Steinbauer's *UB 48*, which failed to reach their rendezvous point in time, leaving him to proceed alone. All but one of Dönitz's crew survived when the boat was scuttled. Decades later he harked back to the incident as key to his development of "wolf pack" tactics for the Second World War.[25] Whether Dönitz lost his boat because a plan went awry or because of his inexperience in dealing with the consequences remains open to debate. Generally, during 1918, the increase in the number of novice commanders in the Mediterranean and the full application there of the antisubmarine countermeasures that had been introduced earlier in northern waters resulted in a decline in the effectiveness of the U-boat force. Of the fifteen German submarines lost in the theater during the entire war, ten succumbed in its last year.

The Mediterranean efforts of the German and Austrian submarines operating out of Pola and Cattaro were supplemented during 1918 by U-boats from the German naval force at Constantinople, whose role had changed after Russia's departure from the war ended the fighting in the Black Sea. Because Sevastopol became part of Ukraine, the Germans gained control of most of the Russian Black Sea fleet (eventually acknowledged by the Soviets as a "loan," under an agreement signed 27 August 1918), raising fears among the Allies that these ships, with the Ottoman flagship *Yavuz Sultan Selim* (ex-*Goeben*), could break out into the Eastern Mediterranean. They never did, and the only such sortie by the flagship and its escort *Midilli* (ex-*Breslau*), on 20 January 1918, ended with the *Midilli* sunk and the *Yavuz Sultan Selim* badly damaged, both by mines. It was left to the U-boats based at Constantinople to exploit the newfound freedom of not having to focus on the Black Sea. Of the four still stationed there in 1918, the most active was *UC 23* (*Kapitänleutnant* Hans Georg Lübbe), which sank twenty-eight ships (17,399 tons) during the war's last year. On a raid into the Aegean Sea in October, Lübbe claimed seventeen victims, most of them small, most of them Greek, totaling 7,158 tons. After sinking three Greek sailing vessels in the Gulf of Salonika on 15 October, *UC 23* returned to Constantinople, where the German presence had been compromised by an offensive the Allied armies launched from northern Greece, which forced Bulgaria to conclude an armistice on 29 September. The loss of Bulgaria devastated the Central Powers, as it also closed the Danube to grain barges from Ukraine, ending their last hope of fending off another hungry winter. The Ottoman Empire soon quit the war, too, signing an armistice with the Allies on 30 October, which forced the Germans to end their naval mission. They departed Constantinople on 2 November, leaving behind the *Yavuz Sultan Selim*, which survived until 1971 as the flagship of the Turkish navy. Lübbe's *UC 23* and the other three U-boats ran for Sevastopol, where they eventually surrendered to the Allies.[26]

REFORM, REVOLUTION, AND RUNNING FOR HOME
Just as the collapse of Bulgaria made the German naval position at Constantinople untenable, the inability of the army to hold the western front after the start of the final Allied offensive (26–28 September) forced the evacuation of the bases at Zeebrugge and Ostend and the dissolution of the Flanders Flotilla. On 29 September, in an emergency meeting at Spa, Ludendorff informed William II and German political leaders that "the condition of the army demands an immediate armistice in order to avoid a catastrophe."[27] Scheer ordered the abandonment of Ostend later that day, followed by Zeebrugge, thirteen miles (21 km) to the east, on 3 October. The loss of the Flemish bases was a significant blow to the continuation of unrestricted submarine warfare. Scheer estimated that the Flanders Flotilla had claimed 23 percent of all Allied tonnage sunk, but operating on the enemy's doorstep had made the price of success very high; Fürbringer, captured by the British in July 1918 after surviving the sinking of

UB 110, his seventh Flanders U-boat, estimated that the flotilla ultimately lost 83 percent of boats that had served in it, a figure far greater than the loss rate of any other German submarine flotilla in the First World War. The decision not to evacuate Ostend and Zeebrugge earlier cost the navy another four U-boats, along with thirteen destroyers and torpedo boats, all of which were scuttled or abandoned when German forces left the area.[28]

Afterward, the generals of the High Command remained shameless in emphasizing the responsibility of the navy in making good their own failures. Indeed, Scheer recalled that "Ludendorff was in favor of keeping to the plan of strengthening the U-boat weapon" even at that late date, because "the threat it contained might be useful for securing the armistice desired by the army."[29] But by then, the generals realized that they faced more than just recriminations within a postwar Second Reich over whether the army or the navy had been most responsible for the failure to achieve the anticipated victory. They had lost the war, and they now advised William II to implement constitutional reforms, reasoning that a government including the Reichstag parties that had supported the Peace Resolution of July 1917 would be in a better position to negotiate with the Allies. This approach also allowed Hindenburg and Ludendorff to avoid responsibility for the defeat in the eyes of the public by putting the politicians they liked the least in the position of having to conclude the unfavorable peace that was certain to follow. The emperor agreed to the changes, and after Hertling resigned the chancellorship on 30 September, the liberal Prince Max of Baden organized a cabinet consisting of leaders of the SPD, the Center Party, and the Progressive People's Party, including Matthias Erzberger as minister without portfolio.

On 2 October, Ludendorff sent his deputy, Major Baron Erich von der Bussche, to tell a shocked Reichstag that "we cannot win the war" and the government would have to seek "the breaking-off of hostilities, so as to spare the German people and their allies further sacrifice."[30] The following day, while the navy completed its evacuation of Zeebrugge, Prince Max officially assumed the duties of chancellor. Rather than approach London or Paris, he cabled Washington to open a dialog with Wilson for an end to the war based on the Fourteen Points, the president's peace program outlined in a speech to the US Congress on 8 January 1918. In Austria-Hungary, Emperor Charles similarly sought to make his regime appear more palatable to Wilson and to identify himself with the American vision of a just peace. On 16 October he proclaimed a constitutional reform promising autonomy to the various nationalities of his empire, as Wilson had specifically demanded

FIGURE 8.1.
Prince Max of Baden
(German Federal Archives)

in the Fourteen Points. The following day, he started to distance Austria-Hungary from Germany by unilaterally ending his own navy's participation in unrestricted submarine warfare.[31]

On 17 October, Scheer joined Hindenburg and Ludendorff for meetings in Berlin. Their discussions with Prince Max and his cabinet focused on the latest correspondence from Wilson, a stern note written in the immediate aftermath of *UB 123*'s deadly sinking of the *Leinster* one week earlier. With the president's attention returning specifically to the U-boat issue, the chancellor recalled that his ministers felt "we could not now break off the armistice action once begun, simply for the sake of maintaining the intensified submarine war."[32] They were all willing to sacrifice the unrestricted campaign in order to keep the negotiations going, but Ludendorff, having succeeded in prompting the prince and the politicians to take responsibility for the peace talks, now distanced himself from his own earlier defeatism. Expressing confidence that the army could continue the fight into 1919, he argued that it was "impossible to abandon submarine warfare" because it was "continually reducing

England's strength."[33] Scheer likewise insisted that the campaign was still working and asserted that "the loss of the two submarine bases in Flanders and in the Mediterranean" would actually have the positive result of freeing the U-boats to "concentrate on the immediate neighborhood of the British Isles."[34] When Scheer reluctantly proposed offering Wilson "the cessation of the U-boat campaign . . . in exchange for the Armistice," Prince Max informed him that Germany was "not in a position to make conditions."[35]

Over the next four days, Scheer joined Ludendorff in continuing to make assertions that left both of them fully discredited in the eyes of Prince Max and his ministers, some of whom already felt "outflanked" by the High Command, seeing clearly that "now we are to be made responsible for losing the already-lost war."[36] At this point the chancellor's direct correspondence with Crown Prince Rupprecht of Bavaria, a field marshal on the western front, was a crucial corrective to the delusions and disinformation of Ludendorff and Scheer. Alluding to the failure of the U-boats to interdict troopships, Rupprecht, on 18 October, doubted that Germany had "any possibility of holding out [past] December, particularly as the Americans are drawing about 300,000 men monthly from beyond the ocean."[37] His estimate was remarkably accurate. By the time of the Armistice just over three weeks later, 2,079,880 US troops had been landed in France, and two-thirds of them, roughly 1.4 million men, were deployed on the western front, where their numbers far eclipsed the French army and, in the war's last days, also surpassed the British and Imperial forces. Over two million additional troops had been mobilized in the United States and would be ready for transport during 1919.[38] The long-term hopelessness of the situation left Prince Max with no alternative to continuing negotiations to avoid the sort of disaster Ludendorff himself had presaged on 29 September.

In light of the events that had triggered the American declaration of war in the first place, the chancellor believed that no serious peace talks with the United States would occur until after Germany had ended unrestricted submarine warfare. The argument that the unrestricted campaign was still "reducing England's strength" also rang hollow, as the tonnage sunk had continued to drop since summer, from 310,180 tons in August to just 171,970 in September and 116,240 in October, figures so low that the Americans believed the Germans had all but given up sinking cargo ships in a vain attempt to focus on troopships.[39] Prince Max felt it necessary, at the least, to include in his next note to Wilson a pledge that passenger ships would no longer be attacked. Scheer rejected the return to cruiser rules necessary to accommodate this pledge and reverted to his earlier position that such restrictions made commerce raiding too risky for submarines. He insisted that, if the chancellor held firm, "all U-boats sent out to make war on commerce must be immediately recalled."[40] Scheer was confident William II would support him against Prince Max and allow the navy to continue the unrestricted campaign, but the chancellor called his bluff and threatened to resign if the emperor took Scheer's side. William II agreed to the text of the note, capitulating "most unwillingly," in Prince Max's recollection. On 21 October, Scheer ordered home all U-boats then at sea, bringing an end to unrestricted submarine warfare.[41]

In sharp contrast to the less scrupulous adherence of U-boat commanders to the *Arabic* pledge and *Sussex* pledge at the end of the first unrestricted campaign, strict obedience to the order of the 21st gave the second round of unrestricted submarine warfare a more definitive ending. The last attack on an unarmed ship before the order was issued occurred earlier that day, when *UB 94* (*Kapitänleutnant* Waldemar Haumann) torpedoed and sank the 362-ton British coastal steamer *Saint Barchan* (8 dead) in Irish waters off the coast of County Down. Thereafter, the only clear case of rogue behavior came on 23 October, when the minelayer *UC 74* (now under *Oberleutnant* Hans Schüler), on patrol in the Eastern Mediterranean, inexplicably shelled and sank the 85-ton Greek sailing vessel *Aghios Gerasimos* in the waters south of Crete. Thanks to mines laid by U-boats earlier, unrestricted submarine warfare had a postscript of 14,057 tons destroyed in the first eleven days of November. Of this total, 10,233 tons were attributable to mines sown by *UC 74* off the mouth of the Suez Canal after 21 October as a consequence of Schüler's defiance (or creative interpretation) of the order to end the campaign against Allied shipping. The order of the 21st was only intended to end submarine activity against unarmed vessels, not warships. The last Allied warship was not sunk until the day before the Armistice, 10 November, when *Oberleutnant* Doemming, now in command of *UB 67* in the North Sea, torpedoed the 810-ton British minesweeper *Ascot* (51 dead).[42]

As the dozens of U-boats then active in the North Sea and Atlantic began to make their way to Wilhelmshaven and Kiel, German submariners operating in the Mediterranean faced nearly a week of uncertainty about what to do; initially they proceeded to Pola or Cattaro and remained there, awaiting further orders. Their comrades in the Austrian surface fleet had been largely inactive since summer, aside from an operation launched in late September to rescue Austrian troops stranded in northern Albania after the Allied Balkan offensive that broke the Bulgarian army made their positions at the western end of the same front untenable. The Austrian navy evacuated the troops via Durazzo and on 2 October fought its last battle there, a rearguard action against superior Allied forces featuring history's last action by an Austrian submarine, in which *U 31* (*Linienschiffsleutnant* Hermann Rigele) torpedoed and damaged the British light cruiser *Weymouth*. For the personnel of the Austrian armed forces, no less than the population of Austria-Hungary as a whole, Emperor Charles's autonomy proclamation of 16 October failed to allay the centrifugal forces and instead had the opposite effect; while the leaders of several nationalities began to create their own provisional governments, the soldiers on the Italian front and sailors at Pola and Cattaro became increasingly anxious about their immediate future. The Italian army struck the decisive blow on 24 October, launching a major offensive that met with little resistance. The Italian navy remained on the defensive, but the collapse of the Austrian army soon left the commercial port of Trieste and the naval base at Pola virtually defenseless from the land side. Charles, whose earlier efforts to quit the war had already been exposed in the "Sixtus Affair," responded to the crisis with a final effort for a separate peace and on 26 October declared an end to his country's alliance with Germany.[43]

While the time had long passed for Austria-Hungary to save itself, Charles's declaration finally triggered orders from Berlin for German submariners to close their Adriatic bases. Niemöller, in Pola as commander of *UC 67*, witnessed the feverish activity touched off by the order, on the 27th, "to get all seaworthy boats ready to return to Germany . . . in order to make them available for a last stand" and to scuttle all boats "that could not be ready to sail within twenty-four hours." At least some Austrians were keen to join them on their run for home; Niemöller reported that "four young Austrian naval officers came aboard" *UC 67* on the 28th, "asking for a passage to Germany," but all such requests were denied. The Germans sank ten submarines judged unable to handle the monthlong cruise home, most notably Steinbauer's *UB 48*. Their officers and crews, along with land-based support personnel, were sent back to Germany by rail. On 28–29 October, *UC 67* and the other seaworthy boats at Pola left for the southern Adriatic to rendezvous with others coming out of Cattaro. *Kapitänleutnant* Klasing had taken *U 34* out on patrol on 18 October, and his colleagues hoped to meet up with him en route, but his boat was never heard from again. Schüler had sortied with *UC 74* even earlier than *U 34*, was still in the Eastern Mediterranean, and would not be able to return to the Adriatic to refuel; thus he had no hope of making it home and ultimately sought refuge at Barcelona.

The disappearance of *U 34* and subsequent internment of *UC 74* in Spain left thirteen German U-boats to make the long voyage from the Adriatic to the Baltic via the Straits of Gibraltar.[44] The extensive turnover of officers in the war's last months had left all of the boats except Siess's *U 33*, Hartwig's *U 63*, and Canaris's *UB 128* in the hands of men who, like Niemöller, had just become commanders during 1918; Siess, the senior officer remaining, led the flotilla. After their departure, Horthy lost control of the Austrian fleet, which Charles soon resolved to turn over to the Yugoslav national council. On 31 October, Horthy presided over the transfer ceremonies in Pola, after which all officers and seamen not belonging to the South Slavic nationalities were furloughed. The following evening, Italian saboteurs infiltrated the harbor there and sank the dreadnought *Viribus Unitis*, just hours after it had become the Yugoslav flagship. While the Allies soon recognized Yugoslavia as the legitimate successor state to Serbia, at Italy's insistence they did not accept the transfer of the Austrian navy. By 9 November Italian flags flew over all of the former Austrian warships at Pola and Cattaro.[45]

The orders of 27 October, recalling the German Mediterranean U-boats "for a last stand," came amid a last-minute crisis between the High Command and Prince Max over the peace negotiations with Wilson, who had taken an increasingly harder line in his communications with the Germans. The chancellor expected a positive response to the end of unrestricted submarine warfare but instead received a note from the president on 24 October which, in Scheer's opinion, "quite clearly demanded complete capitulation."[46] Wilson questioned the constitutional reforms of William II and the legitimacy of Prince Max's government, concluding that if the United States "must deal with the military masters and the monarchical autocrats of Germany . . . it must demand not peace negotiations, but surrender."[47] The generals and Scheer again came to Berlin, this time against the wishes of Prince Max and the cabinet; to make matters worse, on the evening of the 24th, before they left Spa, Hindenburg issued an Order of the Day appealing to the armed forces "to continue our resistance with all our strength."[48] In meetings on 25 October, Scheer joined the generals in arguing for the rejection of Wilson's latest note, but their assurances of the fighting ability of an army that had retreated every day since 8 August, and of a fleet anchored in Wilhelmshaven since 25 April, failed to inspire much confidence. Meanwhile, the High Command's clear attempt to subvert the peace process led William II to accede to Prince Max's demand that Ludendorff be sacked. In an audience the following morning, the emperor held Ludendorff accountable for Hindenburg's defiant order, then dismissed him in favor of General Wilhelm Groener. Scheer, meanwhile, was not willing to have the High Sea Fleet finish the war at anchor. Without consulting William II or Prince Max, he hatched a scheme to take the navy's remaining dreadnoughts and battle cruisers on a sortie to the Thames estuary in the hope of drawing out the Grand Fleet for one last battle.

Scheer's design for the final engagement, known to history as Operations Plan 19, was set in motion via unwritten orders conveyed to Hipper on 22 October, shortly after the U-boats were recalled. Hipper fleshed out the plan over the days that followed, ultimately including in it over two dozen recalled U-boats. The fleet was scheduled to raise steam on the 29th and depart Wilhelmshaven on the 31st, but on the 27th, Hipper's preparations alerted the crews that a final sortie was imminent, and they began to resist orders for what they considered a suicide mission. Scheer soon acknowledged that "the idea had taken root in their minds that they were to be uselessly sacrificed."[49] On the 29th the growing mutiny forced Hipper to cancel the order to raise steam, but only after some of the U-boats with roles in the plan had already left port. These included *U 78* (now under *Oberleutnant* Johann Vollbrecht) which, on the 27th, sank with all hands after being torpedoed by British submarine *G 2* in the North Sea (40 dead) and *UB 116* (*Oberleutnant* Hans Joachim Emsmann) which, on the 28th, sank with all hands in a minefield while trying to infiltrate Scapa Flow (36 dead).[50] They were the last U-boats lost in action before the end of the war.

Hipper reversed course on 30 October and issued a patriotic appeal to the fleet, denying "that the officers of the navy desire a battle with a superior enemy such that the fleet would be shot to pieces and therefore not be surrendered with the armistice." He then sought to reinstate the sortie just for the U-boats and one of the dreadnought squadrons, a half measure that only served to spread the mutiny to that squadron. By the night of 30–31 October, after the mutiny had paralyzed the entire surface fleet, Hipper finally abandoned what was left of Operations Plan 19. He then focused on restoring order, and in the midst of the standoff he turned to his loyal U-boats for help against his mutinous dreadnoughts. At one point he ordered *Kapitänleutnant* Spiess, now in command of *U 135*, to position his boat to torpedo the *Helgoland*, *Ostfriesland*, and *Thüringen* while boarding parties of marines arrested some of their mutineers. But Hipper unwittingly spread the revolution by dispersing the fleet from Wilhelmshaven, sending some ships up the Elbe River and others through the Kiel Canal to the Baltic. On 2 November, the sailors of the squadron Hipper deployed to Kiel spread the mutiny to the shore installations there, and two days later they joined local workers and soldiers in forming a revolutionary council on the Soviet Russian model. As ship after ship raised the red flag, the besieged naval authorities in Kiel, like Hipper in Wilhelmshaven, turned to their most loyal forces, the submariners, to restore order. Valentiner, assigned to the staff of the U-boat school at nearby Eckern-förde after giving up command of *U 157*, had put to sea on the morning of the 4th to lead routine training exercises, only to be summoned to Kiel later in the day along with other senior U-boat commanders to help suppress the unrest. They had no hope of doing so, and by 5 November the U-boat base at Kiel was also in the hands of the revolutionaries. The following day, after word reached Wilhelmshaven that the revolutionary council had been formed in Kiel, mutinous sailors there joined soldiers and local workers in establish-ing a revolutionary council of their own. Through it all, Hipper remained aboard his flagship and, on the evening of 6 November, finally conceded to Scheer that he had lost control of the fleet. Earlier that day, two of the larger boats returning from Atlantic deployments—Arnauld's *U 139* and Franz's *U 152*—received instructions from *Kommodore* Michelsen, U-boat chief of the High Sea Fleet, to sink any red-flagged ships they encountered on their final approaches. Fortunately, neither had to act on the orders.[51]

By then, sailors had already helped spark the revolution in Hamburg and Bremen, while on the western front, increasing numbers of troops sur-rendered to the Allies. By 7 November, revolutionary councils had been established in cities throughout Germany, leading the Allied and German governments alike to recognize the need to conclude peace as soon as possible to prevent the establishment of a soviet-style republic. Prince Max designated Erzberger to lead a delegation to Marshal Foch's headquarters at Compiègne where, on the 8th, the Allies handed down terms that amounted to surren-der. The German army was to return to the country's 1914 borders (minus Alsace-Lorraine, to be ceded immediately to France, and the Rhineland, to be occupied by Allied troops) and then demobilize, while the newest ships of the High Sea Fleet and all U-boats were to be interned in Britain. The Al-lied armies and navies were to remain mobilized, and the blockade would be maintained until the signing of a definitive peace treaty. Given seventy-two hours to sign the Armistice, Erzberger sought further instructions, but neither the High Command at Spa nor Prince Max in Berlin had anything to offer him. At Spa on the morning of 9 November, it fell to Groener to in-form William II that "the army . . . no longer stands behind Your Majesty."[52] Scheer urged him not to abdicate and leave the navy without a commander-in-chief, to which the emperor, alluding to the mutinies, replied, "I no longer have a navy."[53] After mulling abdication for several hours, he was shocked by the news that Prince Max had already announced it, then resigned the chancellorship in favor of the SPD's Friedrich Ebert, head of the Reichstag's largest party. Shortly afterward came word that Ebert's SPD colleague Philipp Scheidemann had proclaimed a republic, apparently to preempt the far Left from proclaiming a soviet republic. Later that day the emperor left Spa for exile in the Netherlands. In the early hours of 11 November, Erzberger and the German delegation returned to Compiègne to sign the Armistice. Admiral Sir Rosslyn Wemyss, Jellicoe's successor as Britain's First Sea Lord, joined Foch in signing for the Allies. The cease-fire went into effect at 11:00 that morning.

The final mutiny of the High Sea Fleet, the collapse of the Second Reich, the proclamation of the republic, and the signing of the Armistice all occurred while the German Mediterranean U-boats were making their way home. Hartwig later recalled that he kept his *U 63* "more or less together" with the rest of the boats until they approached the Allied defenses at the Straits of Gibraltar, where "everything was in readiness for our coming," making an "every man for himself" strategy the only option for a successful passage.[54] Under the orders of 21 October ending unrestricted submarine warfare, they remained free to engage enemy warships, but on the month-long voyage home, only *Oberleutnant* Heinrich Kukat's *UB 50* attempted to target one: the pre-dreadnought *Britannia*, which he torpedoed and sank just after passing Gibraltar on 9 November (50 dead). Three days later, the news of the Armistice reached them via wireless while they were northwest of Spain, rounding Cape Finisterre. Niemöller's *UC 67* was one of several boats that participated in a rendezvous at which the commanders discussed "whether we should continue the voyage home or seek internment in a Spanish port." Their crews wanted to go home, and that decided it, yet Niemöller recalled that "no trouble of any kind was experienced" afterward. Indeed, the discipline of the crews was "absolutely unaffected" by the end of hostilities. They proceeded around the British Isles to the coast of Norway where, according to Hartwig, "we put in at one of the Norwegian fjords, and there got our first news of the revolution in Germany." The thirteen U-boats proceeded together through the Skagerrak and Kattegat and finally reached Kiel on 25 November, entering the harbor in formation, flying their battle flags.[55] By then, all other U-boats deployed in the war's last weeks had returned home, and some had already been turned over to the British under the terms of the Armistice.

NOTES

1. Scheer, *Germany's High Sea Fleet*, 333.
2. Ludendorff, *Ludendorff's Own Story*, 2:358.
3. Halpern, *A Naval History of World War I*, 423.
4. Ullrich, "Die Januarstreik 1918," 50.
5. http://uboat.net/wwi/men/commanders/crews.html.
6. Horn, *German Naval Mutinies*, 215.
7. Halpern, *A Naval History of World War I*, 423; Herwig, *"Luxury" Fleet*, 222; Ludendorff, *Ludendorff's Own Story*, 2:358.
8. Scheer, *Germany's High Sea Fleet*, 330–32.
9. Rössler, *Die deutschen U-Kreuzer*, 103, 108; http://uboat.net/wwi/boats/successes/u156.html; http://uboat.net/wwi/boats/successes/u157.html. The ships detached for the Mediterranean included fifty-five from HH convoys, fifty from HN convoys, and eight from HS convoys. Data compiled from ADM 137/2656, HH, HN, and HS précis of convoy reports.
10. Crowell and Wilson, *The Road to France*, 531; Rössler, *Die deutschen U-Kreuzer*, 109; Hiram W. Winn, *Fighting the Hun on the U.S.S. Huntington* (n.p., 1919), 91–92; http://uboat.net/wwi/boats/successes/u155.html.
11. Rössler, *Die deutschen U-Kreuzer*, 104, 110; http://uboat.net/wwi/boats/successes/u152.html.
12. Gröner, *Die deutschen Kriegsschiffe*, 3:44; *Conway 1906–21*, 179.
13. Gröner, *Die deutschen Kriegsschiffe*, 3:44–45. According to Rose, *Auftauchen!*, 297–98, the boat with the seaplane that was promised to him was scheduled for completion in December; Rössler, *Die deutschen U-Kreuzer*, 175, identifies this boat as *U 144*.
14. Thomas, *Raiders of the Deep*, 129.
15. Rössler, *Die deutschen U-Kreuzer*, 116–22; http://uboat.net/wwi/boats/successes/u140.html. *U 140* is almost certainly the "homeward bound submarine from [the] American coast" cited in ADM 137/2656, HS53, following a convoy that left Sydney on 28 August and reached the Buncrana destroyers on 8 September.
16. Rössler, *Die deutschen U-Kreuzer*, 124–28; http://uboat.net/wwi/boats/successes/u139.html; Arnauld quoted in Thomas, *Raiders of the Deep*, 340.
17. Gröner, *Die deutschen Kriegsschiffe*, 3:41–42; *Conway 1906–21*, 178–79; http://uboat.net/wwi/boats/successes/u117.html; http://uboat.net/wwi/boats/successes/u118.html; http://uboat.net/wwi/boats/successes/u122.html. *U 119* registered no successes on its lone patrol.
18. Herwig, *The First World War: Germany and Austria-Hungary*, 323–24; Rössler, *Die deutschen U-Kreuzer*, 121–22. Kemp, *U-Boats Destroyed*, 36, notes that survivors of at least one boat sunk during the labor unrest of 1917–18, *UC 55*, "blamed sabotage in the dockyard" for the loss of their boat, but the detailed account of the sinking of *UC 55* by one of its survivors, Kagelmann, *Unterseeboot-Minenleger*, 109–14, gives no indication of this suspicion.
19. http://uboat.net/wwi/ships_hit/losses_year.html?date=1918-10&string=September+1918; http://uboat.net/wwi/ships_hit/losses_year.html?date=1918-10&string=October+1918; http://uboat.net/wwi/ships_hit/losses_year.html?date=1918-10&string=November+1918.
20. Halpern, *A Naval History of World War I*, 424.

21. Hashagen, *U-Boats Westward*, 228–30; http://uboat.net/wwi/ships_hit/1759.html.

22. Crowell and Wilson, *The Road to France*, 439–40, 487; http://uboat.net/wwi/ships _hit/4266.html; http://uboat.net/wwi/ships_hit/4155.html.

23. ADM 137/2656, HS51; http://uboat.net/wwi/ships_hit/2200.html; http://uboat.net/ wwi/ships_hit/4178.html; http://uboat.net/wwi/ships_hit/2866.html; http://uboat.net/ wwi/ships_hit/3552.html; Kemp, *U-Boats Destroyed*, 58.

24. Sondhaus, *The Naval Policy of Austria-Hungary*, 329–36; http://uboat.net/wwi/ men/commanders/342.html; http://uboat.net/wwi/men/commanders/113.html.

25. http://uboat.net/wwi/men/commanders/43.html; http://uboat.net/wwi/men/com manders/226.html; http://uboat.net/wwi/men/commanders/55.html; Kemp, *U-Boats Destroyed*, 57. Dönitz, *Memoirs: Ten Years and Twenty Days*, 1–2.

26. Sondhaus, *The Great War at Sea*, 325–28; Eberhard Rössler, *Die Unterseeboote der Kaiserlichen Marine* (Coblenz: Bernard & Graefe Verlag, 1997), 145; http://uboat.net/wwi/ boats/index.html?boat=UC+23.

27. Quoted in Hajo Holborn, *A History of Modern Germany, 1840–1945* (Princeton, NJ: Princeton University Press, 1982), 502.

28. Scheer, *Germany's High Sea Fleet*, 340–41; Fürbringer, *Fips*, 53; *Conway 1906–21*, 169, 172.

29. Scheer, *Germany's High Sea Fleet*, 343.

30. Major Freiherr von der Bussche's Address to the Reichstag of the Recommendations of the German High Command, 2 October 1918, text at http://firstworldwar.com/ source/germancollapse_bussche.htm.

31. Sondhaus, *The Naval Policy of Austria-Hungary*, 348–49.

32. Prince Max of Baden, *The Memoirs of Prince Max of Baden*, trans. W. M. Calder and C. W. H. Sutton, 2 vols. (New York: Scribner, 1928), 2:98.

33. Ludendorff, *Ludendorff's Own Story*, 2:415.

34. Quoted in Max of Baden, *Memoirs*, 2:127.

35. Scheer, *Germany's High Sea Fleet*, 351, 353.

36. Conrad Haussmann (minister without portfolio) and Friedrich von Payer (vice chancellor), quoted in Max of Baden, *Memoirs*, 2:154.

37. Quoted in ibid., 2:158.

38. Kudlick, "Sealift for the AEF," http://www.worldwar1.com/dbc/sealift.htm#a.

39. Crowell and Wilson, *The Road to France*, 427. Mercantile tonnage totals given here are the round numbers cited most often. Data from http://uboat.net total 301,139 for August, 192,909 for September, and 127,453 for October. Most discrepancies stem from when and whether to count armed merchantmen as warships.

40. Scheer, *Germany's High Sea Fleet*, 352.

41. Max of Baden, *Memoirs*, 2:159.

42. http://uboat.net/wwi/ships_hit/5712.html; http://uboat.net/wwi/ships_hit/95.html; http://uboat.net/wwi/ships_hit/481.html; http://uboat.net/wwi/ships_hit/losses_year. html?date=1918-11&string=November+1918.

43. Sondhaus, *The Naval Policy of Austria-Hungary*, 340–50.

44. Niemöller, *From U-Boat to Pulpit*, 112–13. On the fate of *U 34*, see http://uboat.net/ wwi/boats/index.html?boat=34.

45. Sondhaus, *The Naval Policy of Austria-Hungary*, 350–58.

46. Scheer, *Germany's High Sea Fleet*, 354.

47. Wilson's Third Note [under signature of Secretary of State Robert Lansing], 23 October 1918, text in Max of Baden, *Memoirs*, 186–88.

48. Quoted in Ludendorff, *Ludendorff's Own Story*, 2:423.

49. Scheer, *Germany's High Sea Fleet*, 355.

50. Kemp, *U-Boats Destroyed*, 58–59.

51. "Appeal of Admiral Ritter von Hipper to the Enlisted Personnel of the High Sea Fleet," Wilhelmshaven, 30 October 1918, text in Tobias R. Philbin III, *Admiral von Hipper, the Inconvenient Hero* (Amsterdam: John Benjamins, 1982), 165–66. See also Horn, *German Naval Mutinies*, 222–26, 235–45, 261–64; Thomas, *Raiders of the Deep*, 3; Valentiner, *Der Schrecken der Meere*, 277; Rössler, *Die deutschen U-Kreuzer*, 110, 129.

52. Quoted in John W. Wheeler-Bennett, *Wooden Titan: Hindenburg in Twenty Years of German History, 1914–1934* (New York: William Morrow, 1936), 197.

53. Scheer, *Germany's High Sea Fleet*, 358.

54. Quoted in Thomas, *Raiders of the Deep*, 343.

55. Niemöller, *From U-Boat to Pulpit*, 117–18; Hartwig quoted in Thomas, *Raiders of the Deep*, 345.

9

Aftermath

Among U-boat commanders of the First World War, *Oberleutnant* Karl Dönitz counted as one of the fortunate ones. He survived the loss of his boat, *UB 68*, in the Mediterranean in October 1918, then went via Malta to a prisoner-of-war camp in Britain. He was released in July 1919, less than a month after the signing of the Versailles Treaty, and upon his return to Germany he reported to Kiel. There, the naval personnel director expressed confidence that "things won't always be like this" and that "within a couple of years or so . . . we shall once again have U-boats."[1] On that assurance, Dönitz decided to remain in the navy even though it no longer had a submarine service. Too many of his comrades did not live long enough to be given that choice. Of the 402 German submarine commanders on active duty in the years 1914–18 (including flotilla leaders), 396 commanded boats at some point during the war, of whom 150—nearly 40 percent—died in the line of duty. The naval school's Crew 08 and Crew 09, consisting of men aged twenty-seven and twenty-eight in 1918, produced the greatest number of U-boat commanders and also suffered the highest losses, with twenty-six of the forty-eight submariners in Crew 08 dying, and twenty-eight of the fifty-six in Crew 09. Dönitz's own class, Crew 10, had fared better but still lost a third of its submariners, nine of twenty-seven.[2]

The "couple of years" without U-boats turned out to be sixteen, for even after Adolf Hitler came to power, Nazi Germany waited until after Britain gave its permission in the Anglo-German Naval Treaty (18 June 1935) to once again have submarines. In the meantime, Dönitz returned to his roots in the cruiser service. He had begun the First World War aboard the light cruiser *Breslau*, escort of the battle cruiser *Goeben* on its flight to Constantinople in August 1914, and had served there, nominally in the Ottoman navy, until requesting a transfer to the U-boats in 1916. Serving once again in cruisers under the republic, Dönitz rose to the rank of *Fregattenkapitän* and eventually became captain of his own light cruiser, the *Emden*, before the commander of the navy, Admiral Erich Raeder, appointed him to head Nazi Germany's first group of U-boats in July 1935. The navy named the small submarine formation the Weddigen Flotilla to honor the hero of *U 9*. As the force continued to grow, Dönitz remained its commander, ultimately with the title *Führer der Unterseeboote*, en route to succeeding Raeder as Hitler's top admiral.

Dönitz did not rise to such heights because of a stellar record commanding U-boats in the First World War, having sunk just five ships before losing his boat and being captured. Political considerations also played little part, because he never joined the Nazi Party. Rather, he had the benefit of being the right age at the right time (still just forty-three in 1935) and became Hitler's U-boat chief first by outlasting most potential competitors, then by accepting the role at a time when the centrality of submarines in Germany's next naval war was not a foregone conclusion. At least in 1935, Dönitz believed that "in the formation of the new, balanced fleet" of the Third Reich, U-boats would have "only a small and comparatively unimportant part."[3] Until Dönitz's extraordinary promotion to overall navy commander in 1943, fellow former submariners who had remained in the surface fleet and become admirals there appeared to have made the better career decision. These included the fleet commander in 1939–40, Wilhelm Marschall, along with Rolf Carls, Alfred Saalwächter, and Otto von Schrader, all of whom played key roles in the conquest or occupation of Norway in 1940.

U-BOATS, THE ARMISTICE, AND THE TREATY OF VERSAILLES

The Allies wasted no time in insisting upon the implementation of the naval provisions of the Armistice. On the morning of 21 November, just ten days after Erzberger signed the document at Compiègne, the newest ships of the High Sea Fleet steamed across the North Sea from the Helgoland Bight to the mouth of the Firth of Forth. Most were still under the control of mutineers and had to be cajoled into flying their battle flags rather than the red banners of revolution; because Hipper had declined to remain at his post, his successor as head of the battle cruiser squadron, Vice Admiral Ludwig von Reuter, became de facto fleet commander. Upon their arrival, they met the ships of Britain's Grand Fleet, supplemented by a division of American dreadnoughts and three French cruisers. Admiral Beatty formed the Allied vessels into two columns for the German warships to pass between. At the close of the ninety-minute review, the Germans dropped anchor at Rosyth and struck their battle flags. The interned ships were transferred to the Grand Fleet base at Scapa Flow on 25–27 November, after which periodic repatriations gradually sent home over 90 percent of their crews. Less than two thousand were still with the captive fleet on 21 June 1919, one week before the signing of the Treaty of Versailles, when Reuter, in anticipation of having to surrender the ships, ordered them all to scuttle. The German public applauded this final act of defiance, and when the last of the crews finally made it home, they were greeted as heroes.

Germany's U-boats were turned over under a separate process and interned at the British naval base at Harwich, home to the light cruisers and destroyers that had protected the eastern approaches to the Straits of Dover. The German navy ended the war with 134 submarines in commission (one more than at the beginning of 1917, when the decision was made to resume the unrestricted campaign), plus sixteen Type *UC III* minelayers completed but not placed in service. Together, these accounted for most of the 176 boats ultimately sent to Harwich. The remaining twenty-six came from among those deactivated earlier for training purposes, interned in neutral countries, or nearing completion when the war ended. The latter included a small number of boats made seaworthy in order to be turned over, but most of the 224 boats still in the shipyards at various stages of completion were broken up for scrap.[4]

The first twenty U-boats left for the crossing to Harwich on 18 November, a week after the Armistice and a week before the return of the thirteen surviving units of the Mediterranean flotilla. They were accompanied by two accommodation ships (*Wohnschiffe*), the converted merchantmen that functioned as dormitories for submariners during their time in port. They arrived two days later, and after the boats were turned over, the officers and crews returned to Germany aboard their accommodation ships. By 1 December six groups of submarines, 122 in all, were delivered to Harwich in the same manner, among them five boats that had been interned briefly in Sweden by commanders who sought to avoid the revolution at home. The remaining fifty-four made the crossing after the first of the year, fifty in eight smaller groups during the stormy winter months of January, February,

and March, many of which had to be towed, and the last four boats during April, towed individually. These included the thirteen Mediterranean
boats, another seven that had been interned in neutral countries, plus the
sixteen Type *UC III* minelayers and the recently completed boats that had
never been commissioned. Those unable to cross under their own power
included the two extremes: older boats whose engines required repairs too
extensive to be made in the allotted time, and newer ones with machinery
still untested in trials. Five U-boats were lost on the crossing when their
tow lines broke; much to the delight of Otto Hersing, these included *U 21*,
which sank in the North Sea on 22 February. The transfers finally ended on
24 April with the arrival of *UC 109* at Harwich.[5]

The Germans had to account for every submarine deemed remotely capable of offensive action. The British ultimately allowed *U 1* and *U 2* to remain
behind (the former to eventually become an exhibit at the Deutsches Museum
in Munich) but insisted that *U 3* be sent to Harwich, even though it had been
a training boat since before 1914 and never went on patrol during the war.
They rejected a German appeal to keep Weddigen's *U 9* as a "tradition boat"
(*Traditionsboot*) and required its inclusion in the fifth group, which made
the crossing on 25–26 November. The Imperial Navy Office placed the value
of the 176 interned U-boats at 171.5 million Marks. The British also insisted
on the transfer of two submarine dry docks, the salvage ship *Cyklop*, and
machinery from incomplete boats scrapped in Germany, assets collectively
valued at another 45.5 million, bringing the total to 207 million Marks.[6]

The Treaty of Versailles (28 June 1919) included seventeen "naval clauses"
as articles 181 through 197, of the total 440 articles in the full document. All
German warships already interned were declared surrendered, and older
dreadnoughts not given up earlier with the rest of the High Sea Fleet were to
be turned over within two months. The postwar German navy was left with
a core of six obsolete pre-dreadnought battleships, backed by a limited number of light cruisers, destroyers, and torpedo boats. It was prohibited from
replacing its lost dreadnoughts, battle cruisers, and submarines and, owing to
a general ban on German military aviation, could have no aircraft carriers.[7]
The former German U-boats were soon divided among the victorious Allies
as reparations. All were scrapped or used for targets in postwar exercises except for ten boats commissioned by the French navy, most notably Arnauld's
U 139, which remained active until 1935 under the name *Halbronn*, and
seven commissioned by the Japanese navy, all of which served only briefly, in

FIGURE 9.1.   Surrendered U-boats at Harwich (Imperial War Museum)

1920–21. In the dispersal of the much smaller Austrian navy, the French also recovered Austrian *U 14* (ex-*Curie*), captured attempting a raid on Pola early in the war, and recommissioned it under its original name.[8] Germany's use of U-boats as commerce raiders inspired a rekindling of the Jeune École within the French navy, to such an extent that when Britain proposed an outright ban on submarines at the Washington Naval Conference of 1921–22, France took the lead in opposing it. For the five victorious Allied powers (Britain, France, Italy, Japan, and the United States), postwar naval arms control placed strict limits on capital ships, more flexible limits on cruisers and aircraft carriers, and left submarines unregulated, reflecting their ultimate consensus that there was nothing wrong with submarines in general, just German submarines. Because Germany's naval limits were prescribed by the Versailles Treaty rather than the Washington Treaty of 1922, its navy was the only one not allowed to have them.

The Versailles Treaty also envisioned war crimes trials, with U-boat commanders among the defendants. While Article 227 specifically arraigned William II "for a supreme offense against international morality and the sanctity of treaties," Article 228 required Germany to "hand over to the Allied and Associated Powers . . . all persons accused of having committed an act in violation of the laws and customs of war."[9] In February 1920, the Allied countries presented Germany with a list of 890 persons against whom allegations had been leveled, including all of the prominent admirals plus fifty-one submarine officers; aside from Valentiner, wanted by the Italians for sinking the *Ancona* in 1915, all of the naval personnel made the list at the insistence of the British.[10] Ironically, after introducing the notion of treating U-boat officers as war criminals while serving as First Lord of the Admiralty, Churchill, as postwar air minister, blocked the indictment of zeppelin officers who had bombed civilian targets in order not to create a precedent for future RAF personnel to be held accountable for air raids on enemy cities.[11] Such glaring inconsistencies undermined the legitimacy of the process, and from the start, the Dutch government's refusal to extradite William II compromised plans to try alleged war criminals before Allied judges.

The German government likewise refused to extradite any of the 890 men accused under Article 228 and proposed instead trying them before the German supreme court (*Reichsgericht*) in Leipzig. The Allies agreed and also consented to a dramatic reduction in the list of defendants, removing the political leaders and commanding generals, along with Tirpitz, Scheer, and the admirals. Ultimately seventeen defendants were tried in Leipzig between January 1921 and November 1922, six against whom the Germans themselves brought charges, plus eleven indicted by the Allies. The latter included three U-boat officers: Karl Neumann, commander of *UC 67* when it sank the hospital ship *Dover Castle*, and Helmut Patzig's subordinates Ludwig Dithmar and John Claus Boldt, held accountable for *U 86*'s sinking of the hospital ship *Llandovery Castle*. Patzig himself avoided prosecution by seeking refuge in his hometown of Danzig, which was not under the jurisdiction of German courts because the Versailles Treaty had made it a free city under the League of Nations. Of the eleven defendants indicted by the Allies, Dithmar, Boldt, and two of the military men were found guilty, while Neumann and six of the soldiers were found not guilty. Dithmar and Boldt, convicted in July 1921, each received four years' imprisonment, by far the harshest sentences handed down. The proceedings were deeply resented in Germany but were considered farcical by Allied observers. Neumann, for example, was exonerated in June 1921 in a trial that lasted barely two hours. The Allied governments eventually gave up on the whole process, but their experience helped shape the approach to war crimes trials after 1945.[12]

FORMER SUBMARINERS UNDER THE REPUBLIC

While most Germans whom the Allies considered war criminals thus escaped punishment, the court of public opinion within Germany proved to be far less lenient toward the political leaders it held accountable for losing the war. The complete collapse of November 1918 made irrelevant the army's quest to set up the navy as the service responsible for failing to deliver victory, but Ludendorff's cynical maneuvers during the war's last months sufficed to absolve the High Command of responsibility, at least in the eyes of most Germans. By the following autumn, both Hindenburg and Ludendorff had rewritten history to whitewash their own role in encouraging the parties of the Peace Resolution to form the constitutional government and conclude the Armistice, alleging instead that the army had been "stabbed in the back" by the home front, in particular by the leaders of those same parties. The field marshal's public articulation of this viewpoint on 18 November 1919, before a Reichstag committee of inquiry, put Ebert and the leaders of the new republic in a position from which they never recovered.[13] According to the stab-in-the-back myth (*Dolchstosslegende*), prominent liberals and socialists (to whom the anti-Semites added prominent Jews) were responsible for losing the war that the army had won and were collectively branded "the November criminals." But the navy was not completely blameless, at least in the eyes of Prince Max of Baden. He connected the dots from Scheer's ill-conceived Operations Plan 19 to Hipper's botched implementation of it, the ultimate mutiny of the High Sea Fleet, and Hipper's fateful decision to disperse the rebellious ships, which sparked the revolution in Kiel that spread like wildfire to other cities. Prince Max thus held the navy, or at least its leading admirals, responsible for leaving his government with no choice but to accept whatever terms the Allies offered at Compiègne: "No Kiel, no revolution; no revolution, no capitulation on 11 November!"[14]

While the mutinous sailors of the High Sea Fleet indeed played a critical role in the revolution that brought down the Second Reich, amid the chaos of the winter of 1918–19 those serving in the branches of the navy where morale had remained the highest were more likely to rally behind their officers in defense of traditional order. Disproportionate numbers of officers and seamen from the submarine and torpedo boat flotillas joined conservative army colleagues in forming the right-wing paramilitary *Freikorps*, which ultimately included three naval brigades. The *Freikorps* opposed the republic but pragmatically supported Ebert's government against the threat from the far Left and its vision of a soviet republic, most notably in crushing the Spartacist Revolt (5–15 January 1919). Some lesser-known submariners joined the First Marine Brigade, commanded by an army colonel, Emmo von Roden, and *Korvettenkapitän* Hermann Ehrhardt's Second Marine Brigade, which consisted primarily of men from the torpedo flotillas, but more joined the Third Marine Brigade of *Korvettenkapitän* Wilfried von Löwenfeld, a former adjutant to Scheer, which Wilhelm Canaris helped organize. Lothar von Arnauld and Kurt Hartwig were the most prominent U-boat commanders in the Löwenfeld Brigade, but others of note included Constantin Kolbe, Hermann von Fischel, Heinrich Middendorff, Heinrich Kukat, and future SS man Carl-Siegfried von Georg. While the Roden Brigade disbanded in May 1919, the other naval *Freikorps* formations survived until May 1920. In the spring of 1919 the Ehrhardt Brigade ventured as far south as Bavaria to help suppress the Left in Munich. The Löwenfeld Brigade spent most of 1919–20 in Upper Silesia, fighting against Poles in an area where a plebiscite ultimately determined the border between Germany and the restored Polish state.[15]

Once the *Freikorps* had served their purpose, Ebert sought their abolition, which was required in any event under the terms of the Versailles Treaty. His order precipitated an attempt by Tirpitz's old Fatherland Party associate Wolfgang Kapp to overthrow the government, led by the Ehrhardt Brigade in Berlin and supported by the Löwenfeld Brigade in Breslau. The Kapp Putsch (13–17 March 1920) failed when Ebert mobilized the SPD and far Left behind a general strike that paralyzed the country, making it impossible for Kapp to govern. Ironically, after the putsch collapsed, Ebert did not hesitate to use the naval brigades against a communist uprising in the Ruhr, which was crushed in early April; casualties there included Kukat of the Löwenfeld Brigade, the only former U-boat commander to die in Germany's paramilitary violence. Other former submariners participating in the suppression of the Ruhr uprising included Martin Niemöller, who took a break from his postwar theology studies at the University of Münster to command a *Freikorps* student battalion, the *Akademische Wehr Münster*. After the *Freikorps* were dissolved, Ehrhardt recruited several torpedo flotilla veterans into the terrorist group *Organisation Consul*, which assassinated Matthias Erzberger in August 1921 and foreign minister Walther Rathenau, the most prominent Jewish member of the government, in June 1922. In between these murders, some of the same former torpedo officers also masterminded the escape from prison and flight abroad of the navy's two convicted war criminals, Boldt in November 1921 and Dithmar in January 1922, both of whom were free to return to Germany after the *Reichsgericht* overturned their convictions in 1928.[16]

After the disbanding of the *Freikorps*, many veterans of the "gray navy" of the Löwenfeld and Ehrhardt brigades returned to naval service and to an uneasy reintegration with the "blue navy" of officers such as Dönitz, who had sat out the paramilitary violence.[17] Because most submariners were not interested in serving in a navy without submarines, few among those returning were U-boat men. While Dönitz and a handful of other former submariners assumed roles in the surface fleet, at least some of their former colleagues went undercover as civilians to keep Germany active in submarine research and development. The Allied powers unwittingly facilitated this effort by allowing the German navy to keep money from the sales of ships required to be scrapped under the Versailles Treaty. The proceeds amounted to 100 million Marks, enough to establish the Dutch firm *Ingenieurskantoor voor Scheepsbouw* or IvS, a front company for a consortium of three of the top four private German submarine manufacturers (AG Weser, AG Vulcan, and Germania). From 1922 until 1933, IvS built submarines in the Netherlands for export abroad and developed designs for submarines built in other countries. IvS had direct relationships with the navies of Spain, Finland, and Turkey, and its consulting clients included the navies of Italy, Japan, and Argentina. German engineers designed the submarines, which were equipped with German engines. German personnel operated the boats during their trials and delivered those built in the Netherlands to their new owners. Veterans of the Flanders Flotilla played prominent roles as employees of IvS, including Werner Fürbringer, who moved to the Netherlands in the 1920s and later represented the firm in Turkey, and Karl Bartenbach, the former flotilla chief, who supervised submarine construction in Finland and later served as a naval advisor in Argentina. Both eventually reentered German naval service to continue their work after Hitler's accession brought the dissolution of IvS. Meanwhile, the navy of the republic created an antisubmarine warfare section in 1925, a thinly disguised submarine section which allowed aspiring submariners to keep abreast of the latest developments in other navies.[18]

FORMER SUBMARINERS UNDER THE THIRD REICH

The leading U-boat commanders of the First World War played no role in the initial restoration of the German submarine service under the Third Reich. All were seven to nine years older than Dönitz and thus already at least fifty by the time Germany once again had U-boats. Valentiner, Rose, Forstmann, Siess, and Steinbrinck all took the same path of leaving the navy in 1919, sitting out the *Freikorps* violence, and then pursuing successful careers in business and industry before serving in various roles on land during the Second World War. Only two of them ever had anything to do with U-boats again. Valentiner returned to active duty from 1934 to 1945 as a naval staff officer, ultimately supervising wartime submarine construction, while Rose returned in 1939 to serve briefly first on Dönitz's staff, then in command of a U-boat training detachment, before spending 1940–43 in administrative roles in occupied Norway. Forstmann likewise returned to active duty in 1939 and spent 1940–45 in administrative roles in occupied Denmark. After earning a pilot's license as a civilian, Siess joined the Luftwaffe upon its creation in 1935 and retired from it in 1944 at the rank of *Generalleutnant*. Only Steinbrinck became a Nazi, joining the party in 1933 and subsequently also the SS. He returned to naval service in 1939 but spent the war in administrative roles supervising steel production in the occupied territories of the Low Countries and France. Convicted of war crimes, he died in prison in 1949. Valentiner died the same year, but the others lived remarkably long lives, Rose dying at eight-four, Siess at eighty-six, and Forstmann at ninety.[19]

Of the top U-boat aces of 1914–18, only Arnauld died during the Second World War, after also logging more time in naval service than the others. He reentered the navy from the *Freikorps* in 1920 and commanded cruisers before retiring in 1931 at age forty-five. Following six years as a professor at the Turkish naval academy, he returned to Germany in 1938 and to active duty, at the rank of vice admiral, by the time of Hitler's invasion of Poland. After spending 1939–40 in an administrative post at Danzig, he was assigned to Brest following the fall of France, ultimately with the title *Admiral West Frankreich* and the task of organizing the German naval presence on the Bay of Biscay. In February 1941 he was killed in a plane crash at a Paris airport while en route from Bordeaux to Berlin to be briefed on his next assignment. Arnauld died just before his fifty-fifth birthday; had he lived, he would have likely finished the war in some prominent capacity within the navy.[20]

Just two of the surviving U-boat commanders of the First World War also commanded a submarine during the Second. Bruno Mahn sank six ships (7,844 tons) on three patrols as a thirty-year-old reserve *Oberleutnant* commanding *UB 21* during 1918, then sank one ship (7,628 tons) as a *Kapitän zur See* in command of the captured Dutch submarine *UD 5* during 1942 on a single patrol that ended just before his fifty-fifth birthday. Hermann Rigele commanded four Austrian U-boats as a *Linienschiffsleutnant* during the years 1916–18, torpedoing the British cruiser *Weymouth* at the Battle of Durazzo while at the helm of *U 31*; as a citizen of Nazi Germany after the annexation of Austria in 1938, he entered German naval service at the rank of *Fregat-tenkapitän* and sank one ship (5,041 tons) while commanding the captured Dutch submarine *UD 3* on three patrols in 1942–43, during the year after he turned fifty-one. Rigele's colleague Georg von Trapp, whose thirteen naval and mercantile victims (60,294 tons) made him the most successful Austrian U-boat commander of 1914–18, avoided Nazi German service, though not for the reasons given in the heavily fictionalized film *The Sound of Music* (1965), released eighteen years after his death. The widower of the heiress to the Whitehead torpedo fortune, Trapp was fifty-eight when the Germans annexed Austria and was thus an unlikely candidate for active duty; in any event, he chose Italian citizenship after the First World War and could have entered the German navy only as a foreign volunteer. In 1938 Trapp, his second wife, and their musically talented children "escaped" from the Nazis by taking a train to Italy and then eventually emigrating to the United States.[21]

UNRESTRICTED SUBMARINE WARFARE IN TWO WORLD WARS

In the face of superior Allied naval power, the "balanced fleet" of Nazi Germany fared no better than the High Sea Fleet of Imperial Germany. Unrestricted submarine warfare once again became the focal point of the German effort at sea, but only after the surface fleet had failed to make a difference. Otherwise, the German submarine effort of 1939–45 bore little resemblance to the campaign of 1914–18. The conquests of 1940 left Norway and France in German hands, giving U-boats with bases on their coasts free access to the Atlantic. Britain was unable to blockade the Third Reich as it had the Second Reich, and the altered strategic geography made antisubmarine barrages irrelevant. But the other countermeasures of the First World War all returned, in more refined and effective forms. Instead of primitive hydrophones, the Allies had sonar (asdic) to detect U-boats, and a more sophisticated convoy system operated from the onset of the war. Most important of all, aircraft (both land-based and deployed from escort carriers) emerged as the most effective antisubmarine weapon. These factors combined to transform the way U-boats operated, forcing them to carry out the vast majority of their attacks underwater. Whereas in the First World War most targets were sunk with the deck gun, in the Second almost all had to be sunk with torpedoes, and the limited number of torpedoes on board thus limited the damage that could be done even on a successful patrol. In the face of these challenges, Dönitz deployed a force capable of keeping the sea-lanes in play by maintaining the highest standards of training, introducing "wolf pack" tactics

FIGURE 9.2.
Karl Dönitz
(German Federal Archives)

for attacks on convoys and, perhaps most important of all, getting Hitler to agree to the mass production of medium-sized U-boats, thus repudiating the U-cruiser experiments of 1917–18. Of the 1,171 U-boats constructed during the Second World War, 863 of which eventually sortied, few had a surfaced displacement greater than 1,200 tons. The most replicated design, the 568 boats of Type *VIIC*, displaced just 769 tons, with a speed (nearly 18 knots surfaced, nearly 8 knots submerged) only modestly better than the fastest U-boats of the First World War.[22]

In the final analysis, the German submarine campaign of 1914–18 was more successful than that of 1939–45, and at a far lower cost. The U-boats of the Imperial German navy sank 11.9 million tons in a war that lasted fifty-one months, against losses of 178 boats and 4,474 men, while the U-boats of the Nazi German navy sank 14.6 million tons in a war lasting sixty-eight months, at the staggering cost of 754 boats and 27,491 men lost. German submarine service was risky enough during the First World War, when 53 percent (178 of 335) of all boats that sortied did not return and 120 were lost with all hands.[23] It became practically suicidal in the Second World War, when the figure rose to 87 percent (754 of 863) not returning, including 429 for which there were no survivors.[24] In both wars, the most talented U-boat commanders sank a disproportionate share of the Allied shipping, but in the Second World War a remarkable number recorded no successes at all. By one estimate, in the years 1939–45 just 321 U-boats sank or damaged an Allied ship, and 2 percent of the commanders claimed 30 percent of the tonnage.[25] In contrast, in 1914–18 the top 2 percent sank less than 20 percent of the tonnage, despite their number including Arnauld's lopsided achievement of 455,869 tons, a figure that dwarfed the total of his counterpart in the next generation, Otto Kretschmer, whose 273,043 tons sufficed to top the table for 1939–45.

While the leading submariners of the First World War avoided prosecution for war crimes, the Allies held Dönitz accountable for the undersea campaign of the Second World War. Having been appointed, in Hitler's will, to the revived office of Reich president, he could hardly have been excluded from the ranks of the defendants at the Nuremberg trials, even though he functioned as head of state for barely a week, between Hitler's suicide and Germany's unconditional surrender. Of those found guilty in 1946, Dönitz received the shortest sentence, ten years' imprisonment, thanks in part to Admiral Chester Nimitz of the US Navy, who testified that his own country had waged unrestricted submarine warfare in the Pacific. Indeed, American submarines had sunk 5.3 million tons of Japanese shipping in the years 1941–45, in history's third-deadliest unrestricted campaign, trailing only the two German efforts.[26] Dönitz enjoyed nearly a quarter century of freedom before dying in 1980 and thus ranked among the longest-surviving U-boat commanders of the First World War, along with the Austrian Rigele, who died in 1982, and Dönitz's Crew 10 classmate Martin Niemöller, who died in 1984.

CONCLUSION

During the First World War, the German navy in general, and its submariners in particular, valiantly, perhaps foolishly, embraced the notion that unrestricted submarine warfare would enable their country to prevail in a war against a superior array of foes in which every other strategy had failed to achieve victory. Yet they would have succeeded only if the Allies had declined to mobilize the resources at their disposal to counter them. Werner Fürbringer's confession of feeling that the U-boats were "pitted in a gigantic battle against practically all the tonnage in the world"[27] proved to be an accurate assessment of the enormity of the mission they had undertaken. While the volume of shipping sunk in the first months after the resumption of the unrestricted campaign in 1917 caused grave concerns for the Allies, the task they faced, though difficult, proved to be far from impossible, and the linchpin—extensive Anglo-American cooperation, on short notice—ultimately served them well as a model for how to win the next war, too.

During and after the war, the navy's advocates of the unrestricted use of U-boats, from Tirpitz down to the submarine commanders themselves, blamed their failure on the indecision and doubts of the emperor and civilian leaders and argued that a truly ruthless application of submarine warfare would have delivered victory. In their postwar memoirs, many U-boat men echoed Scheer's assertion that the campaign of 1917–18 had come too late, postulating that if the policy had been resumed in the spring of 1916, as Tirpitz wanted, or at the latest, that summer, after Jutland, the outcome would have been different.[28] But their reminiscences were also full of examples of the times when they, or their colleagues, had been extraordinarily scrupulous in the conduct of their duties, sparing potential targets or towing lifeboats to give their victims a better chance at survival. Arnauld was only the most prominent among the large number of officers who operated more or less the same way during the unrestricted periods as he did under the restrictions of cruiser rules. There was, after all, only one *Lusitania* and only one *Llandovery Castle*; the coldbloodedness of a Schwieger in sinking a liner with over a thousand passengers on board, or of a Patzig in firing on the lifeboats of a torpedoed hospital ship, clearly were exceptions to the standard by which most U-boat commanders operated. Notwithstanding their laments about having to fight "fettered,"[29] or "with our hands tied behind our backs,"[30] most were incapable of the very sort of ruthlessness needed for the total war they claimed to desire. No less than the leaders they scorned, they struggled to reconcile policy with principle. Yet in allowing their discourse to be dominated by the argument that the undersea campaign failed because it had not been ruthless enough, they ignored the sobering amount of damage U-boats had done to the Allied war effort during the interlude of restricted submarine warfare, all without provoking the United States into entering the war. They were unwilling to acknowledge that submarine warfare, unrestricted, served the same strategic purpose as it did in the restricted form, as a useful complementary tool in an arsenal of means to disrupt the enemy's war effort, but far from the only or even the primary means.

On the level of policy, far above the pay grade of a *Kapitänleutnant* commanding a U-boat, the emperor, generals, admirals, and most politicians too readily embraced the argument that German unrestricted submarine warfare was the moral equivalent of the British blockade. Even though it had begun as an ad hoc response to Britain's plan to achieve victory by strangling Germany economically, American public and political opinion never accepted its legitimacy. After German leaders ignored clear early signs of this rejection, too many of them dismissed the importance of the United States altogether. During the war Germany pursued its aims in the same clumsy, tone deaf manner that it had in the prewar years, at least since the retirement of Bismarck in 1890, only with far more lethal means. The Allies also torpedoed unarmed ships, used poison gas on the battlefield, and dropped bombs on cities from the air, but the Germans bore the stigma of having done each of these things first. Despite causing more damage to the enemy at a lower cost than history's other great examples of unrestricted submarine warfare, the German U-boat campaign of 1914–18 failed utterly where it mattered most. In rationalizing the risk of renewing unrestricted submarine warfare in February 1917, the German leadership took for granted that U-boats would be able to stop the transport of an American army to France. In taking up the cause of unrestricted submarine warfare after Tirpitz's retirement, Admiral Holtzendorff argued that it was "the right means to bring the war to a victorious end," and also "the only means to that end."[31] But by bringing the United States into the war while also failing to stop the deployment of its troops to Europe, unrestricted submarine warfare caused Germany to lose the war, and to lose it within a political-diplomatic context shaped by American ideals, thereby accelerating the collapse of the Second Reich in favor of a republic that, fatefully, too few Germans were willing to support.

NOTES

1. Dönitz, *Memoirs: Ten Years and Twenty Days*, 5.

2. http://uboat.net/wwi/men/commanders/crews.html. In his account of a 1928 visit to the officers' club in Wilhelmshaven with Arnauld, Thomas, *Raiders of the Deep*, 130–31, refers to the photographs of 151 lost submarine commanders displayed on the walls. The discrepancy of one is almost certainly because of Heinrich Kukat, the only former U-boat officer killed in the postwar *Freikorps* (see section below). The officers leading Austria-Hungary's much smaller undersea effort had a significantly higher survival rate. Of the fifty Austrian U-boat commanders active in the years 1914–18, forty-six commanded boats during the war, of whom five died in action. For details of the Austrian submarine commanders, see Lawrence Sondhaus, "The Austro-Hungarian Naval Officer Corps, 1867–1918," *Austrian History Yearbook* 24 (1993): 77–78.

3. Dönitz, *Memoirs: Ten Years and Twenty Days*, 7.

4. Grant, *U-Boats Destroyed*, 140.

5. Rössler, *Die Unterseeboote*, 145–49.

6. Ibid., 146, 149.

7. "Peace Treaty of Versailles, Articles 159–213: Military, Naval and Air Clauses," text at http://net.lib.byu.edu/~rdh7/wwi/versa/versa4.html.

8. *Conway 1922–46*, 258; http://uboat.net/wwi/fates/listing.html.

9. "Peace Treaty of Versailles, Articles 227–230: Penalties," text at http://net.lib.byu.edu/~rdh7/wwi/versa/versa6.html.

10. Edwin L. James, "7 Nations Demand 890 War Culprits," *New York Times*, 4 February 1920, 1–2. Keith W. Bird, *Weimar, the German Naval Officer Corps, and the Rise of National Socialism* (Amsterdam: B. R. Grüner Publishing, 1977), 66, has twenty-nine "U-boat captains" among 895 names on the final list.

11. Willis, *Prologue to Nuremberg*, 128.

12. Gerd Hankel, *Die Leipziger Prozesse: Deutsche Kriegsverbrechen und ihre strafrechtliche Verfolgung nach dem Ersten Weltkrieg* (Hamburg: Hamburger Edition, 2003), 103, 420–23, 452–64.

13. Wheeler-Bennett, *Wooden Titan*, 233–38.

14. Max of Baden, *Memoirs*, 2:285.

15. The Löwenfeld Brigade also maintained a detachment in Kiel and in July 1919 deployed against striking railway workers. See Bird, *Weimar*, 46–48.

16. Hankel, *Die Leipziger Prozesse*, 464–70, 500–506. Dithmar eventually returned to naval service under the Third Reich; Boldt, who had fled to South America, committed suicide there in 1931.

17. Bird, *Weimar*, 246.

18. Holger H. Herwig, "Innovation Ignored: The Submarine Problem—Germany, Britain, and the United States, 1919–1939," in *Military Innovation in the Interwar Period*, ed. Williamson Murray and Allan R. Millett (Cambridge: Cambridge University Press, 1996), 231–33; Fürbringer, *Fips*, 139–41.

19. Karl-Friedrich Hildebrand and Christian Zweng, *Die Ritter des Ordens Pour le Mérite des I. Weltkriegs*, 3 vols. (Bissendorf: Biblio Verlag, 2011), passim.

20. Yves Dufeil, "Lothar von Arnauld de la Perière," http://www.histomar.net/arnauld/htm/indexarnauld.htm.

21. http://uboat.net/wwi/men/commanders/194.html; http://uboat.net/men/commanders/774.html; http://uboat.net/wwi/men/commanders/531.html; http://uboat.net/men/commanders/1009.html; Sondhaus, *The Naval Policy of Austria-Hungary*, 366–67.

22. http://uboat.net/types/viic.htm.

23. The Austrians suffered proportionally less than the Germans, losing 8 of their 27 U-boats (30 percent), four with all hands, but significantly more than the Allies, among whom the British lost just 43 of 269 submarines (16 percent); the French, 13 of 72 (18 percent); the Italians, 8 of 75 (11 percent); and the Russians, through December 1917, 9 of 61 (15 percent). See *Conway, 1906–21*, 86–94, 207–12, 274–78, 312–17, 342–44.

24. Michael Gannon, *Operation Drumbeat* (New York: Harper & Row, 1990), xxi, 417; Axel Niestlé, *German U-Boat Losses during World War II: Details of Destruction* (Annapolis, MD: Naval Institute Press, 1998), 4, 303; Herwig, "Innovation Ignored," 231. Sources disagree on the exact number of U-boats that sortied and, of those, the number lost; Gannon gives the figure 754 of 863; Niestlé, 757 of 859; and Herwig, 784 of 940.

25. Jak P. Mallman Showell, preface to 2012 reprint ed. of Dönitz, *Memoirs: Ten Years and Twenty Days*, xii.

26. Dönitz, *Memoirs: Ten Years and Twenty Days*, 59n, characterizes Nimitz's Nuremberg testimony of 11 May 1946 as "clear and honest." In the Second World War, the US campaign of unrestricted submarine warfare sank 5.3 million tons in forty-four months at a cost of fifty-two boats and 3,506 American submariners lost.

27. Fürbringer, *Fips*, 89–90.

28. Scheer, *Germany's High Sea Fleet*, 360–61.

29. Hashagen, *U-Boats Westward*, 58.

30. Fürbringer, *Fips*, 60.

31. Holtzendorff to Hindenburg, 22 December 1916, text in Scheer, *Germany's High Sea Fleet*, 248–52.

Bibliography

PRIMARY SOURCES

Bacon, Reginald. *The Dover Patrol, 1915–1917.* 2 vols. New York: George H. Doran, 1919.

Bayly, Lewis. *Pull Together! The Memoirs of Admiral Sir Lewis Bayly.* London: George G. Harrap, 1939.

Bethmann Hollweg, Theobald von. *Betrachtungen zum Weltkriege.* 2 vols. Berlin: Hobbing, 1919–21.

Campbell, Gordon. *My Mystery Ships.* Garden City, NY: Doubleday, Doran & Company, 1929.

Corbett, Julian Stafford. *Some Principles of Naval Strategy.* London: Longmans, Green, 1911.

Crompton, Iwan. *Englands Verbrechen an U 41: Der zweite "Baralong"-Fall im Weltkrieg.* Edited by Werner von Langsdorff. Gütersloh: C. Bertelsmann, 1941.

Domergue, Jean Gabriel. *The Crimes of Germany: Being an Illustrated Synopsis of the Violations of International Law and of Humanity by the Armed Forces of the German Empire.* New York: American Defense Society, 1918.

Dönitz, Karl. *Memoirs: Ten Years and Twenty Days.* Translated by R. H. Stevens. New York: World Publishing Company, 1959.

Erzberger, Matthias. *Erlebnisse im Weltkrieg.* Stuttgart: Deutsche Verlags-Anstalt, 1920.

Fechter, Hans. *In der Alarmkoje von U 35.* Berlin-Wien: Ullstein, 1918.

Forstner, Georg-Günther von. *The Journal of Submarine Commander von Forstner.* Translated by Anna Crafts Codman. Boston: Houghton Mifflin, 1917.

Fürbringer, Werner. *Fips: Legendary U-Boat Commander, 1915–1918.* Translated by Geoffrey Brooks. Original edition 1933. Annapolis, MD: Naval Institute Press, 1999.

Halsey, Francis W. *The Literary Digest History of the World War.* 10 vols. Original edition 1919. Reprint edition New York: Cosimo Classics, 2009.

Hashagen, Ernst. *U-Boats Westward.* Translated by Vesey Ross. New York: Putnam Sons, 1931.

Heimburg, Heino von. *U-Boot gegen U-Boot.* Berlin: Druck und Verlag August Scherl, 1917.

Hersing, Otto. *U 21 rettet die Dardanellen.* Zürich: Amalthea-Verlag, 1932.

Husband, Joseph. *On the Coast of France: The Story of the United States Naval Forces in French Waters.* Chicago: A. C. McClurg, 1919.

Jellicoe, John Rushworth. *The Grand Fleet, 1914–1916: Its Creation, Development, and Work.* New York: George H. Doran, 1919.

Kagelmann, Paul. *Unterseeboot-Minenleger im Weltkrieg: Wir von der I. U-Flottille, Kriegserlebnisse eines U-Boots-Deckoffiziers in der Hochseeflotte und auf Unterseebooten.* Bremen: Anker-Verlag, 1934.

Kirchhoff, Hermann, ed. *Maximilian Graf von Spee, Der Sieger von Coronel: Das Lebensbild und die Erinnerungen eines deutschen Seemanns.* Berlin: Marinedank-Verlag, 1915.

———. *Otto Weddigen und seine Waffe: Aus seinen Tagebüchern und nachgelassenen Papieren.* Berlin: Marinedank-verlag, 1915.

König, Paul. *Voyage of the Deutschland: The First Merchant Submarine.* New York: Hearst's International Library Co., 1917.

Kramsta, Joachim. *Aus dem Logbuch des 1. Wachoffiziers U 66: Auszüge aus Briefen und Tagebuchblättern.* Bremen: Industrie- und Handelsverlag G.m.b.H., 1931.

Ludendorff, Erich. *Ludendorff's Own Story.* 2 vols. New York: Harper, 1919.

Lloyd George, David. *War Memoirs.* 6 vols. Boston: Little, Brown, 1933–37.

Marschall, Wilhelm. *Torpedo achtung! Los! Erlebnisse im U-bootkrieg, 1917/18.* Berlin: Im Deutschen Verlag, 1938.

Max of Baden, Prince. *The Memoirs of Prince Max of Baden.* Translated by W. M. Calder and C. W. H. Sutton. 2 vols. New York: Scribner, 1928.

Moraht, Robert. *Die Versenkung des "Danton": meine U-Boots-Erlebnisse von der Ostsee bis zum Mittelmeer.* Berlin: Hutten Verlag, 1917.

Neureuther, Karl, and Claus Bergen, eds. *U-Boat Stories: Narratives of German U-Boat Sailors.* Translated by Eric Sutton. London: Constable, 1931.

Niemöller, Martin. *From U-Boat to Pulpit.* Translated by D. Hastie Smith. Chicago: Willett, Clark, 1937.

Pohl, Hugo von. *Aus Aufzeichnungen und Briefen während der Kriegszeit.* Berlin: Karl Siegismund, 1920.

Rose, Hans. *Auftauchen! Kriegsfahrten von "U 53."* Essen: Essener Verlagsanstalt, 1939.

Scheer, Reinhard. *Germany's High Sea Fleet in the World War.* London: Cassell, 1920.

Sims, William Snowden. *The Victory at Sea.* With Burton J. Hendrick. Garden City, NY: Doubleday, Page, 1920.

Spiess, Johannes. *U 9 auf Kriegsfahrt.* Gütersloh: C. Bertelsmann Verlag, n.d.

Taussig, Joseph K. *The Queenstown Patrol, 1917: The Diary of Commander Joseph Knefler Taussig, U.S. Navy.* Edited by William N. Still Jr. Newport, RI: Naval War College Press, 1996.

Terry, Charles Sanford. *Ostend and Zeebrugge, April 23–May 19, 1918: The Dispatches of Vice-Admiral Sir Roger Keyes and Other Narratives of the Operations.* London: Oxford University Press, 1919.

Tirpitz, Alfred von. *Deutsche Ohnmachtspolitik im Weltkriege.* Hamburg: Hanseatische Verlagsanstalt, 1926.

———. *Erinnerungen.* Leipzig: Verlag von K. F. Koehler, 1920.

———. *My Memoirs.* 2 vols. New York: Dodd, Mead, 1919.

United Kingdom. National Archives. Admiralty. Convoy Reports, 1917–18. ADM 137/2656.

United Kingdom. National Archives. Admiralty. Information Obtained from Survivors of U-Boats. ADM 137/3872/2.

United States Congress. *Congressional Record.* 65th Congress, 1st Session.

United States Congress. Senate. Committee on Naval Affairs. *Naval Investigation: Hearings before the Subcommittee of the Committee on Naval Affairs.* 66th Congress, 2nd Session.

United States Congress. Senate. Committee on Commerce. *United States Shipping Board Emergency Fleet Corporation: Hearings before the Committee on Commerce.* 65th Congress, 2nd and 3rd Sessions.

United States Department of State. *Papers Relating to the Foreign Relations of the United States, 1915.* Supplement: *The World War.* Available online at https://history.state.gov/historicaldocuments/frus1915Supp.

United States Navy Department. *The Northern Barrage and Other Mining Activities.* Washington, DC: US Government Printing Service, 1920.

Valentiner, Max. *Der Schrecken der Meere: Meine U-Boot-Abenteuer.* Leipzig: Amalthea-Verlag, 1931.

Winn, Hiram W. *Fighting the Hun on the U.S.S. Huntington.* N.p., 1919.

SECONDARY SOURCES

Abbatiello, John J. *Anti-Submarine Warfare in World War I: British Naval Aviation and the Defeat of the U-Boats.* London: Routledge, 2006.

Allen, Keith. "Food and the German Home Front: Evidence from Berlin." In *Evidence, History and the Great War: Historians and the Impact of 1914–18*, ed. Gail Braybon, 172–97. New York: Berghahn Books, 2003.

Barrett, Michael B. *Operation Albion: The German Conquest of the Baltic Islands.* Bloomington: Indiana University Press, 2008.

Bird, Keith W. *Weimar, the German Naval Officer Corps, and the Rise of National Socialism.* Amsterdam: B. R. Grüner Publishing, 1977.

Black, Nicholas. *The British Naval Staff in the First World War.* Woodbridge: Boydell Press, 2009.

Boghardt, Thomas. *The Zimmermann Telegram: Intelligence, Diplomacy, and America's Entry into World War I.* Annapolis, MD: Naval Institute Press, 2012.

Chatterton, E. Keble. *Q-Ships and Their Story.* London: Sidgwick & Jackson, 1922.

Compton-Hall, Richard. *Submarines and the War at Sea, 1914–1918.* London: Macmillan, 1991.

Corbett, Julian Stafford. *History of the Great War: Naval Operations.* 5 vols. London: Longmans, Green, 1920–31.

Crowell, Benedict, and Robert Forrest Wilson. *The Road to France.* Vol. 2, *The Transportation of Troops and Military Supplies, 1917–1918.* New Haven, CT: Yale University Press, 1921.

Delany, Walter S. *Bayly's Navy.* Washington, DC: Naval Historical Foundation, 1980.

Doenecke, Justus D. *Nothing Less Than War: A New History of America's Entry into World War I.* Lexington: University Press of Kentucky, 2011.

Dufeil, Yves. *Dictionnaire biografique des commandants de la Marine Impériale allemande.* N.p.: Histomar Publications, 2016. Available online at http://en.calameo.com/read/000802552841bc1ae847e.

Frey, Marc. *Der Erste Weltkrieg und die Niederlande: Ein neutrales land im politischen und wirtschaftlichen Kalkül der Kriegsgegner.* Berlin: Akademie Verlag, 1998.

Gannon, Michael. *Operation Drumbeat.* New York: Harper & Row, 1990.

Gibson, R. H., and Maurice Prendergast. *The German Submarine War, 1914–1918.* London: Constable, 1931.

Grant, Robert M. *U-Boat Intelligence, 1914–1918.* Hamden, CT: Archon Books, 1969.

Gray, Edwyn. *The Killing Time.* Original edition 1972. Reprinted as *The U-Boat War, 1914–1918.* London: Leo Cooper, 1994.

Gregory, Adrian. *The Last Great War: British Society and the First World War.* Cambridge: Cambridge University Press, 2008.

Hadley, Michael L., and Roger Sarty. *Tin-Pots and Pirate Ships: Canadian Naval Forces and German Sea Raiders, 1880–1918.* Montreal: McGill-Queen's University Press, 1991.

Halpern, Paul G. *The Naval War in the Mediterranean.* Annapolis, MD: Naval Institute Press, 1987.

———. *A Naval History of World War I.* Annapolis, MD: Naval Institute Press, 1994.

———. *The Battle of the Otranto Straits: Controlling the Gateway to the Adriatic in World War I.* Bloomington: Indiana University Press, 2004.

Hankel, Gerd. *Die Leipziger Prozesse: Deutsche Kriegsverbrechen und ihre strafrechtliche Verfolgung nach dem Ersten Weltkrieg.* Hamburg: Hamburger Edition, 2003.

Headrick, Daniel R. *The Invisible Weapon: Telecommunications and International Politics, 1851–1945.* Oxford: Oxford University Press, 1991.

Herwig, Holger H. "Innovation Ignored: The Submarine Problem—Germany, Britain, and the United States, 1919–1939." In *Military Innovation in the Interwar Period,* ed. Williamson Murray and Allan R. Millett, 227–64. Cambridge: Cambridge University Press, 1996.

———. *The First World War: Germany and Austria-Hungary, 1914–1918.* London: Arnold, 1997.

———. "Total Rhetoric, Limited War: Germany's U-Boat Campaign 1917–1918." *Journal of Military and Strategic Studies* 1, no. 1 (1998). Text at http://jmss.org/jmss/index.php/jmss/article/view/19/18.

Hildebrand, Karl-Friedrich, and Christian Zweng. *Die Ritter des Ordens Pour le Mérite des I. Weltkriegs.* 3 vols. Bissendorf: Biblio Verlag, 2011.

Holborn, Hajo. *A History of Modern Germany, 1840–1945*. Princeton, NJ: Princeton University Press, 1982.

Horn, Daniel. *The German Naval Mutinies of World War I*. New Brunswick, NJ: Rutgers University Press, 1969.

Hughes, Thomas. "Learning to Fight: Bill Halsey and the Early American Destroyer Force." *Journal of Military History* 77, no. 1 (January 2013): 71–90.

Johnston, William. "The Royal Canadian Navy and the First World War." In *The Naval Service of Canada, 1910–2010: The Centennial Story*, ed. Richard H. Gimblett, 23–40. Toronto: Dundurn Press, 2009.

Jones, Jerry W. *U.S. Battleship Operations in World War I*. Annapolis, MD: Naval Institute Press, 1998.

Kelly, Patrick J. *Tirpitz and the Imperial German Navy*. Bloomington: Indiana University Press, 2011.

Kiraly, Béla, Peter Pastor, and Ivan Sanders, eds. *Essays on World War I: Total War and Peacemaking*. New York: Brooklyn College Press, 1982.

Klim, Jake. *Attack on Orleans: The World War I Submarine Raid on Cape Cod*. Charleston, SC: History Press, 2014.

Lambert, Nicholas A. *Planning Armageddon: British Economic Warfare and the First World War*. Cambridge, MA: Harvard University Press, 2012.

Langensiepen, Bernd, and Ahmet Güleryüz. *The Ottoman Steam Navy, 1828–1923*. London: Conway Maritime Press, 1995.

Langensiepen, Bernd, Dirk Nottelmann, and Jochen Krüsmann. *Halbmond und Kaiseradler: Goeben und Breslau am Bosporus, 1914–1918*. Hamburg: Verlag E. S. Mittler & Sohn, 1999.

Larzelere, Alex R. *The Coast Guard in World War I: An Untold Story*. Annapolis, MD: Naval Institute Press, 2003.

Link, Arthur S. *Wilson*. Vol. 3, *The Struggle for Neutrality, 1914–1915*. Princeton, NJ: Princeton University Press, 1960. Paperback edition, 2015.

Massie, Robert. *Castles of Steel*. New York: Random House, 2003.

McKee, Fraser M. "An Explosive Story: The Rise and Fall of the Depth Charge." *Northern Mariner* 3 (1993): 45–58.

Morison, Elting E. *Admiral Sims and the Modern American Navy*. Boston: Houghton Mifflin, 1942.

Niestlé, Axel. *German U-Boat Losses during World War II: Details of Destruction*. Annapolis, MD: Naval Institute Press, 1998.

Offer, Avner. *The First World War: An Agrarian Interpretation*. Oxford: Clarendon Press, 1989.

Osborne, Eric W. *Britain's Economic Blockade of Germany, 1914–1919*. London: Frank Cass, 2004.

Philbin, Tobias R., III. *Admiral von Hipper, the Inconvenient Hero*. Amsterdam: John Benjamins, 1982.

Preston, Diana. *Lusitania: An Epic Tragedy*. New York: Walker Publishing, 2002.

———. *A Higher Form of Killing: Six Weeks in World War I That Forever Changed the Nature of Warfare*. New York: Bloomsbury Press, 2015.

Ritschl, Albrecht. "The Pity of Peace: Germany's Economy at War, 1914–1918 and Beyond." In *The Economics of World War I*, ed. Stephen Broadberry and Mark Harrison, 41–76. Cambridge: Cambridge University Press, 2005.

Rössler, Eberhard. *Die Unterseeboote der Kaiserlichen Marine.* Coblenz: Bernard & Graefe Verlag, 1997.

———. *Die deutschen U-Kreuzer und Transport-U-Boote.* Bonn: Bernard & Graefe Verlag, 2003.

Scheck, Raffael. *Alfred von Tirpitz and German Right-Wing Politics.* Atlantic Highlands, NJ: Humanities Press, 1998.

Solis, Gary D. "Obedience of Orders and the Law of War: Judicial Application in American Forums." *American University International Law Review* 15, no. 2 (1999): 482–525.

Sondhaus, Lawrence. "Strategy, Tactics, and the Politics of Penury: The Austro-Hungarian Navy and the *Jeune Ecole.*" *Journal of Military History* 56 (1992): 587–602.

———. "The Austro-Hungarian Naval Officer Corps, 1867–1918," *Austrian History Yearbook* 24 (1993): 51–78.

———. *The Naval Policy of Austria-Hungary: Navalism, Industrial Development, and the Politics of Dualism, 1867–1918.* West Lafayette, IN: Purdue University Press, 1994.

———. *Naval Warfare, 1815–1914.* London: Routledge, 2001.

———. *World War One: The Global Revolution.* Cambridge: Cambridge University Press, 2011.

———. *The Great War at Sea: A Naval History of the First World War.* Cambridge: Cambridge University Press, 2014.

Thomas, Lowell. *Raiders of the Deep.* Original edition 1928. Reprint edition Penzance, UK: Periscope Publishing, 2002.

Ullrich, Volker. "Die Januarstreik 1918 in Hamburg, Kiel und Bremen: Eine vergleichende Studie zur Geschichte der Streikbewegungen im Ersten Weltkrieg." *Zeitschrift des Vereins für Hamburgische Geschichte* 71 (1985): 45–74.

Vogt, Adolf. *Oberst Max Bauer: Generalstabsoffizier im Zwielicht, 1869–1929.* Osnabrück: Biblio Verlag, 1974.

Wheeler-Bennett, John W. *Wooden Titan: Hindenburg in Twenty Years of German History, 1914–1934.* New York: William Morrow, 1936.

Williamson, Gordon. *U-Boats of the Kaiser's Navy.* Oxford: Osprey, 2002.

Willis, James F. *Prologue to Nuremberg: The Politics and Diplomacy of Punishing War Criminals of the First World War.* Westport, CT: Greenwood, 1982.

Wilson, George Grafton. "Report of the International Commission of Inquiry in the Loss of the Dutch Steamer *Tubantia.*" *American Journal of International Law* 16 (1922): 432.

Zacher, Dale E. *The Scripps Newspapers Go to War, 1914–1918.* Urbana: University of Illinois Press, 2008.

Zieger, Robert H. *America's Great War: World War I and the American Experience.* Lanham, MD: Rowman & Littlefield, 2000.

DATA SOURCES

Ayres, Leonard P. *War with Germany: A Statistical Summary.* Washington, DC: US Government Printing Office, 1919.

Conway's All the World's Fighting Ships, 1906–1921. London: Conway Maritime Press, 1985.

Grant, Robert M. *U-Boats Destroyed: The Effect of Anti-Submarine Warfare, 1914–1918.* London: Putnam, 1964.

Gröner, Erich. *Die deutschen Kriegsschiffe 1815–1945.* 8 vols. Coblenz: Bernard & Graefe Verlag, 1982–94.

Helgason, Guðmundur. "U-Boat War in World War One." http://www.uboat.net/wwi.

Kemp, Paul. *U-Boats Destroyed: German Submarine Losses in the Two World Wars.* Annapolis, MD: Naval Institute Press, 1997.

King, William C., ed. *King's Complete History of the World War.* Springfield, MA: History Associates, 1922.

OTHER INTERNET RESOURCES

http://archives.chicagotribune.com

http://islayhistory.blogspot.com

http://net.lib.byu.edu

http://newspaperarchive.com

http://query.nytimes.com

http://trove.nla.gov.au/newspaper

http://www.archeosousmarine.net

http://www.archivespasdecalais.fr

http://www.firstworldwar.com

http://www.rmslusitania.info

http://www.whitestarhistory.com

http://www.worldwar1.com

http://www.wwvets.com/Submarines.html

http://www.wrecksite.eu

https://www.history.navy.mil/research/histories/ship-histories/danfs.html

Index

Note: Page references for figures are italicized. All officers and warships indexed are German, unless otherwise indicated.

Aaland Islands, 35

Aboukir, British armored cruiser, 1–2, 4–5, 45

Acton, British Q-ship, 155

Adam, Hans, *Kapitänleutnant*, 40, 65, 168

Adriatic Sea, 37–41, 49, 52, 66, 69–70, 74, 79, 128–29, 155–56, 180–82, 200, 207

AEG (Allgemeine Elektricitäts-Gesellschaft), as engine manufacturer, 101

Aegean Sea, 202

Aghios Gerasimos, Greek sailing vessel, 206

Alaunia, British steamer, 71

Albania, 72, 79, 128–29, 206–7

Alexandria, 117, 126–27, 170

Alfonso XIII, king of Spain, 68

Algeria, 169

Algonquin, American steamer, 114, 116

Allen, C. H., British lieutenant, 179

Alsace-Lorraine, 104, 210

Amalfi, Italian armored cruiser, 39

Amazon, British steamer, 167

Amberger, Gustav, *Kapitänleutnant*, 154

Amiens, Battle of (1918), 184

Amiral Charner, French armored cruiser, 69

Amiral Ganteaume, French steamer, 14, 21n21

Amsterdam, 33, 63

Ancona, Italian passenger liner, 57–59, 80n1, 220

Andania, British steamer, 166

Anglo-German Naval Treaty (1935), 215–16

antisubmarine warfare, 73–80, 152–58, 175–82; in Second World War, 225

Antivari (Bar), 37

Antwerp, 36

Antwerp, British Q-ship, 75

Arabic, British passenger liner, and the "*Arabic* pledge," 49–51, 58–59, 75–76, 93, 116, 157, 206

Arcadia, British troopship, 117

Archangel, 48, 72, 87, 91, 128, 151–52

Arctic Circle, 87, 92, 144

Arctic Sea, 48, 91, 128, 151–52

Argentina, 192, 223

Ariadne, British protected cruiser, 146

Armenian, British steamer, 47

Armistice, between Germany and the Allies (1918), 210–11

Arnauld de la Perière, Lothar von,
Kapitänleutnant, 65, 66, 67–70, 76–77,
79–80, 81n14, 91–92, 112, 118, 143,
149, 158, 177, 182, 195–96, 200, 218,
222, 224, 227
Athos, French steamer, 113
Atlantic, Battle of the (1942–43), 166, 173
Atlantic Ocean, 73, 78, 91–92, 113, 120,
144, 172–73, 182, 192–98. See also
convoys
Atlaswerke, shipyard, 100
Aube, Théophile, French admiral, 6
Audacious, British dreadnought, 5, 15
Auguste Conseil, French steamer, 34
Aurania, British steamer, 166
Australia, 73, 118
Australia, British battle cruiser, 21n33.
Austria-Hungary, 19, 27, 37–41, 52, 89,
141; final disintegration of, 207–8;
relations of, with United States, 58–59,
104, 203–4; seeks separate peace with
Allies, 104, 207; wartime strikes in, 165,
175
Austrian navy: casualties among U-boat
officers in, 229; and double-numbering
of German U-boats in Mediterranean,
39–40, 51, 58–60; first submarines of,
9–10; morale in, 142–3, 200; mutinies
in, 175, 200; seaplanes of, 154; and
unrestricted submarine warfare, 37–41,
96, 104, 109, 204; victory of, at Otranto
Straits (1917), 128–29, 155
Avenger, British armed merchant cruiser,
130
Azores, 144, 149, 171, 193–94, 196

Bachmann, Gustav, Admiral, 30–31, 45,
49–51, 66
Bacon, Reginald, British rear admiral, 80,
156, 179, 181
Balfour, Arthur, First Lord of the
Admiralty, 46
Balkan Wars (1912–13), 12
Ballarat, British troopship, 118
Baltic, British passenger liner, 123–24
Baltic Sea, 12, 35–36, 48–49, 157, 209
Baralong, British Q-ship, 75
Barcelona, 207

barrages, antisubmarine, 77–80, 92, 128–
29, 153, 156
Bartenbach, Karl, Kapitänleutnant, 36, 223
Bauer, Hermann, Fregattenkapitän, 14
Bauer, Max von, colonel, 136–39
Bayano, British armed merchant cruiser,
35
Bayly, Sir Lewis, British admiral, 33, 120,
123–24, 126, 147
Beachy Head, 34, 146–47
Beatty, Sir David, British admiral, 29, 85,
88, 92, 122, 157, 179
Becker, Franz, Oberleutnant-
Kapitänleutnant, 72, 169
Behncke, Paul, German vice admiral, 185,
190
Beitzen, Curt, Kapitänleutnant, 71, 87
Belgium, 34, 36, 73. See also Flanders
Belleau Wood, Battle of (1918), 184
Belridge, Norwegian tanker, 33–34
Benghazi, 170
Benz, engine manufacturer, 101
Berckheim, Egewolf von, Baron,
Kapitänleutnant, 14, 35, 48
Bergen, 48, 93, 179
Berger, Gerhard, Kapitänleutnant, 113
Bermuda, 123, 172
Bernstorff, Johann von, Count, German
ambassador to US, 49, 103, 111
Bethmann Hollweg, Theobald von,
German chancellor, 18, 23, 27–31, 44–
45, 49–50, 59–60, 62, 90, 98–99, 102–3,
109–11, 110, 136–39
Bieber, Thomas, Oberleutnant, 118
Biscay, Bay of, 92, 155
Black, Nicholas, historian, 122
Black Sea, 16, 18, 38–39, 47, 49, 52, 69, 95,
98, 159, 165, 201–2
Black Tom Island explosion (1916), 65
blockade, Allied: American opinion of, 15,
19, 26, 228–29; of Austria-Hungary,
37–38; of Germany, 15, 24, 27, 31, 44,
52, 77, 105, 166, 228
Blohm & Voss, shipbuilder, 72, 99–101,
190
Blücher, armored cruiser, 29
Boldt, John Claus, Leutnant, 220, 222,
230n16

Bolshevik Revolution (1917), 102, 119, 140, 152, 172

Borkum, 73

Bostonian, British escort merchant ship, 146

Bothmer, Thorwald von, *Kapitänleutnant*, 88

Boxer Rebellion (1900), 120

Boy-Ed, Karl, *Fregattenkapitän*, 64

Brazil, 117

Bremen, shipyards in, 48, 72, 100, 136, 175, 210

Bremen, German merchant submarine, 96, 107n23

Bremer Vulcan, 100

Bremerhaven, 95

Bremse, light cruiser, 148, 178

Breslau, light cruiser, 16, 216

Brest, destroyer base and port of, 124, 128, 130, 146–47, 167–69, 176, 198–99

Brest-Litovsk, Treaty of (1918), 159, 165

Brindisi, 79, 128

Bristol, 168

Britain: Ireland's Easter Rising against, 63; merchant marine of, 19, 51; relations of, with United States, 19, 24, 64; supplies Russia via the Arctic, 48, 72, 87, 91, 128, 151–52; trade of, with neutral countries, 47; war plans of, against Germany, 15, 21n25, 27

Britannia, British pre-dreadnought, 211

Britannic, British hospital ship, 72, 177

British army: British Expeditionary Force (BEF) of, 5, 36; Egyptian Expeditionary Force (EEF) of, 117, 127; Royal Flying Corps of, 180

British navy: Adriatic Squadron of, 79, 155; Auxiliary Patrol of, 74, 156; Buncrana force of, 124–25, 146, 167, 196; Devonport force of, 124, 147, 167; Dover Patrol of, 80, 179, 181; first submarines of, 9–13; Grand Fleet of, 5, 18, 29, 34, 62, 64, 71, 73–74, 87–88, 92, 122, 157, 179, 209; Harwich force of, 88, 105, 122, 217; hydrophones used by, 153, 155; Mediterranean Fleet of, 155; North American and West Indian station of, 123; and

postwar naval arms control, 219; prewar expansion of, 4, 10; Q-ships of, 74–77, 130, 153–55; Royal Naval Air Service of, 130, 154, 180; Seventh Cruiser Squadron of, 1; and strategy of "distant blockade," 5, 12, 15; wireless technology and codebreaking of, 73–74, 114, 145, 152

Bruges (Brugge), 36, 73–74, 98, 156, 179, 189

Brummer, light cruiser, 148, 178

Bryan, William Jennings, US secretary of state, 44–45

Bulgaria, and Bulgarian navy, 38, 60, 117, 202

Buncrana, destroyer base at, 124–25, 146, 167, 196

Burdigala, French troopship, 72

Burián, István, Count, Austrian foreign minister, 58–59

Bussche, Erich, Baron von der, Major, 203

Calais, 14

Calgarian, British armed merchant cruiser, 167

California, British passenger steamer, 112

Calvados, French troopship, 57

Cambank, British freighter, 34

Cameronia, British troopship, 117, 132n20

Campbell, Gordon, British lieutenant commander, 76, 130, 155

Canada, 173, 193. *See also* Halifax; Montreal; Sydney

Canaris, Wilhelm, *Kapitänleutnant*, 201, 208, 222

Canary Islands, 98, 150, 196

Candidate, British steamer, 42

Cantigny, Battle of (1918), 184

Cape Blanco, 150

Cape Cod, 173

Cape Finisterre, 196, 211

Cape Hatteras, 196–97

Cape Helles, 38

Cape Matapan, 113, 200

Cape Santa Maria di Leuca, 38, 80, 128, 180

Cape St. Vincent, 172

Cape Verde Islands, 98, 171

Capelle, Eduard von, Admiral, 62, 138, 141–42, 159, 185
Caporetto, Battle of (1917), 156, 159
Carlisle Castle, British freighter, 167
Carloforte, 170
Carls, Rolf, *Kapitänleutnant*, 197, 216
Carolina, American passenger steamer, 172
Carpathia, British steamer, 169
Cartagena, 67
Carthage, French troopship, 38
Casement, Sir Roger, Irish nationalist, 63, 81n10
Catalonia, 127
Cattaro, 37–38, 40, 47, 69–70, 78–80, 104, 128–29, 149, 154, 156, 201; mutiny at base in (1918), 175, 200, 206–8
Center Party, 19, 99, 137–39, 142, 203
Central Powers, 16, 19, 38–40, 48, 58, 60, 70, 79–80, 95, 99, 101–2, 104, 114, 142, 152, 159–60, 164–65, 202
Centurion, British steamer, 42
Cephalonia, 38
Channel, English, 1, 14, 30, 33–34, 71, 74, 88, 92, 125, 146–47, 157, 167–68, 177
Channel Islands, 115
Charles, Habsburg emperor, 104, 175, 203–4, 207–8
Chateau-Thierry, 184
Chile, and Chilean navy, 16–18, 69, 192, 201
China, and Chinese laborers, 16, 113, 120
Churchill, Winston, First Lord of the Admiralty, 15, 35–36, 46, 220
City of Memphis, American steamer, 114
Civil War, American (1861–65), 6
Conservative Party, German, 99
Constantinople, 16, 38–40, 47, 69–70, 165, 201–2
convoys, Allied, 121–27, 143–48, 167–69, 175–79, 193–94, 198–99; of First World War, compared to Second, 123; HD (Dakar) 7, 146; HH (Halifax), 123–24, 146–47, 168; HN (New York), 123–25, 167–69; HS (Sydney, Nova Scotia), 123–24, 126, 167, 196, 199; HX (Halifax), 123, 167
Corbett, Sir Julian, British naval strategist, 121

Corfu, 79–80, 180
Cornwall, 34, 44, 47, 76, 112, 114, 146, 168, 170
Cornwallis, British pre-dreadnought, 69
Coronel, Battle of (1914), 16–17
Courageous, British battle cruiser, 157
Covington, American troopship, 169
Cressy, British armored cruiser, 1–2, 4–5, 45
Crete, 59, 72, 206
Crimean War (1853–56), 6
cruiser rules, 6, 14, 50, 57, 59, 64, 74, 90, 95, 112, 192, 205. *See also* international law
Cuba, 117
Curie, French submarine, 37
Cushing, American tanker, 43–45
Cuxhaven 73
Cyklop, submarine salvage ship, 218
Cymric, British passenger liner, 64
Czernin, Ottokar, Count, Austrian foreign minister, 104

Daimler, engine manufacturer, 11, 101
Dakar, 127, 146, 169, 171
Dalmatia, 37, 47, 200
Damao, Portuguese steamer, 168
Damascus, 98
Dandolo, Italian steamer, 67
Danton, French pre-dreadnought, 129, 169
Danube River, 202
Danzig, base and navy yard in, 10, 13, 48, 72, 101
Dardanelles, 38, 46
Dartmouth, British light cruiser, 129
Delfin, Greek submarine, 12
Delmarva Peninsula, 172
Denmark, 47, 85, 87, 93, 105, 112
depth charges, 76, 153–54, 158, 167, 176, 178
d'Equevilley-Montjustin, Raimundo, Spanish naval engineer, 10
Deutschland, German merchant submarine, 96, 106n23
Devon, 34, 118
Devonian, British steamer, 146
Devonport, destroyer base at, 124, 147, 167

Dieckmann, Victor, *Kapitänleutnant*, 147
Dieppe, 33
Diesel, Rudolf, and diesel-electric engines, 10–11
Dinorah, French collier, 33
Ditfurth, Benno von, *Oberleutnant*, 154
Dithmar, Ludwig, *Leutnant*, 220, 222, 230n16
Djemmah, French transport, 170
Doemming, Hellmuth von, *Oberleutnant*, 170, 206
Dogger Bank, 47, 87; Battle of (1915), 29–30
Dönitz, Karl, *Oberleutnant*, 144–45, 201, 215–16, 223–24, *226*, 227
Dover, and Straits of, 35–36, 77–80, 92, 128, 130, 153, 155–56, 180–82
Dover Castle, British hospital ship, 127–28, 220
Doyle, Sir Arthur Conan, British author, 29
Drake, British armored cruiser, 146
Dreadnought, British battleship, 4, 10, 34
Dresden, light cruiser, 16–17, 69, 201
Drina, British steamer, 114
Dröscher, Otto, *Kapitänleutnant*, 14, 28, 87, 197
Drummond, John, British captain, 2
Dublin, 199
Duff, Alexander, British rear admiral, 123
Dulwich, British steamer, 33
Dungeness, 167
Dunkirk, 33, 180
Dupetit-Thouars, French armored cruiser, 198
Durazzo (Durrës), 79, 128; Battle of (1918), 207, 224
Durward, British steamer, 33
Dwinsk, British steamer, 172

E 1, British submarine, 94
E 3, British submarine, 14
E 9, British submarine, 4
E 11, British submarine, 39
E 23, British submarine, 88
E 35, British submarine, 172
E 42, British submarine, 179
E 48, British submarine, 150
Eastern Prince, British freighter, 146

Ebert, Friedrich, German chancellor, 211, 221–22
Eckelmann, Erich, *Korvettenkapitän*, 171, 193, 195
Eckernförde, U-boat school at, 175, 191, 210
Eckhardt, Heinrich von, German ambassador to Mexico, 113
Edeling, Karl, *Kapitänleutnant*, 146, 156
Elbe River, 209
Electric Boat Company, American submarine manufacturer, 9
Emden, base at, 13, 36, 63, 200
Ems River, 14
Emsmann, Hans Joachim, *Oberleutnant*, 209
English Channel. *See* Channel
Erhardt, Hermann, *Korvettenkapitän*, 222
Erzberger, Matthias, German politician, 19, 62, 135–41, *136*, 203, 210–11, 216, 222
Estonia, 73
Estrella Da Bissao, Portuguese sailing vessel, 151

Fähndrich, Friedrich, *Linienschiffsleutnant*, 128
Falaba, British passenger steamer, 35, 42–45
Falkenhayn, Erich von, General, 50, 60–62, 86, 89
Falkhausen, Hugo von, Austrian *Linienschiffsleutnant*, 79
Falklands, Battle of the (1914), 16, 18, 69, 73, 200
Falmouth, British light cruiser, 88
Fanning, British destroyer, 154
Farnborough (ex-*Loderer*), British Q-ship, 76, 130, 155
Faroe Islands, 48, 197
Fatherland Party, 141–2, 185
Fechter, Hans, engineer, 92
Feldkirchner, Johannes, *Kapitänleutnant*, 5–6, 128–29
Feldt, Richard, *Kapitänleutnant*, 171–73, 192–93, 196
Fessenden, Reginald, Canadian inventor, 153

Fife Ness, 35
Finland, 49, 63, 165, 178, 223
Finland, Gulf of, 14, 48, 165
Firth of Forth, 4
Fischel, Hermann von, *Kapitänleutnant*,
    113, 222
Fisher, Sir John, British admiral, 15
Flanders, U-boat bases in, 30, 34, 36, 63,
    78, 92, 98, 156, 179–80, 184, 190, 202–
    3. *See also* Bruges; Ostend; Zeebrugge
Flavia, British steamer, 199
Flensburger Schiffbau, shipyard, 100
Fletcher, Frank, American officer, 126
Foch, Ferdinand, French marshal, 184,
    210–11
Folkestone, 33
Formidable, British pre-dreadnought, 33
Forstmann, Walter, *Kapitänleutnant*,
    14, 52, 59, 65, 68, 113, 129, 177, 200,
    223–24
Forstner, Georg-Günther,
    Kapitänleutnant, 35
Foucault, French submarine, 154
France, and French navy, 6, 8–11, 37, 61,
    78, 125, 140, 219
Francis Joseph, Habsburg emperor, 104
Franconia, British troopship, 69
Franz, Adolf, *Kapitänleutnant*, 194
Freetown, 127, 151
Freikorps, postwar, 221–24
Friedrich der Grosse, dreadnought, 171
Friedrichsort torpedo factory, 100, 136,
    174, 197
Frisian Islands, 73, 157
Fröhner, Eberhard, *Oberleutnant*, 70
Fulton (1904), submarine prototype, 9
Fürbringer, Werner, *Kapitänleutnant*, 36,
    78, 143–44, 202–3, 223, 227

G 2, British submarine, 209
Gäa, Austrian depot ship, 40
Gallia, French troopship, 70, 79
Gallipoli, 38–39, 46, 79, 153
Gansser, Konrad, *Kapitänleutnant*, 52, 59,
    65, 68, 149–50
Garrett, George, British submarine
    pioneer, 8
Gaulois, French pre-dreadnought, 69

Genoa, 118, 127
Georg, Carl-Siegfried von,
    Kapitänleutnant, 91, 93, 222
George G. Henry, American tanker, 194
Georgia, 63, 165
Gercke, Hermann, *Korvettenkapitän*,
    171–72
German navy: auxiliary cruisers of, 17;
    Baltic Flotilla of, 95, 165; battle cruiser
    squadron (I Scouting Group) of, 16, 29,
    64, 85, 87, 178–79; casualties among
    U-boat officers in, 229; Courland
    Flotilla of, 165; East Asiatic Squadron
    of, 16–17, 21n33; first submarines
    of, 10–12; Flanders Flotilla of, 36, 49,
    78, 83n45, 87–88, 92, 113, 128, 130,
    144, 156–57, 179–80, 187n39, 190,
    202–3; High Sea Fleet of, 3, 12, 17–18,
    29–30, 36, 50, 61–62, 64, 66, 71, 73, 78,
    85–88, 90, 92–95, 101, 136, 140, 142,
    178–79, 185, 209–11; and the Jeune
    École, 7; Mediterranean Division of,
    16; morale in, 142–3; organization of
    U-boat flotillas in, 13–14, 36, 40, 69,
    95, 128, 159, 165; prewar expansion of,
    4, 10, 17; as scapegoat for Germany's
    lost war, 140, 164, 189, 203; in Second
    World War, 117, 151, 180, 191, 201,
    224–27; strikes and mutinies in,
    136, 141–42, 192, 209–11; Torpedo
    Inspection of, 7, 10; U-boat Office
    of, 159, 174, 190; under Naval High
    Command (*Seekriegsleitung*), 185, 189,
    192–93; under the Republic (1918–33),
    221–23; and Versailles Treaty, 215,
    217–20; wireless technology and
    codebreaking of, 73–74, 98, 145,
    152–53
Germania shipyard, 10–11, 72, 100–101,
    105, 136, 174, 190, 195, 223
Germany: final offensive of, in France
    (1918), 163–66; interned merchant
    ships of, seized for Allied use, 131,
    174; Nazi era in, 201; public support
    in, for unrestricted submarine warfare,
    26–27, 49–50; relations of, with Italy,
    39, 60; relations of, with United States,
    19, 42–47, 49–51, 64, 90, 96, 102,

111, 114, 137; trade of, with neutral countries, 47; wartime food rationing in, 27, 105, 110–11, 136, 143, 164, 183; wartime strikes in, 135–36, 165, 174–75, 197

Gerth, Georg, *Oberleutnant*, 130

Gibraltar, Straits of, 38, 57–58, 66, 72, 126–27, 149, 155–56, 171–72, 181–82, 193, 211

Giuseppe Garibaldi, Italian armored cruiser, 47

Glasenapp, Alfred von, *Kapitänleutnant*, 129, 168

Glasgow, 124

Glencarron, British steamer, 168

Glitra, British merchant steamer, 5–6, 14–15, 74

Glorious, British battle cruiser, 157

Goeben, battle cruiser, 16, 18, 216

Goetting, Gernot, *Korvettenkapitän*, 171–72

Gough-Calthorpe, Sir Somerset, British admiral, 155

Graeff, Ernst, *Kapitänleutnant*, 75 82n35

Grant, Sir William, British admiral, 123, 132n31, 173

Great Northern, American troopship, 177

Great Yarmouth, 16, 48

Greece, and Greek navy, 12, 112, 202

Grelhame, British freighter, 146

Grey, Sir Edward, British foreign secretary, 15, 21n21

Grodno, British freighter, 48

Groener, Wilhelm, General, 209–10

Gross, Karl, *Oberleutnant*, 75

Grösser Kurfürst, dreadnought, 22n34, 94

Grünert, Franz, *Kapitänleutnant*, 93

Gryfevale, British steamer, 150

Guinea, Gulf of, 151

Gulflight, American tanker, 43–45

Güntzel, Ludwig, *Kapitänleutnant*, 76

Gymnôte, French submarine, 8

Haagen, Rudolf, *Leutnant*, 191

Halifax, 123, 126, 168–70

Halpern, Paul, historian, 182, 192

Halsey, William "Bull," American officer, 126

Hamburg, shipyards in, 48, 72, 100, 174, 210

Hampshire, British armored cruiser, 71, 87

Hampton Roads, 47, 123–24, 126, 146, 172–73

Hansen, Claus, *Kapitänleutnant*, 33–34, 47, 76

Hartlepool, 16

Hartwig, Kurt, *Kapitänleutnant*, 69, 119, 200–201, 208, 211, 222

Harwich, British base at, 88, 105, 122, 217

Hashagen, Ernst, *Kapitänleutnant*, 114–15, 146, 172, 198

Hattie Dunn, American schooner, 172

Haumann, Waldemar, *Kapitänleutnant*, 206

Haus, Anton, Austrian admiral, 104

Haverford, British steamer, 128

heat, aboard submarines, 149, 161n46

Hebrides, 146

Heimburg, Heino von, *Oberleutnant*, 39, 47

Hela, light cruiser, 4

Helgoland, dreadnought, 209

Helgoland, and Helgoland Bight, 3, 4, 12–13, 16, 29, 63, 73, 156, 179; First Battle of (1914), 16, 29; Second Battle of (1917), 157

Henderson, Reginald, British commander, 122

Henry, Prince of Prussia, Admiral, 68, 171

Herbert, Godfrey, British lieutenant commander, 75–76

Hermes, British seaplane carrier, 14

Hersing, Otto, *Kapitänleutnant*, 4, 14, 33, 38–40, 47, 52, 65, 69, 113, 118, 143, 218

Hertling, Georg von, German chancellor, 142, 184, 203

Hertwig, Wolf Hans, *Kapitänleutnant*, 199

Herwig, Holger, historian, 192

Hesperian, British passenger liner, 50

Hillebrand, Leo, *Kapitänleutnant*, 91, 151–52, 166

Hindenburg, Paul von, Field Marshal, 88–90, 95, 101–3, 109, 119, 135, 137–41, 183, 184, 189, 203, 208, 221

Hindenburg Program, 89, 98–100, 183, 190

Hipper, Franz von, Admiral, 16, 29, 64, 85, 87, 103, 178, 185, 209–10, 216, 221
Hirano Maru, Japanese passenger liner, 199
Hitler, Adolf, 64, 201, 215, 223, 227
Hoek van Holland, 1, 4
Hogue, British armored cruiser, 1–2, 4–5, 45
Holland, John Philip, American submarine pioneer, 9
Holland, American submarine, 9
Holstein. See Schleswig-Holstein
Holtzendorff, Henning von, Admiral, 50, 61–63, 74, 89–90, 102–4, 111, 121, 128, 130, 135, 138–39, 142, 158, 184–85, 189, 192, 229,
Holyhead, 199
Hoppe, Bruno, Kapitänleutnant, 31, 130, 224
Horns Reef, 93–94, 157
Horthy, Miklós, Austrian rear admiral, 128–29, 155, 175, 200, 208
Horton, Max, British lieutenant commander, 4
Housatonic, American freighter, 112–13, 115
House, Edward, advisor to Woodrow Wilson, 49, 58
Hoy, Elizabeth, American socialite, 113
Hoy, Mary, American socialite, 113
Hufnagel, Hans, Kapitänleutnant, 149
Hughes, Guy D'Oyly, British lieutenant, 172
Humber River, 198
hydrophones, 153, 155

Iceland, 149, 171
Illinois, American tanker, 115
Independent Social Democratic Party (USPD), 136–37, 141–3
India, British armed merchant cruiser, 48
Inflexible, British battle cruiser, 21n33.
Ingeneurskantoor voor Scheepsbouw (IvS), 223
Ingenohl, Friedrich von, Admiral, 16–17, 23, 28–30
international law, 6, 14–15, 68, 91, 111
Inverlyon, British Q-ship, 75, 82n36

Invincible, British battle cruiser, 21n33
Iola, British collier, 91
Ionian Islands, 38
Ionian Sea, 38, 119
Ireland, 19, 41–42, 63–64, 75–76, 91–92, 112–14, 118, 124–25, 127–30, 146–47, 152, 154–55, 167, 169, 199
Irish Sea, 34, 124, 158, 199
Islay, 166, 185n6
Italy, and Italian navy, 39–40, 57–60, 78, 86, 89, 155–56, 207–8, 219, 223
Ivernia, British troopship, 69

J 1, British submarine, 94
Jacob Jones, American destroyer, 147–48
Jagow, Gottlieb von, German foreign secretary, 23, 43–46, 50, 64, 90, 103
Japan, and Japanese navy, 9, 12, 72, 114–15, 127, 156, 219, 223; in Second World War, 227, 231n26
Jean Bart, French dreadnought, 37
Jellicoe, Sir John, British admiral, 5, 87–88, 92–93, 120–22, 130, 157–58, 211
Jeune École, naval strategy, 6–8, 11, 219
Justicia, British liner, 169, 186n14, 187n33
Jutland, Battle of (1916), 71, 85–87, 178

Kaiser, dreadnought, 157
Kaiserin, dreadnought, 157
Kapitänleutnant Schwieger. See U 139
Kapitänleutnant Weddigen. See U 140
Kapp, Wolfgang, German politician, 141, 222
Karp, Russian submarine, 10
Kattegat, 149, 157, 211
Kelly, Sir Howard, British commodore, 155
Kerr, Mark, British rear admiral, 80, 128–29, 155
Keyes, Sir Roger, British vice admiral, 179
Kiel, shipyards and base in, 10, 12, 66, 99, 128, 136, 149, 151, 171–72, 174, 194–97, 206, 209–11
Kiel Canal, 157, 209
Kingstonian, British steamer, 170
Kirchner, Johannes, Oberleutnant, 72
Kitchener, Horatio Herbert, 1st Earl, British field marshal, 71, 87

Klasing, Johannes, *Kapitänleutnant*, 127, 155, 207
Kléber, French armored cruiser, 130
Kolbe, Constantin, *Kapitänleutnant*, 33, 171, 195, 222
König, dreadnought, 22n34.
Kophamel, Waldemar, *Kapitänleutnant*, 52, 59, 65–66, 149–50, 172, 195–97, 201
Körting, engine manufacturer, 11, 101
Kramsta, Joachim, *Leutnant*, 135
Kratzsch, Hans, *Kapitänleutnant*, 35
Kretschmer, Otto, *Fregattenkapitän*, 227
Kroll, Carl Albrecht, *Korvettenkapitän*, 167
Kronprinz, dreadnought, 94
Krupp, arms manufacturer, 7
Kukat, Heinrich, *Oberleutnant*, 211, 222, 229n2

La Follette, Robert, US senator, 116
labor, shipyard, 98–100, 189–91; strikes by, 105, 135–36, 139, 143, 174–75, 197
Laconia, British Cunard liner, 113
Ladoga (ex-*Minin*), Russian minelayer, 49
Lake, Simon, American submarine pioneer, 9
Lakemoor, American steamer, 168
Landrail, British destroyer, 154
Lansing, Robert, US secretary of state, 45, 49, 58–59, 64, 75
Latvia, 48, 74
Laurence, Noel, British lieutenant commander, 94
Laurentic, British armed merchant cruiser, 129
Le Havre, 14, 33
Lebeuf, Maxime, French naval engineer, 8–10
Leinster, British steamer, 199, 204
Lenin, Vladimir Ilyich Ulianov, Bolshevik leader and Russian premier, 119, 140, 152, 159, 165
Léon Gambetta, French armored cruiser, 38
Lerch, Egon, Austrian *Linienschiffsleutnant*, 37
Levetzow, Magnus von, Rear Admiral, 29
Leviathan (ex-*Vaterland*), American troopship, 174, 176–77, 187n33

Libau (Liepaja), 48, 74, 95, 165
Liberia, 171
Liechtenstein, Johannes, Prince von und zu, Austrian *Korvettenkapitän*, 128–29
Lisbon, 63, 171, 193
Lissa, Battle of (1866), 40
Liverpool, 19, 33–35, 41–42, 49–50, 64, 124, 166, 168–69, 199
Llandovery Castle, Canadian hospital ship, 170, 220, 228
Lloyd George, David, British prime minister, 105, 122, 166
Loch Ewe, 5
Lodge, Henry Cabot, US senator, 116
Lohs, Johannes, *Oberleutnant*, 167
London, Declaration of (1909), 15, 31, 105
Long Island, 172
Lough Swilly, 5, 15, 124, 126. *See also* Buncrana
Löwenfeld, Wilfried von, *Korvettenkapitän*, 222
Lübbe, Hans Georg, *Kapitänleutnant*, 202
Lucia, American steamer, 193–94
Luckner, Felix von, Count, *Kapitänleutnant*, 82n35
Ludendorff, Erich, General, 88–90, 95, 98, 101–3, 119, 136–41, 165–66, *183*, 184–85, 189–90, 192, 202–5, 208, 221
Lugano, British freighter, 146
Luppis, Johann, Austrian officer, 6
Lusitania, British Cunard liner, 41–47, 49–50, 52, 70, 75, 93, 116, 155, 228
Lyman M. Law, American schooner, 112–13

Madeira, 65, 149, 171–72, 182, 193
Magdeburg, light cruiser, 73
Mahan, Alfred Thayer, American officer, 8
Mahn, Bruno, *Oberleutnant*, 224
Majestic, British pre-dreadnought, 38
Malachite, British steamer, 14
Maloja, British steamer, 71
Malta, 37, 69, 72, 104, 126–27, 146, 153, 156, 169–70, 181, 201
Mann-Tiechler, Ernst von, Vice Admiral, 159, 174, 190
Margit, British Q-ship, 76–77
Marmara, Sea of, 39

Marmora, British armed merchant cruiser, 169
Marne, Second Battle of the (1918), 184
Marschall, Wilhelm, *Kapitänleutnant*, 117, 170, 216
Maschinenfabrik Augsburg-Nürnberg (MAN), 11, 101
Mashobra, British steamer, 118
Marseilles, 113, 117, 127, 180, 193
Mauretania, 150
Max, Prince of Baden, German chancellor, 203–6, *204*, 208–11, 221
Mayo, Henry T., American admiral, 120, 123
Mecidiye, Ottoman cruiser, 12
Medina, British passenger liner, 118
Mediterranean Sea, 16, 37–40, 47, 51, 57, 59–60, 65–72, 74, 76, 79–80, 86, 92, 98, 104, 112–13, 117–18, 126, 128, 146, 149, 155–56, 159, 169–70, 174, 177, 200–202, 206–8, 211
Medjerda, French steamer, 127
Medusa, Italian submarine, 39
Merion, British decoy ship, 38
Merton Hall, British freighter, 167
Messina, Strait of, 170
Metz, Arthur, *Oberleutnant*, 63
Meusel, Karl, *Kapitänleutnant*, 149, 170–71
Meyer, Wilhelm, *Kapitänleutnant*, 166
Michaelis, Georg, German chancellor, 140–42
Michelsen, Andreas, *Kommodore*, 14, 210
Middendorff, Heinrich, *Kapitänleutnant*, 198–99, 222
Midilli (ex-*Breslau*), Ottoman light cruiser, 16, 202
Milazzo, Italian cargo ship, 146
Milos, 200
Milwaukee, British transport, 199
Minas, Italian troopship, 113
minelaying submarines, 48, 51, 60, 63, 70–72, 87, 91–92, 96–97, 101, 117, 146, 152–53, 174, 191, 198, 200, 209, 217–18
mines, development of, 48
Minnehaha, British steamer, 146
Minnesota, American pre-dreadnought, 197

Minnetonka, British steamer, 169
Minnewaska, British troopship, 72
Mira, British tanker, 147
Missanabie, British steamer, 199
Missourian, American freighter, 118
Moltke, battle cruiser, 93–94, 142, 178–79
Monge, French submarine, 78–79
Montenegro, 37
Montreal, 50, 168
Moraht, Robert, *Kapitänleutnant*, 129, 169
Morillot, Roland, French lieutenant, 78–79
Mount Vernon (ex-*Kronprinzessin Cecilie*), American troopship, 198–99
Myrtle Branch, British steamer, 168

Nantucket, 91, 196
Napier, T. W. D., British vice admiral, 157
Naples, 57
Narval, French submarine 8, 10
Nasmith, Martin, British lieutenant commander, 39
National Liberal Party, 99
Nauen, wireless transmitter at, 98, 151
Neptune, British dreadnought, 35
Netherlands, and Dutch merchant marine, 30, 63, 101, 105, 112, 117, 122, 131, 174, 211, 220, 223
Neumann, Karl, *Oberleutnant*, 127–28, 220
Neumünster, German cryptanalysts at, 74, 148, 175
Neureuther, Karl, *Kapitänleutnant*, 168
New York, 41–42, 48, 57, 64–65, 118, 123–24, 126, 166–69, 173, 176, 198–99
New Zealand, 114
Newcastle, 88
Newfoundland, 197
Newport, 91, 112, 120
Nicholas II, tsar of Russia, 60, 114, 119, 137
Nicosian, British freighter, 75
Niemöller, Martin, *Oberleutnant*, 40, 150, 180–81, 201, 207, 211, 222, 227
Niger, British minesweeper, 14
Nimitz, Chester, American admiral, 227
Nivelle offensive, by French army (1917), 140, 159

Njegovan, Maximilian, Austrian admiral, 104, 175
Nordenfelt, Thorsten, Swedish arms manufacturer, 8
Nordenfelt I (1885), early submarine, 8
Nordenfelt IV (1888), early submarine, 8
Norefos, Norwegian freighter, 150–51
Norris, George, US senator, 116
North Cape, 91, 151
North Channel, 124, 126, 166–68
North Rona Island, 75
North Sea, 5, 12, 15–16, 18, 24, 27, 29–30, 36, 38, 60, 62, 73–74, 77, 85, 87–88, 118, 149, 156–57, 194, 196, 206, 209
Northern Barrage, 181, 187n43, 193, 199
Northern Pacific, American troopship, 177
Norway, and Norwegian merchant marine 5–6, 30, 47–48, 77, 93, 101, 112, 126, 148–51, 178, 211
Nostitz und Jänckendorff, Heinrich von, *Korvettenkapitän*, 171–72, 192, 194
Nottingham, British light cruiser, 88
Nova Scotia, 123–24, 173
Novara, Austrian light cruiser, 128–29
Noya, British freighter, 146

O. B. Jennings, American tanker, 196
Obry, Ludwig, Austrian officer, 11
Ocean City, Maryland, 197
Odessa, 38
Old Head of Kinsale, 42, 49
Olive Branch, British steamer, 151–52
Olympic, British troopship, 177
Oopack, British steamer, 201
Orama, British armed merchant cruiser, 146
Oran, 57
Organisation Consul, postwar terrorist group, 222
Oriole, British steamer, 33
Orkney Islands, 5, 71, 181
Orleans, Massachusetts, 173
Oronsa, British steamer, 168
Ostend, submarine base at, 34, 36, 156, 179–80, 184, 202–3
Ostfriesland, dreadnought, 209
Otranto, Straits of, 37–38, 77–80, 153, 155–56, 180–81

Otranto Straits, Battle of the (1917), 128–29, 155, 200
Ottoman Empire, and Ottoman navy, 6, 16, 18, 38–39, 117, 202, 216
Otway, British armed merchant cruiser, 146

Palestine, 117
Pallada, Russian cruiser, 14
Papen, Franz von, Captain, 64
Pargust, British Q-ship, 155
Paris, Declaration of (1856), 6
Passchendaele, Battle of (1917), 156, 159, 184
Patagonia, British freighter, 38
Pathfinder, British light cruiser, 4, 14
Patriotic Auxiliary Service Law (1916), 98, 135, 137, 190
Patzig, Helmut, *Oberleutnant*, 169–70, 220, 228
Pentland Firth, 34
Peresviet, Russian pre-dreadnought, 72
Pershing, John J., American general, 120, 123, 184
Persia, British auxiliary cruiser, 59
Petri, Karl, *Kapitänleutnant*, 146, 199
Petrograd, 48, 152; soviet in, 141
Petz, Willy, *Kapitänleutnant*, 112, 130
Philadelphian, British steamer, 168
Platsch, Erich, *Oberleutnant*, 154
Pohl, Hugo von, Admiral, 5, 15–18, 23, 27–31, 33, 35, 47, 50, 61–62, 65–66, 109
Pola (Pula), base and arsenal in, 9, 37–40, 47, 66–67, 69, 74, 79, 98, 149, 155, 175, 200–201, 206–8
Portland, 33
Porto di Rodi, Italian steamer, 119
Portugal, 63, 65, 113, 171
Prásil, Leo, Austrian *Linienschiffsleutnant*, 118
President Lincoln, American troopship, 169
Primo, British steamer, 14
Prince Charles, British Q-ship, 75
Princess Royal, British battle cruiser, 21n33.
Principe Umberto, Italian troopship, 69–70, 79

Prinzregent Luitpold, dreadnought, 136, 141
prisoners of war, 35–36, 46, 99, 100, 118, 148, 190
privateers, and privateering, 6
Privet, British Q-ship, 130, 155, 162n57, 182
Prize, British Q-ship, 130
prize rules. *See* cruiser rules
Progressive People's Party, 98, 137–39, 203
Protector (1902), submarine prototype, 9
Provence, French troopship, 69, 79
Pustkuchen, Herbert, *Oberleutnant*, 64, 114–15, 130, 154, 158

Q-ships, 74–77, 130, 147, 153–55
Queenstown (Cobh), destroyer base at, 33, 50, 123–26, 147–48, 167, 169, 198

Raeder, Erich, Admiral, 216
Ramm, Robert, *Oberleutnant*, 199
Rathenau, Walther, German politician, 222
rationing and food shortages, 27, 105, 110–11, 136, 141, 143–4, 164–66, 183, 185n2
Rave, Ortwin, *Korvettenkapitän*, 171, 193–94
Regina Margherita, Italian pre-dreadnought, 72
Reichstag, German parliament, 4, 18, 28, 50, 98–99, 109, 111, 114, 137, 142, 211; Peace Resolution of (1917), 138–41, 143, 203
Reiherstiegwerft, shipyard, 100
Remy, Walter, *Kapitänleutnant*, 169
restricted submarine warfare. *See* submarine warfare, restricted
Resurgam (1879), early submarine, 8
Reuß zu Köstritz, Heinrich XXXVII, Prinz, *Kapitänleutnant*, 170
Reuter, Ludwig von, German vice admiral, 216–17
Rhodesia, British freighter, 147
Riga, Battle of (1915), 94; Battle of (1917), 142
Rigele, Hermann, Austrian *Linienschiffsleutnant*, 207, 224–25, 227

Roden, Emmo von, Colonel, 222
Rohrbeck, Otto, *Kapitänleutnant*, 146
Roland Morillot (ex-*UB 26*), French submarine, 78
Romania, 89–90, 101–2
Roosevelt, Franklin, US president, 115
Roosevelt, Theodore, US president, 44
Rose, Hans, *Kapitänleutnant*, 91, 112, 115, 127, 143, 145–46, 167, 192, 195, 223–24
Rosenberg-Grusczyski, Erich von, *Kapitänleutnant*, 34, 43
Rosenow, Ernst, *Oberleutnant*, 155
Rosyth, 179
Rotorua, British steamer, 114
Rowanmore, British steamer, 91
Royal Air Force (RAF), British, 180, 220
Royal Edward, British troopship, 39
Rücker, *Claus, Kapitänleutnant*, 52, 59, 65, 68, 177–78
Rucketeschell, Hellmuth von, *Oberleutnant*, 186n14
Rupprecht, Crown Prince of Bavaria, Field Marshal, 205
Russell, British pre-dreadnought, 72
Russia, and Russian navy, 6, 8–12, 19, 27, 48, 60, 73, 86, 89, 91, 94–95, 102, 137, 140, 142, 159, 184, 201–2
Russian Civil War (1918–20), 165
Russo-Japanese War (1904–5), 9, 11–12
Russo-Turkish War (1877–78), 6, 48

Saalwächter, Alfred, *Kapitänleutnant*, 128, 216
Saint Barchan, British coastal steamer, 206
Salonika (Thessaloniki), 79, 104, 113, 117, 170, 202
Saltzwedel, Reinhold, *Oberleutnant*, 115, 157
San Diego, American armored cruiser, 172
Sant Anna, French troopship, 170
Santee, American Q-ship, 147
Sardinia, 112, 129, 170
Scapa Flow, 5, 34, 71, 93, 130, 179, 209
Scarborough, 16
Scheer, Reinhard, Admiral: and Battle of Jutland (1916), 85–86; as commander of High Sea Fleet, 61–62, 87–89, 92–94, 171, 178–79; as head of Naval High

Command (*Seekriegsleitung*), 185, 189–
  93, 198, 203–6, 208–10, 222; pictured,
  164; and submarine warfare, 64–65, 74,
  86, 90, 95, 98, 101–3, 142, 148, 156–57,
  159, 163, 181; war crimes allegations
  against, 220
Scheer Program (1918), 190–92
Scheidemann, Philipp, German politician,
  211
Scheldt River, 180
Schleswig-Holstein, 73–74, 157
Schlosser, Friedrich, Austrian
  Linienschiffsleutnant, 69
Schmettow, Count Matthias von,
  Oberleutnant, 71, 130, 158
Schmidt, Georg, *Kapitänleutnant*, 128,
  151–52
Schneider, Rudolf, *Kapitänleutnant*, 14,
  33, 47, 157
Schrader, Otto von, *Kapitänleutnant*,
  168–69, 216
Schüler, Hans, *Oberleutnant*, 206
Schultze, Otto, *Kapitänleutnant*, 88, 127
Schulz, Gerhard, *Kapitänleutnant*, 166
Schwarz, Kurt, *Oberleutnant*, 165
Schwieger, Walther, *Kapitänleutnant*, 33,
  41, 42, 45, 64, 81n10, 93–94, 155, 157,
  228
Scilly Islands, 130, 148
Scotland, 35, 63, 75, 77–78, 87, 92–93, 124,
  126, 148–49, 171, 178, 197
Senegal, 127
Serbia, 37, 60, 79, 208
Seuffer, Rudolf, *Kapitänleutnant*, 147
Sevastopol, 201–2
Shenandoah, Confederate cruiser, 6
Shetland Islands, 30, 47, 129
Sicily, 57
Sierra Leone, 35, 127, 151
Siess, Gustav, *Kapitänleutnant*, 71–72, 200,
  208, 223–24
Siewert, Kurt, *Kapitänleutnant*, 199
Sigismund, Prince of Prussia,
  Oberleutnant, 68
Sims, William S., American admiral, 120–
  24, 126, 131, 147, 158
Singule, Rudolf, Austrian
  Linienschiffsleutnant, 47

Sittenfeld, Erich, *Kapitänleutnant*, 128
Sixtus, Prince of Bourbon-Parma, and the
  "Sixtus Affair," 104, 207
Skagerrak, 93, 149, 157, 211
Smiths, Wilhelm, *Oberleutnant*, 78
Social Democratic Party (SPD), German,
  27, 135–38, 203, 211, 222
Somme, Battle of the (1916), 89, 156, 183
Southland, British steamer, 127
Spa, German headquarters, 185, 192, 202,
  208, 210–11
Spain, 67–68, 112, 192, 208, 211, 223
Spee, Maximilian von, Count, Vice
  Admiral, 16–17, 73
Spiegel von und zu Peckelsheim, Edgar
  von, *Kapitänleutnant*, 118, 130
Spiess, Johannes, *Kapitänleutnant*, 1, 158,
  167, 209
Sprenger, Robert, *Oberleutnant*, 72
Spring Rice, Sir Cecil, British ambassador
  to US, 44
St. Nazaire, 124, 147, 168, 176
Stavanger, 5, 178
Stein, Hermann von, general, 141
Steinbauer, Wolfgang, *Oberleutnant*, 69,
  170, 200–201
Steinbrinck, Otto, *Oberleutnant*, 36, 113,
  146, 223–24
Sterope, Italian freighter, 171
Stifinder, Norwegian bark, 194
Stinnes, Hugo, German industrialist, 62
Stone, William J., US senator, 116
Stonecrop, British Q-ship, 155
Stoss, Alfred, *Kapitänleutnant*, 34, 78
Strackerjan, Friedrich, *Kapitänleutnant*,
  149, 199
Studt, Ferdinand, *Korvettenkapitän*,
  193–94
Stülcken & Sohn, shipyard, 100
Sturdee, Sir Doveton, British admiral,
  21n33
submarine chasers, 147, 173, 182
submarine warfare, restricted, 51, 57–80,
  86–95, 228
submarine warfare, unrestricted: American
  opinion of, 18–20, 23–26, 29, 31,
  42–47, 49–51; Bethmann Hollweg and,
  29–30, 44–45, 49–50, 60, 90, 102, 109–

10; decision to resume (1917), 102–5, 109–11; decision to stop (1918), 205–6; first phase of (1915), 30–51; German assumptions regarding, 25, 103, 119, 121, 130–31, 135, 138–39, 144, 158–59, 176; German public support of, 26–27, 29, 44, 52, 105; initial proposal for, 15–16, 18–20; postwar recriminations over, 228; resumption of, debated, 85–95, 101–102; second phase of (1917–18), 112–31, 135–60, 163–85, 189–206; in Second World War, 225–27; William II and, 29–30, 44–45, 49–50, 102, 206

submarines, Allied, wartime losses of, 230n23

Suez Canal, 72, 113, 206

Suffren, French pre-dreadnought, 69

Sunderland, 87–88

superstitions, of U-boat crews, 78, 83n46

Sussex, French passenger ferry, and the "*Sussex* pledge," 63–65, 71, 74, 86, 90, 93, 111, 116, 130, 206

Sweden, 47, 112

Switzerland, 105

Sydney, Nova Scotia, 123–24, 126

Szent István, Austrian dreadnought, 200

Tagus, British steamer, 143

Taranto, 70

Taylor, Frederick H., British lieutenant, 150

Tegetthoff, Wilhelm von, Austrian admiral, 40

Terschelling, 2, 149, 155, 157

Texel Island, Battle of (1914), 16, 29, 73

Thames River, 19, 34, 105, 124, 209

Thomas, Lowell, American journalist, 180, 187n39, 195

Thüringen, dreadnought, 209

Thursby, Cecil, British rear admiral, 79–80

Ticonderoga, American freighter, 194

Tiger, British battle cruiser, 38

Tirpitz, Alfred von, Admiral: early doubts of, about submarine warfare, 4–5, 10, 18–19; and Fatherland Party (1917), 141–42, 185, 222; pictured, *24*; political aspirations of, 28, 141; resignation of (1916), 62, 86; and Torpedo Inspection,

7, 10, 62; and unrestricted submarine warfare, 15, 23–31, 44–45, 49–50, 52, 60–62; war crimes allegations against, 220; in wartime retirement, 89, 103

Titanic, British passenger liner, 72, 153, 169, 177

Transylvania, British troopship, 127

Trapp, Georg von, Austrian *Linienschiffsleutnant*, 38, 146, 225

Trieste, 207

Triumph, British pre-dreadnought, 38

Triumph, Canadian trawler, 173

Tsingtao (Qingdao), 16–17

Tubantia, Dutch passenger liner, 63

Tunisia, 170

Turkey, Republic of, 223. *See also* Ottoman Empire, and Ottoman navy

Turkish navy, 224. *See also* Ottoman Empire, and Ottoman navy

Turner, R. R., British lieutenant commander, 88

Tuscania, British troopship, 167, 185n6

Tyne River, 198

U 1, 10, *11*, 13, 31, 36, 218

U 1, Austrian, 9

U 2, 10–11, 31, 218

U 2, Austrian, 9

U 3, 31, 218

U 3, Austrian, 10

U 4, 31

U 4, Austrian, 10, 47

U 5, 32

U 5, Austrian, 38, 69

U 6, Austrian, 79–80, 128

U 7, 31

U 8, 34–36, 46, 78

U 9, 1–5, 14, 34, 158, 216, 218

U 10 (ex-*UB 1*), Austrian, 39

U 11 (ex-*UB 15*), Austrian, 39

U 12, 14, 35–36, 46

U 12, Austrian, 37

U 14 (ex-*Curie*), Austrian, 39, 146, 219

U 16, 32–34, 47

U 17, 5, 14–15, 74

U 19, 11, 32–33, 63, 81n10, 101, 167, 171

U 20, 14, 28, 33, 41–43, 45, 81n10, 93, *94*, 155

U 21, 4, 14, 33, 38–40, 52, 65, 69, 72, 113, 118, 143, 218
U 22, 31
U 24, 14, 33, 47, 75
U 26, 14, 35, 48
U 27, 14, 35, 75–76
U 28, 35, 43, 128, 151–52
U 29, 34–35, 118
U 30, 34, 43, 93–94
U 30, Austrian, 128
U 31, 10, 68
U 31, Austrian, 207, 224
U 32, 69, 119, 200
U 33, 52, 59, 65, 117, 149, 200, 208
U 34, 52, 59, 65, 127, 155, 162n57, 177, 201, 207–8
U 35, 52, 59, 65–70, 77, 91–92, 112, 118, 143, 149, 158, 182, 195, 200
U 36, 75, 82n35
U 38, 47, 52, 57, *58*, 59, 65, 155, 158, 182, 200–201
U 39, 52, 59, 65, 113, 129, 200
U 41, 48, 76
U 43, 32
U 43 (ex-*UB 43*), Austrian, 40
U 44, 32
U 45, 128
U 46, 91, 151–52, 166
U 47 (ex-*UB 47*), Austrian, 40
U 48, 156
U 50, 113
U 51, 68
U 52, 69, 88, 118
U 53, *90,* 91, 112, 125, 127, 143, 145–47, 167, 192, 195
U 54, 186n14
U 55, 169
U 57, 93
U 58, 154
U 61, 147
U 62, 114, 146, 172, 198
U 63, 88, 200, 208, 211
U 64, 129, 169
U 65, 113
U 66, 88, 135
U 68, 76, 127
U 69, 129, 157
U 70, 114, 127

U 71, 70
U 73, 71–72, 200
U 75, 71, 87, 91
U 76, 91
U 78, 87, 209
U 79, 146, 191
U 80, 70
U 81, 148
U 82, 168, 198–99
U 83, 130
U 85, 112, 130
U 86, 169–70, 220
U 87, 157–58
U 88, 155
U 90, 169
U 91, 168
U 92, 187n43
U 93, 97–98, 100, 118, 130, 144, 148–50
U 94, 128
U 102, 187n43
U 103, 177–78
U 105, 148–49, 199
U 106, 149
U 107, 199
U 110, 167
U 117, 196–98
U 118, 197
U 119, 197
U 120, 196
U 122, 196–97
U 124, 197
U 126, 196
U 135, 209
U 139, 194–96, 198, 200, 210
U 140, 194–98
U 141, 195
U 142, 195
U 144, 195
U 151, 149–50, 171–72, 192–96, 201
U 152, 171, 194–95, 198
U 153, 171–72
U 154, 171–72
U 155 (ex-*Deutschland*), 96, *97,* 149, 170–71, 193–96, 198
U 156, 149–50, 153, 172–73, 187n43, 192–93, 196, 198
U 157, 149–51, 153, 155, 198, 200, 210
UB 2, 36, 78

UB 3, 37–38
UB 4, 75
UB 7, 37–38
UB 8, 37–38
UB 10, 36
UB 13, 63
UB 14, 37–39
UB 21, 224
UB 26, 78
UB 29, 63, 154
UB 31, 118
UB 32, 118, 154
UB 39, 143
UB 42, 165
UB 44, 70
UB 47, 69, 200
UB 48, 170, 200–201, 207
UB 50, 92, 169, 211
UB 57, 167
UB 64, 168–69
UB 67, 166, 206
UB 68, 201, 215
UB 73, 168
UB 77, 166
UB 81, 157
UB 87, 199
UB 91, 199
UB 94, 206
UB 104, 187n43
UB 105, 161n46, 170
UB 110, 148, 203
UB 116, 209
UB 123, 187n43, 199, 204
UB 124, 169, 186n14
UB 127, 187n43
UB 128, 201, 208
UB boats, 32–33, 48, 51, 63, 69, 72, 87,
    96–97, 101, 117, 152, 174, 198
UC 2, 48
UC 4, 49
UC 6, 71
UC 12, 70
UC 14, 72, 169
UC 16, 70–71
UC 17, 114
UC 21, 115
UC 23, 72, 202

UC 25, 128–29, 201
UC 26, 130
UC 29, 155
UC 34, 72
UC 49, 146
UC 50, 147
UC 52, 170
UC 54, 170
UC 55, 148
UC 57, 165
UC 61, 130
UC 65, 113–14, 146
UC 66, 130, 133n44, 154
UC 67, 127, 180–81, 201, 207, 211, 220
UC 72, 155, 162n57
UC 74, 117, 206–8
UC 79, 70
UC 109, 218
UC boats, 48, 51, 60, 63, 70–72, 87, 92, 96–
    97, 101, 117, 152–53, 174, 198, 217–18
UE I boats. *See U 71–80*
UE II boats. *See U 117–120* and *U 122–126*
Ukraine, 86, 89, 165, 201–2
Ulster, 35, 124
Ultonia, British steamer, 127
United States: declares war on Austria-
    Hungary, 117; declares war on
    Germany, 116, 137; deploys American
    Expeditionary Force (AEF), 120, 123–
    24, 159, 168, 184, 205, 229; relations of,
    with Austria-Hungary, 39, 58–59, 117;
    relations of, with Britain, 19, 24, 64;
    relations of, with Germany, 19, 42–47,
    49–51, 64, 90, 102, 111, 114; shipyards
    of, 174; U-boat cruises to coast of, 91,
    172–73; and unrestricted submarine
    warfare, 23–26, 31, 42–47, 103
United States navy: and antisubmarine
    barrages, 181–82; Atlantic Fleet of,
    120; base at Brest, 124, 147, 167, 169,
    198–99; base at Queenstown, 123–26,
    147–48, 167, 169, 198; contingent
    of, at Gibraltar, 156, 182, 187n45;
    dreadnought division of, with Grand
    Fleet, 120, 124, 178; first submarines of,
    9; and postwar naval arms control, 219;
    prepares for war (1917), 115; in Second

World War, 227, 231n26; War College of, 120

unrestricted submarine warfare. *See* submarine warfare, unrestricted

Urbino, British steamer, 76

Ushant, 167

Valentiner, Max, *Kapitänleutnant*, 40, 47, 57–59, 68, 80, 149–51, 155, 158, 177, 182, 193, 200–201, 210, 220, 223–24

Valona (Vlorë), 72, 79, 128

Venice, 39

Verdun, Battle of (1916), 61–62, 86–87, 89, 140

Verona, Italian troopship, 170

Versailles Treaty (1919), 103, 116, 215, 218–20, 223

Vesper, Karl, *Oberleutnant*, 49

Vickers, British arms manufacturer, 9

Viebeg, Max, *Kapitänleutnant*, 118

Vigilancia, American steamer, 114–15

Ville de Lille, French steamer, 33–34

Vindictive, British light cruiser, 179–80

Viribus Unitis, Austrian dreadnought, 208

Vittoria, British Q-ship, 74

Voigt, Ernst, *Oberleutnant*, 155

Voigt, Ernst von, *Oberleutnant*, 38

Vollbrecht, Johann, *Oberleutnant*, 209

Voltaire, French pre-dreadnought, 200

Volturno, Italian steamer, 169

Vulcan, AG, shipbuilder, 48, 72, 100–101, 190, 223

Wäger, Franz, *Oberleutnant*, 70

Walther, Hans, *Kapitänleutnant*, 69, 88, 118

war crimes, allegations of, involving U-boat personnel, 35–36, 46, 128, 170

War Council, British steamer, 200

Wardlaw, Mark, British lieutenant, 75

Washington Naval Treaty (1922), 219

Weddigen, Otto, *Kapitänleutnant*, 1–5, *3*, 13–14, 34–35, 45, 51, 158, 216, 218

Wegener, Bernd, *Kapitänleutnant*, 14, 35, 51, 75–76

Weisbach, Raimund, *Oberleutnant*, 63, 81n10

Wemyss, Sir Rosslyn, British admiral, 211

Wenninger, Ralph, *Oberleutnant*, 114

Werner, Egon von, *Oberleutnant*, 71

Werner, Wilhelm, *Kapitänleutnant*, 38, 169

Weser, AG, shipbuilder, 48, 72, 100–101, 105, 136, 174, 190, 223

Western Sahara, 150

Westfalen, dreadnought, 88

Weymouth, British light cruiser, 207, 224

Whitby, 16

Whitehead, Robert, and Whitehead torpedoes, 6, 8, 11, 225

Wickes, American destroyer, 177

Wiegand, Karl von, German-American journalist, 19, 23–30, 52, 137, 176

Wilhelms, Ernst, *Kapitänleutnant*, 129, 157

Wilhelmshaven, High Sea Fleet base at, 3–5, 13, 23, 29, 38, 63, 85, 88, 93, 99, 136, 142, 148, 178–79, 185, 195, 206, 208–10

William, Crown Prince, 138

William II, German emperor: abdication of, 210–11; agrees to constitutional reforms, 202–3, 208; indictment of, for war crimes, 219–20; pictured, *183*; supports naval expansion, 17; and unrestricted submarine warfare, 28–31, 34–35, 44–45, 50, 62, 85–87, 94–95, 206, 208–11; as wartime leader, 23, 49–50, 60, 68, 88–89, 138, 141, 185

Williams, John Sharp, US senator, 116

Wilmot-Smith, A., British lieutenant commander, 76

Wilson, Edith, First Lady, 113

Wilson, Henry B., American rear admiral, 147

Wilson, Woodrow, US president: after outbreak of war in Europe (1914), 23; and American declaration of war (1917), 115–17; and final negotiations with Germany (1918), 204–5, 208; Fourteen Points of, 203–4; mediation efforts of, 102–3, 110–11; reelection of (1916), 91; reluctance of, to criticize British actions, 64, 75, 116; responses

of, to unrestricted submarine warfare (1915), 31, 42–47, 49–50; and restricted submarine warfare, 58–59; and resumption of unrestricted submarine warfare (1917), 111–15; as wartime leader, 119–20
wireless radio technology and codes, 73–74, 98, 145, 152–53
Wissmann, Friedrich, *Kapitänleutnant*, 165
women, as shipyard workers, 100, 190
Wünsche, Otto, *Kapitänleutnant*, 114, 127
Wutsdorff, Hans Oscar, *Oberleutnant*, 169
Wyandra (ex-*Baralong*), British Q-ship, 76

Yarmouth, 75
Yavuz Sultan Selim (ex-*Goeben*), Ottoman battle cruiser, 16, 202
Yenisei, Russian minelayer, 48
Ypres, Second Battle of (1915), 36
Yugoslavia, 208

Zédé, Gustave, French naval engineer, 8
Zeebrugge, submarine base at, 36, 92, 156, 179–80, 184, 190, 202–3
zeppelins and zeppelin raids, 36, 66, 220
Ziegner, Wilhelm, *Oberleutnant*, 130
Zimmermann, Arthur, German foreign secretary, 103–4, 113–14

Total War

Series Editors

MICHAEL B. BARRETT and KYLE SINISI

Total war implies the mobilization of the entire resources of the state and the adoption of military objectives that blur or erase traditional distinctions between civil and military populations. Epitomized by the Second World War, a conflict that literally spanned the globe, total war saw civilian populations and factories become targets of importance equal to tank columns or shipping convoys. Nationalities were uprooted, and entire cities disappeared in flames or atomic flashes. However, many of the hallmarks of total war were already evident in previous struggles. Rowman & Littlefield's "Total War" series examines the nature of total war and its ramifications, not only in its popular association with the Second World War, but its devastating appearance, wholly or partially, in earlier conflicts. Through concise and provocative accounts, readers will be drawn into the debate about total war through compelling narratives that make history come alive.

Marc Gallicchio, *The Scramble for Asia: U.S. Military Power in the Aftermath of the Pacific War*

Geoffrey Megargee, *War of Annihilation: Combat and Genocide on the Eastern Front, 1941*

Lawrence Sondhaus, *German Submarine Warfare in World War I: The Onset of Total War at Sea*

Haruo Tohmatsu and H. P. Willmott, *A Gathering Darkness: The Coming of War to the Far East and the Pacific, 1921–1942*

H. P. Willmott, *The War with Japan: The Period of Balance, May 1942– October 1943*

Thomas W. Zeiler, *Unconditional Defeat: Japan, America, and the End of World War II*